DESIGN AND IMPLEMENTATION OF
COMPUTER-BASED INFORMATION SYSTEMS

DESIGN AND IMPLEMENTATION OF COMPUTER-BASED INFORMATION SYSTEMS

edited by

Norbert Szyperski
Erwin Grochla

SIJTHOFF & NOORDHOFF   1979
Alphen aan den Rijn, The Netherlands
Germantown, Maryland, USA

Proceedings of the BIFOA Symposium, September 18-20, 1978, Bensberg/Cologne, edited by

Norbert Szyperski
Professor of Business Administration and Planning
Theory, Director of BIFOA, University of Cologne,
Cologne, Federal Republic of Germany

Erwin Grochla
Professor of Business Administration and Organization
Theory, Executive Director of BIFOA, University of Cologne,
Cologne, Federal Republic of Germany

BIFOA is the Institute for Business Administration, Organization and Automation at the University of Cologne, Federal Republic of Germany.

© 1979 Sijthoff & Noordhoff International Publishers B.V., Alphen aan den Rijn, The Netherlands
Softcover reprint of the hardcover 1st edition 1979

ISBN 978-94-009-9570-3   ISBN 978-94-009-9568-0   (eBook)
DOI   10.1007/978-94-009-9568-0

Table of Contents

Preface

From 18th to 20th September, 1978, about forty scientists and practitioners from Australia, Canada, Denmark, Finland, Great Britain, the United States and the Federal Republic of Germany joined in an international symposium entitled "Design and Implementation of Computer-based Information Systems".

This symposium was initiated by the invitation of the BIFOA (*Betriebswirtschaftliches Institut für Organisation und Automation an der Universität zu Köln*) as a part of the institute's research project IMPLAN (Development of Tools for the IMPLementation of Computer-based PLANning Systems).

This book includes the opening address, the papers presented at the symposium —revised by the authors after presentation—the chairmen's summaries of the various working group sessions, and an edited version of the concluding "Blueprint for Research on Implementation".

Acknowledgements

The symposium was made possible by a federal grant from the *Bundesminister für Forschung und Technologie* (BMFT), Bonn, represented by the *Gesellschaft für Mathematik und Datenverarbeitung* (GMD), St. Augustin, who sponsored the whole IMPLAN research project and the symposium. We are extremely appreciative of their valuable cooperation and support; in this respect our special thanks go to Mrs. Katharina Gregor and Dr. Jürgen Marock of the GMD.

Our sincere thanks and appreciation are due to the authors for the many hours of work, for their contributions and for preparing and revising them after the symposium. We appreciate the valuable help of the chairmen for conducting the working sessions and preparing summaries of the sessions.

We should also like to extend our thanks to Mr. Frank Kolf, Mr. Hans-Jürgen Oppelland and Dr. Thilo Tilemann (all of the BIFOA) for their help in preparing the concept of the symposium. We appreciate the unstinting efforts of Mr. Hartwig Garmers and Mr. Albrecht Windler (both of the BIFOA) for their help in the organising and smooth running of the symposium. They also made valuable contributions towards the preparation of the present book.

Finally we express our sincere thanks to Sijthoff & Noordhoff International Publishers, especially to Mr. Arne Visser and Mr. Robert Lyng, for their support in editing the proceedings of the symposium and for the excellent care they have taken over printing this publication.

Cologne, August 1979
Erwin Grochla
Norbert Szyperski

Opening Address

by Prof. Erwin Grochla, Ph.D.

It is a great pleasure for me to welcome all of you as participants of this symposium. Since many of you are attending a BIFOA-symposium for the first time, I would like to give you some general information about our institute, its scope of activities and its research philosophy. BIFOA is an abbreviation which stands for Betriebswirtschaftliches Institut für Organisation und Automation an der Universität zu Köln. The institute was founded in 1963 by me in cooperation with managers from business practice. The main purpose of the institute has been to intensify research in the fields of Business Administration and Management as well as Organization and Automation.

Throughout the past years the institute developed its particular research philosophy which has proved to be very successful up to now. To make this clearer let me shed some more light on this particular aspect. First of all, the institute attempts to emphasize the practical application of its research results. This is achieved through a close cooperation with pilot user-companies and software companies in the various projects that have been undertaken by the institute and through the manifold seminars and workshops that are offered by the institute for managers from business practice.

Apart from this close cooperation with business practice, the institute emphasizes the permanency of its contacts with academic institutions such as universities. Especially to be mentioned are personal relationships with the *Seminar für Allgemeine Betriebswirtschafslehre und Organisationslehre* (Department for Business Administration and Organization), the *Seminar für Allgemeine Betriebswirtschaftslehre und Planung* (Department for Business Administration and Planning), the *Institut für Informatik* (Institute for Informatics), all of which belong to the University of Cologne. Apart from this, the BIFOA has a strong personal relationship with the University of Essen.

The activities of the BIFOA are to communicate, show applications, and to elaborate research results in special study circles consisting of members from the institute and from business practice, in workshops, seminars, and international symposia as well as in publications. To be able to undertake its projects, the institute participates in governmental programs such as the Federal Government programs for the development of automatic data processing, information and documentation, and the humanization of work organization. It is essential for the institute to perform all of its activities in close cooperation and with intensive feedback from German industry. German industry is represented in an association that was founded for the financial and nonfinancial support of the institute. This association was founded in 1963 by fourty business firms; currently this association has about 140 member firms.

The milestones in the past work of BIFOA were:

—First memorandum of BIFOA published in 1968:

"Application Systems for Automated Date Processing: The Gap between Research and Education in the Federal Republic of West Germany."

—Second memorandum, published in 1969:

"Business Informatics as a Necessary Application Oriented Supplement to General Informatics."

—Model for the Development of an Integrated Data Processing System (KIM— *Kölner Integrationsmodell*)

—Proposition of a MIS-research program to the Federal Ministry of Education and Science.

Currently the institute has a broad range of research activities which seem to be of high practical interest. One field is the production of data. Another field of research is office automation and automated text processing, both being of utmost importance in German industry. Yet another subject of BIFOA-research are methods of systems planning and documentation. Besides this, a broad field is the development of practical aids for particular managerial decisions. The three decision areas currently studied are materials management, organizational delegation and the selection of ADP-facilities. Another area of BIFOA-research is the organizational implementation of systems which is the topic of this symposium.

Former symposia were held on

—Model and Computer-based Corporate Planning

—Management Information Systems—A Challenge to Research and Development

—Organizational Structure and Structure of Information Systems

—Man-Computer-Interaction in Management Planning

—Modelling Tools for Corporate Planning.

After these introductory remarks let me try to give a first definition of what is to be understood by implementation, and let me equally describe the context of the present symposium.

The general purpose of implementation is to transfer conceptual schemes into reality, that is to say into actual running systems. Implementation processes always have to focus upon two aspects, a systems technical aspect, and an organizational aspect. Both are equally important and require a broad set of concepts and techniques in order to be performed in an efficient way.

The organizational implementation includes the setting of systems-specific and organizational rules for the users of a prospective system as well as the systematic training of the users to enable them to interact with the system. The system implementation process thus covers a whole set of technical, organizational, and, last but not least, psychological problems that still require thorough research.

The background of the present symposium is the BIFOA project IMPLAN (as mentioned in the foreword). The structure of the proceedings reflects that this project is composed of two related subprojects of the institute. The first is PORGI which stands for Planning of Organizational Implementation. It deals with organizational and human aspects of implementation, as an attempt to develop procedural and substantial concepts and tools for preventing and overcoming implementation problems. The second is APIS which stands for Development of Models for Analysis and Planning in Interactive Systems. APIS deals with problems of modeling methods and data processing-technical questions in the design and implementation of systems. It is intended to give procedural help especially for medium-sized firms.

Due to our experience in the development of running systems (ISAS, CORPIS) and methods (SIMMIS) in MIS-research, we became aware of the problems of organizational implementation. Our experiences gave us the know-how that is necessary for dealing with the problems. We discovered a lack of knowledge especially in the following respects:

—Organizational and human resistance in the development of systems
—There are few efficient instruments for overcoming the problems of resistance and a lacking acceptance.
—It is necessary to analyze which strategies are efficient in which situations and how to design and shape them in an operational way.
—It is necessary to analyze which of the relevant factors can be influenced at all and in which way they can be influenced.
—It is necessary to analyze which support can be offered to system designers in order to enable them to evaluate design alternatives and alternative models and to identify their consequences.

It has been the objective of this symposium to discuss the problems mentioned so far and possibly others with the participants, and to discuss the results of the project IMPLAN achieved so far and to compare them with other research results and developments.

I would like to emphasize the working atmosphere of this symposium which can already be seen from the fact that most of the participants out of the reasonably small number will present a paper here. Contributions from all of us are needed to tackle the broad set of problems lying ahead of us. The institute therefore highly appreciates all of your submitted papers and welcomes your contributions to the discussions that are to be expected.

A.
Basic Considerations on Design and Implemenation of Computer-based Information Systems

I. INTRODUCTION

1. State of the Art of Implementation Research on Computer-based Information Systems

by Norbert Szyperski

1 INTRODUCTION

To give some idea of the actual state of the art of implementation research it might be helpful to start with our understanding of "implementation", which is used in a rather broad sense: implementation is a set of actions or activities which should help that the intended use, realization or application of an idea, method, concept, plan, program, procedure or system will not be a failure.

To overcome noise—in the sense of this word in system theory—is a central task of implementation activities. As long as there is no noise, no disturbance, is it necessary to do anything in order to implement something? No. Things will work out as we would like. But in the moment noise comes up we have to do something: we have to overcome noise, and disturbance. And there are many faces to these disturbances which actually call for adequate implementation acts. In this picture, implementation is an overall process which complements all the creating, designing, changing activities in developing and using systems. That means above all that implementation is not confined to a final stage of handing over a once-developed system to its intended user (see Figure 1).

> IMPLEMENTATION should:
>
> —help that the intended use, realization or application of an idea, method, concept, plan, program, procedure, system, will not be a failure
> —to overcome noise and disturbances.
> —be an overall process, complementing all the creating, changing activities developing and using systems.

Figure 1. Implementation

Asking what the state of the art might be we can consider two parts of the question: (1) What is that "state"? It is hard to pin down who is knowing, doing, controlling what. The given state has many facets: there is the state written in literature, the state in practice, the state in the mind of people experienced in this area.

(2) What kind of art do we really mean? Are we right in thinking that it is still an art to implement planning systems—and not just a technological job?

Here we concentrate on the implementation problems related to planning systems. Planning is the process that creates and determines programs for deci sions—that means setting up goals and action requirements at the very different levels of problem solving, the different layers, stratums or hierarchies. And that often makes the implementation problem rather difficult, as experiences have shown. In my further consideration of implementation I want to look at it as something of a game [4a]. Therefore, I would like to ask: What is the game like which requires some artistry in order to implement with success?

2 BASIC NOTES ON THE IMPLEMENTATION GAME

Looking at the implementation game there are eight questions which I think can frame the scope of our considerations and therefore the structure of my presentation. The synopsis of these principal questions is shown in Figure 2.

1. What are the objectives?
2. Who are the players?
3. What is the playground like?
4. What are the rules of the game?
5. Which are the instruments used to play the game?
6. Are there basic implementation strategies at hand?
7. System development process as an implementation game?
8. Multi-stage-implementation game?

Figure 2. Principal questions related to the implementation game

2.1 Objectives of Implementation

The first question, focussing on the objectives of playing implementation games, is related to four goals. Maybe there are some others, but in many respects those four are the most relevant ones (see Figure 3).

To get understanding: That means to overcome the noise that we have in our know ledge system in the perception and awareness of problems; it refers to our ability to understand, to take over information from the outside. That means specifically that there are difficulties of recognizing, isolating and discussing the right prob lem and handling and understanding the adequate methods and procedures in or der to solve these problems sufficiently.

To get acceptance: In many cases this goal seems to be the most important one, even if it should not be the only one in implementation research. The objective of getting acceptance can be seen as a two-folded, maybe even three-folded problem:

—To get acceptance by the individual is one problem;

—To get acceptance by a group is quite a different problem: you may get acceptance by every single individual, and you possibly won't get acceptance of the group of these individuals;

—To get the organizational acceptance. Organizations are subcultures, they have their own rules; group acceptance does not lead necessarily to an organizational acceptance.

To get action: To get action is important, but yields nothing as long as people you would like to do something are not able to get actions: if they would like to do it, if they will do it, but if they can't do it, what then? We have to do something to overcome noise as far as the capability of going into action is concerned; there are aspects of technical feasibilities, aspects of controlled behaviour.

To get results: We are not just interested in actions; that only would make the world a little bit busier, but we want some results, which are to be measured in the sense of efficiency *and* effectiveness.

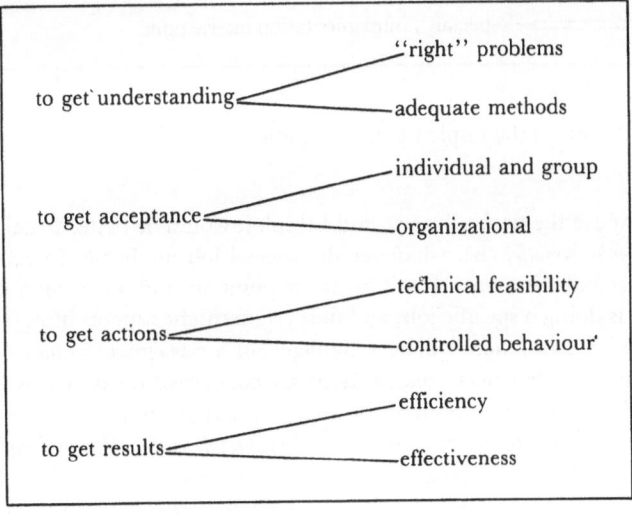

to get understanding
— "right" problems
— adequate methods

to get acceptance
— individual and group
— organizational

to get actions
— technical feasibility
— controlled behaviour'

to get results
— efficiency
— effectiveness

Figure 3. Objectives of the implementation game

2.2 Players of the Implementation Game

If we try to distinguish in a functional approach those people who are playing the implementation game we will find a minimum set of players, as shown in Figure 4.

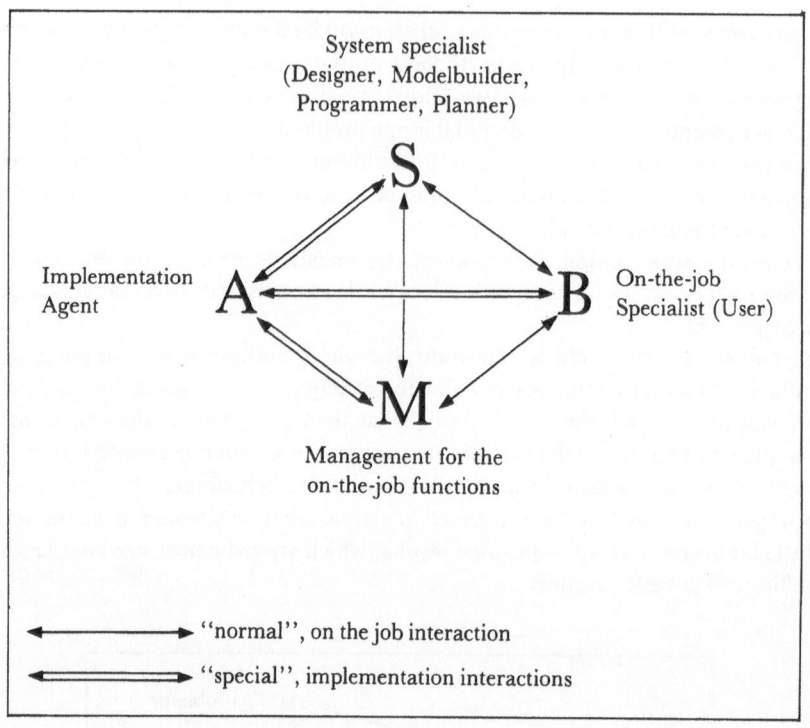

Figure 4. Players of the implementation game

I hesitate to use the name ''user'' and I think it would be better to call this player and *on-the-job specialist* (B), whatever the special job might be. In relation to the system he actually is a user, but it turns the point around: he is not only using the system, he is doing a specific job, and the system might support him.

On the other hand there will be a manager, or a *management for the on-the-job-function* (M). As far as business organizations are concerned we say (B) is reporting to (M). For the system development process—and later on for the technical system operating—we have to introduce some *system specialists* (S). These people might be designer, model builder, programmer, operation research specialist. And I think if we use a functional appraoch, there is a functional role of an implementation agent (A) or an implementator. In a real-world situation the manager (M) or the system specialist (S) could play that role, too.

In the formal scheme of Figure 4 the single lines indicate the ''normal'' interactions of defining and setting the requirements, designing the system, and using the system later on. The double lines refer to a special kind of interaction for the implementation of the system.

2.3 Playground of the Implementation Game

Now—asking *what type of playground* we are playing in—I can reply briefly that Harold Leavitt answered that question many years ago; his scheme has been used many times since (See Figure 5): we are looking at organization as task-driven, goal-oriented entities, regarding men as members of it, structured in one or the other sense, depending on the task and depending on technology (including the use of methods).

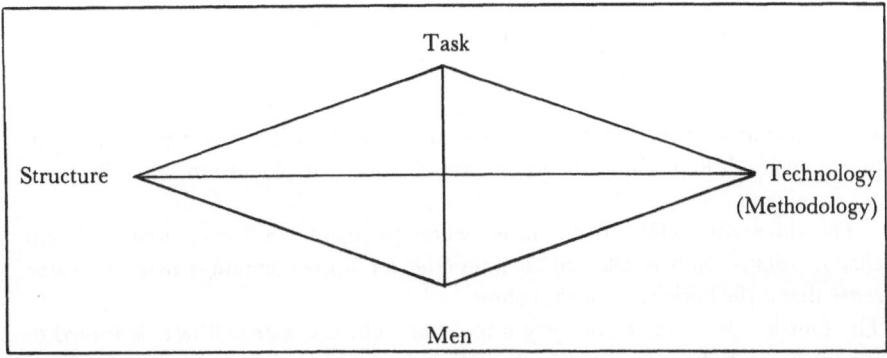

Figure 5. Playground of the implementation game

What we can learn from this is that the implementation game we are playing takes place in the same playground as all the other business activities. There is no special implementation world we can take for us as regarded. We can't say: let's try to take the implementation problem out of the real-world organization and put it into a laboratory or some isolated experimental design. We are forced to solve the whole problem within the same set of conditions we are playing a normal organizational business game in.

2.4 Rules of the Implementation Game

Some of the basic rules of an implementation game should be stressed here (see Figure 6).

One of the rules is: the systems should be implemented to serve and to support users. That means actually we are playing a service game; it is not a real production game or a "real doing" game; but it is a game in which we would like to help in one or the other way to avoid a failure.

And the second rule means: in many cases we have no choice, we have no idealized organization in order to make implementation easier. We cannot change

9

> Systems should be implemented to serve and support users;
>
> at a given playground, with given players;
>
> an implementation agent might help;
>
> the user will not be forced to change his task-driven work.

Figure 6. Rules of the implementation game

all the personnel just to make it easer to implement an idea; we have to go with the given conditions within the given organization: the playground and the players are given.

The third rule refers to an implementation agent—you even may call him change agent—who is allowed to intervene for implementation help. In some sense that is the basic rule for that game.

The fourth rule seems to be very important, too: the user will not be forced to change his task-driven work. He should not be asked to "please the system" and to forget his own job at the same time. We have to accept the person as he is, and we have only limited strategies in order to change the situation.

2.5 Implementation Instruments

Using the same distinction as for topic (2.1)—referring to the goals of implementation—let us look at the subsets of instruments which are available to help those persons who are in charge of implementation. Figure 7 gives a synopsis of various

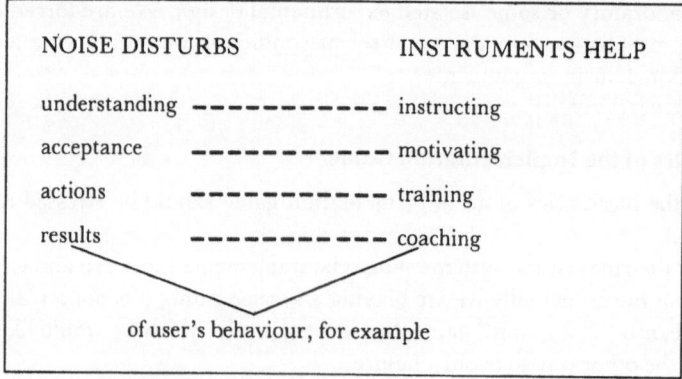

Figure 7. Implementation instruments

instruments corresponding to the already known objectives.

Instructing in the sense of giving help to understand corresponds to the point of disturbance in understanding. And *motivating* helps to provide a better condition for acceptance. *Training* actually is an aid in getting a controlled behaviour: quite often you know everything, you know the rules of the soccer game, or of the football-game; you are able to accept the game, and you even accept the function one would like you to play; but you won't be able to play without a good goal-keeper. Therefore you have to train him; and training is a prerequisite to doing something really. To get good results by doing everything best is a problem of controlling the environment. We have to have help to prevent disturbance from the outside—that might be disturbance from other departments, disturbance from other people, from other companies—from interactive interfering. The related function in the world of sports is *coaching*. It means: to get noise out of the environment of that player who is trying to do his best.

2.6 Implementation Strategies

Consideration of implementation strategies has to deal with the problems of how to analyse given noise and how to get noise out of the game—with support by given instruments. In order to analyze the implementation situation, we have to ask three important questions:
—What system is subject to change?
—What style of change is used and given?
—What do we know of the expected noise and expected behaviour?

If we take the first question—the *system subject to change* (see Figure 8)—you will find that there are two relevant dimensions: (a) the degree of intended integration (isolated tasks, integrated islands, full integration); (b) the degree of autonomy re-

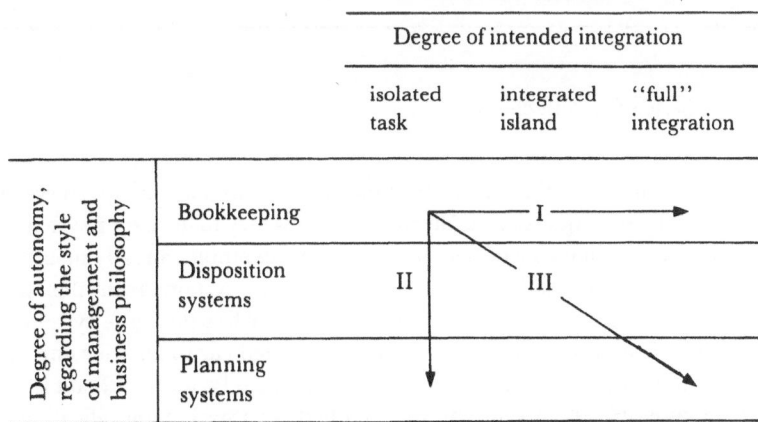

Figure 8. Systems subject to change

lated to the very steady aspects of business organizations: the style of management and the basic business philosophy. To change it in the subculture "business organization" is a very hard work. The more the system to be designed and implemented will interfere with management style and business philosophy, the more difficult the implementation job will be.

Going along the arrows in Figure 8 implementation conditions will become tougher. There is an order of difficulties ranging from Type I to Type III: if we try to get more and more integration (I) or if we go from a bookkeeping system to some type of disposition or planning system (II); and if we do both, of course, then we possibly will run into more severe problems.

As to our next question: what is the *style of system change* like? Here again we differentiate two dimensions: one refers to the kind of innovation step related to the existing system in the organization. For instance, for those organizations with a given bookkeeping system it is quite a step to get any kind of planning or disposition system. The other dimension refers to the state of art of the system technology (see Figure 9).

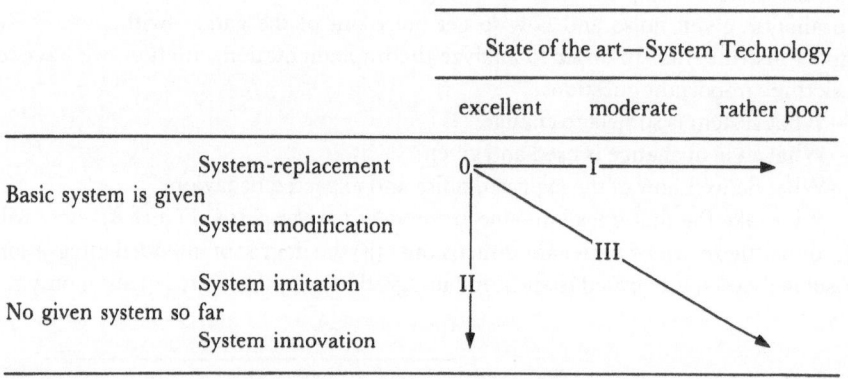

Figure 9. Style of system change

I want to explain these dimensions in some detail. If we have no given system we can ask the following question: is the new system we try to develop a system imitation? (then we have a frame of reference and some examples already in existence). Or is it a system innovation? And if we have the basic system given, then it might be just a replacement, but a replacement in more or less the same system mode. For instance, if we are changing from an accustomed car to another one, it is almost the same, not a tremendous change; but it would be more difficult to go into a system that is slightly or more or less modified; so a system modification might come up. But it is not worthwhile to discuss these stages without understanding what actually is the state of the art. That means:

—How far are we able to control the development process?

—How far do we know and can control the "production" of these systems?

And that actually means the state of art of system technology. It might be related to programming technology or system engineering, but if we take into account the point discussed earlier, it goes far beyond that into the social context. So it is a part of social technology, of course, too.

The third question in the frame of the implementation strategies refers to what we have to understand before trying to implement and use some implementation strategies: What actually is the *expected behaviour* of the people we have to look at like? Is there any noise we should expect? But if we are going back to our playground and to the objectives, then we remember that the problem is not just set up to something that would be going into work without any noise. What we are asking for is the service system, a system that helps to do something, so solve problems.

Therefore we have to ask in addition: is the system we designed, the model we would like to apply, the method we would like to use related to the given problem in a way that we could say, there is a problem fitting (regardless if you can measure it or not)? And if we can answer "yes", then it means the system or the subject we would like to implement is worthwhile of being implemented. And then and only then it is reasonable to ask: is there any noise, is there any disturbance we have to get rid of? Only if there is no disturbance, we have no implementation problem (see Figure 10).

		noise to be expected?	
		no	yes
problem fitting?	yes	no implementation problems	what noise? what can be done? who can help? what implementation strategy?
	no	Why not? How can we get awareness?	Implementation activities will be harmful!

Figure 10. Expected behaviour

If there is expected noise, and the problem fitting seems to be guaranteed, then we have to ask: what kind of noise, what is the type of noise; how dangerous is it to have these disturbances? And: what can be done?, who can help?, what implementing strategy should we choose?

But we have the other cases, too. And quite a part of implementation research is just looking on these cases. They are not asking: what is the expected noise like?

But they take just one special type of noise, the noise changing the ability to accept something, and ask "acceptance: yes or no?" But if the answer is "yes", and we have to realize the fact of "no problem fitting", then of course we have to ask: why do and why should people accept a worthless system? And are we not obliged to make them aware of it so that they should not accept it?

On the contrary, if we will have a situation with expected noise, we will make a lot of implementation effort while the very system and methods we are looking at won't help to solve the problems at all. Then implementation activities will be very harmful, because they create cost a second time. We not only have the cost for developing and using a terrible system, but we also have the cost for promoting and training and doing everything in order to get this system accepted and in use; we have to recognize that it would be just nonsense in that case to try to implement the system.

Confining some possible *implementation strategies* we have to look at two of the players in our game: one is the on-the-job specialist (B), and the other is the system specialist (S). These relations are related to types of specialization and differentiating in working systems.

A basic relation in the business world is the *ordering strategy*. That means the user defines his requirements, and tells the system specialist what he would like to have. And the system specialist will realize the system. Another very common type can be called the *marketing strategy*. In that case the system specialist will define the system, and will realize it; then he has to solve the problem of getting the very product "sold" to the user. Some other aspects of implementation are related to *participating*. In the case of full participating (B) and (S) will define the system, and (B) and (S) will realize it later on. The types of partial participating are shown in Figure 11. In addition we have to take into account that quite often the user and on-the-job specialist will just refuse any help—any help of the three types mentioned above. He will say: I would like *to do it myself*. And quite often he thinks he is the only one who really can do it. The "helping yourself" strategy is coming up again in the world of minis and micros.

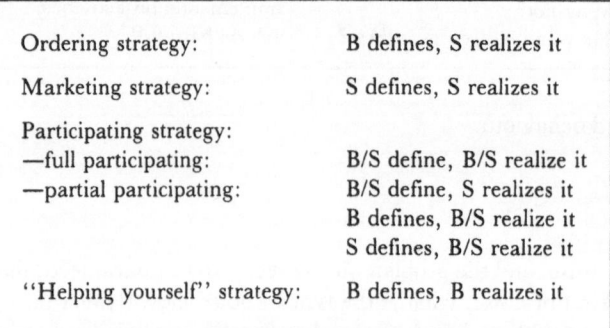

Figure 11. Implementation strategies

2.7 System Development Process

Differentiating the strategies of implementation, we have to be very careful in order to understand the process we are looking at. We need to consider it in a slightly different way than we are accustomed to, discussing its stages by just trying to understand some relevant activities. If we will block these processes into:

—problem definition, information needs and system requirements as one block;
—design concepts, models, procedures;
—technical solutions, programming, testing, operating;
—individual use, organizational actions, and
—successful behaviour in order to solve the real problem;

then we have actually three different groups of problems within the implementation process (see Figure 12).

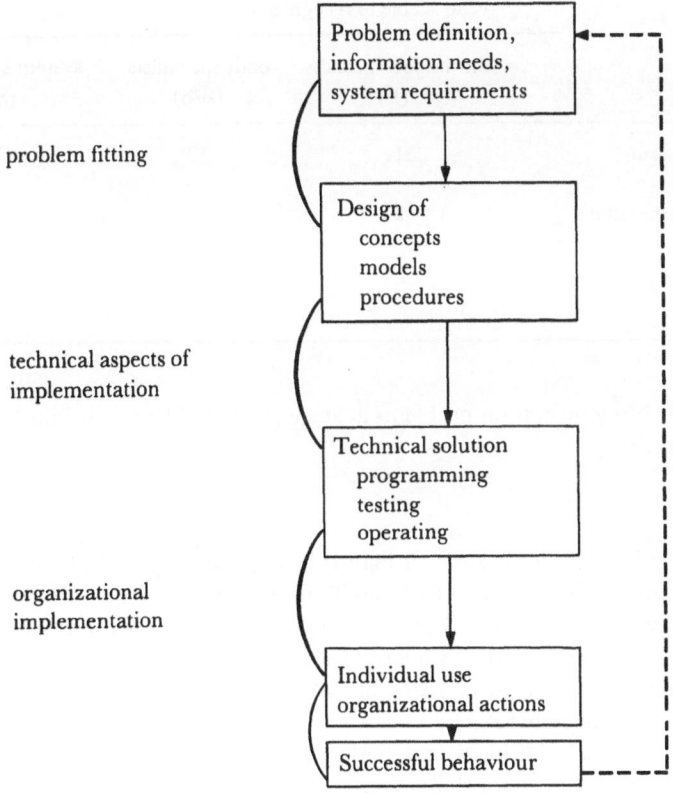

Figure 12. System development process

15

One aspect is very much related to the *problem fitting*; another is related to the *technical aspects of implementation*, and a third would be the *organizational implementation* (and quite often the individual behaviour related to it).

If we now try to understand this process and its problems, then we have to cover actually every stage and go very closely and very carefully into these problems. Let us first take the implementation problem at the stage (I) "problem definition and information needs" (see Figure 13).

		on-the-job specialist (B)	both specialists (B/S)	system specialist (S)
	a priori	11	12	13
	processual	21	22	23
	a posteriori	31	32	33

conditions, impacts?
coaching—results
training—actions
motivation—acceptance
understanding—instructions

Who is able to recognize it?

When is it possible to recognize?

Figure 13. Implementation problems at stage (I): "Problem definition and information needs"

If we just look at the columns of Figure 13 we could say in applying the traditional approach: (B) is doing it by himself, or (S) is doing it, just with the marketing strategy alone, or (B) and (S) are cooperating, and it's a participative approach. But discussing just this question would not be enough. It may only answer the question: who is recognizing the problem, who is recognizing what information needs somebody has?

In this case the additional and perhaps more difficult problem is: at what time—related to the actual doing—somebody ((B) or (S)) is able to recognize what to do? By mixing these two aspects, we will get the real picture for the implementation problem. For instance, in many cases it might not be possible to recognize some needs or some problems a priori. But by starting and by doing something one understands the problem of the subject one is dealing with. And it

16

might be that the best way to do it is just with the man who really is doing it. But in many cases—take a man who is in bookkeeping—the problems and the best way of solving them is to ask the bookkeeping specialist because he has broad scope of looking at subjects and problems.

So we could go through the matrix of Figure 13 and will find different situations for starting the process and for using various strategies, especially for the implementation aspects. The conditions and impacts of these situations are related to the type of noise and the instruments of implementation we are looking at. What are the conditions of understanding likely to be? Who understands better? Quite often two people coming from different sides are complementing one another; suddenly they understand the problem better than anyone alone by himself. This effect of synergy might come up as far as working together and growing understanding is concerned.

Furthermore we can go on to our second objective and ask: what does the interaction mean as far as motivation or acceptance is concerned? Is there growing acceptance depending on the personality of one or the other man? Are interactions stimulating acceptance or do they bring up additional resistance?

In the same line we might question the training and the coaching aspect.

The main problem, as far as I can see it, is that there are special conditions for doing the implementation job in the best way within the very stages of the overall system development process on one hand, and various impacts from understanding to accepting and to training, and from acceptance to training and back and forth. Besides that we have to look at these cross-related impacts from one stage to another.

So we could go through the following stages of the process considered, differentiating the relevant aspects for implementation strategies. Figure 14, for instance, shows for stage (II), "design of concepts, models, procedures", the set of possible situations of implementation.

	who has knowledge or can develop it?		
knowledge for sufficient design?	B	B/S	S
given	11	12	13
partly given	21	22	23
not given	31	32	33

Figure 14. Implementation situations at the stage (II): "Design of concepts, models, procedures"

17

We could develop analog schemes for stages (III) and (IV). I won't do so here, but what we need is an integrated consideration of process stages and the interrelated sets of implementation problems.

2.8 Multi-Dimensional and Multi-Stage Implementation Dynamics

Therefore, I want to suppose understanding the implementation game as multidimensional and multi-stage dynamics. One dimension is related to—if we take these very broad terms—problem definition, system design, system realization and system use as the stages of an implementation process. The second dimension—as shown in Figure 15—refers to the above-mentioned objectives of understanding, acceptance, actions, results. As a third dimension we see the differentiation of concerned members of our organization (B, S). They have to be considered at each element of the matrix in Figure 15. So, my multi-interrelationships of these dimensions we have a very difficult dynamic implementation process, for which we can define a multi-stage and multi-dimensional implementation problem chart.

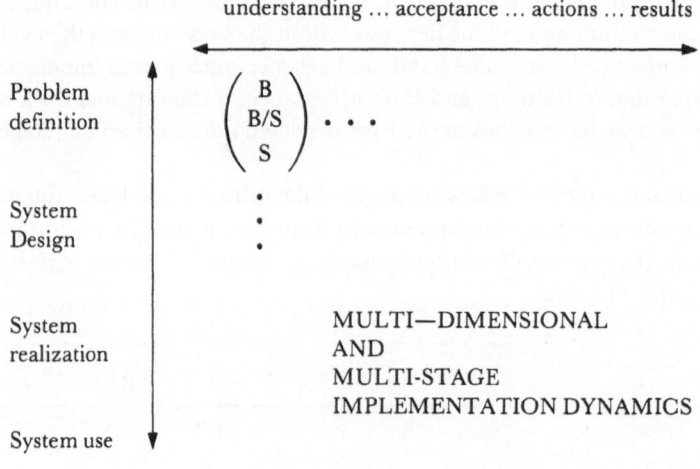

Figure 15. Multi-dimensional and multi-stage implementation dynamics

To discuss this in some detail, we can say, for instance, that being involved in problem definition it is easier for a man to accept the system design. Or we may state: a man who is trying to be involved in the system design process is better trained in advance to use the system. And even with respect to system use we can ask: who is the man the system is designed for; is he really able to use it by himself? Or must he have support from the system specialist all of the time in using

18

the system? In many cases only the system individual who designs the system will be able to use it. So quite often there is actually no direct use by the man the system is designed for. We will get most of the problems of implementation confined and disclosed within this multi-stage and multi-dimensional approach.

3   CONTRIBUTIONS FROM RESEARCH TO SYSTEM DESIGN AND IMPLEMENTATION

3.1   Aspects of System Design and Technical Implementation

It is quite clear that the success of implementation at least partly depends on the results of the activities carried out earlier. In fact, implementation in this sense means implementation of a programmed or computer system, a meaning which has remained the most wide-spread until now (e.g., [29]). Giving a broader sense to implementation we can ask, what is implemented in the three preceding phases? Possible answers are: programming is the implementation of a system, e.g., a planning or information system; the modeling process can be regarded as the implementation of a model, a method or a concept, depending on the type of system to be built; and problem analysis, finally, is the implementation of an idea. So we can regard implementation as a process with a changing object. A point of view that is becoming more common now (e.g., [15]).

Considering now various contributions of research to the process of system design and implementation, we ought to distinguish between research with regard to the different phases. This is necessary, firstly, in order to get an idea of the respective contributions of the specific tools to implementation success and, secondly, in order to be fair regarding many of these tools, which promote implementation now, but originally had not been developed in the context of the design process as a whole and especially not with regard to implementation success.

3.1.1   Problem Analysis

Here we can ask the question: how much did we do on the research side in order to understand the problem analysis process?

If we are going to analyze the literature of the very early years of scientific work, we see that people were thinking in a philosophical way about how to fight the right problems; and for a long time there was actually no structure out of which a process could be gotten. And if we are looking at the applications and literature right now, of course we will find some techniques for problem analysis, assessment methods or anything similar. For instance for the subphases of problem opportunity identification [16], methodological help developed much earlier is now being recommended: problem analysis and assessment methods [30], creativity techniques, such as brainstorming [10] and synectics [18], and methods for technological forecasting and assessment [49]. Especially the creativity techniques are interesting in the sense that they are doing nothing else but trying to get the noise out of our minds in order to let us understand the real problem.

Most of them were neglected in the discussion as far as implementation is concerned because it is very easy to say one has a problem, and the problem is easy to describe, but nobody knows whether it is a problem or whether it is just a fiction of one's ideas that might be a problem. And at the point, we can see that not to understand the real problem means to spend a lot of money for nothing. It might be very interesting in an intellectual or aesthetical sense to design a system and to run this system, but it is a failure if nobody really can use it.

As to the results of different research activities and practical experiences we can see that problem analysis has to focus on the next steps of system design and is consequently oriented towards an implementation success. But it is still difficult to estimate consequences of problem analyses for implementation success. To achieve a more technical and reproducable proceeding, suggestions have been made about how to use interactive procedures [7] or interactive simulation models in problem analysis [11] or to follow a systems approach which has been well accepted for strategic planing purposes and should be extended to the planning process of information systems in order to "identify all problems and study their relationship before solving any one problem" [17, p. 50].

As a result we can suppose that in the area of problem definition and problem analysis we are lacking in methods and practice; we are not using these instruments sufficiently enough.

3.1.2 System Modeling

For a long time the process of modeling has not been paid the attention it deserves. Models and methods had been developed for nearly every task. And it seemed to be a question of adaptation and fine-tuning to find new applications for OR-models, simulation techniques, optimizing and forecasting methods. As these grew out of the experimentation stage the model builders were no longer model users and so new information and orientation were needed for successful implementation. Some procedures for the choice between models and methods have been developed [38], and suggestions have been made about how to assess the value of a certain model in a certain situation. Considering the difficulties associated with this we should not wonder when recommendations on alternative models and methods are made rather than decision processes programmed [40] or just information on models is gathered and distributed.

In fact, there were several activities besides the straightforward approach to a modelling methodology, advancing the thinking on modeling. Obviously easy-to-use models were developed by Forrester [13] and models of a new type were implemented (e.g., [37]), and soon criticized (e.g., [19]). These problems are still under discussion, but first conclusions have already been drawn. One of the most important is that a modeling methodology not only forces demands on and influences the models themselves but also the phases of development directly adjacent to the modeling process. The models which are implemented should not only be easy to understand [29, 40] and easy and comfortable to use, but problem analysis and programming should contribute their part to meet the requirements concerning the models. So a strong effect on the trend to integrating the different phases results from the modeling process.

Let me emphasize this: we are talking quite often about the problem of implementing a model, but nobody asked the question: is that the right model? Even if we have the right problem, it's hard to decide if we have the right model for the problem. And modeling something actually means: setting up an instrument, building up a tool. And if a man tries to build a tool, he has to know what to do with it; he has to evaluate and check his own tool.

So it is not only a question of how to get an easily-used model, but how to find the models really structured to meet the requirements of our objectives. That is a substantial problem. And that asks for a lot of knowledge; not just formal, mathematical, but experienced, substantial knowledge in the field we would like to work in.

3.1.3 Programming Technology

As to the contributions to programming technology, these contributions are characterized by two developments. On one hand, we can see that the designer of program languages tries to design very powerful languages for limited applications— and these relate to one another. If the language actually is very powerful it is most of the time related to a very special subject. On the other hand, we can find more and more discussion related to the question of how to organize, how to structure the programming process. And programming actually means to get some concepts into a set of orders, orders understandable by somebody, maybe some machine. But the process of setting up these lines of orders, this system of orders, is almost independent of the type of programming language you would like to use later on. So the basic structure of program systems, e.g., does not depend 1:1 on a special programming language. We can see both: very friendly, powerful languages, programming languages on one hand; and on the other a lot of discussion as far as the basic structuring of programs is concerned.

Some remarks on the actual state in programming technology may illustrate this in somewhat more detail: regarding the problems arising in the process of system design and implementation, the help which can be found by adopting the new techniques and languages is enormous. Especially, insight into the model or method, documentation and modifiability are supported. The contribution of the new programming languages in this field has been discussed very often and the use of interpreters instead of compilers, e.g., for a broad area of application, are nearly generally recognized.

The diffusion of the principles of programming technology has not gone ahead satisfactorily until now. For example, flow charts are still much more often in use than Nassi-Shneiderman-diagrams [45]. This may be due to the origin of the research, which is in informatics and mathematics. In fact, this research is not really conducted with regard to implementation, but rather from an EDP-technical point of view. Secondly, these developments are rather new. Böhm and Jacopini

[6] published the principles of structured programming in 1966 and Mills the mathematical foundations in 1972 [39]. Principles for structuring real-time and multiprogrammed programs have recently been developed [55].

These techniques simultaneously support all phases from requirements specification over programming, coding to documentation. So, adopting these techniques leads to a process where significant parts of the original programming phase are to be done earlier, i.e., in the modeling phase or even during requirements specification. On the other hand certain organizational consequences are implied by structured programming [4], whose influence on the process of implementation should be discovered.

Programming technology has now and will have even greater influence in the future on any of the stages of system implementation, mainly when it coincides with the development of programming languages, and structured languages such as PASCAL.

3.1.4 Integrated System Design

There are some contributions to the very important need of integrating the stepwise activities in system design. Integration in this sense does not mean to stop thinking in steps, but to bring the separate steps, phases, or stages of system design together. At last within this technical aspect we would like to overcome the highly specialized differentiation between different stages and different groups working in these areas.

Two major forces can be detected, stimulating the process of integrating the separated steps of system design. One has already been emphasized in connection with the description of the different steps, more precisely, in connection with the tools developed for these steps: it is the tendency to determine and consider the influence of one step on another. First it is the influence or feed-forward from problem analysis to modeling and programming. Second we have the requirements of a certain step, which involve feedback on the earlier steps. These problems have been recognized now, but solved only partially.

The second major force is the diffusion of the MIS idea, which has been stated in numerous approaches. One of the latest, dealing with the German situation, is the one of Köhler and Heinzelbecker, who found out that in 1975 nearly all of the big companies were concerned with considerations on MIS [31, p. 268]. Smaller companies have begun to implement planning models and MIS and they particularly need professional tools because of their limited resources as far as financial power and qualification of personnel are regarded. The EDP barrier is now becoming slightly less important.

Integrating the process of system development will lead to considerable savings in every respect. So efforts have been undertaken to support this process. Mere sequencing of activities has been detected as unvaluable, but it may serve as a basis for further activities. Roberts recently gave recommendations on the individual steps emphasizing the implementation-affecting aspects [50]. Manuals have been produced on this for specific design and implementation problems. The

22

suppliers of such manuals now aim at a broader range of application. Certainly, the procedural aid intended will only be given if the methodological questions arising in system design can be solved. Müller-Merbach [41] has been researching into this field and will elaborate on the topic.

3.2 Aspects of Organizational Implementation

Now I want to focus our interest on the important area of organizational aspects of design and implementation. On the one hand there are a lot of publications on system development of computer-based planning systems as an interactional process of organizational innovation, knowledge from the social sciences in general, from social psychology, organization theory can be claimed to be effective contributions to implementation research.

But what does that mean? We are learning that the situation in designing and implementing is not a unique problem, but that people around the world, trying to implement governmental policies e.g., are facing the same basic problem. So what we really can learn is an understanding of the implementation process in different areas. We should not look merely at the very problem of getting the right program language in order to implement the system, and we should not believe that implementing a computer-based planning system is—as far as the implementation problem is concerned—a unique task. It is a very common problem to get something and somewhat implemented!

There are many contributions, especially by empirical studies dealing with personal and organizational aspects of system development process. These studies can be differentiated as follows:

3.2.1 Factor Studies

Several contributions stress the enormous importance of factors like
—user participation [34, 8],
—top management support [48, 47],
—overcoming user resistance to change [27]. Most of these studies support their statements with results from relatively small samples and analysis of factors that differ strongly among the studies. Most of their consequences are somewhat normative but claim to have general validity, the range of their consequences seldom is discussed.

3.2.2 Impact Studies

In a second group, we will find these special impact papers: impacts of computer-based information or planning systems on individuals or small groups [12, 52, 32, 51, 54, 56]; impacts of certain technological components or special forms of the computer-based systems on decision behaviour [25; 9]; the impacts on the organizational structure [54, 35, 5]; but most of these investigations represent just a monocausal explanation; they are trying to use just one variable and study its impact on some other variable.

3.2.3 Relational Studies

A third kind of study analyzes the relations between certain factors or groups of factors and the success of implementation. Ginzberg [14] gives a very comprehensive survey on such factor studies. The problem with them is the variety of factors investigated. The studies concentrate on different groups of factors, on different types of information systems and different organizational and personal settings of computer-based information systems (CBIS) [20, 46, 36, 5].

There are many other studies, but they all do approve one main problem: there is no type of coordination between them. You can use their very different single statements, but you cannot find a path to an integrated result of these empirical efforts. There is no common frame of reference for these research activities.

Most of these studies are trying to understand something that has happened. They have a retrospective orientation. Relations between factors are analyzed ex post. Empirical data are mostly collected after system development has been finished. There are only a few statements on the process of system development. This leads to the fact that system people do not find much information in these studies which could help them directly in their daily work. Therefore, in the following passages I would like to focus on contributions predominantly dealing with the constructive and procedural side of overcoming implementation problems.

3.2.4 Comprehensive Approaches

Some contributions we know can be called comprehensive because they deal with the whole implementation process. One of these comprehensive approaches we see in the "ETHICS: Method of Socio-Technical System Design", providing a tool for structuring the principal social and technical components of systems implementation, serving as a basis for detailed specification and adjustment of these components to be incorporated in the system [43, 44, 00, 57].

The PORGI-approach is to be seen—hopefully—as another contribution. The aim of the BIFOA research project PORGI is to supply procedural as well as substantial aid to systems implementation. Both approaches—ETHICS and PORGI—will be presented extensively later on.

Additionally, in this group we find different kinds of handbooks (e.g., advor—620 [1]; HIPO [26]; IFA-PASS [28]; ORGWARE II [2]; ORGWARE IV [3]) providing guidelines for formal aspects of the system development organization. Some support to *evaluation activities* in system implementation is supplied by contributions of *utility analysis* [59], for instance BASYC [21, 22]. You can consider BASYC as a procedural scheme for integrating different dimensions of utility analysis in a multi-personal context.

4 SOME PRELIMINARY REMARKS ON CONSEQUENCES FOR IMPLEMENTATION RESEARCH

What are the principal requirements that implementation research should fulfil in order to be a real help to implementation practice—related to the previously-stated implementation objectives? Implementation research should of course continue to derive general knowledge about implementation processes; special attention, however, should be drawn to developing tools, instrumental knowledge, applicable in special cases, considering the contextual peculiarities of a given situation, suited to guide preventive action, system- as well as process-oriented. For this purpose, a mere retrospective orientation, producing ''a posteriori'' knowledge, is not sufficient. Although many insights have been gained by studies with the main concern ''why systems fail...'', what we need to know is ''why systems succeed''. Similarly: if, during the construction of a machine, we have been able to control most of the relevant factors, and the machine will explode anyhow: what insights did we gain? We might be able to reproduce the machine, but the risk that the new one will explode, too, is relatively high. We have gained little insight in order to be able to build a machine that succeeds. What does this mean for system implementation? We need positive examples to derive experience from. To return to our machine: copying a functioning one in a similar setting will probably prove more successful.

To develop such positive experiences the researcher should take an active role in ongoing implementation processes. And referring to the social reality we have to play the implementation game. Implementation technology should be seen as a part of social technology.

Finally, I would like to make some general remarks on what implementation research is today and what it should be. Talking about the ''State of the Art of Implementation Research'' cannot reasonably be done neglecting the ''State of the Art of Implementation Practice''. If there has really been considerable progress in implementation research—and our symposium will show that much work has been done—why then is the state of implementation practice still so poor, many systems being insufficiently developed, dissipating resources, frustrating system specialists, management, and users?

If there is a gap between the knowledge produced in implementation research and the degree of its application in implementation practice, this gap, at least in part, is caused by the researchers themselves; the quality and validity of their results, the practicability of their methodological contributions, the intelligibleness of their publications, all determine the actual degree of knowledge and competence transfer from research into practice. This we should have in mind: implementation research is not a more or less contemplative activity; to make its results really be effective, they themselves will have to be implemented.

REFERENCES

1. ADV/ORGA F.A. Meyer KG, *Advor-620: Projektmanagement System,* Wilhelmshaven.

2. ADV/ORGA F.A. Meyer KG, *ORGWARE II: Planung und Implementierung aktueller DV-Aufgaben,* Wilhelmshaven.

3. ADV/ORGA F.A. Meyer KG (ed.), *ORGWARE IV: Planung und Implementierung von Informationssystemen,* Wilhelmshaven.

4. Baker, F.T., "Chief Programmer Teams: Principles and Procedures," IBM Report FSC71-5108, Gaithersburg, Md., 1971.

4a. Bardach, E., *The Implementation Game: What Happens After a Bill Becomes a Law,* Cambridge, Mass./London, England, 1977.

5. Bean, A.S., R.D. Neal, M. Radnor and D.A. Tansik, "Structural and Behavioral Correlates of Implementation in U.S. Business Organizations," in R.L. Schultz and D.P. Slevin (eds.), *Implementing Operations Research/Management Science,* New York, 1975, pp. 77-132.

6. Böhm, C. and G. Jacopini, "Flow Diagrams, Turing Machines, and Languages With Only Two Formation Rules," *Communications ACM* 9 (1966): 366-371.

7. Boland, R.J., "The Process and Product of System Design," *Management Science* 24(9) (1978): 887-898.

8. Carter, M., L. Gibson and A. Rademacher, "A Study of Critical Factors in Management Information Systems in the U.S. Air Force," Colorado State University, Information Systems Series 460-2, 1973.

9. Chervany, N.L. and G.W. Dickson, "An Experimental Evaluation of Information Overload in a Production Environment," *Management Science* 20 (1974): 1335-1344.

10. Clark, C.H., *Brainstorming: Methoden der Zusammenarbeit und Ideenfindung* (German translation), Munich, 1966.

11. Davis, K.R., "The Process of Problem Finding: a Production-Marketing Example," *Interfaces* 8(1) (1977): 82-86.

12. Dyckmann, T.R., "Management Implementation of Scientific Research: An Attitudinal Study," *Management Science* 13(10) (1967): B612-B620.

13. Forrester, J.W., *Industrial Dynamics,* Cambridge, Mass., 1961.

14. Ginzberg, M.J., "A Detailed Look at Implementation Research," Report CISR-4, Sloan School of Management, MIT, Working Paper 753-4, November 1974.

15. Ginzberg, M., "Steps Toward More Effective Implementation of MS and MIS," *Interfaces* 8(3) (1978): 57-63.

16. Graham, R.J., "Problem and Opportunity Identification in Management Science," *Interfaces* 6(4) (1976): 79-82.

17. Graham, R.J. and M. Jahani, "People, Problems and Planning: A Systems Approach to Problem Identification," *Interfaces* 8(1) (1977): 50-55.

18. Gordon, W.J.J., *Synectics, the Development of Creative Capacity,* New York, 1961.

19. Hansmann, F., "Modelle zur Energieplanung: Eine kritische Betrachtung," in F. Schober and H.D. Plötzeneder (eds.), *Ökonometrische Modelle und Systeme,* Munich-Vienna, 1978, pp. 249-59.

20. Harvey, A., "Factors making for Implementation Success and Failure," *Management Science* 16(6) (1970): B312-B321.

21. Hawgood, J., "A formal framework for participative benefit assessment," Paper submitted to IFIP Congress 77, Durham.

22. Hawgood, J., E. Mumford, F.F. Land and C.M. Reddington, "Evaluation and management of computer-based systems: an interdisciplinary approach," *Information Processing 71,* Amsterdam: North Holland Publ. Co., 1972.

23. Hawgood, J., F.F. Land and E. Mumford, "Comparison of alternative strategies and systems," *Datenverarbeitung im Europäischen Raum* (Arbeitsgemeinschaft für Datenverarbeitung), Vienna, 1972, pp. 283-287.

24. Hawgood, J., "Quinquevalent quantification of computer benefits," *Proceedings of the International Symposium on Economics of Informatics*, IBI 1974, pp. 96-105.

25. Hedberg, B., *On Man-Computer Interaction in Organizational Decision-Making: A Behavioral Approach*, Gothenburg, 1970.

26. HIPO: A Design and Documentation Technique, IBM-Form: GC20-1851-1, 2nd ed., 1975.

27. Huysmann, J.H.B.M., *The Implementation Research: An Approach to the Joint Consideration of Social and Technological Aspects*, New York: 1970.

28. IFA-Beratungsgesellschaft für Automation GmbH, "IFA-PASS: Projekt-Management-, Administrations- und -Steuerungs-System," Düsseldorf.

29. Kallina, C., "Development and Implementation of a Simple Short Range Forecasting Model—a Case Study," *Interfaces* 8(3) (1978): 32-41.

30. Kepner, Ch.H. and B.B. Tregoe, *Managemententscheidungen vorbereiten und richtig treffen*, Munich, 1967, 3rd ed., 1971.

31. Köhler, R. and K. Heinzelbecker, "Informationssysteme für die Unternehmungsführung," *Die Betriebswirtschaft* 37(2) (1977): 267-82.

32. Ladd, D.E., "Report on a Group's Reaction to the 'Researcher and the Manager': A Dialectic of Implementation," *Management Science* 12(2) (1965): B24-B25.

33. Leavitt, H.J., "Applied Organizational Change in Industry: Structural Technological and Humanistic Approaches," in J.G. March (ed.), *Handbook of Organizations*, Skokill, Ill., 1965, pp. 1144-70.

34. Little, J.D.C., "Models and Managers: The Concept of a Decision Calculus," *Management Science*, 16(8) (1970): B466-B483.

35. Lucas, H.C., Jr., "Performance and the Use of an Information System," *Management Science* 21(8) (1975a): B908-B919.

36. Lucas, H.C., Jr., *Why Information Systems Fail*, New York/London, 1975.

37. Meadows, D.L., *The Limits to Growth*, New York, 1972.

38. Mertens, P., W. Neuwirth and W. Schmitt, "Verknüpfung von Daten- und Modellbanken, dargestellt am Beispiel der Analyse von Marktforschungsdaten," in H.D. Plötzeneder (ed.), *Computergestützte Unternehmungsplanung/Computer Assisted Corporate Planning*, Stuttgart, 1977, pp. 291-334.

39. Mills, H.D., "Mathematical Foundations for Structured Programming," IBM Document FSC72-6012, Gaithersburg, Md., 1972.

40. Mohn, N., and J.C. Reid, "Some Practical Guidelines for the Corporate Forecaster," *Interfaces* 7(3) (1977): 70-75.

41. Müller-Merbach, H., "Quantitative Entscheidungsvorbereitung, Erwartungen, Enttäuschungen, Chancen," *Die Betriebswirtschaft* 37(1) (1977): 11-23.

42. Mumford, E., "Job satisfaction: a major objective in the system design process," *Management Informatics* 2(4) (1973).

43. Mumford, E., *Job Satisfaction: A Study of computer specialists*, London, 1972.

44. Mumford, E., *Systems Design for People: Economic Evaluation of Computer Based Systems*, Book 3, Manchester, 1971.

45. Nassi, I., and B. Shneidermann, "Flow Chart Techniques for Structured Programming," *SIGPLAN Notices* 8(12) (1973).

46. Powers, R.F. and G. Dickson, "MIS Project Management: Myths, Opinions, and Reality," *California Management Review* 15(3) (1973): 147-56.

47. Radnor, M., A.H. Rubenstein and A.S. Bean, "Integration and Utilization of Management Science Activities in Organizations," *Operations Research Quarterly* 19(2) (1968): 117-141.

48. Radnor, M., A.H. Rubenstein and D.A. Tansik, "Implementation in Operations Research and R&D in Government and Business Organizations," *Operations Research* 18(1970): 967-91.

49. Roberts, E.B., "Explanatory and Normative Technological Forecasting: a Critical Appraisal," in M.J. Cetron and J.D. Goldhar (eds.), *The Science of Managing Organized Technology*, Vol. 2, New York/London/Paris, 1970, pp. 891-909.

50. Roberts, E.B., "Strategies for Effective Implementation of Complex Corporate Models," *Interfaces* 8(1) (1977): 26-33.

51. Schultz, R.L. and D.P. Slevin, "Implementation and Organizational Validity: An Empirical Investigation," in R.L. Schultz and D.P. Slevin (eds.), *Implementing Operations Research/Management Science*, New York, 1975, pp. 153-182.

52. Shaw, E., *Group Dynamics: The Psychology of Small Group Behaviour*, New York, 1971.

53. Smith, D.M., "Job design: from research to application," *The Journal of Industrial Engineering* 19(10) (1968): 477-481.

54. Sorensen, R.E., and D.E. Zand, "Improving the Implementation of OR/MS Models by Applying the Lewin-Schein-Theory of Change," in R.L. Schultz and D.P. Slevin (eds.), *Implementing Operations Research/Management Science*, New York, 1975, pp. 217-36.

55. Tausworthe, R.C., *Standardized Development of Computer Software*, Englewood Cliffs, N.J., 1977.

56. Vertinsky, I., R.T. Barth and V.F. Mitchell, "A Study of OR/MS Implementation as a Social Change Process," in R.L. Schultz and D.P. Slevin (eds.), *Implementing Operations Research/Management Science*, New York, 1975, pp. 253-69.

57. Weir, M., "Effectiveness of Computer Systems in Creating Satisfying Jobs for Users: A Method of Assessment," in A.B. Frielink (ed.), *Economics of Informatics*, Proceedings of the IBI-ICC International Symposium, Mainz, 16-20 September 1974, Amsterdam/Oxford/New York, 1975, pp. 421-26.

58. Whisler, T.L., *The Impact of Computers on Organizations*, New York, 1970.

59. Zangemeister, C., *Nutzwertanalyse in der Systemtechnik*, 2nd ed., Munich, 1971.

2. Evaluating the Quality of Information Systems

by Charles H. Kriebel

1 INTRODUCTION

One clever paradigm I have seen used in discussions on the management of system development serves to illustrate a common pitfall which confronts many project managers. Imagine four circles that serve to represent "control dials" arranged in the pattern of a square. Circle number one in the upper left-hand corner of the square is labeled "Scope of the Project". Suppose in a hypothetical situation it has been decided to set the project scope at a level of magnitude which corresponds to a "three o'clock" reading on this dial. The second circle immediately below the first, in the lower left-hand corner of the sqaure, is labeled "Resources". Now suppose through negotiation it is agreed that project resources of people and money are to be at a level corresponding, say to a "five o'clock" reading on the second control dial. The third circle in the lower right-hand corner is labeled "Quality". In the current context this might involve consideration for issues such as documentation, component systems testing, and management reviews. Let us say, given the previous settings, that this dial is positioned at a "four o'clock" reading. The fourth circle in the upper right-hand corner of the square is labeled "Schedule" and the position of this control dial is the end result of the other three settings. Now imagine a belt or cable which connects all four dials around the perimeter of the square. Often in practice line management is tempted to try to turn back on the "Schedule" control dial while simultaneously holding fixed the first two dials (scope and resources) at their original values. If the mechanical analogy is valid, the result of this behavior has inevitable impact on the third control dial, "Quality". Despite the litany of case histories, learning from experience is expensive and seems to be painfully slow.

The notion of information system *quality* is ambiguous, although it is pervasive in the literature. In the preceding allegory I finessed the question with the imagery of a "quality control dial". It would be nice if it were that simple. I suspect most would agree with the allegory's message, however, the instrumentation for the "quality control dial" no doubt would engender a lively discussion among the experts.

To initiate a meaningful dialogue on the subject requires attention in my judgment to four interrelated process elements. First, the quality characteristic (or attributes) must be identified and defined. Secondly, the surrogates that will serve as objective measures of the quality characteristics must be specified. Thirdly, the measurement instrument (or data collection mechanisms) for monitoring the surrogates must be devised. And, finally, the basis for evaluating performance and validating the results must be determined.

In the balance of this papaer I will attempt to review the current status of work on the evaluation of information systems quality in organizations. To provide perspective the following section outlines several open conceptual and operational issues on the performance evaluation question. Next, a survey of the research literature is given. The paper concludes with some ideas for future research.

2 CONCEPTUAL AND OPERATIONAL ISSUES

The prescription of criteria for performance evaluation is bounded by purpose and environment, which presupposes answers to several questions. For instance, does interest center on problems relating to planning, managerial control or administrative incentives? What level within the organizational hierarchy is to be accommodated: the individual, the departemental or work unit level, or the overall organization? Are inter-organizational comparisons important? Should the analytical reference involve comparative statics or comparative dynamics in addressing intertemporal elements? Does interest focus primarily on existing systems, new developments, or both?

Much of the recent literature on information systems evaluation has stressed the distinction between two performance concepts: efficiency and effectiveness. Efficiency measures pertain to the amount of input resources required to deliver a unit of output—an information service or product. A common application of technical efficiency measures is in monitoring computer equipment resource utilization [4]. Limiting attention to efficiency measures raises difficulties in performance evaluation, however, because the immediate service or observable output received by a user is typically only the means by which the system's resources are being utilized to achieve other purposes of the user. For example, a report generated by a computational session represents an intermediate good that a user may require to make a decision. A more macro view of performance evaluation is to measure the *effectiveness* of the user as a result of having received the output or service. The efficiency vis-à-vis effectiveness perspectives have been paraphrased, respectively, as addressing the questions: "Are we doing things right?" and "Are we doing the right things?" While there appears to be agreement that the effectiveness perspective is the more relevant evaluation concept, there is less consensus on how to define and measure it.

It is obvious that the notion of effectiveness even for an individual is a multi-dimensional concept. For the moment I will defer consideration of the specific dimensions in detail. Operationally, is it necessary or desirable to aggregate the various dimensions into a single performance index? What are the units of "effectiveness"? For example, how does one measure the effectiveness of a manager in performing his job? (By his economic compensation?) Is it feasible to measure the incremental contribution of an information service to a user in a "value added" sense? How are individual differences among and across users to be reconciled? A similar question arises regarding potential tradeoffs between various dimensions of the vector of effectiveness. No doubt many performance indicators of quality will be highly correlated. Does this imply that measurements will be biased or that only relatively crude, ordinal evaluations can be made? More positively, can a procedure be developed or a technique identified (such as goal programming) that would yield a priority ordering for "leading" quality indicators?

Usually one does not consider the quality of a product in absolute terms, but rather it is considered in a comparative sense relative to some "standard of performance" (e.g., for a product class) or to an expectation or to a performance goal. The comparison might also be made relative to a departure from the status quo or an equilibrium condition. This immediately raises the questions of what constitutes a norm and how is it established? As we shall see, one common practice reported in the literature is to survey the population of users or consumers of the output, e.g., employing semantic differentials of users' attitudes on various quality dimensions. If the survey's results are uniformly good (or bad) the evaluation may be straightforward, but such an outcome typically is the exception. With mixed results, how should the data be interpreted? Presumably, a survey of users would be a stratified sample perhaps by function and management level. Should an attempt be made to weight the responses according to some logic? There is some evidence which suggests that senior management's views and opinions have an impact on their subordinates. As a source of bias should one attempt to correct for this effect or ignore it? Moral hazard and incentive compatible considerations also enter here. That is, is it in the respondent's own best interests to be truthful even if the control of anonymity is included? The position and requirements of an individual's job relative to the formal information system of an organization influence his attitudes and perception of the system's utility [9; 35]. Not surprisingly, those more job dependent on the system tend to be more knowledgeable about it and correspondingly may overvalue its capabilities. How should one evaluate different perceptions by active and passive users of the system, especially where the latter class tend to be technically unsophisticated but operationally more important to the organization?

To evaluate information system performance the majority opinion still holds that one must go to the users for their evaluation even though we recognize some operational pitfalls. Users, we know, are complex cognitive and organizational entities. Observational data from users on performance may involve goals or aspirations, expectations or perceptions, or actual realizations, i.e., the service delivered. For any of these a user may be reporting his most recent episode or the cumulation of his experience. Should one isolate these distinctions to ensure consistency and objectivity in data reporting and analysis?

For example, consider the following simple model of user behavior. Suppose in two dimensions we plot on the ordinate axis a user's information-driven utility or satisfaction level as a function of quality where the quality characteristic is, say, timeliness as measured on the abscissa by turnaround time or response time. We can envision the functional relationship to be determined primarily by two user-specific parameters corresponding to threshold aspirations. One threshold value represents an ideal point in that at this value or better (below in this case) the user is satisfied completely, indifferent or satiated. The other threshold corresponds to a rejection point; when quality reaches this level or worse the user is so dissatisfied that he withdraws his consumption and seeks alterative means to meet his requirements. I have no strong empirical argument on the functional form of the graph between the threshold parameters; it could be linear, convex, concave or anything else, depending, I suppose, on the user's utility function. Outside of the threshold range it is flat or a saturation function by assumption. Side-stepping whether or not this model appears reasonable, empirical questions remain. I do not know if users would identify with the specification or how difficult it would be for them to articulate their threshold parameters (especially where multiple quality dimensions are involved.)* One would also conjecture that an individual's thresholds would adapt over time as a function of experience. For example, if the quality realized was consistently above a user's ideal point, then most likely over time the user would accordingly raise his aspirations, as well as his expectations.

Data analysis presupposes data availability and hence data collection instruments. Where performance evaluation primarily concerns technical efficiency as defined above, the data tends to be longitudinal or a cross-sectional and longitudinal series of objective measurements on physical operations. Instruments here include hardware monitors, various online software devices such as trace routines, benchmarking experiments, Kiviat graphs and simulation analysis [4 or 34]. Where the focus of evaluation is on effectiveness the majority of the work reported in the literature involves cross-sectional data. Common instruments employed here include survey questionnaires, interviews, panel media (for users or experts), nominal group sessions, laboratory experiments, field studies and combinations of these. In addition to the prescription of the sampling or monitor design parameters, these instruments require special attention to validity issues (e.g., on content, prediction and construct). Outside of the research community, a recent survey of U.S. industry by Diebold [7] indicated the following evaluation methods in use: capital-investment analysis, charge out, simulated profit centers, performance auditing, quality statistics and user surveys, to name several. It is apparent from the variety in this list that line management seeks multiple measurements of longitudinal and cross-sectional data in many dimensions as a hedge against risk.

The principal conclusion of the Diebold survey was that all firms employ several methods in consort for information system evaluation. No one method dominated in preference and the specific portfolio implemented differed across those firms surveyed in depth with no obvious generalization. The prominence of individual differences suggests a contingent theory construct for the evaluation issue although the conclusion is premature on this evidence alone. It comes as no surprise that answering many of the questions posed is not a simple task and it depends significantly on the particular organization and environmental constraints.

* On the surface at least such an exercise appears comparable to the behavioral experiments on utility functions in economics and decision analysis.

We now look to the research literature and attempt to refine the concept of information system quality.

3 A SURVEY OF THE RESEARCH LITERATURE

In the space available it is impossible to deal comprehensively with the extensive literature on this subject in general. To this end I refer the interested reader to recent bibliographies [4; 5; 21; 29; 33; 34; 35] and the secondary references cited in the publications discussed below. For the balance I will review work that I believe is representative of this research with apologies to those omitted due to space constraints or oversight.

The evaluation by management of information system performance is mixed, notwithstanding the billions of dollars invested [2; 7; 12; 16; 30; 32]. For instance, Gupta [12] surveyed 150 of the 500 largest U.S. companies and found that not one of the respondents was satisfied with their system development, citing the lack of "relevant output" as a primary reason. In the Peat, Marwick, Mitchell and Company survey [30] of 147 computer users, less than one third were satisfied with the return on their EDP investment; although more than ninety percent of the same users expected their information system resources over the next five years to be more important to the organization's profitability and performance. Adams [2] interviewed seventy-five managers in ten major corporations and found that management user attitudes toward the information systems were quite favorable. Such conflicting empirical data underscores the need to better understand the effectiveness construct and how to calibrate it.

All authors agree that system effectiveness is multidimensional. For example, the popular Davis textbook [6] lists the following related characteristics: purpose, mode and format, rate, frequency, redundancy/efficiency, deterministic or probabilistic states, cost, value, reliability, and validity. Mumford [24] identifies and defines four "variables" affecting implementation success: degree of stability, user perception, strategy for change, and role perception of the systems analyst. Emery [8] discusses information quality in terms of data base content, response time, accuracy, reliability, generality, flexibility, and the selectivity of displayed data. Gorry and Scott-Morton [11] consider the primary characteristics to be scope, level of aggregation, time-horizon, currency, required accuracy, and frequency of use. In the structured interviews by Adams [2] system quality involved accuracy, precision, age, repetitiveness, summarization, content, relevance, and source. The Powers and Dickson study [31] considered thirty-four factors and studied eleven of them using four evaluation criteria: time, cost, user satisfaction, and the computer operations impact; the authors concluded that user satisfaction was the most important criterion. Each of these authors provides comparable definitions for the characteristics considered, although the characteristics might best be defined by the objective measure used to monitor it. Perhaps the most comprehensive recent study is the work by Pearson [29] who considered thirty-nine characteristics related to performance. For reference Pearson's list and the accompanying definitions are given in the Appendix.

Many authors argue that to be operationally useful in an evaluation context, the several dimensions of system quality should be combined into a single index of performance. The most common aggregation procedure employed is a weighted linear combination of either the raw score or the difference between an ideal and the realized scores for each dimension. These authors [6; 23; 28; 29; 31; 33] suggest that system effectiveness is synonymous with the concept of user satisfaction or user appreciation (and involvement) [36]. For example, in the recent series of seminars on productivity conducted at Ohio State University, Morris [23] found that user satisfaction with information services was most often identified by the participants as the dominant measure.

Representative of a direct approach to the measurement of user satisfaction is the work by Seward and Nolan [28; 33]. This work was motivated by questions concerning the feasibility in practice of employing "effective and efficient" decision analysis as a procedure to determine the information requirements of managers. The authors perceived a need to separate the tasks of information system evaluation from information system design and for analysis purposes to decouple information from its antecedent decisions. However, this required a surrogate for the utility of information in decision making; the surrogate chosen was "user satisfaction" which includes the user's aspirations and the satisfaction received through repetitive interactions with the formal information system that reinforce positive or negative experience. The authors tested their construct in an empirical study involving the users of a governmental system that provided contractor financial information to the U.S. Department of Defense procurement agencies. Users were surveyed by questionnaire regarding several reports provided by the system. The dimensions of quality considered were currency of reporting (i.e., how often received by user), level of detail, and format.

An interesting series of studies related to user satisfaction is provided in the work by Lucas [16; 18]. For example, in [16] the interest centers on how user reactions to information systems can be improved where favorable user attitudes are taken as one measure of effectiveness. User perceptions were solicited on five characteristics: the quality of output and of input, the training received, the involvement reported, and the perceived management support. Data was also obtained on company computer practices as defined by four management practices (e.g., method of charging for services) and six system design practices (e.g., presence of an online system). The cross-sectional data base analyzed consisted of survey questionnaires from 616 employees in seven manufacturing companies.

In Lucas [17; 19] a descriptive model of information system use and (job) performance in an organization is proposed. For instance, in [19] the use of an information system (U) is hypothesized to depend directly on attitudes and perceptions (A), decision style (D), and performance (P). Attitudes (A), as described by the computer's potential and management computer support, depend in turn on system quality (measured here by perceptions on the timelines, accuracy, and usefulness of computer output). Performance (P), and hence use (U), is also influenced by various situational (S) and personal factors (I) for the user, such as indicators of environmental activity levels and age or education. The model was tested in an empirical study of a sales organization.

The work by Pearson [29] focused primarily on the prescription and development of an explicit instrument (in this case a robust survey questionnaire) to measure user satisfaction. His thesis concludes with such an instrument which consists of a semantic differential type of questionnaire on the thirty-nine factors listed in the appendix. For example, the typical format for a question on one of the factors is shown in Figure 1.

12. Processing of requests for changes to existing systems

fast:__:__:__:__:__:__:__:__:slow
timely:__:__:__:__:__:__:__:__:untimely
simple:__:__:__:__:__:__:__:__:complex
flexible:__:__:__:__:__:__:__:__:rigid
satisfactory:__:__:__:__:__:__:unsatisfactory

To me, this factor is

important:__:__:__:__:__:__:__:unimportant

Figure 1. Sample Survey Question from Pearson [25]

As indicated, the user responding is also requested to provide a weighting for each factor. Instructions for the questionnaire also emphasize that the user should "... judge the factors based on *your* feelings."

Pearson's initial analysis of the literature identified thirty-six factors* related to user satisfaction which were grouped into five categories corresponding to the components of a schematic model. In brief, the model postulates that the relationships between users and information services exist within an "Organizational Context" (factors 1 to 4 in the appendix). The source of the services is identified with an "EDP Center, Staff and Policies" (factors 5 to 12). The user receives the services through an "Interface" (factors 13 to 15) and the "Quality of the Systems" (factors 16 to 28) will influence satisfaction. Finally, each individual posesses certain "User Constructs" (factors 29 to 36) which determine his feelings and circumscribe the reference for his evaluation of performance. A subsequent test of this model using Factor Analysis produced some, but not conclusive, corroboration.

For instance, on a seven point scale (-3.0 to +3.0) the industrial subjects uniformly identified as "extremely important" (+3.0) the following factors: accuracy (+2.59), reliability (+2.48), timeliness (+2.38) and relevancy (+2.28). The factor analysis loaded accuracy and reliability together, and output format, precision and completeness along a dimension that might readily be labeled "Quality of information products". The respondents also identified the factors

---

* These are the first twenty-six defined in the appendix; the last three factors were added on the advice of "independent judges" or advisors who reviewed the analysis.

most often leading to dissatisfaction (in rank order) as: time required for new development, unresponsiveness to change requests, flexibility, integration, degree of training provided, top management involvement, and documentation. The factor analysis loaded the first two together with top management involvement; a category that might be labeled "Change and development".

From the author's reading of Pearson's work it would seem that one should be aware of two major influence categories in evaluation: the information services organization and the (reference) user "group". Within each of these, various key sub-categories should be monitored through measurements on factor characteristics. For the information services organization three sub-categories seem to dominate: ongoing product quality, direct user relations (structural and behavioral), and (response to) change and development. For the user group the important considerations appear to relate to user perceptions (beliefs and attitudes) and the user task domain (i.e., ongoing experience of job impact). We recognize that many of the individual factor characteristics (such as those listed in the appendix) will be highly correlated in sample measurements due to interdependence. Consequently, it probably is not critical for evaluation purposes to attempt to measure most such factors, let alone the thirty-nine listed by Pearson.* It certainly is not economical and it could be dysfunctional. For instance, a recent study by Neumann and Segev [27] surveyed bank branch managers along the quality characteristics of accuracy, content, frequency and recency. They analyzed eighty-one data sets and found content to be the determinant factor with spill-over effects on the others. They conclude that this confounding of effects (and bias) may mislead design efforts based on user evaluation surveys. That is, the user has a "holistic perception" of the information he receives and, for example, faced with a lack of information he may also claim a need in the system for more accuracy or frequency, or one of the other quality characteristics.

There have been several other authors who have focused on performance evaluation by users without direct consideration of the user satisfaction construct. For example, in Gallagher's thesis [10] managers were asked to stipulate the maximum amount of (real) money they would be willing to pay out of their budgets for various reports or services they received. In the "P&D" (planning and development) approach by Nadler, et al. [25] user groups are convened and through structured discussions the users are asked to rank order system goals and priorities. Morris [23] and Adam, et al. [1] have also focused more on the process for user participation, rather than on the content or specific quality criteria to be measured, employing a combination of nominal group sessions and the Delphi method to elicit user responses. Their efforts appear to have been reasonably successful, however, the quality criteria developed are very specific to the organizational environments studied.

* Curiously perhaps, even in Pearson's exhaustive listing *cost* per se is *not* considered a factor of satisfaction, except in the indirect sense of the fourth characteristic, "charge-back method of payment".

During the past three years this author has been a co-principal investigator on a joint industry-university research project concerned with productivity measurement for computing and information systems [13]. Productivity here was defined in terms of efficiency and effectiveness, as described above. Work on the project evolved along three separate but related avenues of approach: (1) behavioral science models, (2) an economics framework, and (3) a total factor model. The behavioral science group, led by Dr. Anthony Debons of the University of Pittsburgh, focused on the intellectual functions or tasks required of a user in the performance of his job and the contribution the information system or service makes to the accomplishment of such functions. Some laboratory experiments were carried out of the "with and without treatment" variety demonstrating the feasibility of this approach [13]. Although this research effort was embryonic due to time and resource constraints, similar work on a larger scale has been done by others [35].

Modeling information systems in an economics context is not a new idea, e.g., see [8; 26]. Our approach here, however, was to view the organization in its totality as a marketplace for computing and information services containing analytic components of supply and demand. The theory is that efficiency measures concern partial equilibrium analyses of the market (e.g., the production process with demand exogenous) and effectiveness measures concern general equilibrium analyses. In brief, a model of the production process for information services was developed which quantitavely related input resources and output products; the model also incorporated output quality within the process. Various measures of production efficiency were defined based on this model. The analysis then proceeded to suggest how one can incorporate consideration of user demand for services into the analysis and derive an objective function for system effectiveness (e.g., based on constructs analogous to consumer's surplus in welfare economics [22; also see 14]). The former analysis was refined and pilot-tested initially at a university site. Subsequently, the approach was validated at two additional sites: an industrial and a municipal data processing center [15]. In all three cases only the supply model was implemented. Our experience in attempting to implement the demand analysis produced mixed results due to administrative and pragmatic reasons. It appears our failure here was a consequence of the existing organizational environments which had conditioned user behavior. That is, the assumption of a "competitive marketplace" was not operational since users did not behave as "conventional" price-quality taking consumers. At each site the information services facilities are essentially a monopoly. This and related factors create a situation where demand is relatively inelastic and typically users regard information services as a "public good" relying on other non-market devices (e.g., bureaucratic negotiations) to obtain satisfaction. The resolution of this issue invariably lies in areas of incentives and organization design. The project effort in the total factor area was also field tested at two sites, however, in the context of theory it was shown that this framework was actually a special case of the economics supply model for certain derived efficiency measures.

To summarize this discussion, it is evident that the research literature is rich and a variety of methods and measures have been developed. The following list proposes and defines several evaluation criteria which appear germaine to the problem of choosing from among alternatives. At this juncture these criteria will simply be recommended for consideration, since the list is not intended to be exhaustive.

Evaluation Criteria for Performance Measurement Methods

1. *Validity* (Relevance). How well does the method measure what it is supposed to measure? Is it measuring what is thought of as performance by the people who are interested in this problem?
2. *Practicability*. Will it cost too much? Will it take too much time? Will it disrupt too much of the activity that is being measured?
3. *Informativeness*. In addition to producing a numerical index, will the method have any potential for aiding in decision-making or in identifying problem areas?
4. *Completeness*. Does the method incorporate important inputs? Can it react to possible events that may occur on a regular basis, such as major or minor breakdowns?
5. *Generality* (Transferability). Is the method general enough to apply to most computers and information centers? If it is developed and calibrated with respect to one site, will it be applicable, without major modifications, to another?
6. *Reproducibility* (Stability, Reliability). If applied under similar conditions, will the method produce similar results?
7. *Sensitivity*. Does it respond to changes in the environment? (In some senses this is antithetic to Reproducibility in that at one extreme are methods that always produce "the same" result and so are insensitive whereas at the other extreme are methods that are unstable in that they may vary for no apparent reason.)
8. *Non-reactivity*. Does the measurement process avoid influencing the process being measured?

4 CONCLUSION

The theme of last year's Ninth Annual Conference of the Society for Management Information Systems was "MIS Productivity: Achieving Gains in Efficiency and Effectiveness through MIS." The proceedings from that conference [37] have recently become available; they contain a number of papers that provide very pragmatic discussions on the various issues involved and of different methods authors have employed to deal with them. Many of the methods described are validated on the basis of the author's experience. While there appears to be agreement on the relative issues, there is some diversity in the advice on methods. Clearly this involves empirical questions which can only be answered properly through research.

In the brief survey of the literature several studies were mentioned which this author thinks are beginning to circumscribe the relevant behavorial areas of concern, e.g., the work by Lucas and by Pearson. But the empirical reference for these models is still very limited. The statistical data base needs to be expanded and further study performed on cross validation and refinement to better understand the implications for management. I do not believe such effort will be of value if it is devoted towards the testing of trivial hypotheses which many might take to be axioms. For example, the literature now contains a number of reports on laboratory experiments concerned with the influence of cognitive style on user behavior; unfortunately, most of these studies are repetitious in reporting simply that an influence exists and not substantively what should be done about it. In contrast a refined behavioral model that gives insight into the organizational and policy conditions which lead to greater user satisfaction could result in better decisions for establishing those conditions. Developing an understanding of these circumstances would also enhance our ability to define target goals for the information systems unit in the organization and to measure progress toward those goals.

Dr. Ruth Davis of the U.S. National Bureau of Standards remarked recently that "the main problem for productivity improvement (in computer-based information system efforts) is motivation." Our recent completed study supported by the National Science Foundation made the obvious apparent in that organizational parameters dominate economics in influencing user behavior. With this commonplace wisdom we have embarked on a new study of some of these issues in a framework of organizational design and incentives as viewed by economists. That is, the design of an organization is viewed as the prescription of formal mechanisms which determine the interaction of information, authority, incentives and performance under various exogenous environments. Once determined in the formal sense, these mechanisms can then be translated into operating policies and procedures for resource allocation and implemented in an organization. Our goal here is to draw upon recent economics research on the theory of agency relationships as a means to understanding certain organizational constructs at a more fundamental level of analysis. The research plan includes a pilot testing of the theoretical results at an industrial site.

Many of the readers are aware of the activities of the I.F.I.P. Technical Committees, especially TC8 - "Information Systems" and its two Working Groups: WG8.1 - "Design and Evaluation of Information Systems" and WG8.2 - "The Interaction of Information Systems and the Organization". It seems fitting to end this article with a recognition of these continuing efforts and the forum they provide for enlightened discussion and professional development.

APPENDIX. CHARACTERISTICS AFFECTING COMPUTER USER SATISFACTION
Source: [29, pp. 230-32]

1. *Top management involvement:* The positive or negative degree of interest, enthusiasm, support, or participation of any management level above the respondent's own level toward computer-based information systems or services or toward the computer staff which supports them.

2. *Organizational competition with the EDP unit:* The contention between the respondent's organizational unit and the EDP unit when vying for organizational resources or for responsability for success or failure of computer-based information systems or services of interest to both parties.

3. *Organizational position of EDP function:* The hierarchical relationship of the EDP function to the overall organizational structure.

4. *Priorities determination:* Policies and procedures which establish precedence for the allocation of EDP resources and services between different organizational units and their requests.

5. *Charge-back method of payment for services:* The schedule of charges and the procedures for assessing users a pro rato basis for the EDP resources and services that they utilize.

6. *Relationship with the EDP staff:* The manner and methods of interaction, conduct, and association between the user and EDP staff.

7. *Communications with the EDP staff:* The manner and methods of information exchange between the user and the EDP staff.

8. *Technical Competence of the EDP staff:* The computer technology skills and expertise exhibited by the EDP staff.

9. *Attitude of the EDP staff:* The willingness and commitment of the EDP staff to subjugate external, professional goals in favor of organizationally directed goals and tasks.

10. *Schedule of products and services:* The EDP center time-table for production of information system outputs and for provision of computer-based services.

11. *Time required for new development:* The elapsed time between the user's request for new applications and the design, development and/or implementation of the application systems by the EDP staff.

12. *Processing of change requests:* The manner, method, and required time with which the EDP staff responds to user requests for changes in existing computer-based information systems or services.

13. *Vendor support:* The type and quality of the service rendered by a vendor, either directly or indirectly, to the user to maintain the hardware or software required by that user. A vendor is distinguished by his external organizational status.

14. *Response/turnaround time:* The elapsed time between a user-initiated request for service or action and a reply to that request. Response time generally refers to the elapsed time for a terminal type request or entry. Turnaround time generally refers to the elapsed time for execution of a program submitted or requested by a user and the return of the output to that user.

15. *Mode of interface:* The method and medium by which a user inputs data to and receives output from the EDP center.

16.   *Convenience of access:* The ease or difficulty with which the user may act to utilize the capability of the computer system.

17.   *Quality of systems:* The degree of excellence of the computer-based information systems as manifested in the six attributes of the system outputs—accuracy, timeliness, precision, reliability, currency, and completeness.

18.   *Accuracy:* The correctness of the output information.

19.   *Timeliness:* The availability of the output information at a time suitable for its use.

20.   *Precision:* The variability of the output information from that which it purports to measure.

21.   *Reliability:* The consistency and dependability of the output information.

22.   *Currency:* The age of the output information.

23.   *Completeness:* The comprehensiveness of the output information content.

24.   *Flexibility:* The capacity of the information system to change or to adjust in response to new conditions, demands, or circumstances.

25.   *Format of output:* The material design of the layout and display of the output contents.

26.   *Language:* The set of vocabulary, syntax, and grammatical rules used to interact with the computer systems.

27.   *Volume of output:* The amount of information conveyed to a user from computer-based systems. This is expressed by not only the number of reports or outputs but also by the voluminousness of the output contents.

28.   *Relevancy:* The degree of congruence between what the user wants or requires and what is provided by the information products and services.

29.   *Error recovery:* The methods and policies governing correction and rerun of system outputs that are incorrect.

30.   *Security of data:* The safeguarding of data from misappropriation or unauthorized alteration or loss.

31.   *Documentation:* The recorded description of an information system. This includes formal instructions for the utilization of the system.

32.   *Expectations:* The set of attributes or features of the computer-based information products or services that a user considers reasonable and due from the computer-based information support rendered within his organization.

33.   *Understanding of systems:* The degree of comprehension that a user possesses about the computer-based information systems or services that are provided to him.

34.   *Perceived utility:* The user's judgment about the relative balance between the cost and the considered usefulness of the computer-based information products or services that are provided. The costs include any costs related to providing the resource, including money, time, manpower, and opportunity. The usefulness includes any benefits that the user believes that he derives from the support.

35.   *Confidence in the systems:* The user's feelings of assurance or certainty about the systems which support him.

36.   *Feeling of participation:* The degree of involvement and commitment which the user shares with the EDP staff and others toward the functioning of the computer-based information systems and services.

37.   *Degree of training:* The amount of specialized instruction and practice that is afforded to the user to increase his proficiency in utilizing the computer capability that is available to him.

38. *Job effects:* The changes in job freedom and job performance that are ascertained by the user as resulting from modifications induced by the computer-based information systems and services.

39. *Feeling of control:* The user's awareness of his power or lack of power to regulate, direct or dominate the development, alteration and/or execution of the computer-based information systems or services which serve him in his perceived function.

REFERENCES

1. Adam, Jr., E.E., J.C. Hershauer, and W.A. Ruch. "Measuring the Quality Dimension of Service Productivity," Final Report National Science Foundation Grant No. APR 76-07140, College of Business and Public Administration, University of Missouri-Columbia and College of Business Administration, Arizona State University (January, 1978).

2. Adams, C.R., "How management users view information systems," *Decision Sciences* 6 (1975):337-45.

3. Adams, C.R. and R.G. Schroeder, "Managers and MIS: 'They Get What They Want'," *Business Horizons* 16 (1973):63-68.

4. Agajanian, A.H., "A Bibliography on System Performance Evaluation," *Computer* (IEEE), November, 1975.

5. Campbell, J.P., D.A. Bowman, N.G. Peterson and M.D. Dunnette, "The Measurement of Organizational Effectiveness: A Review of Relevant Research and Opinion," Personnel Decisions, Inc., Minneapolis, Minn., NPRDC TR 75-1, Naval Personnel Research and Development Center, San Diego, Cal. 92152 (July 1974).

6. Davis, G.B., *Management Information Systems: Conceptual Foundations, Structure and Development.* New York: McGraw-Hill, 1974.

7. The Diebold Research Program, "Key Measurement Indicators of ADP Performance," E Report No. E153, Document number S25 (1977).

8. Emery, J.C., "Cost/Benefit Analysis of Information Systems," S.M.I.S. Workshop Reprint No. 1 (1971).

9. Galbraith, J., *Designing Complex Organizations.* Addison-Wesley, 1973.

10. Gallagher, C.A., "Measuring and Analysis of Manager's Perceptions of the Value of Selected Management Information," Unpublished Dissertation, Florida State University, Gainsville, Florida, 1971.

11. Gorry, A.G. and M.S. Scott-Morton, "A Framework for Management Information Systems," *Sloan Management Review* 13 (1971):55-70.

12. Gupta, R., "Information Manager: His Role in Corporate Management," *Data Management* 12 (1974):26-29.

13. Hanes, L.F. and C.H. Kriebel (eds.), "Productivity Measurement Systems for Administrative Services: Computing and Information Services," Final Report National Science Foundation Grant No. APR75-20546, Westinghouse Electric Corporation, Carnegie-Mellon University and University of Pittsburgh, Pittsburgh, Pa. (July 1978).

14. Kriebel, C.H. and A. Raviv, "An Economics Approach to Modeling the Productivity of Information Systems," Working Paper (January 1978), G.S.I.A., Carnegie-Mellon University.

15. Kriebel, C.H. and A. Raviv, "Modeling the Productivity of Information Systems: Empirical Analysis, Implementation and Evaluation," Working Paper (May 1978), G.S.I.A., Carnegie-Mellon University.

16. Lucas, H.C., Jr., "User Reactions and the Management Information of Services," *Management Informatics* 2(1973):165-172.

17. Lucas, H.C., Jr., "A Descriptive Model of Information Systems in the Context of the Organization," *Data Base* 5 (1973):27-39.

18. Lucas, H.C., Jr., *Toward Creative Systems Design*. New York: Columbia University Press, 1974.

19. Lucas, H.C., Jr., "Performance and the use of an information system," *Management Science* 21 (1975):908-19.

20. McFarlan, F.M., "Management Audit of the EDP Department," *Harvard Business Review* 51 (1973):131-42.

21. McLean, C., R.O. Mason, and S. Foote, "Behavioral, Organizational Aspects of Computers, Allied Technology: A Partial Bibliography," *Data Base* 6 (1975):15-26.

22. Mehra, R., "Consumer Surplus with Quality Variation: An Application to Multipriority Pricing," Working Paper, G.S.I.A., Carnegie-Mellon University (November 1975).

23. Morris, W.T., "The Development of Productivity Measurement Systems for Administrative Computing and Information Services," Unpublished working paper, Department of Industrial Engineering, Ohio State University, 1976.

24. Mumford,E., "Implementing EDP Systems—A Sociological Perspective," *The Computer Bulletin* (U.K.), January 1969, pp. 10-13.

25. Nadler, G., J.T. Johnston, and J.E. Bailey, Design Concepts for Information Systems, Monograph C/IS/-72-2-Rev., American Institute of Industrial Engineers, Norcross, Ga., 1975.

26. Nelson, E.A., "The VOPIR Technique for the Evaluation of Computer Augmented Administrative Systems," SP-2765 (17 May 1967), Systems Development Corporation.

27. Neumann, S. and E. Segev, "User Evaluation of Information Characteristics," Working Paper No. 558/78, Tel-Aviv University (June 1978).

28. Nolan, R.L. and H.H. Seward, "Measuring User Satisfaction to Evaluate Information Systems," in R.L. Nolan, ed., *Managing the Data Resource Function*. West Publishing Co., 1974.

29. Pearson, S.W., "Measurement of Computer User Satisfaction," Unpublished Doctoral Dissertation, Arizona State University, Tempe, Arizona, 1977.

30. Peat, Marwick, Mitchell, and Co., "Benchmarks," *Datamation* 22 (1976):162:

31. Powers, R.F. and G.W. Dickson, "MIS Project Management: Myths, Opinions, and Reality," *California Management Review* 15 (1973): 147-56.

32. Schussel, G., "Scoring DP Performance," *Infosystems* 21 (1974):59-62.

33. Seward, H.H., "Measuring User Satisfaction to Evaluate Information Systems," Unpublished Dissertation, Harvard Business School, Boston, Mass. 1973.

34. Stewart, R.J., "Productivity Measurement in Computing and Information Services," Technical Report NSF APR 75-20546/TR-1 (February 4, 1976), Westinghouse R&D Center.

35. Streeter, D.N., *The Scientific Process and the Computer*. John Wiley, 1974.

36. Swanson, E.B., "Management Information Systems: Appreciation and Involvement," *Management Science* 21 (1974).

37. The Society for Management Information Systems, "MIS Productivity: Achieving Gains in Efficiency and Effectiveness Through MIS," *Proceedings of Ninth Annual Conference* (September 26-28, 1977; Los Angeles), S.M.I.S., July 1978, Chicago.

II. TECHNICAL ASPECTS OF SYSTEMS DESIGN AND IMPLEMENTATION

3. The Modeling Process: Steps Versus Components

by H. Müller-Merbach

1 THE TOPIC

There are quite a few books and articles on model building, design of planning systems, system analysis, planning, etc., in which the (modeling, design, or planning) *process* is presented as a *sequence of steps*.

The author of this contribution takes an opposite stand. He suggests organizing these processes as *assemblages of components*.

The question "steps or components" is not purely academic. The author is convinced that the organization of modeling, design, and planning processes, etc., is the central key to success or failure. And arguments exist that the *assemblage-of-components concept* allows for a more flexible and adaptable organization of the process than the *sequence-of-steps concept*.

The main arguments for this are as follows:

The *sequence-of-steps concept* suggests that steps are carried out in a given sequence. Although overlapping of steps, repetitions, and revisions of earlier steps are not explicitly excluded, the *ideal* of this concept is that one step is completed after another and that at any step one can rely upon the results of the preceding steps. Many arguments can be quoted to support this concept, e.g., "You cannot solve a problem unless you have first formulated it."

In contrast to that, the *assemblage-of-components concept* denies (1) the *practicability* as well as (2) the *psychological justification* of the sequence-of-steps concept. The total process is taken instead as a complicated net of feedback relations which makes it necessary that the components have to be free from the sequence ideal. A basic statement which is characteristic for this concept says: "Problem formulation is a never ending process" [1]. It is certainly trivial that a not yet formulated problem cannot be solved; however, might a solution not provide new insight into the problem such that a reformulation will follow consequently? The belief in such feedback relations excludes the acceptance of steps. The *ideal* of the assemblage-of-components concept might lie in the *never ending continuation* of all components. The endlessness is certainly not acceptable; therefore, the process has to be structured and controlled carefully and halted after some time.

The plea for the assemblage-of-components concept will be continued in section 3. This will be preceded by a discussion of the role that models play in planning

47

systems (section 2). The main components of modeling processes will be outlined in section 4. The paper closes with a brief discussion about whether modeling is an *art* or a *science*.

2   THE ROLE OF THE MODEL

The author considers models as the *heart* of planning systems. Therefore, he will use the terms "model", "modeling" or "model design" instead of "planning system" or "planning system design", respectively, even if "planning system" is used in the title of the Symposium. Although a model is not a planning system, the author considers the modeling process as a synonym for the *planning system design process*. That means that all the aspects which have to be considered are the same.

In this paper, the term "system" will be used in a sense which is quite distinct from the term "planning system". The term "system" shall rather be applied to indicate the *reality* and parts of it. In particular, those parts of the reality will be called "system" which are to be represented by a *model*.

A *model has to serve purposes*. In the following, a distinction will be made between the *technical* purposes and the *social* or *organizational* purposes of the model.

2.1   The Technical Purposes of the Model

The technical purposes of a model lie in the *transformation of information*. A model is fed with *input information* and should be able to transform this into such *output information* which has the *potential* to allow for better understanding of the system represented by the model, as sketched in Figure 1.

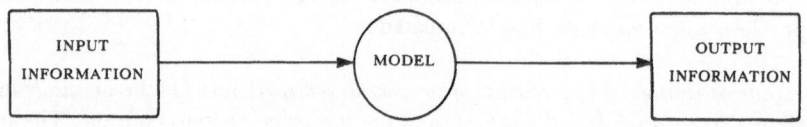

Figure 1. The technical purposes of a model

2.2   The Social or Organizational Purposes of a Model

The *potential* for the better understanding of a real system through the output information of a model does not necessarily guarantee that such a better understanding will in fact be achieved. It is not automatic that output information of "objectively" high quality leads to a good understanding of the system. Rather, there is a *subjective and personal dimension* which has to be considered. It cannot be sufficient that a model provides "objectively" good information. In addition, the information must be *mentally accessible* for those who are or ought to be the users and beneficiaries of the model. This leads from the *technical* purposes to the *social* or *organizational* purposes of the model.

The *technical* purposes require "objectively" high-quality information, while the social or organizational purposes have to do with the subjective usefulness and usage of this information.

It might be relatively easy to build a model which serves *technical* purposes satisfactorily, but in general it is much more difficult to design models which serve the *social* or *organizational* purposes as well. This might become clearer through the following argument:

Consider a man-machine system with several individual members. Some of them may be concerned with a problem arising within a subsystem and will develop an individual *mental image* of the subsystem and the problem. No two of the mental images will be identical. And each individual mental image will change over time, due to the perception of new aspects, etc.

If now a model of the subsystem is developed and made accessible to the individuals, they might develop a mental image of the *model* as well (if they take notice of it at all). Some of them might find that their two mental images (of the subsystem and of the model) have some properties in common and hence tend to accept the model. Over time, both images might come closer and closer and finally, the individuals might find it useful to understand certain properties of the real subsystem *through* the model, and they might actively use the model, put questions to it and feed it with input information and derive increased insight into the subsystem by means of the output information. Other members might not be willing to follow this path and perhaps refuse to accept the model.

It seems to be quite difficult to design models which are accepted by the potential beneficiaries. It is not at all surprising that models will not be accepted by those individuals who are not familiar with models in general, or with the structure of and the theory behind a particular model; or, as Woolsey put it: "A manager would rather live with a problem he cannot solve, than accept a solution he cannot understand" [17, p. 505].

The relations between the subsystem, the model and individuals are outlined in Figure 2, in which the arcs represent the following connections:

1. The individuals perceive the (real) subsystem and build a mental image of it (which might change over time).
2. The individuals (or some of them) make decisions and change the subsystem through them.
3. The individuals perceive the model and build a mental image of the model which may or may not be close to their mental image of the subsystem. The mental image of the model might also change over time.
4. Some individuals may find that their two mental images (of the subsystem and of the model) have properties in common. They will therefore begin to use the model in that they try to understand certain properties of the subsystem *through* the model. The model takes the role of an "interpreter".

49

5. The individuals might start to feed the model with input information and put questions to the model.
6. The model "answers" the questions and provides output information which will be received by the individuals.

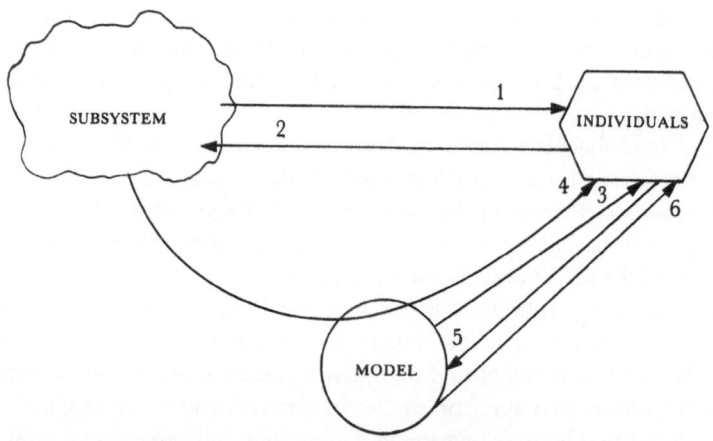

Figure 2. The relations between the subsystem, the model and individuals

For those individuals who like to use the model, the (information) flows through the arcs 3-6 tend to be quite intensive. These flows are near to zero for those individuals who are not prepared or willing to use the model at all.

A model serves the *social* or *organizational* purposes the better, the more intensively the arcs 3-6 are utilized.

2.3 The Purposeful Design of a Model

The discussion of the *technical* purposes of models (section 2.1) did not include individuals. In connection with the *social* or *organizational* purposes of models, *one* group of individuals was considered: the group of the potential *users* or *beneficiaries*. Another group of individuals is important when discussing model design: the *model designers*.

The model designers have to build models which serve technical as well as social or organizational purposes.

This means that the model designers have to develop a good understanding of the *man-machine system*, a subsystem of which is to be modeled. It is *not* sufficient that they study the subsystem. They have to make themselves familiar with the *whole* man-machine system. This means that they—among others—have to become acquainted with the individuals who should become users of the model.

By the perception of the man-machine system the model designers will develop individual mental images of the man-machine system and of the subsystem which is to be modeled. These mental images will generally be quite different from the mental images which the potential users of the model might have. It is important though that the model designers' mental images include knowledge about the mental images which the potential users have.

In parallel to the development of the mental images, the model designers will be building a model of the very subsystem.

It is important to emphasize that the model depends highly upon the model designers, their personalities, their psychological types, their mental structures, their modeling styles, etc. It is very likely that two different model designers (or two different groups of model designers) will model the same subsystem in a quite different way and will come up with quite different models. Different models might serve the technical and social or organizational purposes equally well, but in most cases they will not be equally good.

The general procedure of the modeling process is shown in Figure 3. It demonstrates that model design goes through the individual designers and that the model is subject to the designers' perception of the subsystem.

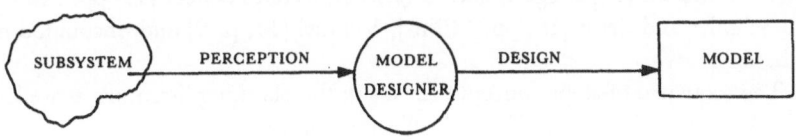

Figure 3. The process of model design

3 THE PLEA FOR THE ASSEMBLAGE-OF-COMPONENTS CONCEPT

The model design team—in particular its leader—has to organize the modeling process. It is a widely believed and frequently repeated piece of folklore that the modeling process has to follow the *sequence-of-steps concept*. Such concepts have been suggested in many *operations research* textbooks, e.g., [2, p. 13]:

1. Formulating the problem.
2. Constructing a mathematical model to represent the system under study.
3. Deriving a solution from the model.
4. Testing the model and the solution derived from it.
5. Establishing controls over the solution.
6. Putting the solution to work: implementation.

A similar sequence-of-steps concept was suggested by Wagner [15, pp. 9 ff.]. A finer grid of steps was presented by Hanssmann [3, pp. 5 ff.]:

After these remarks it seems clear that the analyst must go through the following steps:

1. General orientation about the decision-making situation.
2. Choice of suitable decision criteria (E).
3. Development of alternative environments, especially definition of suitable environmental parameters (Y).
4. Development of decision alternatives (X).
5. "Model construction", that is, the formulation of functional relationships between decision alternatives and environments, on one hand, and decision criteria on the other hand [E = f(X,Y)].
6. Estimation and forecasting of environmental parameters.
7. Computation of outcome matrix based on the model relationships; identification of particularly interesting decision alternatives.
8. Presentation of outcome matrix (or equivalent information) to management as a basis for its selection of a particular alternative.
9. Implementation and modification of the decision; repeat cycles of the analysis.

Based on Hanssmann, the author suggested an even finer grid of 13 steps [10, p. 20] from which he would like to dissociate today.

Quite similar sequence-of-steps concepts are common in *systems analysis* literature. Wedekind [16] suggests such a concept, as does Scheer [12, pp. 340 ff.], as do Schmitz and Seibt [13, pp. 140 ff.], Vemuri [14, p. 9] and uncounted many others.

The sequence-of-steps concept prevails in the planning literature as well, e.g., Hax [4], Koch [7], Müller [8, pp. 37 ff.] and many others.

More than ten years ago, Witte (1968a, 1968b) reported on empirical experience according to which there was no evidence on the existence of sequence-of-steps procedures in certain practical planning processes. This does not at all prove that the sequence-of-steps concept is not applicable or desirable. Could not the leaders of planning teams (or of model design teams) organize the working process of the teams according to the sequence-of-steps concept? They will certainly be able to try to do so. But they will find that steps have to overlap, that they will have to be repeated and revised and that the practice is far away from *one* sequence of steps. It is rather a network of steps with almost as many *backward* movements to earlier steps as *foreward* movements to subsequent steps.

The frequency of backward movements as such is not critical at all. But the team might lose its confidence in its professional efficiency if it has to violate its ideal of *completing* one step after another (without backward movements).

Backward movements are natural and should not be questioned by believing in a nonpractical ideal.

This is the point where the suggestion of the *assemblage-of-components concept* arises as a natural consequence. The components replace the steps and cover similar contents. But they are *not* arranged in a sequence. Rather, the components are treated in parallel. This does not mean that all the components are equally important throughout the whole process. Some components may be important and more work-intensive in the beginning of the process, others in the middle, some at the end.

But all of them are "open for development and revision" throughout the whole process.

This could certainly lead to absolutely chaotic situations where key decisions on any component are revised just in front of the approaching end of the process such that the findings and decisions on every other component have to be revised again. The project leader has to prevent the process from such chaos by careful planning and structuring. He will certainly use some sort of network planning which covers all the components. And in such a network he will certainly indicate the key decisions and will take these decisions with particular care in order to reduce the danger of their revision to a minimum.

The single components which are suggested by the author are presented in section 4. Beforehand, it might be useful to discuss some examples which support the *assemblage-of-components concept*:

Example 1. It seems to be logical that the "steps" *problem recognition* and *problem formulation* have to precede the "step" *problem solution* since a not yet stated problem cannot be solved. On the other hand, Checkland [1] considers problem formulation as a never ending process. That means that one learns so much about the problem from the "component" *problem solution* that one might find it necessary to revise the "component" *problem formulation*.

Example 2. An optimization model can only be treated mathematically if the objective function is defined beforehand. Otherwise, the model would not know whether to maximize profit, to minimize costs, or to maximize turnover, etc. On the other hand, no executive will definitely choose a certain objective function before knowing the consequences, i.e., the results provided by the model. That means that the *decision on the decision criteria* (such as the objective function) is not a single "step". It is a *process* which has to be carried out in parallel to the other components of the total process.

Example 3. It is logical that a model should be completed before the computation of solutions makes sense. On the other hand, it is generally agreed that a model will never be completed as long as it is in use. That is, a network planning model (like CPM, etc.) is usually completed not earlier than the project which is represented by the network. This means that at all the earlier stages the model was an incomplete and defective representation of the project. However, working with imperfect models at earlier stages of planning and of project realization was the main purpose of the model. From this it follows that model design is a *continual process*. This does not only hold for network planning models.

These examples support the opinion that *dominant* directions in the sense of "B follows A" do not exist between different "steps". It seems rather to be closer to reality to state sequential dependencies in the sense of "B follows A as A follows B". If this is accepted, the "components" A and B have to be developed in parallel where the development of each single component depends highly upon the development of *all* the other components.

4 THE COMPONENTS OF THE MODELING PROCESS

In section 3 the author tried to show the advantages of the *assemblage-of-components concept* over the *sequence-of-steps concept*. Not yet discussed is *which* components have to be considered and developed in a model design process. This discussion follows now.

The *totality* of the components should cover *all* the important activities which have to be carried out in connection with model design. With respect to this totality requirement there is no principal difference between the *assemblage-of-components concept* and the *sequence-of-steps concept*. However, the *single* components and their coverage differ to some extent from the *single* steps (which are suggested in the literature), because they do not have to fit into a unique sequence.

In the following, fourteen components will be outlined. They form a rough frame for the modeling process in practical situations. Since the problems and tasks in the real world vary over wide ranges, the author is far away from claiming that *each* of these components has to be considered in every practical case. This means that the single components are of altering importance from case to case.

The fourteen components will be presented in front of the background of the following scenario: There is a *man-machine system* with different individuals (decision makers, planners, model builders, ..., workers, etc.) as its members. A (not yet precisely defined) *problem* may arise in a *subsystem* of the man-machine system. A *team* will be formed in order to yield solutions to the problem. The team may find it useful to develop a *model* (or models) of the subsystem (where the model represents the heart of the planning system; see section 2). The model should be able to provide deeper insight into the subsystem and to test decisions and decision alternatives.

The key words used in this scenario (and in the following descriptions) are *man-machine system, subsystem, problem, team,* and *model*. Further termini will be defined when they are introduced.

The fourteen components are:

Component 1—Problem recognition and problem formulation:
The problem has to be recognized, (increasingly) better understood, defined, and formulated. This process can in some cases be supported by creativity techniques, by time series analysis and alarm systems, by forecasting techniques, etc. The process will be fed continually from the experience gathered from the other components.

Component 2—Analysis and design of the organizational structure of the man-machine system:
Since the problem occurred within a man-machine system, its organizational structure (the formal and informal links) has to be evaluated. In connection with this structure, the position of the team has to be defined (such as project management). In addition, the possible changes of the organizational structure through the solution of the problem might be anticipated and developed.

54

Component 3—Analysis and design of the relevant process structure within the man-machine system:

The problem may have to do with working processes, information processes, etc. Therefore, the structures of the relevant processes have to be evaluated. Possible changes in the processes which may be imposed by the model have to be anticipated and tested. Additionally, the modeling process itself has to be planned and controlled.

Component 4—Analysis of the subsystem:

Since a model of the subsystem is to be designed (Component 8), the subsystem itself has to be analyzed thoroughly. Of particular value for this analysis could be the conceptual frame of the *systems approach*. This means that (1) the relevant *elements* of the system and (2) their relevant *attributes* will be defined, and (3) the *links* between the elements will be stated.

Component 5—Analysis of the goal system and definition of the decision criteria:

Since the problem arose within a man-machine system, the solutions have to consider the goals and objectives of the man-machine system. In general, no defined *goals of the system* itself will be available. But there will be goals, desires, aims, etc. of the *individuals* within the system; see Kirsch [5, pp. III/32 ff.] and Müller [9]. They have to be evaluated and transformed into operational *decision criteria*. Component 5 contains three particular difficulties. (1) The goals, desires and aims of the individuals (or their groups) have to be evaluated and defined. (2) A decision has to be taken on the weighting of the different goals of the different individuals and groups. (3) The weighted goals, etc., have to be transformed into operational decision criteria.

Component 6—Analysis and prediction of environmental development:

Any subsystem will have an *environment* within and outside the man-machine system. In general, the development of the subsystem will depend upon the development of the environment. Therefore, those *parts* of the environment which have influence on the subsystem have to be *identified*. In addition, the *development* of these parts of the environment has to be *predicted*. This is particularly difficult in many cases. Quite often one cannot do more than show the possible and probable paths of development. In general, this component covers much more of investigation than only the application of statistical forecasting techniques.

Component 7—Creation of decision alternatives:

The model which has to be developed shall be able to *test decisions* or to *find optimal decisions* within defined decision spaces. The decisions or decision spaces, respectively, have to be stated by the modeling team. In most cases, there is not only *one* decision or *one* decision space, there are many of them which have to be created.

Component 8—Construction of the model(s):

The model has to be constructed in its details. This can be carried out in close connection with the *systems approach* of Component 4 in that the *elements* of the system are represented by the *indexes* of the model, the *attributes* of the elements are represented by *variables* and the *links* between the elements will be represented by *equalities* and *inequalities*.

Component 9—Analysis of data quality; data gathering; data base design, etc..
There are close dependencies between the *model* and the *data quality*. Therefore, the data quality has to be evaluated very carefully. Additionally, the single data have to be gathered and made accessible to the model. And if the model is to be used continually over a period of time, data bases might have to be designed in which the relevant data are kept. This component covers all the *data activities*.

Component 10—Selection and/or design of algorithms:
The model (Component 8) is the device to transform input information into output information (see Figure 1). *Algorithms* have to be provided for this transformation process. In many cases, the algorithms are quite simple from the mathematical point of view; in other cases advanced mathematics is necessary. Today, many *standard algorithms* are available, many of which were developed in the 1950s and 1960s, particularly under the roof of Operations Research [10, pp. 13 ff.] and under the influence of new computer technology. However, they apply only to *standard models. Nonstandard models* tend to require *tailormade algorithms* (e.g., in the field of combinatorial optimization).

Component 11—Selection and/or design of EDP programs:
If computers are necessary to do the computation (because of the *quantity of data* or because of the *complexity of the algorithm*), the EDP programs have to be selected *or* designed. These programs not only realize the algorithm (Component 10), but also cover the organization of the data input and data output and the data management (Component 9) and the management of the model (Component 8). In some cases, *standard EDP programs* are available which are applicable after some minor or major modifications. In other cases, *tailormade EDP programs* are necessary.

Component 12—Computation:
The algorithms (Component 10) and EDP programs (Component 11) have to be applied to the models (Component 8) using the adequate data (Component 9). Component 12 refers to the organization of the "working runs" and covers all the aspects of actual computation.

Component 13—Interpretation of the model results and their analysis:
The model results have to be analysed and organized in a format which can easily be understood by the decision makers, i.e., all those individuals who are the users or beneficiaries of the model. This requires a careful analysis and interpretation of the real meaning of the output information. A *report generator* could support this activity considerably.

56

Component 14—Implementation and maintenance of the model:
The *aim* of the model design is *implementation*. Therefore, implementation has to be prepared and planned throughout the *whole* design process. This component has to consider particularly the *social* or *organizational purposes* (section 2.2) of the model. A part of implementation is the maintenance of the model which has to be organized in advance.

There is no doubt that cutting the total modeling process into fourteen (or any other number of) components is rather arbitrary. These components are neither separate nor separable. They are closely interrelated.

However, the separation of the components has the purpose of emphasizing the most important areas of activities throughout the modeling process. In addition, the separation may also be a key for splitting the total task into subtasks and assigning them to team members who work on the project at the same time. This organizational aspect indicates another advantage of the assemblage-of-components concept over the sequence-of-steps concepts.

Again, it is emphasized that the fourteen components given above form only a general frame. There are projects where Components 10 and 11 cannot be separated at all. In other cases, there might be such close interdependencies between the models and the algorithms that the Components 8 and 10 are almost identical. And it might occasionally be advantageous to combine the analysis of the system and the construction of the model (Components 4 and 8), etc.

There is another advantage of the assemblage-of-components concept over the sequence-of-steps concept. The *ideal* of the assemblage-of-components concept leaves room for the application of the *top down approach* to the *whole* process. The sequence-of-steps concept allows only for the application of the top down approach *within each step*.

The overall top down approach in combination with assemblage-of-components concept allows for a quite rough first round through all the components, a first refinement in the second round, etc.

The step-oriented top down approach in combination with the sequence-of-steps concept asks for the final completion of one step before the first round of next step begins. This is not advantageous.

5 MODELING, AN ART OR A SCIENCE?

In this paper, the following positions were taken:

1. *Models* are the *heart* of "planning systems". They are representations of *sub-systems* within *man-machine systems*. The model has to serve *technical* as well as *social* or *organizational purposes*.

2. The *modeling process* (or model design process, or planning system design process) has to aim at *total coverage*, represented in this paper by the fourteen components. It is an *integrative* approach.

3. The modeling process has to be organized. The author tried to show the ad-

57

vantages of the *assemblage-of-components concept* over the *sequence-of-steps concept.*

In connection with such topics it might be interesting to put the question of whether modeling is an art or a science.

Model design has many properties in common with any other *design task,* such as computer program design. There is a fascinating discussion by Knuth [6] about whether *computer programming* is an art or a science. He comes to the conclusion that it is an art. And it is the author's opinion that *modeling* is an art as well. But no branch of art can exist without theories, principles, concepts, methods, rules, laws, techniques, tools, etc. These have to be developed and the development requires *scientific research and investigation.* The research and investigation into model design can be called "science of modelling".

The purpose of the science of modeling is to provide theories, principles, concepts, methods, rules, laws, techniques, tools, etc. of modeling which should be applicable to actual modeling.

Actual modeling, however, remains an art but depends highly upon the results of the science of modeling.

And education in modeling has some parallel to education in composition in the following sense: "In this respect I feel akin to the teacher of composition at a conservatory: He does not teach his pupils how to compose a particular symphony, he must help his pupils to find their own style and must explain to them what is implied by this" [6, p. 670, quoting Dijkstra]. Modeling depends upon individual styles as well. It is not a mechanical application of rules, laws and techniques.

REFERENCES

1. Checkland, Peter B. "The Problem of Problem Formulation in the Application of a Systems Approach." in *Education in Systems Science* edited by B.A. Bayraktar et al. London, 1979, pp. 318-26.

2. Churchman, C. West, Russell L. Ackoff and E. Leonard Arnoff. *Introduction to Operations Research.* New York, 1957.

3. Hanssmann, Fred. *Operations Research Techniques for Capital Investment* (2nd ed.). Huntington, N.Y., 1974.

4. Hax, Karl. "Planung und Organisation als Instrumente der Unternehmensführung." *Zeitschrift für handelswissenschaftliche Forschung* 11 (1959): 605-15.

5. Kirsch, Werner. *Einführung in die Theorie der Entscheidungsprozesse* (2nd ed.). Wiesbaden, 1977.

6. Knuth, Donald. "Computer Programming as an Art." *Comm. of the ACM* 17 (12) (1974): 667-73.

7. Koch, Helmut. *Aufbau der Unternehmungsplanung.* Wiesbaden, 1977.

8. Müller, Max. *Planung als Prozess und System.* Zürich, 1974.

9. Müller, Werner R. "Ziele von Organisationen." *Die Unternehmung* 31 (1) (1977): 1-19.

10. Müller-Merbach, Heiner. "Quantitative Entscheidungsvorbereitung: Erwartungen, Enttäuschungen, Chancen." *Die Betriebswirtschaft* 37(1) (1977):11-23.

11. Müller-Merbach, Heiner. "Tendenzen der Verwendung quantitativer Ansätze in der betriebswirtschaftlichen Forschung und Praxis." in *Quantitative Ansätze in der Betriebswirtschaftslehre*, edited by H. Müller-Merbach. Munich, 1978, pp. 11-27.

12. Scheer, August-Wilhelm. *Wirtschafts- und Betriebsinformatik*. Munich, 1978.

13. Schmitz, Paul and Dietrich Seibt. *Einführung in die anwendungsorientierte Informatik*. Munich, 1975.

14. Vemuri, V. *Modeling of Complex Systems: An Introduction*. New York, 1978.

15. Wagner, Harvey M. *Principles of Operations Research* (2nd ed.). London, 1975.

16. Wedekind, Hartmut. *Systemanalyse* (2nd ed.). Munich/Vienna, 1976.

17. Woolsey, R.E.D. "How to do integer programming in the real world." in *Integer Programming*, edited by H.M. Salkin. Reading, Mass., 1975, pp. 505-26.

4. Implementation of Planning Models: Presentation of the APIS Approach

by Thilo Tilemann

1 INTRODUCTION

The expression "data processing task" sometimes is interpreted in two different ways. Some people use this notion to describe a data processing problem for which a solution has still to be found, i.e., a "task" of an organisation. Others imply a set of instructions already controlling the automatic solution of the problem, i.e., a "task" of a computer. With planning problems, however, the step from the problem statement to an adequate planning model usually is a big one. The ambiguous use of "data processing task" there can be regarded as symptomatic for the poor perception of modeling problems as well as for the underdeveloped state of modeling methodologies.

1.1 Characteristics of Analysis and Planning Models

Models in this context are purposeful images of real companies, artificial managerial constructs (e.g., systems of financial variables) and markets or parts of those. They are represented in computable equations or inequalities to serve decision makers as quantitative tools in analysis and planning processes.

In computer aided planning systems we distinguish analysis and planning problems. Analysis models and methods are used to:

—aid selection and aggregation decisions refering to model variables,
—estimate and validate model parameters,
—analyse and forecast input data and to
—examine (alternative) model outputs.

Planning models apply mainly to:
—the evaluation of the effects of alternative values of key variables ("What-if" or "consequence calculation"),
—the (optimal) choice out of alternatives ("What to do to achieve calculation") and to
—transformation calculations of arbitrary planning data (Table 1)

Table 1. Planning model features and applications

Type of calculation / Model features	What if?	What to do to achieve?	Transformation
values of model variables	1. hypothetical management decisions 2. estimated external parameters 3. states of the firm	1.a. target values 1.b. objective functions 2. conditions, restrictions	arbitrary planning data
model types	Simulation models	a. Simulation b. Ms/OR Models	Transformation Models, e.g., Report Generators
model outputs	consequences	a. target oriented developments b. possible decisions	1. aggregations/ disaggregations 2. selections 3. consolidations of planning data

Source: [17]

1.2 Design Versus Implementation

The development of planning systems is considerably more difficult than that of accounting systems. This is mainly due to the existence of:

—different possible starting points for the problem specification,
—different possible approaches of solution,
—structural uncertainty which is also caused by changes in the modeled phenomena, and
—reduced availability and reliability of future related data.

The transformation of an application model on the concept level to an application program on the software level is commonly acknowledged as an implementation process. A similar process but much more important for a satisfying model: problem fit is often neglected, the implementation of abstract models into an individual application situation [22]. This is a crucial point in practical modelling. The pattern independent "zero base" design of models being as much an exception as the plug compatible fit of so-called standard planning models.

Usually the model builder orientates his work either at model concepts underlying similar realisations or at abstract model types, (e.g., LP model) in literature (Figure 1). Abstract model types can only provide a very rough and basic idea of some possible structural elements. So in modelling processes starting from abstract model types the analysis and choice activities tend to need less resources than the design and implementation activities. This used to be vice versa starting from other model realisations which come close to the needed model.

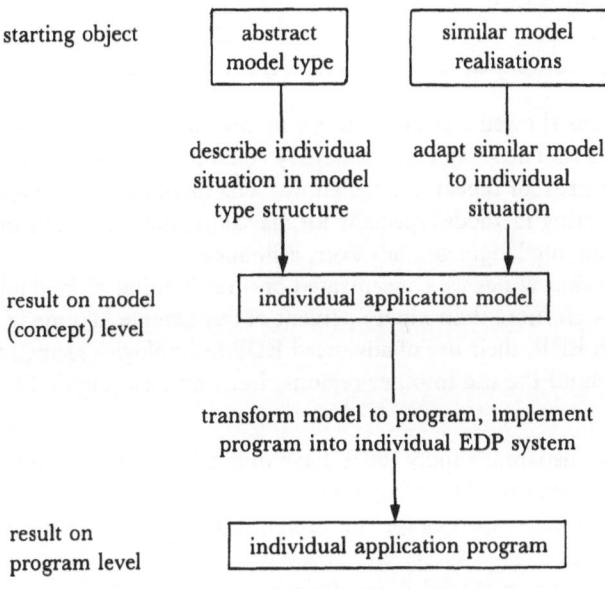

Figure 1. Pragmatic model implementation.

2 DIAGNOSIS OF PROBLEM AREAS

2.1 Supply and Demand of Planning Software

In order to find out how the practical development and use of computer-based planning models could be supported we analyzed the German situation [23] and compared it to that in the U.S. [15] and in Great Britain [4]. For this purpose we distinguished three categories of planning software:

—planning languages and generators [6]
—programmed packages with analysis and forecasting methods and
—programmed application models.

The sold computer use per category indicates which type of tool is demanded (Table 2).

Table 2. Planning Software in Time Sharing Networks
in the Federal Republic of Germany

Planning Software Category \ Distribution	available programs	sold computer time (2 market leaders)
languages and generators	41%	50%
packages	39%	38%
models	20%	12%

The analysis showed a stronger trend to flexible software tools than to prefabricated models. The small model category contains only some financial models and several macros for repeated calculations. The main use of packages is on analysis and forecasting methods especially for marketing purposes. The main application area of planning languages, however, is finance.

On the *demand side* we concentrated on the situation of medium sized companies. Though more than ninety percent of our sample had made positive experience with EDP, their use of advanced EDP technologies seemed to range significantly behind the use in other regions, i.e., samples (Figure 2). This is mainly due to:

1. the intransparent supply (60% have only a rough idea or no idea of decision oriented software) and the "bad quality" of software,

2. the necessary expenses for the prerequisites (e.g., learning development resources), and

3. the bad support of realisation of planning models, which more than 90% want to be individually tailored to their (data) situation [8].

2.2 Current Modelling Approaches

The literature on system development methodology contains a lot of general phase approaches structuring the development process of computer-based systems. They differ in the degree of differentiation of single activities and in the weight given to specific factors influencing the process and its product. Originally initiated by necessities of managing conventional software projects they also can serve as guidelines for design and development of planning models. We analyzed three types of phase approaches:

1. *EDP oriented approaches* consider in particular the conditions of hard and software tools. They are available as phase schemes [5] or as detailed handbooks with practical rules and instruments (checklists, forms, etc.) [1]. The definition of the planning problem and the conception of its solution is not supported. In so far these approaches aim at programmers rather than modelers.

2. *Procedure or algorithm oriented approaches* reflect the type of model or method which

REGION (SAMPLE) MODES OF EDP USE	GREAT BRITAIN 50 COMPANIES GRINYER & WOOLLER 1973	MAINLY USA 323 COMPANIES NAYLOR & JEFFRES 1974	FRG 80 MEDIUM SIZED COMPANIES TILEMANN ET AL. 1976

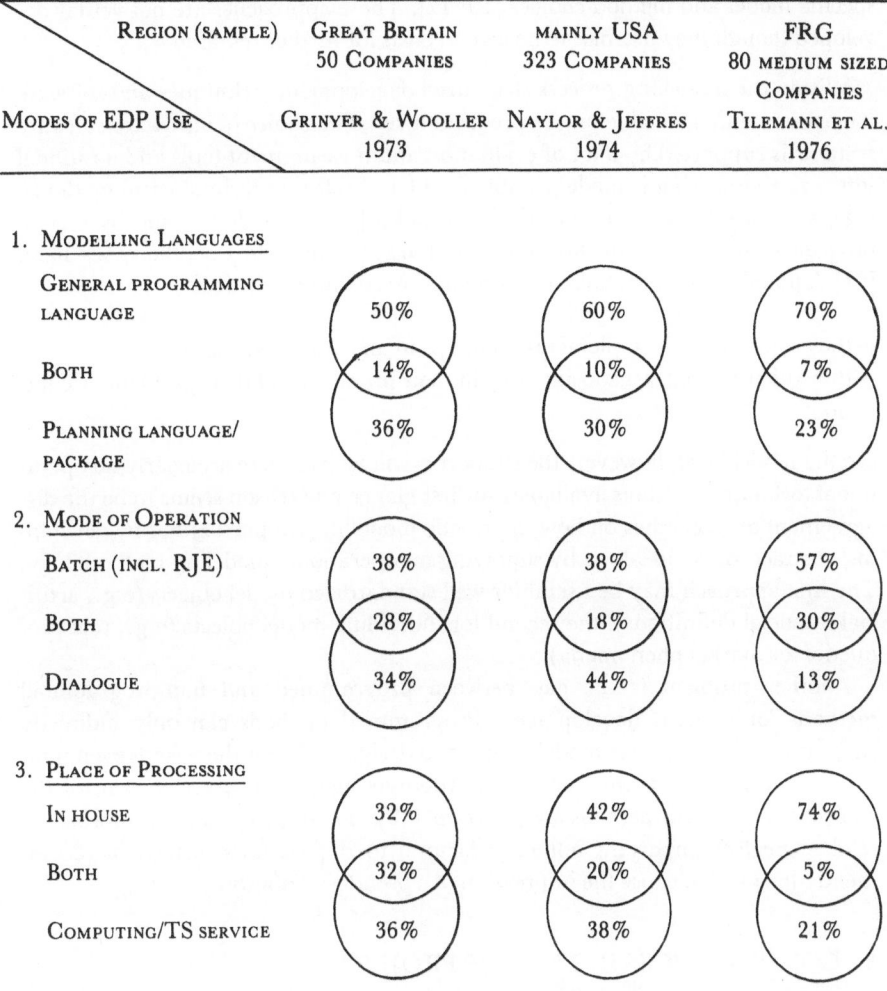

1. MODELLING LANGUAGES

	Great Britain	mainly USA	FRG
GENERAL PROGRAMMING LANGUAGE	50%	60%	70%
BOTH	14%	10%	7%
PLANNING LANGUAGE/ PACKAGE	36%	30%	23%

2. MODE OF OPERATION

	Great Britain	mainly USA	FRG
BATCH (INCL. RJE)	38%	38%	57%
BOTH	28%	18%	30%
DIALOGUE	34%	44%	13%

3. PLACE OF PROCESSING

	Great Britain	mainly USA	FRG
IN HOUSE	32%	42%	74%
BOTH	32%	20%	5%
COMPUTING/TS SERVICE	36%	38%	21%

Figure 2. Modes of EDP Use for Planning Purposes

shall be used for the solution. Regarding organizational and personal factors as given, the development steps describe for example activities concerned with decision models [16] or with dynamic simulation models [14]. Once the problem is stated and the model type chosen these approaches can support model implementation.

3. *Problemoriented approaches* try to overcome the disadvantages of the former approaches in different ways. For example, they relate algorithm oriented approaches to typical implementation situations, e.g., specific structures, processes, planning problems and planning software [18] or they try to support problem

specific model and method choices [10; 12]. These approaches are not yet far developed though they promise to be a good basis for further research.

Within the modelling process structured development techniques and software tools are mainly available on the program level. The choice of hardware/software systems is supported by a lot of evaluation and measurement tools and a rational software engineering is made possible by a lot of software technological methods, e.g., structured programming, decision tables [7] on one hand, and by service programs (generators, on line programming systems, etc.) on the other hand [21]. Though abundant, these instruments are still problematic as

—they support single implementation steps in an isolated way and
—they differ or contrast considerably in their premises and their problem orientation.

On the model level, however, the support is still worse: there are nearly no operational techniques or tools available. At first glance one reason seems to be the disagreement of researches on how to provide modelling support: either by developing abstract model ideals or by supplying an operational modeling methodology. The first approach may be useful for well standardized model objects (e.g., artificial financial definitions), the second for individual model objects (e.g., real production or market phenomena).

Another problem is the gap between programmed and non-programmed methods for systems development. Programmed methods can only indirectly support creative steps like model choice and design [13]. For these steps even non-programmed methods are very rare. Attempts have been made to control the choice of analytical methods by program [12]. These programmed approaches tend to neglect important influence factors, to impose laws instead of recommendations and to cause the impression of a pseudo-reliability.

3   CONSEQUENCES IN THE APIS PROJECT

How can the gap between the abundant supply of planning tools and its poor practical application be reduced? The project APIS tries to provide some support for this on the model and the program levels. (The acronym APIS is an abbreviation for ''Development of Analysis and Planning Models in Interactive Systems''.)

3.1   APIS Objectives

APIS investigates problems in design and implementation of planning models in advanced EDP environments (Figure 3).The project concentrates on analysis and planning problems of medium sized companies. These companies shall be supported in different ways:

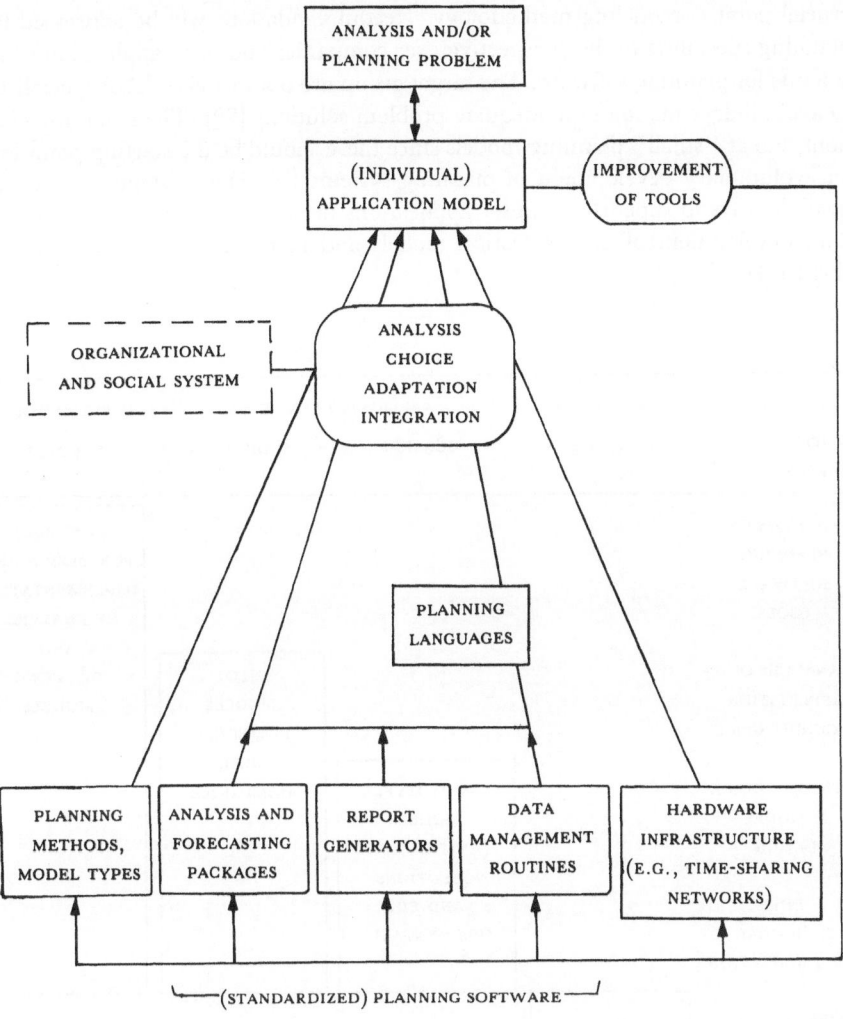

Figure 3. Research and Development Field in APIS.

—by pattern model solutions generated for typical planning areas and demonstrated to practice,

—by recommendations which, regarding the contents of planning problems, systemize the solution of modeling and programming questions and

—by proposals for the improvement of planning tools.

Organizational and personal factors of implementation are taken as non-manipulable constraints in APIS. Software technological methods being abundant the crucial point is modeling methodology. Recommendations will be addressed to planning specialists in the prospective user companies and/or to application consultants for planning software. The target group are not model or EDP specialists to avoid indoctrination of inadequate problem solutions [20]. The recommendations aim at "small" planning models since these should be the starting point for an evolutionary development of planning systems [2]. The existence of several possible ways to support computer applications in planning is recognized by the joint development of demonstration models and methical recommendations (Figure 4).

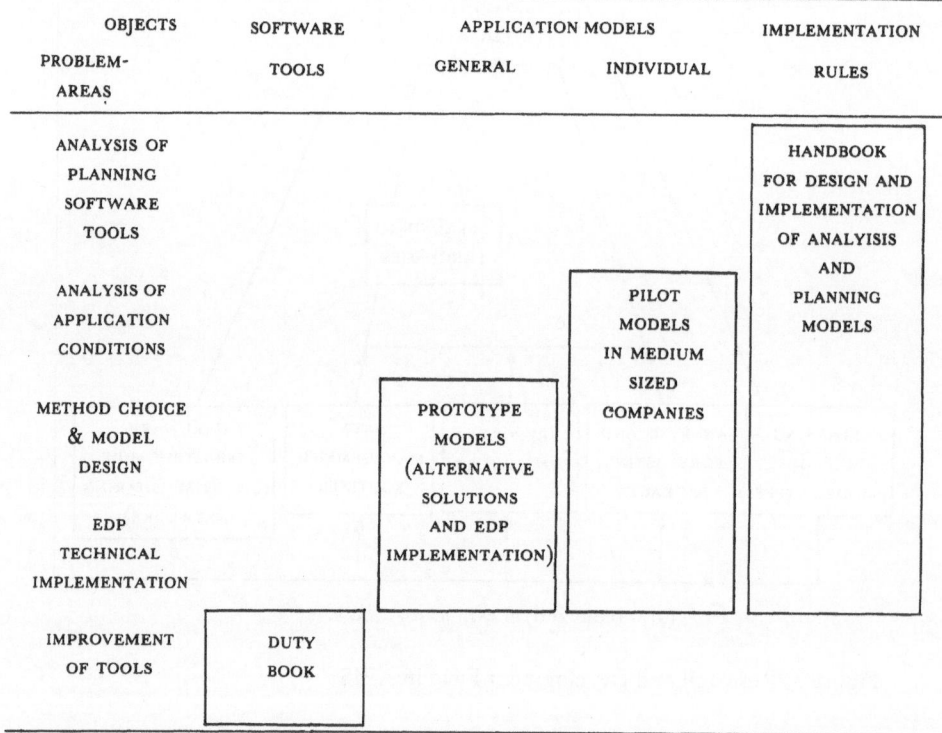

PROBLEM-AREAS \ OBJECTS	SOFTWARE TOOLS	APPLICATION MODELS		IMPLEMENTATION RULES
		GENERAL	INDIVIDUAL	
ANALYSIS OF PLANNING SOFTWARE TOOLS				HANDBOOK FOR DESIGN AND IMPLEMENTATION OF ANALYISIS AND PLANNING MODELS
ANALYSIS OF APPLICATION CONDITIONS			PILOT MODELS IN MEDIUM SIZED COMPANIES	
METHOD CHOICE & MODEL DESIGN		PROTOTYPE MODELS (ALTERNATIVE SOLUTIONS AND EDP IMPLEMENTATION)		
EDP TECHNICAL IMPLEMENTATION				
IMPROVEMENT OF TOOLS	DUTY BOOK			

Figure 4. Planned Results of the APIS Project.

3.2 APIS Methodology

The research and development activities in APIS combine empirical induction with top down conception. They follow a complex methodological setting which is intended to yield synergetic effects (Figure 5). The main characteristics are:

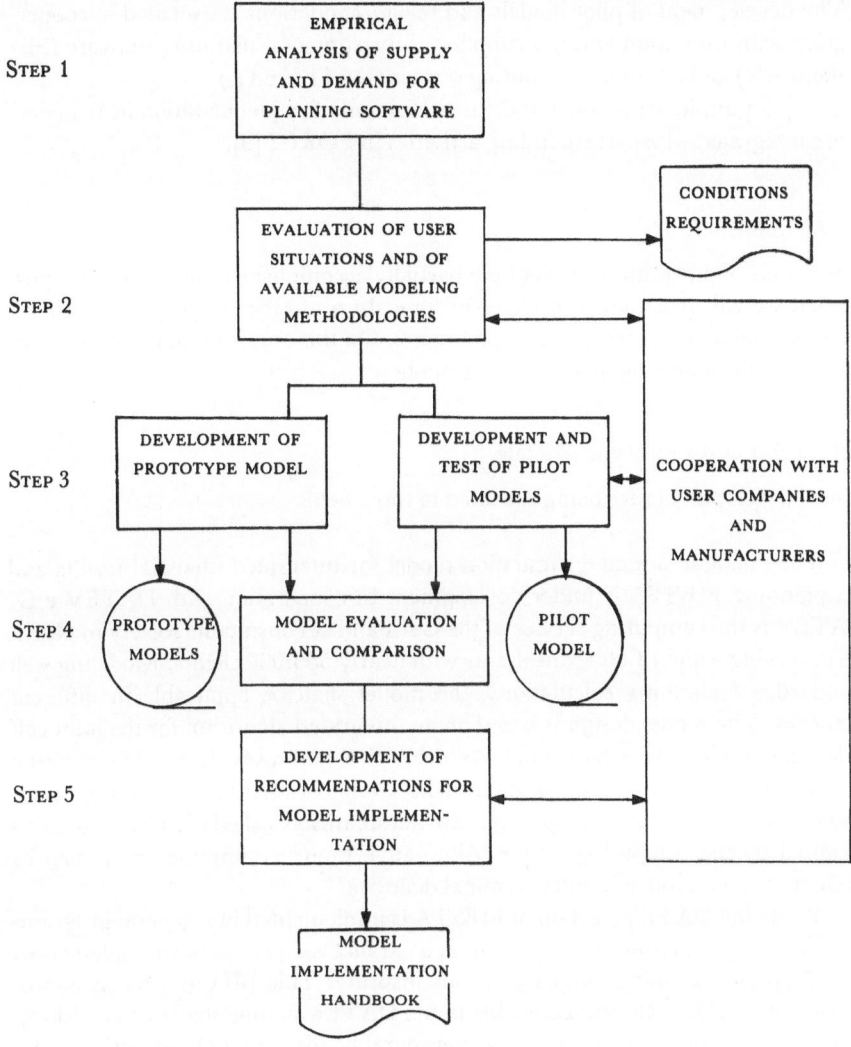

Figure 5. Process of Research by Development in APIS.

—The modeling activities have been divided into two groups: one supplying "pilot models" which are designed and implemented in real companies, and another developing parallel solutions for the same problem in form of "prototype models". The latter use an alternative solution structure and EDP environment in order to allow practical comparisons of these alternatives.

—Available modeling methodologies are used for the development of different models. The development experiences are used to improve the methodologies and supply further methodical recommendations.

—The development of pilot models and recommendations is executed in cooperation with user companies, a supplier of instrumental planning software (Siemens AG) and a leading computing service (DATEV e.G.).

—One pilot implementation and the development of implementation instruments are integrated with corresponding activities in PORGI [9].

4 APIS RESULTS

The results of our project are yet only partially accomplished, but we are optimistic that we will reach our objectives in time. In a number of project reports we have documented the results of Steps 1 and 2. On this empirical and literary basis we started the following model developments.

4.1 Pilot and Prototype Models

Model developments are being executed in three fields:

1. The dialogue oriented simulation model for integrated financial results and tax planning FIESTA is under development in cooperation with DATEV e.G. DATEV is the computing service of the German tax consultants society in Nürnberg, serving some 13,000 consultants with nearly 500,000 clients. Modeling well standardized planning calculations, the model shall be applicable in different branches. The model design is based on an integrated algorithm for the joint calculation of dividends, interests on external capital and taxes. In a special division of labor the consultants play an intermediate role between the computing center and the end user. Constant input data are automatically called off the consultant's terminal by the computing center. Alternative input assumptions may then be evaluated in a remote job-entry terminal dialogue.

2. While the DATEV version of FIESTA is implemented in a general programming language to reduce execution time, a parallel version has been implemented with a special planning language in our institute. This BIFOA version is programmed in BUSTER and accessible in the DATEMA time sharing network[3]. The first valuable experience was a considerably shorter implementation time. The BIFOA version allows simple logic changes and thus serves as a prototype: practical demonstrations and experiments on logic and data are permanently influencing the pilot development with DATEV. Figure 6 shows the rough concept of both versions.

3. A different pilot model is under construction with the pharmaceutical company SANOL. This model is implemented with the Siemens Planning Software COMET [19]. The CPS model comprises what-if calculations for marketing, cost and financial planning. Especially in the marketing and cost subsystems it is necessarily tailored to SANOL conditions. Experiences in this case refered to effects of the pre-project decision for COMET on the solution and the procedures followed in design and implementation.

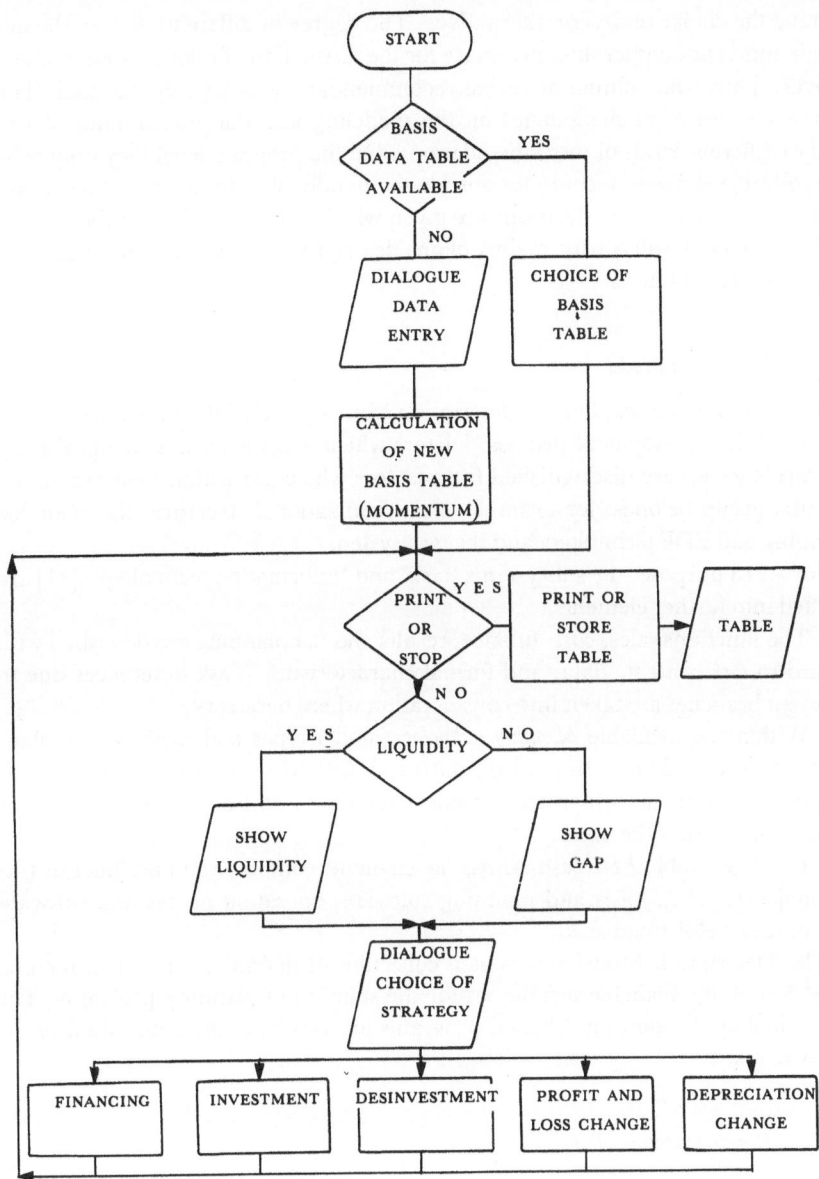

Figure 6. Pilot Model FIESTA (Overview).

4.2 Model Implementation Handbook

The APIS Handbook deals primarily with the problem analysis, model choice and implementation phases. It aims at reducing uncertainty in development situations where model builders have to decide between alternative solutions. The investigation of an analysis or planning problem seizes those factors which de-

71

termine the choice of design alternatives. The degree of differentiation of the determinants is not higher than necessary for the distinction of relevant design alternatives. Thus, the volume of verbal recommendations is kept operational. The different states of methodologies on the modeling and the programming levels lead to different kinds of recommendations. On the program level they only refer to applicable software techniques outside the handbook. On the model level procedures for development decisions are given which are part of the handbook. The APIS Handbook will consist mainly of one descriptive and two instrumental parts plus several appendices.

4.2.1 Description Model

The descriptive part contains a Description Model (DM) of the constants and variables of the development process. Factors which usually are not changeable by the target group are distinguished from factors which are within their reach. To the first group belongs, for example, the organizational structure, the available planning and EDP technology and the task system.

For APIS purposes the subsystems 'task' and 'information technology' [11] are splitted into further elements.

1. The functions sales, cost, finance, results and tax planning are described with regard to *task* content, data, and formal characteristics. Task differences due to different branches are taken into consideration where necessary.

2. Within the available *planning technology* model types and methods for planning, analysis and forecasting (e.g., statistical, OR/MS, intuitive) are described. These form a choice which has practical relevance and does not expect great qualifications from the users.

3. In the available *EDP basis systems* the elements computer and peripherals (including networks), basis and planning software, operation modes and software techniques are distinguished.

The Description Model serves as a collection of definitions and as a method base describing available techniques for the solution of planning problems. The individual application models and programs are results of the application of the following part.

4.2.2 Recommendations Part

The main instrumental part is the Recommendations Part (RP) advising on how to proceed in the development process and which solutions to take. Since different decision situations within the process depend on different determinants, the gathering of information can be split into subactivities for each relevant determinant group. Thus, a partial problem analysis makes a corresponding partial decision possible. The decision points can be regarded as nodes in tree structures which connect possible solutions of subproblems to those of higher problems.

The Recommendations Part consists of the following components:

Table 3. Example of Phase Scheme with Indication of Solution Alternatives.

Phase Scheme (section)	Description Model (section)

⋮

2. MODEL DESIGN	1. Data processing task
2.1. CHOICE OF MODEL APPROACH	1.1. Functions
	1.1.1. Finance
	⋮
2.1.1. Definitions of Outputs	1.1.1.2. Output Forms —Profit and Loss —Balance —Coefficients

2.1.2. Choice of Model Type
2.1.3. Choice of Method (Class)
2.1.4. Input Data Requirements
2.1.5. Analysis of Restrictions

2.2. DESIGN AND ADAPTATION
2.2.1. Definition of Variables
2.2.2. Definition of Aggregation
2.2.3. Definition of Period & Horizon
2.2.4. Definition of Goals/Objectives
2.2.5. Definition of Functional
        Relations
2.2.6. Model Validation

⋮

1.   A *phase scheme* classifying modeling related decision problems. The sequential listing is no law for a sequential processing of the problems. Wherever it is possible control information for jumps or iterations is given.

2.   Attached to each subproblem, *indications* are given to possible solution alternatives (Table 3), and if the choice is difficult to special tools supporting the choice. The indications use elementary tools such as classification schemes, lists of criteria or checklists. Complex tools such as questionnaires are stored separately in the third part of the Handbook.

3.   After having applied these tools to his modeling problem the user has to associate the results of his investigation to typical *problem profiles*. These are groups of conditions for which recommendations are contained in the next component.

4. The *recommendations* are divided into three groups according to the possibility of generalization of implementation practices. The first contains proposals of specific solution parts (e.g., model type, special method), the second advises on general proceeding principles or method classes, while the third is non-conceptual. It contains pointers to solution possibilities which are not proposed in the Handbook.

4.2.3 Tool Kit

The third part is a sort of *tool kit* containing complex tools. These are especially problem analysis methods in form of voluminous checklists and questionnaires, description and evaluation methods. The Tool Kit, thus, provides aids for the solution of design and implementation problems, not for the solution of planning problems. The latter are contained in the Description Model.

The tools are refered to by indications in the Recommendations Part. However, a separate storage seems useful especially for complex tools because they would disturb the transparency of the decision flow in the Recommendations Part.

4.2.4 An Interaction Example

To illustrate the interaction of the different Handbook components we will present a simple example. In the development phase 'Model Design', we consider the two subproblems 'choice of model type' and 'choice of method'. Table 4 shows corresponding solution alternatives. The subproblem indicators refer to corresponding tools which support the intelligence phase of solution choice. In our example these are checklists with general, technical and data oriented criteria. The application of the checklists results in data which are partially presented in Table 5. The user has to check the correspondence of these results with pre-defined values of the criteria. In our example, two solutions (i.e., the decision or what-if model) are related to two different value combinations (problem profiles). By evaluating which problem profile best meets the individual results the user finds the recommended solution.

5 CONCLUSION

The APIS results are hoped to support a broader application of computer-based planning by absorbing uncertainty about alternative planning and EDP solutions. They provide a systematic framework for model implementation decisions. The framework tries to be open to individual modeling styles but to avoid too sophisticated or too expensive solutions. As positive side effects, we credit the contribution to more transparency and sensitivity related to business analysis and planning problems.

The concepts are not only restricted to a special type of implementation decisions but also consider determinants only partially. So they risk becoming invalid if neglected determinants win an overriding influence. Another limit is the small empirical basis APIS has been able to establish until now. Further research could enlarge this basis, add further recommendations and calibrate the Handbook to the most useful level of detail.

Table 4. Interaction Example of Phase Scheme, Description Model and Tool Kit

Phase Scheme (Section)	Description Model	Tool Kit (e.g. Checklists)
2. MODEL DESIGN 2.1. CHOICE OF MODEL APPROACH		
	2. Planning Technology	
2.1.2. Choice of Model Type	2.1. Model Types 2.1.1. What-if 2.1.2. What to do to achieve 2.1.3. Transformation	5. Determinants of Model Choice CH MODW GEN CH MODW TEC
2.1.3. Choice of Method (Class)	2.2. Method Classes 2.2.1. Statistics 2.2.2. Simulation 2.2.2.1. Time Constant —Determined —Probability —Monte Carlo 2.2.3. Optimization 2.2.4. Heuristics	6. Determinants of Method Choice CH METW GEN CH METW TEC CH METW DAT

Table 5. Interaction Example of Problem Profiles and Recommendations.

Evaluation of Checklists (individual results e.g.)	Problem Profiles	Recommendation (individual evaluation)

CH MODW GEN:
1. Most objectives quantifiable
2. Important objectives not commensurable
3. Modelling of multiple objectives difficult
4. Few alternatives for decisions

CH MODW TEC:
1. Low OR qualification of user
2. Low EDP capacity available

Correspondence Checking

PP MODW GEN:
1. Objectives quantifiable?
2. Objectives commensurable?
3. Model solution for multiple objectives available?
4. No decision alternatives?

PP MODW TEC:
1. Necessary OR qualification?
2. Necessary EDP capacity?

MAIN VALUE

DECISION MODEL	WHAT-IF MODEL
yes	no
yes	no
yes	no
yes	
high	low
high	low

Evaluation corresponds mainly to WHAT–IF MODEL → choose WHAT-IF MODEL

REFERENCES

1. ADV/ORGA, F.A. Meyer KG (ed.), Orgware, Vols. 1-5, Wilhelmshaven, 1975.

2. Boulden, J.B. "Instant Modelling," in A.N. Schrieber (ed.) *Corporate Simulation Models.* Washington, 1970, pp. 578-599.

3. DATEMA (ed.) BUSTER Anwender Handbuch, Frankfurt, 1975.

4. Grinyer, P.H. and J. Wooller. "Computer Models for Corporate Planning." *Long Range Planning* 8 (1975): 14-25.

5. Hice, G.E., W.S. Turner and L.F. Cashwell. *System Development Methodology.* Amsterdam and Oxford: 1974.

6. Hurst, G.E. jr. and T. Tilemann. "Characteristics of Planning Systems." in A. Ralston and C.L. Meek (eds.) *Encyclopedia of Computer Science.* New York: 1976, pp. 1077-82.

7. Jackson, M.A. *Principles of program design.* London: 1975.

8. Köhler, R. and K. Heinzelbecker. "Informationssysteme für die Unternehmungsführung. Zur MIS-Entwicklung in der Praxis im Zeitraum 1970/1975." *Die Betriebswirtschaft* 37 (1977): 267-82.

9. Kolf, F., H.J. Oppelland, D. Seibt and N. Szyperski. "Instrumentarium zur organisatorischen Implementierung von rechnergestützten Informationssystemen." *Angewandte Informatik* (1978): 299-310.

10. Laager, F. *Die Bildung problemangepaßter Entscheidungsmodelle.* Zürich: 1974.

11. Leavitt, H.J. and T.L. Whisler. "Management in the 1980s." *Harvard Business Review* 36 (1958): 41-48.

12. Mertens, P., W. Neuwirth and W. Schmitt. "Verknüpfung von Daten- und Methodenbanken, dargestellt am Beispiel der Analyse von Marktforschungsdaten." in H.D. Plötzeneder (ed.) *Computer Assisted Corporate Planning.* Stuttgart et al.: 1977, pp. 291-332.

13. Müller-Merbach, H. "Quantitative Entscheidungsvorbereitung—Erwartungen, Enttäuschungen, Chancen." *Die Betriebswirtschaft* 37 (1977): 11-23.

14. Mirham, G.A. "Simulation Methodology." *Theory and Decision* 7 (1976): 67-94.

15. Naylor, R. and C. Jeffress. "Corporate Simulation Models: A Survey." *Simulation* 24 (1975): 171-76.

16. Rivett, P. *Principles of Model Building: The Construction of Models for Decision Analysis.* London: 1971.

17. Rosenkranz, F. "Status and Future Use of Corporate Planning and Simulation Models: Case Studies and Conclusions." in H.D. Plötzeneder (ed.) *Computer Assisted Corporate Planning.* Stuttgart: 1977, pp. 143-79.

18. Rosenkranz, F. and S. Pellegrini. "Corporate Modelling: Methodology and Computer-based Model Design Procedure." *Angewandte Informatik* 6 (1976): 259-67.

19. Siemens AG (ed.) Siemens-Systeme 7000 und 4004: Software-Produkt COMET. Computergestütztes marketing-orientiertes Entscheidungs- und Kontrollsystem. Anwendungsbeschreibung. München: 1977.

20. Szyperski, N. "Realisierung von Informationssystemen in deutschen Unternehmungen." in H. Müller-Merbach (ed.) *Quantitative Ansätze in der Betriebswirtschaftslehre.* Darmstadt: 1977, pp. 67-86.

21. Teichroew, D., and H. Susieni. "Automation of System Building." *Datamation* (August 1971): 25-30.

22. Tilemann, T. *Implementierung linearer Optimierungsmodelle für die Produktionsplanung in der Grundstoffchemie.* Köln: 1977.

23. Tilemann, T., H. Roden, W. Emde and H.P. Klütsch. *Betriebswirtschaftliche Analyse- und Planungssoftware: Struktur von Angebot und Nachfrage in der Bundesrepublik Deutschland.* Köln: 1977.

III. ORGANIZATIONAL ASPECTS OF SYSTEMS DESIGN AND IMPLEMENTATION

5. Basic Considerations in Organizational and Human Aspects in Systems Design: the State of the Art of Implementation Research

by Henry C. Lucas, Jr.

1 INTRODUCTION

The purpose of this paper is to discuss the state of the art of implementation research. The implementation of computer-based information systems and operations research/management science (OR/MS) projects is usually described as the process during which a system or model is adopted for use by individuals in an organization.

Popular data processing literature often describes implementation as a two week stage in the systems life cycle coming just after conversion and prior to the time that a system is considered operational. Most researchers in the field argue for a broader definition of implementation: it is best to consider implementation as the process that begins when the first idea for a system is generated and ends after a system has achieved a substantial level of use.

This paper describes several different approaches to research on implementation and illustrates them with two examples. The paper proposes a framework for combining these different approaches to implementation research and makes suggestions for the direction of future research efforts.

2 APPROACHES TO IMPLEMENTATION RESEARCH

2.1 Measures of Success

One problem in implementation research is defining success. A number of different indicators have been suggested, including:

1. The payoff to the organization from a system,
2. The use of a system as measured by intended or actual use such as the number of inquiries made of an on-line system,
3. The degree to which a system accomplishes its original objectives,
4. User satisfaction through a self-report measure on a questionnaire or interview,

5. Favorable user attitudes,
6. Favorable user attitudes where the attitudes are good predictors of system use,
7. Cost benefit analysis.

There has been relatively little emphasis on costs versus benefits as a definition of implementation success primarily because of measurement difficulties. It is difficult to obtain data on the costs of a system and the benefits from an information system may not be quantifiable. For more advanced systems beyond those which just process transactions, savings often cannot be demonstrated with any certainty. Transactions processing systems sometimes produce labor savings or improve operations, for example, by a reduction in average inventory balances. However, it is difficult to evaluate the benefits of a strategic planning model. Even if organizational performance improves, can the use of the model be given credit? Also, researchers in the implementation field generally feel that the most important problems to consider are human and organizational; they are unlikely to include costs and benefits in their research.

Cost/benefit measures are important; however, because of the problems of developing realistic estimates as described above, an indicator of success like use is more appropriate. Use is unsuitable as a measure for all information systems because there are systems where use is involuntary. A sales representative has to complete an order form for a computer-based order entry system: the use of such a system is involuntary. Here it is necessary to use another success criteria like satisfaction. For the sales manager who receives a sales analysis report for an order entry system, use is an appropriate measure of system success. This manager may use the report extensively or ignore it at his or her discretion.

Information systems are designed to change some information processing procedure; individuals have to change their activities in order to work with a new system. Therefore, implementation research is largely concerned with organizational and individual behavior. The theories and research to be discussed in this paper can best be classified in the field of a social science rather than engineering or computer science. As a result, most implementation research is empirical; data of some type are collected to test hypotheses or provide insights about implementation.

2.2 Research Designs

There are a number of ways to classify research on implementation. Firstly, there are philosophies and proposals. Some researchers would call these *theories*, though they are really not scientific for the most part. It is often difficult to develop testable hypotheses from these theories; they are informal and describe different approaches to implementation. However, the ideas contained in these writings provide insights and ideas to be used in implementing computer-based information systems. There is no guarantee that the suggestions will improve implementation success. Researchers have conducted surveys of factors which are thought to be important in successful implementation; many variables have been identified through this type of research. Finally, there are articles describing the process of implementation usually in a form of different case studies. Such case studies present insights, though it is often hard to generalize from the cases to other situations.

2.3 Research Models

There are several types of models for guiding implementation research. A descriptive model attempts to explain some phenomena through a description of the underlying dynamics of a process. Predictive models are used to forecast future events; given a set of inputs what outcome is predicted by the model? Normative models, on the other hand, suggest the best way to proceed. For example, many operations research models suggest an optimum solution to a problem.

Empirical research in a field generally begins with descriptive models. A researcher collects data and processes them to increase his or her understanding of the relationship among key variables. A descriptive model can be modified, refined and validated through repeated studies. The validated descriptive model is often used for the purposes of prediction. The researcher who has gained an understanding of other relationships between dependent and independent variables can predict future outcomes. It is possible that descriptive and predictive models have normative implications. If the researcher has confidence in the relationship among the variables, he or she may suggest normative guidelines for action. However, it is unlikely, that empirical models will ever present optimal solutions because it is so difficult to state objective functions and measure variables in these models.

The first task of the researcher is to identify dependent variables. What outcome is of interest? The most popular dependent variables in the study of implementation have been attitudes or some measure of actual or intended use. Some studies include multiple dependent variables such as intended use and actual frequency of use. The presence of multiple dependent variables offers the advantage of greater reliability, particularly when the variables can be measured with data collected from different sources. An independent variable, in principle, can be manipulated to influence dependent variables. Simple models include the relationship between one dependent and one independent variable. More complex models include multiple independent variables which are hypothesized to be related in some way to the dependent variable. The most complex models include intervening variables forming chains of relationships among variables. More complex models are usually quite difficult to validate and place stringent requirements on data collection and analysis. In any empirical research generally one is trying to demonstrate causality, that is, variable A causes variable B. However, one can never really prove causality conclusively in the social sciences. Instead the researcher attempts to provide evidence supportive of causal relationships. Just, because two variables are highly correlated does not mean that one necessarily causes the other; X may cause Y, Y may cause X or some third variable Z may cause both X and Y to move together.

2.4 Measuring Variables

The researcher must also measure variables in the research model. Sometimes researchers have developed classes of variables which are operationalized in each study. A class like attitudes toward a system is quite general and the researcher must specify what system and what attitudes are to be measured.

In implementation research one can employ several sources of data: observation, interviews, and questionnaires are good examples. Observation is the method frequently associated with case studies. Interviews can be highly structured or very unstructured. They provide an opportunity to explain questions and to follow a trend of thought. However, interviews are costly and sometimes the interviewer can lead a subject and introduce bias. Questionnaires, on the other hand, are generally highly structured. The advantage of the questionnaire is the ability to administer it economically to a large sample. However, do the assumptions and the questions mean the same thing to each respondent?

3 RESEARCH DESIGNS

There are many different research designs, though implementation research has tended to employ mostly laboratory and field research for evaluating these different designs including:

1. Control over confounding variables,
2. The presence of a random sample,
3. Possible interaction of the researcher and the research instruments,
4. Replicability of the study,
5. Realism,
6. Strength of causal inferences,
7. Generalizability.

One is interested in control over confounding variables because they can seriously bias the results of a study. If an important variable is omitted then the results of the research may be misleading.

It is unusual in empirical research to select a truly random sample. In field research, participants are frequently selected because they are willing to become involved in research. In a laboratory study, the researcher may have limited choice in selecting subjects. All statistical tests of inference for generalizing results to a population assume random sampling. A researcher must argue that the sample in the study does not differ significantly from a truly random sample. It is also possible that there is interaction between a researcher, the research instruments and the subjects. An evaluator should be concerned about the replicability of research. Can other researchers conduct similar studies? Can the results of research be transferred to an actual implementation effort? The most popular research designs on implementation have been laboratory or field studies. In a laboratory study the researcher has better control over the environment and the results of the research usually offer stronger evidence of causality than field research. However, it is frequently difficult to develop realistic laboratory settings for studies of implementation. Field research takes place in an organization as opposed to a laboratory. Field studies may involve survey research which is frequently cross sectional, that is, the data are collected at one point in time. As a result it is very difficult to make causal inferences because changes and variables are not observed over time. Case studies also generally occur in the field; the researcher is often an observer or a participant observer in an implementation effort. Cases offer insights into the implementation process, but are often difficult to generalize to other circumstances.

How these different types of research are related is shown in Figure 1. Philosophies and theories provide the basis for planning research. Exploratory case studies are useful for providing insights on the implementation process. These insights lead to further case studies which stress the process of implementation. Similarly factor studies identify variables potentially important in the implementation process. These factors and the results of case and process studies are used to modify and extend theories. Laboratory experiments allow the researcher to explore relationships among factors and test theories. All of the popular forms of implementation research are complimentary. The results of implementation research will improve knowledge and understanding and should hopefully provide guidelines which increase the chances of successfull implementation.

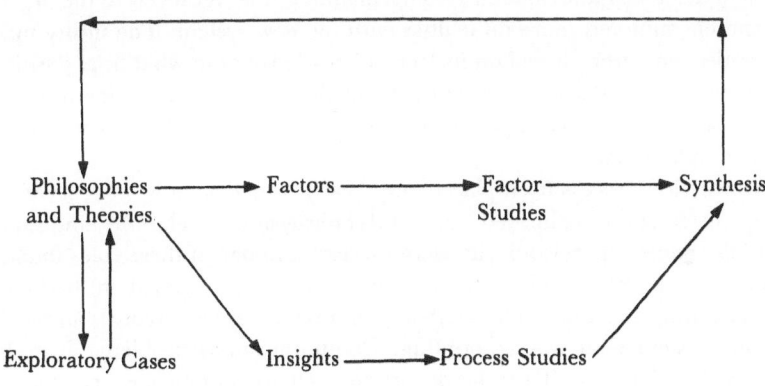

Figure 1. Implementation Research: A synthesis

4 THREE EXAMPLES

This section contains three examples to illustrate case studies and field research on implementation (for further information on theories and philosophies, see Lucas [2]).

4.1 A Case Study

Mann and Williams [3] present a case study of the implementation of a data processing system. This paper contains many insights on the implementation process and the impact of computers on an electric utility. The utility, located in the Midwest, had over a million customers. There were two accounting divisions, one of which was concerned with bills and records and the other with customer contact and service. The central office had eight hundred employees and fifteen hundred workers were in geographically distributed offices. The new system represented a first attempt at computer-based processing for the company; the system was designed to maintain customer accounts. Previous processing had been on electronic tabulating equipment.

The new system was announced in October 1953 and the computer arrived three years later. Conversian began in January of 1957 and by 1958 the initial problems of conversion had smoothed and permanent work assignments were established. The utility took the opportunity of the new system to review the entire organization; management undertook a very broad rethinking of organizational structures. One of the changes was the movement of bookkeeping functions from the district to the central office. Customer contact was centralized in the sales area; for example, the meter reading function was moved from accounting to sales.

The authors observed the change and felt that the participative management style of the accounting division helped them respond well to changes. The sales department delegated information systems planning to lower levels in the organization and encountered more difficulties with the new system. The utility made all job grades temporary based on its lack of knowledge as to what final positions would involve. This decision created a great deal of uncertainty for the work force; almost all employees expected upgrading of jobs and higher pay to result from the computer system.

The conversion process itself placed very heavy time demands on everyone in the company. Supervisors needed a mix of technical, human relations, and supervisory skills. Some supervisors who were successful in one of these roles found it very difficult to handle problems in other areas. The sales department had more trouble adjusting according to the authors, because it was less involved in the design of the system than was accounting. Communications problems arose between these two divisions. The sales department felt accounting was unconcerned about customers and was only interested in records and lower costs. Many individuals mistrusted the information produced by the system. Some of these people kept all records manually rather than relying on a computer system. There were a large number of errors in processing and there seem to be difficulties in correcting them. The situation reached the point where a consulting firm was hired to examine the errors. The consulting report indicated that the number of errors was not unusual for this type of system and the presentation of the report forced the sales department and accounting to work together to resolve these problems.

The process of developing final job assignments after the system was installed was difficult. A complicated procedure was used; the highest level job was filled first and then lower grade positions were assigned. Supervisors tried to find the best fit assignments, though it was difficult to resolve problems, because no supervisor wanted to take anyone but the best candidates.

The authors concluded from their study that the computer system accelerated the level of formalization and appeared to reduce the status of some decision-makers. There was less autonomy for individuals and work groups and there were more deadlines. Greater dependencies were created along with a need for more coordination. Contrary to management goals there appeared to be a shift toward organizational centralization. However, many of the jobs replaced were routine and tedious and there was an increase in employment in the computer area. There was some job enlargement, but there was a greater identification of errors and more responsibility for employees.

4.2 An Experiment

Huysmans [1] conducted a laboratory experiment to test the effectiveness of the cognitive style constraint on the implementation of operations research proposals. Cognitive style measures were used to classify subjects according to two typical ways of reasoning. An analytic subject reduces problem situations to a core of underlying causal relationships. The heuristic subject develops workable solutions to total problem situations, often by finding analogies to familiar, solved problems.

The experimental design included four simulated managers, two analytic and two heuristic. Communications came from the accounting manager who was interested in an overall solution to a problem; this manager presented findings on a mathematical model of the firm's operations. The accounting manager's communications employed two different implementation strategies, one for gaining the subject's explicit and the other for obtaining his integral understanding of the operations research proposal. The two proposals were similar except the explicit understanding approach contained mathematical formulas. Huysmans calculated an adoption measure and kept track of communications among the subject and the simulated managers. His hypotheses can be summarized as:

1. Analytic subjects will have a higher degree of implementation and be at least equal in acceptance to heuristic subjects if the accounting manager uses the explicit understanding approach.
2. Heuristic and analytic subjects who receive the integral understanding approach will reach a higher degree of implementation and be at least equal in acceptance to the heuristic subjects receiving the explicit understanding approach.
3. Heuristic subjects receiving the integral understanding approach will include analytic arguments in communications; heuristics receiving explicit understanding approaches will suppress analytic arguments in their communications.

Huysmans designed an experiment to test the above hypotheses with thirty-five subjects. His results indicated that cognitive style may operate as an effective constraint on the implementation of operations research recommendations. The operations researcher can enhance the chances off successful implementation by taking this constraint into account. If, however, the cognitive style propensities of the manager and operations researcher do not agree, the manager may discard the operations researcher completely as a source of information; the solution may not be implemented no matter how appealing the arguments are in favor of the model.

This experiment dealt with operations research proposals; however, the findings seem generalizable to information systems development. An information systems is an abstract model of information processing procedures. While such a system probably does not optimize as might the model of an operations researcher, it shares many of the same characteristics as an operations research model when viewed from the perspective of a user.

4.3 A Field Study

Swanson [4] examined the use of a computer-based retrieval system in the management of engineering projects. The engineering department had more than 200 employees and was responsible for production quality control in an electronics company's West Coast manufacturing plant that employed several thousand individuals. The system for activity reporting was a vehicle for self-management; most of the engineering group's budget consisted of wages and the allocation of manpower to various tasks at hand was a significant management problem. The system gathered data on the planned and actual work activity of the group's members and made it available to management on a need-to-know basis. Each department manager had access to the data within his or her formally defined area of responsibility; access was limited to the people reporting to the manager. The system made two data files available to the manager for inquiry. The activity status file contained work activity data from the most recent thirteen weeks at a level of detail of the individual group member. The second file, derived from the first, maintained an eighteen month summary of work activity at the department level. Even though the files were relatively simple, a large number of reports could be produced through a generalized inquiry facility. For example, one could obtain a summary of man-hours charged to a particular product type during a recent month, broken down by employee skill code. Inquiries could be made from a number of terminals throughout the plant.

The author's research model provided the following hypotheses:

1. A priori involvement with a system increases MIS appreciation.
2. An increase in MIS appreciation increases inquiry involvement and vice versa.
3. An increase in the a priori involvement of an individual with an MIS will increase inquiry involvement.

Data were collected from thirty-seven managers to test the hypotheses. An index of a priori involvement was developed which included questions concerning the system changes requested by the participants in the study. MIS appreciation was measured by a scale of thirty-eight questionnaire items which measured the respondent's rating of items like the quality of reports and the benefits the user received from the system. Inquiry involvement was measured by monitoring actual usage of the system for a thirty day period.

The results indicated that a priori involvement was associated with MIS appreciation and the MIS appreciation was associated with a high level of system use. A priori involvement was also associated with appreciation and actual use. The data support a model in which appreciation is an intervening variable between a priori involvement and actual use. Swanson suggests that a priori involvement and actual use co-produce favorable attitudes and in turn are coproduced by favorable attitudes.

4.4 Conclusions

The Mann and Williams case study was exploratory; there appears to be no theory which guided the researchers. However, this early case provided insights which influenced subsequent researchers and helped them develop hypotheses. Huysmans' experiment tested for a hypothesized relationship between one variable and implementation. The rigor of the laboratory design provides more credibility for hypothesized causal relationships. Swanson used multiple sources of data in a field study which tested an explicit research model. All of these studies have made a contribution to knowledge about implementation.

5 FUTURE RESEARCH

What are the most important areas for future research on implementation? There are several directions for research which would contribute to a further understanding of implementation.

1. Factor studies and survey research should concentrate on testing hypotheses derived models or theories. A large number of factors have been identified and associated with implementation success; now researchers need to demonstrate the nature of the relationship between such factors and successful implementation.

2. Laboratory research should be expanded; this type of research design makes it possible to study the relationship among a few variables with much greater control than most field studies.

3. Further case studies are needed, but it is important to design such research to either produce new insights, test a theory or new approach to implementation, or to develop a research design which makes it possible to generalize from the study.

4. Field or survey research should attempt to include a longitudinal design and control groups. By measuring changes over time, researchers will learn much more about possible causal relationships.

5. A new and promising area for implementation research is the development of structural models of implementation. These models similar to the ones used in economics or marketing, can then be tested and refined with data.

6. Finally, research should attempt to develop the implications for their work in the form of guidelines for practitioners. Can the results of research be used to improve the implementation process itself?

In summary, past research has contributed a great deal of knowledge about the implementation process. Now is the time to build on this past work to refine and extend what has been learned to date.

REFERENCES

1. Huysmans, J., "The Effectiveness of the Cognitive-Style Constraint in Implementing Operations Research Proposals," *Management Science* 17 (1970): 92-104.
2. Lucas, Henry C., Jr., *Implementation: The Key to Successful Information Systems*. New York: Columbia University Press, forthcoming.
3. Mann, F. and L. Williams, "Observations On The Dynamics of The Change to Electronic Data Processing Equipment." *Administrative Science Quarterly* 5 (1960): 217-56.
4. Swanson, E.B., "Management Information Systems: Appreciation and Involvement," *Management Science* 21 (1974): 178-88.

6. A Design-oriented Approach in Implementation Research: The Project PORGI

by Frank Kolf, Hans Jürgen Oppelland

1 STATEMENT OF THE PROBLEM

Literature on the development of CBIS as well as activities of system analysts and system designers have been and still are dominated by many attempts to solve technological questions (concerning computers, programs, data bases, methods, models, etc.). There exists a continuously growing number of tools to support these activities (e.g., techniques for program design, interactive programming support systems, documentation methods and systems, etc.).

Since roughly 1970, some large organizations (companies etc.) have been trying to achieve computer-based management information systems especially to support management planning and control processes. These systems not seldom perform multiple functions and/or serve users in multiple areas of the organization. They provide users with access to data and analytical capabilities which previously were not available to them. In trying to develop such systems a special kind of "implementation" problem originated, which system designers used to attribute to the fact that "users" have only insufficient technological knowledge and, therefore, are not able to make optimal use of CBIS. More and more it became clear that the introduction and usage of CBIS in existing organizational environments was confronted with large difficulties comparable to those which originate with implantations of artificial organs into the human body. In many cases potential user departments put the new systems under a boycott. As a consequence, diligent system analysts invented an additional phase in the development process, the core of which was "user-training". At the same time they were active in seeking out the necessary modifications of user behavior and of the organizational structures and tried to convince management to perform those modifications. But then new difficulties arose in the form of feed-back-effects to the technological solutions designed in earlier phases of the development process. In many cases "trained users" were no longer satisfied with the system they themselves had previously defined, as they had experienced learning processes. They changed their demands and needs. New incompatibilities between the future system and its environment arose. The date of system-delivery to the user had to be postponed, planned budgets could not be held to; this being only few out of a large number of frustrations which hit users and system analysts participating in these situations.

Some consequences had to be drawn from these experiences. The traditional understanding of "organizational implementation" and of its position in the process of system development had to be modified:

—objects of system development are not only the technological components, but simultaneously and equally important the organizational and personal components of an information system (as a socio-technical system)
—the core of system development is to produce a fit between technological, organizational and personal system components. System development can only be successful if activities to produce this fit, to integrate system components, start with the beginning of the design phases. *Organizational implementation is understood here as this central process of integrating, mutually adjusting system components.*

From another point of view, system development is a special form of "planned change or organizational innovation", a term which is influenced by social science thinking. This approach is not very new. Many authors have already mentioned this point. There are a lot of publications especially on empirical studies dealing with the personal and organizational aspects of system development processes:

1.   Several papers stress the enormous importance of factors like
—user participation [2; 13],
—top management support [18; 19],
—overcoming user resistance to change [8].
Authors of these papers always have only relatively small samples at hand on which they base their statements. Most of their consequences are of a normative nature and claim to have general validity. In most cases the range of these consequences is not discussed.
2.   Some studies concentrate on "impacts": impacts of CBIS on individuals or small groups [4; 11; 21; 22; 23; 24], impacts of certain technological components or special forms of CBIS on decision behavior [3; 7], or impacts of CBIS on organization structure [1; 14; 25]. Most of these investigations represent mono-causal explanations, i.e., impacts studied are attributed solely or mainly to the introduction of CBIS or traced back exclusively to changes of technological system components.
3.   In a third kind of studies the relations between certain factors or groups of factors and success of CBIS-implementation are analysed [5]. The problem here is the variety of factors investigated. Studies are concentrating on different groups of factors, on different types of information systems and different organizational and personal settings of CBIS [1; 6; 15; 17]. In many cases, the results of these studies are contradictory. One finds a large number of single statements without any help how to coordinate them.
4.   Many studies have a retrospective orientation. Relations between factors are analysed ex-post. Empirical data are mostly collected after system development has been finished. There are only few statements on the process of system devel-

opment. This leads to the fact, that system people don't find much information in these studies which could help them directly with their daily work.

We think that implementation research in the field of CBIS as a special form of technological research should produce tools to improve the effectiveness of system development activities. Moreover, it should generate empirically founded statements about how to use these tools in an individual context. It should stress important attributes of organizational implementation in different situations. The management of system development is context-dependent. General rules and general statements must be substituted by specialized combinations of methods and techniques which take account of the specialized conditions of implementation cases.

These and other objectives are pursued in research project PORGI (Planning Model of the Organizational Implementation), which is sponsored by the German Federal Ministry for Research and Technology. Within this project we try to generate instruments for CBIS development

—which help to measure the fit (or mis-fit) respectively the degree of integration between technological, organizational and personal system components (specialized methods for analysis/diagnosis)
—which help to produce a better fit between system components by concentrating on these fitting problems.

2   RESEARCH DESIGN OF PROJECT PORGI

A multi-staged research and design process is provided for this project:

Stage 1. Design of a first global version of a descriptional framework, which contains all important factors by which OI-situations may be characterized.

Stage 2. Empirical research: interviews with fifty experts in the field of information systems (twenty-two cases). One purpose of these interviews was to examine the descriptional framework and to detail it in such a way that it is able to map all factors which are named by the experts as being important factors in their individual OI-cases. A second purpose was to generate context-dependent hypotheses about how implementation processes have been performed in different organizational settings, which tools have been or not been used to produce a fit between system components.

Stage 3. Classification of typical implementation situations, problem and process profiles of these situations based on the expert interviews.

Stage 4. Development of techniques and methods to measure implementation situations, to diagnose problems and to derive specialized recommendations to overcome these problems.

Stage 4a. Application of these techniques and methods in a certain number of cases in order to examine and continuously improve them in the practice of system development. The research team has participated in CBIS projects in two German companies. The same purpose of examination and methodological improvement is pursued in a working group consisting of several German CBIS-experts belonging to different institutions and the members of the PORGI team.

Stage 5 (actual state of project PORGI). Collection and comprehension of all tools in a *Handbook for organizational implementation of CBIS*, which will support practitioners in system development and will be the basis for training courses performed to disseminate this kind of know-how.

3 PORGI-IMPLEMENTATION HANDBOOK: THE CONCEPT

The PORGI-Implementation Handbook (IHB) as a collection and comprehension of tools to support practitioners in handling human and organizational problems in CBIS development consists basically of five elements which will be portrayed in short.

The *Descriptional framework (DF)* serves as a common terminological basis for all the tools and guidelines of the IHB, not as an explanatory model. The DF contains all those principal elements which constitute specific implementational situations. That does not mean *all* elements have to occur in a specific situation. According to the underlying implementation philosophy we have to differentiate two areas of analysis:

—analysis of the fit between the system components "man, organizational structure, information technology and the task" to be supported (System Fit) in analogy to Leavitt [12].
—analysis of the design process (the project organization, project management, etc.) (Process Fit).

The principal categories of the DF are grouped into the four modules [9; 10] Personal System, Task, Information Technology, Organization Structure.

The Procedural Scheme (PROC) consists of a sequence of well-known design activities. Associated with the different design activities are implementational aspects and specific tools to support the analysis of these aspects. The conception of that procedural scheme has been guided by the following principles:

—Based on our definition of the organizational implementation as a process of securing the well-tuned design of the system components Man, Task, Structure and Information Technology there have to be planned specific activities which enable us to verify that tuning from the start-up-phase of the project.
—The design activities have to be supplemented by specific analytical steps. By

performing repeated status analyses of *all* the system components we get information about the design status of the different components and FIT of these components. The evaluation of actual and planned status indicates specific (potential) problem areas early in the design process which have to be counteracted.

—Those who are concerned with system design and system usage have to be involved to the degree of their individual concern. Therefore, we have to plan activities which ensure that the organization of the design process becomes a design variable too.

The following abstract from the PORGI-Procedural-Scheme shows the realization of these principles.

The *Pool of Methods (METH)* consists of instruments, tools and methods for Analyzing and Diagnosing implementational situations. The above mentioned Procedural Scheme (PROC) for all design activities points to such aspects, which have to be considered in the view what we call *Organizational Implementation*. Problem-oriented questionnaires, checklists, lists of criteria, etc. support the diagnosis and analysis of constellations of variables (in the terminology of the DF), which are relevant to organizational implementation activities in this specific situation (Table 1).

To analyze issues relevant to the process fit there are available:

—Checklist for the identification of those members of the organization who are concerned with the development process and/or will be system users;
—Questionnaire for identification of actual and required participation in system development activities.

To analyze issues relevant to the system fit there are available:

—Checklist for the identification and definition of the problem which shall be solved by designing a new CBIS;
—Checklist and questionnaire for the definition of project and system objectives;
—Questionnaire and checklist for identification and analysis of the required/planned innovatorial step and its importance regarding the system components: Task, Personal System, Information Technology and Organization Structure, e.g., task content, procedures, communication.

The *Pool of Implementation Problems (PROB)* for the contextual analysis and diagnosis consists of specific implementation problems which can be identified by a situational profile. These profiles describe those empirical situations in which that specific implementation problem has occurred repeatedly, e.g., results or consequences of specific actions in the design process which deteriorate the intended implementation success. These problems lead to *economically* and/or *socially* insufficient results of the system design process or system usage. Descriptions of these

Table 1. Abstract from the PORGI-Procedural-Scheme

DESIGN ACTIVITIES	OI-ASPECTS	ANALYTICAL TOOLS
(1) Problem Definition		
—Identification and Description of the problem	Identification of the "interested" people	PORGI-Checklist PROB
—Information about the problem	—Who has the problem?	PORGI-Descriptional Framework
—Evaluation of the problem	—Who articulates the problem?	
—Decision about the realization of Problem Analysis	—Who participates in the evaluation (priorities etc.) of the problem?	PORGI-Checklist BTR Group-evaluation methods (e.g., BASYC)
	—Who decides upon the realization of the Problem Analysis	PORGI-Questionnaire BEW
(2) Problem Analysis		
—Analysis of the different elements of the problem and its context	—Analysis of problematic areas in/between the system components —Man —Task —Structure —Information Technology	PORGI-Questionnaire 1-69 PORGI-Checklist ZIE PORGI-Checklist INN
—Analysis of possible causes	—Identification of the interests of the people concerned	PORGI-Criteria-List EIG-1; AUS-1 Group-evaluation-methods
—Specification of the requirements for the system components		PORGI-Checklist PROB
	—Group consensus about the required characteristics of the different system components	PORGI-Questionnaire INFBED

implementation problems use the categories of the descriptional framework and are based on those problems which have been identified in our expert interviews to be typical for specific situations [16]. Additionally it contains theoretically or empirically based implementation problems found in literature, case studies and unique design experiences of the members of the PORGI-team. Objective of the diagnosis is the comparison of the characteristics of the individual situation and the situative profile of the implementation problems of PROB in order to identify possible problem areas in the actual situation. Follow-up activities focus on the analysis of possible causes for that problem and possible solutions.

The *Pool of Design Concepts (CON)* supports the solution of these problems identified by the use of METH and PROB in offering appropriated implementational actions. The choice of appropriated implementational actions is supported by offering *general design* principles and *situative design* proposals, which can be seen as sufficiently tested and confirmed by the system development praxis. The description of these design concepts is also oriented at the categories of the descriptional framework, thus their situative applicability could be better evaluated in actual situations by the project manager, implementor or other people responsible for the system development.

The design concepts contain as possible implementational actions proposals to correct (or confirm) social and organizational behavior and its rules regarding the different aspects of organization and procedures of design and implementation processes, and the design of mutually adjusted system components.

The procedural interactions of these instruments during a CBIS-project are as follows (Table 2):

The procedural scheme (PROC) works as a directory which tells us what next steps should be undertaken and what kind of implementational aspects should be considered. The details of such an OI-aspect (e.g., (5.1.1) Participation) are compiled in the Descriptional Framework (DF), in that example the elements of the group 1113: Kind of Participation. The Pool of Methods (METH) offers for the analysis of these OI-aspects specific analytical tools, in the example the PORGI Questionnaire BET. After having gathered facts about the specific situation by use of the PORGI tools the problem-oriented analysis of that situation is being performed by searching the pool of implementation problems (PROB). The objective of that search is to find out whether the situative profile just gathered is similar to one of those situative profiles in the problem pool in which specific implementation problems have repeatedly occurred. Then the pool of Design Concepts (CON) is to be searched for whether it contains a possible solution with a similar situation profile, i.e., a solution which has proven to be useful in similar situations.

Table 2. Schematic Description of the Application of PORGI-Instruments

PROCEDURAL SCHEME (PROC)		DESCRIPTIONAL FRAMEWORK (DF)		QUESTIONNAIRE/ CHECKLIST-ITEMS
Systems Design Activities	OI-Aspects			
(1) ...	...	1	Personal System	
(2) ...	...	11	People participating in system design	
(3) ...	...			
(4) ...	...	1113	Kind of participation	
(5) Raw Concepts	Analysis of Design Process (Process FIT) (5.1)	...	...	
	Participation (5.1.1)	11133	Consultancy	PORGI-BET
	Concern (5.1.2)	11134	Cooperation	BET-2.0 thru BET-2.3
	Analysis of Conception (System fit planning) (5.2)	11135	Responsibility	
	Man (5.2.1)	12	People concerned with system application	
	Task (5.2.2)		...	
	Structure (5.2.3)	1213	Indiv. eval. of being concerned	
	Inf. Technology (5.2.4)	12131	—Work Flow	PORGI-BTR
		12132	—Decision Autonomy	BTR-1.1
		12133	—Information	BTR-2.1
		12134	—Communication Relations	BTR-2.2
		5	Organizational Structure	
		51	User organization	
			...	
		513	Cooperation with other organizational units	PORGI-ORG/INT
(6) ...		5301	—Tuning with other units	ORG-INT 1.0
(7) ...		5302	—Procedure of reconcilation	ORG-INT 2.0
(8) ...		5303	—Dependency on other units	ORG-INT 3.0
(9) ...				
(10) ...				

REFERENCES

1. Bean, A.S., R.D. Neal, M. Radnor, and D.A. Tansik. "Structural and Behavioral Correlates of Implementation in U.S. Business Organizations." in *Implementing Operations Research/Management Science* edited by Schultz, Slevin (1975) pp. 77-132.

2. Carter, D.M., H.L. Gibson, and R.A. Rademacher. "A Study of Critical Factors in Management Information Systems in the U.S. Air Force." Colorado State University, Information Systems Series 460-2, 1973.

3. Chervany, N.L. and G.W. Dickson. "An Experimental Evaluation of Information Overload in a Production Environment." *Management Science* 20 (1974): 1335-44.

4. Dyckmann, T.R. "Management Implementation of Scientific Research: An Attitudinal Study." *Management Science* 13 (1967): B612-B620.

5. Ginzberg, M.J. "A Detailed Look at Implementation Research." Report CISR-4, Sloan School of Management, MIT, Working Paper 753-4, November 1974.

6. Harvey, A. "Factors making for Implementation Success and Failure." *Management Science* 16 (1970): B312-B321.

7. Hedberg, B. *On Man-Computer Interaction in Organizational Decision-Making. A Behavioral Approach.* Gothenburg, 1970.

8. Huysmans, J.H.B.M. *The Implementation of Operations Research: An Approach to the Joint Consideration of Social and Technological Aspects.* New York, 1970.

9. Kolf, F., J. Claus, H.J. Oppelland. "Grundlagen und Konzeption eines Modells zur Beschreibung organisatorischer Implementierungssituationen." PORGI-Projektbericht Nr. 1, Köln, 1977.

10. Kolf, F., H.J. Oppelland, D. Seibt, N.Szyperski. "Instrumentarium zur organisatorischen Implementierung von rechnergestützten Informationssystemen." *Angewandte Informatik* 20 (1978): 299-310.

11. Ladd, D.E. "Report on a Group's Reaction to the 'Researcher and the Manager': A Dialectic of Implementation." *Management Science* 12 (1965): B24-B25.

12. Leavitt, H.J. "Applied Organizational Change in Industry. Structural, Technological and Humanistic Approaches." in March J.G. (ed.) *Handbook of Organizations.* Skokill, Ill., 1965, pp. 1144-1170.

13. Little, J.D.C. "Models and Managers: The Concept of a Decision Calculus." *Management Science* 16 (1970): B466-B483.

14. Lucas, H.C. "Performance and the Use of an Information System." *Management Science* 21 (1975): B908-B919.

15. Lucas, H.C. *Why Information Systems Fail.* New York, London, 1975.

16. Oppelland, H.J., F. Kolf, J. Claus. "Dokumentation der Ergebnisse einer Expertenbefragung zur Entwicklung und Einführung rechnergestützter Informationssysteme." PORGI Projektbericht Nr. 5, Köln, 1977.

17. Powers, R.F., W. Dickson. "MIS Project Management: Myths, Opinions, and Reality." *California Management Review* 15 (1973):147-156.

18. Radnor, M., A.H. Rubenstein and A.S. Bean. "Integration and Utilization of Management Science Activities in Organizations." *Operations Research Quarterly* 19 (1968): 117-141.

19. Radnor, M., A.H. Rubenstein and D.A. Tansik. "Implementation in Operations Research and R&D in Government and Business Organizations." *Operations Research* 18 (1970): 967-991.

20. Schultz, R.L. and D.P. Slevin (eds.) *Implementing Operations Research/Management Science:* New York-London-Amsterdam, 1975.

21. Schultz, R.L., D.P. Slevin. "Implementation and Organizational Validity: An Empirical Investigation." in Schultz, Slevin, 1975, pp. 153-82.

22. Shaw, M.E. *Group Dynamics: The Psychology of Small Group Behavior*. New York, 1971.

23. Sorensen, R.E. and D.E. Zand. "Improving the Implementation of OR/MS Models by Applying the Lewin-Schein Theory of Change." in Schultz, Slevin, 1975, pp. 217-36.

24. Vertinsky, I., R.T. Barth and V.F. Mitchell. "A Study of OR/MS Implementation as a Social Change Process." in Schultz, Slevin, 1975, pp. 253-69.

25. Whisler, T.L. *The Impact of Computers on Management*. 1970.

B.
Working Group:
Technical Aspects of Systems Design and Implementation

I. SELECTION OF PLANNING METHODS

Chairman: Charles H. Kriebel

Applications of computer-based technology in modern organizations have evolved from the data processing of routine business transactions to systems that provide support capabilities for management decisions. Decision support system (DSS) applications are not homogeneous with respect to the type of management support provided and how that support is accomplished. This variety has prompted authors to categorize these systems as a guide for design and development. Classifications in this context are also useful for addressing methodological questions related to system applications and alternatives.

In a recent paper Alter* proposes a taxonomy for DSSs which appears especially useful, based on what he calls the "degree of action implication of system outputs (i.e., the degree to which the system's outputs could directly determine the decision)." The basic idea is that a DSS can be classified according to the generic operations it performs, independent of the functional area, problem type, computer technology, modeling approach, etc. Alter's framework results in seven reasonably distinct categories of decision support systems which he identifies as follows:

1. *File drawer systems* allow immediate access to data items, e.g., the simple retrieval of a single data item.
2. *Data analysis systems* allow the manipulation of data by means of operators tailored to the task or operators of a general nature to provide mechanisms for ad hoc data analysis.
3. *Analysis information systems* provide access to a series of data bases and small models.
4. *Accounting models* calculate the consequences of planned actions based on accounting definitions, e.g., to provide prespecified aggregations of data in the form of reports.
5. *Representational models* estimate the consequences of actions based on models which are partially non-definitional, such as simulation.
6. *Optimization models* provide guidelines for action by generating the optimal solutions consistent with a series of constraints, such as a linear programming application.

* S.L. Alter, "A Taxonomy of Decision Support Systems," *Sloan Management Review* (Fall 1977), pp. 39-56.

7. *Suggestion models* perform mechanical work leading to a specific suggested decision for a fairly structured task, i.e. performing a calculation whose output is "the answer".

The first three categories are data-oriented systems whereas the last four types are essentially model-oriented systems. Within the latter group, Alter's study of fifty-six applications revealed that accounting, representational and optimization models (categories 4, 5 and 6) were the ones primarily used for planning tasks.

It may be constructive in a discussion on the "selection of planning methods" to relate to this taxonomy in considering how new methods or approaches contribute to these systems and enhance the accomplishment of planning by managers.

Dipl.-Volksw. Bernhard Bleuel: "Evolution and Feasibility Problems of a Cost Planning Model"

Mr. Bleuel described a system developed and installed at the Mannesmann AG Hüttenwerke in Essen. The system is used to aid short range planning (quarterly) and control of steel production decisions; it includes accounting and optimization models of the DSS taxonomy. The system employs IBM 5100s as intelligent terminals linked to a central complex employing two CPs, IBM 370/158 and 370/168. The system has been under development for the past five years and is still being modified and updated. Mr. Bleuel discussed several problems related to the feasibility and evolution of the system. Anticipated future developments within the system will include: (1) multi-period planning with stockpiling (e.g., investment analysis and linkage to five-year plans), (2) mixed-integer problems (e.g., to accommodate personnel shifts or melting weights), and (3) financial planning.

Dr. Horst Burwick: "Application Areas for Planning Software"

Dr. Burwick's talk covered the following topics: the purpose, categories and features of planning software, matrix-oriented languages, which companies use planning languages and what problems planning languages help to solve. In discussing matrix-oriented planning languages, Dr. Burwick traced his involvement with their evolution beginning in 1969 at IBM with the development of PLATO (PLAnning TOol), to PSI in 1971, to ITS/73 and its current version ITS/DMS. He described some of the features of ITS and some "unexpected" applications, such as for LP reporting and component forecasting, subsequent to its installation in client companies.

7. The Feasibility of Linear Planning Models in Business Administration

by Bernhard Bleuel

1 SURVEY

The problem deals with the production-cost planning in a metallurgical plant, which has a capacity of five million metric tons of crude steel per annum. Roughly speaking, the plant consists of an ore-agglomeration plant, five blast-furnaces of different capacity, two basic oxygen-steel plants, four open-hearth furnaces and one electric furnace; furthermore, two continuous-casting plants, one ingot-slab mill and one tube-rounds mill. The sales revenue is about 2 billion DM. The number of employed people nearly reaches 10,000.

2 METHODS AND TOOLS FOR PLANNING

Table 1 shows periods, contents and repetition or timing of planning.

Table 1. Planning Methods

Part of Planning-System	Contents of Plan	Cycle
long-range planning	definition of goals, fields of activity, concept of investment, organizational structure	not fixed
5-year-planning	costs, sales, yield, investments	annually revolving
1-year-planning	measures of production program planning, according to the fixed goals	annually with quarterly revisions

Long-range planning is essentially the appointment of principles. Planning under the five-year horizon concentrates mainly on investments. The planning under short-term conditions deals with production, cost and revenue. Only the latter is under consideration here.

The essential core of the system is demonstrated in Figure 1. As easily can be seen it has a twofold structure. One branch aims at deterministic calculations with the aid of a matrix-algorithm, the other one uses an LP-model for alternative con-

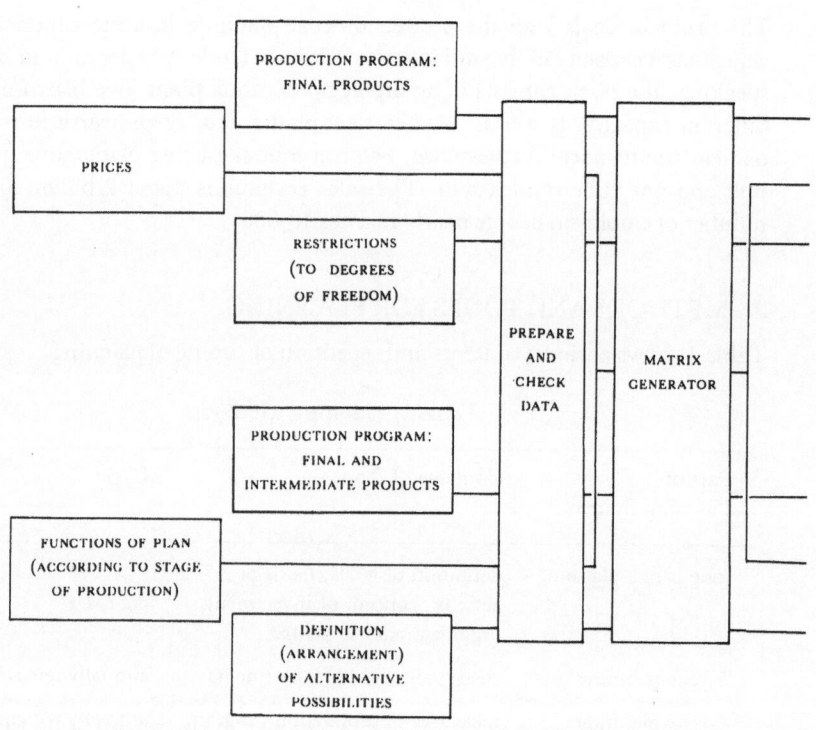

Figure 1. Core of the System.

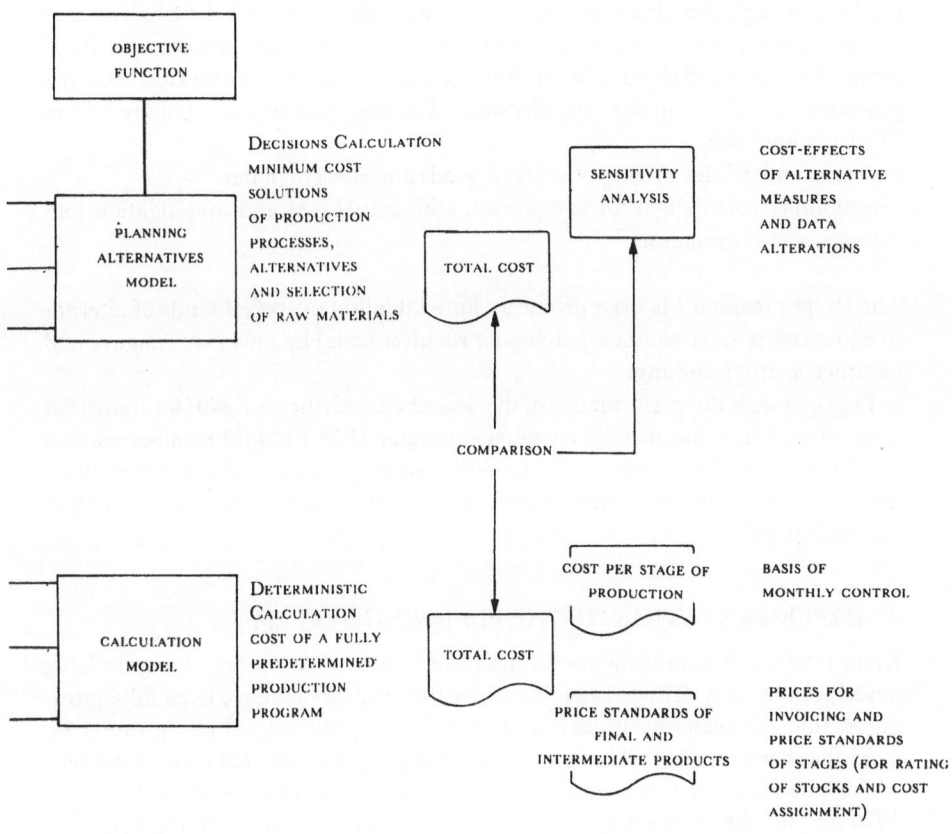

siderations. In both cases well-known software packages (Matsys resp. MPSX/370) are used.

There is a unique data-base for both kinds of problems to be solved, comprising the functions describing all interdependencies between final products and all kinds of input as well as prices for these inputs.

In case of the LP model there are of course the additional data needed, i.e., restrictive functions as to capacities, availabilities, etc., and, furthermore, the functional aiming at cost-minimization; while in the calculation model all chances of choice must be abolished by deterministic functions. Complex models like these need a thorough checking and preparing of input-data, which is done by two matrix-generators, one for each model because of the different structure of data-input. The results derived from both models are primarily "Total Cost" for the planning period are under consideration. Further informations gathered from "Calculation" are

—price standards for pricing of shipped goods and stock on hand
—a monthly cost-budget for comparison with actual cost and investigation into the causes of deviations.

The "Optimization" is used primarily for evaluation of special kinds of alternative processing (adaptation on changing requirements) by means of ranging and parametric programming.

Engaged with the performance of the described activities is a staff for industrial economics, which has its own terminal-computer IBM 5100 for stand-alone and terminal applications under TSO or APL. In a remote computer center there may be used alternatively three installed computer systems, in general an IBM system 370/168.

3 IMPLEMENTATION OF THE PLANNING SYSTEM

Right now the deterministic model has been in use for two years, the optimizing model for one year. This means, that since then the models have been fully introduced into the planning process and, if any, the prior way of doing things by hand, has been replaced. There was an overlapping development on both models, which extends for the deterministic model from the end of 1974 up to the end of 1976 and for the optimizing model from the middle of 1976 up to the middle of 1977. According to the experience gained it seems to be very important, that the user engages himself in the first line, because no complex system of this kind will work efficiently, if it is forced upon the user, no matter whether this is done by advice or by order. Furthermore, it must be emphasized, that the continuous development of such a system, necessarily in a top-down-approach, should be directed by the user in a sequence, which results from his practical needs, i.e., his requirements for preparing decisions.

4   PROBLEMS OF EVOLUTION

Subsequent to what has been said before, to overcome difficulties in various stages of evolution and implementation, the user must not only be engaged, but he has to initiate and take the helm in the project-management.

There is always the necessity to have realistic figures to work with; textbook examples do not have persuasive power for management. In the case of cost and revenue each company has such figures respectively estimates used for pricing. Because nothing is more disappointing than repeated incorrect solutions due to errors in input-data, the greatest importance must be attached to a fool-proof checking before the execution of a job. A computer program for plausibility control cannot cover all aspects of a specific problem.

The next claim from the user's point of view is *not* to start on a highly sophisticated and detailed level. In the context of the described models the necessity of refinement is proven by the monthly discussions about deviations between the predictions of the model and the actual figures for the past period.

5   FEASIBILITY PROBLEMS

Feasibility problems are not the same in each corporate model. The following are some which have so far emerged during implementation and application of both models.

The standard presentation of input and output as regards Matsys and MPSX is quite unsatisfactory for practical, i.e., quick application. New report programs had to be written in order to meet the requirement for better checking and interpreting the solution. Also batch-processing cannot afford the necessary speed in answering questions. The user must be enabled to start a job and to get results in a time-sharing mode. In our case a dialog-version of the MPSX/370 program itself is being installed, especially for a more sophisticated investigation into alternative decisions on actual problems. Different questions do not need the same extensive presentation of results. Therefore, different stages (at present six) of condensing or aggregating the model are used.

The user must be in a position to relieve himself of keeping in his mind all new information; instead he must be able to check whether changes in the latest used data are relevant or not. This can be done by means of sensitivity analysis. In the same respect the user must supervise and keep under his control the data base, especially as regards the implementation of new vectors and the cancellation of old ones.

The volume of solution output in general is tremendous. For efficient use of such comprehensive corporate models there should be a possibility to select deliberately the most interesting values of any solution.

Optimization is an ambitious objective and it is needless to say that management decisions have to be optimized. But each manager has his own way of making decisions. Therefore, he does not like to get ready-served solutions. Hence, it is often necessary to go from ex-post supporting of a decision to step-by-step ex-ante preparation of decisions. Voluntarily accepted, on the other hand, are references to critical values of important variables (prices, production-volume, capacities, etc.) pointing at necessary reviewing of foregoing decisions whenever these critical values become actual. This is perhaps the most important use of parametric programming within an LP model.

6 FUTURE DEVELOPMENT

Attention is given in the future especially to investment evaluation and investigation into the five-year planning period. Regarding the different kinds of adaptation to changing requirements, there are many integer variables, which have to be considered in order to achieve more realistic solutions in detail. Some testing has already been done with a mixed-integer-version of the LP.

From the calculation model there may be derived information about demand of input-goods and for financial planning.

Finally we must realize, that none of our instruments will ever be perfect.

8. Application Areas for Planning Software

by Horst L. Burwick

INTRODUCTION

In recent years many software tools have been developed to support the set-up of computerized planning systems. I personally was involved in this process and the following presentation is based on my experience in this area.

The subject matter has been divided into five major points.

1 The Purpose of Planning Software
2 Categories of Planning Software
3 Features of Planning Software
4 The Planning Languages PLATO, PS1, ITS/73, ITS/DMS
5 Various Applications of a Planning Language.

Points 1 through 3 discuss planning languages in general terms. In point 4 the discussion draws specifically upon those planning languages I have developed since 1969. Point 5 provides the reader with a list of diverse applications of the Planning Language ITS/73.

1 THE PURPOSE OF PLANNING SOFTWARE

1.1 User Participation in Model Implementation

A fundamental purpose of planning software is to engage the user in model implementation. A model which is not used or accepted by the user is an academic model and not a tool for effectively running a company or for supporting a decision-making process. The planning software must, therefore, facilitate user participation in setting up and implementing models. The more people working with a system, the simpler the system should be. This requirement should be kept in mind when the discussion turns to the various approaches to setting up planning systems.

1.2 A Guide to Organizing Data

Data can be stored in numerous ways, and the decision on how files should be organized, how they should be related, etc. can be a very time consuming task. It is of great help when the software relieves the user of some of these decisions. This attribute should reduce the large variety of possible storage methods without being restrictive, however.

111

1.3 A Guide to Structuring Programs

The above problem also applies to program structure. The possibilities are in fact so manifold, that months could be spent coming to a conclusion on how the programs supporting a planning system are to be structured. In principle, some guidance can be given to solving this problem. We have, for example, found that program structuring can be generalized. The principle is that the organisational structure of the company is defined within tables or connected files, which are used as control structures for the programs. The control structures of the planning languages ITS/73 and ITS/DMS correspond to this principle, as does the program control in the more general language GOGOL, which is presently being used in the ITT Reporting System in Europe.

1.4 Providing a Procedure Service

Planning systems sometimes require high level techniques. These techniques should, however, be prepared to a degree where their execution can be initiated by a simple instruction. For example, the solving of linear equations should be possible by simply instructing the system "to solve these equations". The user should not be encumbered with programming the solutions of linear equations. The same applies to optimizing models, like LP models, simulation models, etc.

1.5 Abbreviate the Implementation Phase of Systems

A project in data processing requiring two or three months to complete can be considered a short project. However, it is not unusual that large projects, like setting up reporting or planning systems must be completed within much less time. I give as an example the six week time limit set for developing all programs for consolidating and analysing the actual reports and planning reports of the European activities of one of the world's largest corporations, starting from scratch. Since it is not the exception that planning systems, reporting systems and other systems have to be set up under similar time pressure, a planning language must facilitate a relatively short implementation phase.

1.6 Enable Quick Changes of Programs

The planning software must facilitate the quick change of modules, since final requirements are often made known only hours before an analysis is to be presented to top management. Therefore, a time-sharing service for the planning software is desirable. As these services are usually only offered by external computer service centers, the integration of planning figures and actual figures becomes a technical problem. I suggest using transaction oriented systems which are usually available on the in-house computer (like CICS, or IMS) in combination with time-sharing versions of planning languages. My company proved the technical feasibility of this concept within a project for setting up a computerized financial

112

reporting system at Unilever. The computer center in Rotterdam provides the financial departments in London and Rotterdam with a time-sharing service which allows an immediate access to data and programs.

2 CATEGORIES OF PLANNING SOFTWARE

Planning software can be divided into three major groups..The division made here is similar to the grouping into packages, languages and models, presented by T. Tielemann. Deviating from this concept, I prefer to group models and packages together and to introduce a further group of software tools, which cannot be considered related to either of the other two.

2.1 Packages for Solving Mathematical Problems

This category of planning software comprises advanced mathematical algorithms for optimizing or analysing complex relations, for example, linear programs or statistical methods. Whether the methods of linear programming, statistical methods and simulation software should constitute a part of planning languages is a question which will be discussed later. It may be desirable, but technical problems are involved.

2.2 Project Planning and Control Systems

Project planning and control systems show a structure deviating from other software packages. They are based on the network model; actions which are to be planned and controlled are predefined. Using these systems the availability and allocation of time, costs and capacity is planned. People with project planning experience are aware that the planning and construction of the model is a continuous task requiring constant revision for the duration of the project. For larger and complex projects this task can only be solved with computer programs.

2.3 Languages for Corporate Planning

There are numerous languages and many systems for corporate planning which are called languages. The multitude makes classification according to system type extremely difficult. Generally, two types can be distinguished: line oriented systems and matrix oriented systems.

2.3.1 Line Oriented Systems

The development of line oriented systems was stimulated by the chart of accounts. A line corresponds to an account. The model consists of arithmetic relations between accounts. Mainly the Balance Sheet and Profit and Loss Sheet are derived from these models which are based on some assumptions on sales and related cost items. An example of a line oriented system, given by G.W. Gershefski, is the FP/70 package developed by Bonner & Moore.

2.3.2 Matrix Oriented Systems

A second approach to corporate planning is to use matrix oriented systems. These systems can be divided into two types, those for handling large matrices and those for handling small matrices. It is my opinion that the systems for handling large matrices are not too well suited to deal with commercial problems. For example, a few years ago a large German steel company decided to use a matrix oriented system to tackle their cost problem. Costs were grouped by departments and types of costs. This led to one large sparse matrix. The company decided to process this information with MATLAN, a software package which was developed for solving technical problems mainly related to stress analysis. Of course, problems arose as can always be expected when a high level software is applied to problems for which is not designed. Here a lack of suitable reporting features made additional FORTRAN programs necessary.

A second type of matrix oriented systems comprises those which handle small matrices which can be presented on a sheet of paper. These matrices correspond to the quantitative information which is processed in all staff and line departments involved in the planning process.

3   FEATURES OF PLANNING LANGUAGES

3.1   Data Base (Volume, Structure, Access Time)

Usually a planning language has dedicated data management system. Important aspects of planning languages are the size of the data base and the volume of data which can be processed within a reasonable time, the structure of the data base and the access time for selected data.

The software market offers hundreds of systems, and most are capable of handling up to about 50-100 reports. When the number of reports exceeds this number, there is an appreciable decrease in performance. Very few systems can produce thousands of reports within a reasonable time. Another handicap is that planning languages often force the user to structure data in a predefined file layout. In such a case, the only alternative is to restructure the thinking of a company or not to use the system.

3.2   Flexibility of Reports

The flexibility of reports is an important aspect of a system related to its acceptability. When a computerized planning language is introduced, a manually prepared draft of a system usually exists. The planning language is intended to support and improve this system. The reports are presented to top management to meet their specific information demands, and expecting an improvement in quality, a change in the form of these reports is usually not desired. Every sign, word, all figure formats and spaces between them, etc. must remain unaltered. Consequently, a flexible system producing any desired form of output is most practical.

114

3.3 Data Manipulations

Data manipulations can be grouped into arithmetic and string operations, corresponding to numeric and alpha-numeric data presented in planning reports; a planning software should permit the manipulation of both data types. Since a computerized planning system is mainly oriented to processing quantitative information, a powerful arithmetic is of primary importance, but string manipulations should also be possible to allow the addition of an individual text to reports if desirable.

What should the arithmetic of a planning language comprise? Obviously, it must include the basic operations of addition, subtraction, multiplication and division, and beside these, a limited number of functions. Very powerful functions are the exponential and logarithm functions and the absolute value. From these a variety of other functions can be derived. An additional technique for introducing subroutines in which these functions are hidden permits a facile calculation of more difficult functions like compound interests, compound growth rates, etc. Some accounting minded managers also find important the possibility of rounding figures internally, thus permitting figures on external reports to add up. The question of rounding, a minor problem in planning, is too often discussed in practice.

3.4 Access to Other Files

To be able to access files with operational data is a necessary feature of any planning software. Planning models should be based on data which is already stored in operational files combined with manual input like assumptions about sales increase, workload formulas, etc. The plans must be periodically compared with actual figures. Thus, access to files outside the planning system, that is, to data outside the dedicated data base, is essential.

A host language system for languages such as COBOL, PL/1 and FORTRAN, by which the dedicated data base containing management information for planning and reporting can be combined with operational data files, is the best solution to this problem. If such a system is available, the bridge programs can be written by programmers in a language with which they are familiar. The dedicated data base will thus easily be provided with the required information, despite the programmer's lack of knowledge of the planning language and the related data organisation.

3.5 Ease of Handling the Software

People with no data processing experience must also be able to work with planning languages. Therefore, the languages must be easy to learn. Meeting this requirement of simplicity presents a minor problem. Ideally, a planning language should be easy to learn, that means the technical aspects involved with the language elements should be minimized, and at the same time it should be powerful in order to reduce the work in setting up systems. The latter demand is more difficult to meet. In order to minimize development time, the planning system must be powerful. A longer time requirement for learning the planning language is acceptable if the difficult language features involved finally lead to an overall shortening of the development phase of the planning systems. This is substantially more difficult to achieve. Since final requirements for planning and reporting may be given only hours before a program run, a quick alteration of any part of the system must be possible. When choosing a planning language it is recommendable to take into consideration all aspects mentioned above.

3.6 Advanced Methods

The question arises whether planning languages should comprise the methods mentioned under 2.1. On the one hand, technical reasons suggest they should, since to employ two different systems for one application is impractical. One powerful tool is preferable to changing tools when concentrating on one problem area. On the other hand, to develop a software of higher level methods to solve manifold problems is a difficult task, and the resulting programs are excessively large. Combining several large systems of completely different characteristics does not lead to an optimal technical solution. However, the lesser evil would be to employ different systems and allow all of them access to the same data, since many advanced methods can not well be incorporated in one software package. In this context I should mention that I do not consider a simple statement for solving linear equations or multiple regression analysis to be advanced. On the other hand, the solution of a linear programming model with thousands of equations and variables is a completely different subject. Here an optimized dedicated system is required. However, planning languages can be applied to provide the model with data and to process the results of the advanced algorithms.

4 THE PLANNING LANGUAGES PLATO, PS1, ITS/73, ITS/DMS

4.1 The Report as Basic Data Element

Before advancing to applications, a general remark about presenting quantitative data is necessary. Numerical data can be presented within a text, or it can be structured in lines and columns with separate text sections. The latter is the usual form in commercial applications. The structure may be modified according to individual requirements and tastes, but from an analytical point of view, reports consist of two main parts, the text and the matrix. Within the systems discussed here, the text consists of three parts (format modules) because of the modular usages of headings, column headings and line descriptions. Many reports contain the same columns, but different line items, or different columns but the same line items.

All the systems mentioned contain a dedicated data management system for storing and retrieving reports. Furthermore, only the PLATO system and ITS/DMS can handle different types of data structures; arrays and sequential files in PLATO software, and networks of arbitrary files in ITS/DMS.

4.2 The Concept of the PLATO System

The PLATO language (abbreviation for planning tools) was designed in 1969 within a project for developing software tools to support the planning process within IBM, it was intended for handling the reports of the operating plan as well as the reports for monthly control figures, strategic planning, marketing plans, etc. The PLATO planning system comprised four processors. The purpose of these processors is described briefly below.

4.2.1 The Planning Processor

This processor was intended as a tool for setting up planning models. The main part of this processor was a powerful arithmetic for processing multi-dimensional arrays which were dynamically declared by processing sequential files with operating data.

4.2.2 The Finance Processor

The results of the planning models should be treated as entries into a small accounting model based on a chart of accounts which represented a condensed form of the complete chart of accounts of the company. From this model the balance sheet and profit and loss sheet could be derived.

4.2.3 The Report Processor

Reporting the results of the planning models should be separated from the models themselves. Therefore, a report processor was designed to print the figures which were calculated by the planning processor and the finance processor. These reports could be stored and retrieved by this processor, and a minimum of arithmetic operations for consolidating and analysing could be applied to those reports within this processor.

4.2.4 The Control Processor

Working on a large planning system, a large number of people and many programs are involved. The defined program sequence must strictly be adhered to. The control processor should monitor the submission of all planning jobs and their coordination during the short time of operation, preventing any misunderstanding of program sequences. The basis of this monitoring was a network embracing all planning activities.

4.3   Experience with the PLATO System

Practice showed that ninety-five percent of all requirements of the planning departments was covered by the report processor. The planning processor was applied within the Budget Method Department only, since it was intended for constructing very complex models, for example, IBM's salary planning model, and was thus a tool for mathematicians.

The report processor had an unbelievable success. Within one year it was installed in twelve departments within IBM Germany, and a year later, in thirty different countries at all IBM Headquarters. The reason for this success was that people are used to handling information in report form, and the PLATO report processor was designed for just this type of application. Nevertheless, the limited number of arithmetic operations led to a permanent enlargement of the processor. From a software development point of view this was not acceptable, therefore, I decided to change the concept completely within the next planning language PS1, which was used by the German Ministry for Economic Cooperation to prepare the OECD report. This language can only handle reports, but all types of arithmetic instructions can be executed with the report matrices. Some powerful addressing operators and a special subroutine technique enables the user to introduce individual, convenient, higher level functions. This technique was further developed in ITS/73, the successor system of PS1.

4.4   Processing Hierarchical Structures

The subroutine technique of ITS/73 is a generalization of the usual subroutine techniques in programming languages. The call of a subroutine is not executed with a set of parameters, but rather with a table, where every line of the table represents a set of parameters. For every line of the table the subroutine is executed once. The actual parameters in the table can be values, sets for addressing, or names or arbitrary parts of names. Especially the names can be names of subroutines or tables. Within a subroutine another subroutine call, combined with a table, can occur, which will then lead to an iterative execution of another subroutine. By this technique the programs are controlled through a hierarchy of tables. This very powerful control technique, which enables the ITS/73 system to process thousands of reports in one program, was further generalized in the following form within ITS/DMS. Instead of executing a subroutine for each of the lines of a table, the subroutine can be executed for every record of a sequential file or every record in a chain of member records in a hierarchical data management system. As the data management system DMS/77, which is connected with ITS/73, can handle any network files, this planning language became a tool for simple data base programming. That this concept can also be applied to programming languages with a wider range of applications is shown by the application oriented language GOGOL, which also proved very effective for setting up reporting and planning systems, but is not dedicated to this area.

118

5 VARIOUS APPLICATIONS OF A PLANNING LANGUAGE

The preparation of sales plans, budgets, profit and loss sheet, balance sheet, monthly control figures and similar reports belongs to the expected applications of a software supporting the planning process. But due to the general character of a language more difficult tasks are sometimes solved with planning languages. In the following selection diverse applications of ITS/73 are given.

5.1 Reporting Systems of Multi-National Corporations

The financial and marketing reports of hundreds of companies must be consolidated and analysed within a few days, several times a month. This requires a system which is able to store and retrieve more than ten thousand matrices at high speed. The data manipulation features must be flexible enough to meet all information demands of the different staff departments at Headquarters.

5.2 Simulation of the Coupled Production of Four Chemical Plants

This application required the processing of a very complex data structure combined with difficult calculations. Although the data relations could be presented by connected tables, I would suggest, in such difficult applications, the support of a data management system as it is provided within ITS/DMS.

5.3 Budgeting the Cost Items Related to the Flights of an International Airline

Budgeting the flights of an airline is complex because cost items of the various types of airplanes differ, and prices for fuel and landing fees vary at different airports in all parts of the world. Special difficulties arise from the fact that within the reports at the lower level only a few types of airplanes occur, but in consolidating different flights of a country, an area, a continent, an increasing number of aircraft types is involved. This problem can only be handled with very flexible addressing and reporting features.

5.4 Branch Office Statistics for Savings Bank

To analyse the operations of a Savings Bank with a planning language requires full integration of the planning language with the data stored in operational files. This problem can easily be solved if Host Language Systems for COBOL or PL/1 can bridge the data from those files to the report-oriented data base of the planning language.

5.5 Components Sales Forecast Based on Circuit Diagrams of Future Products

A very exceptional application using the very flexible addressing technique of ITS/73 is a forecasting system based on the bill of materials of circuit diagrams presented in sparse matrices. In this application the index position and values are stored in reports. Expanding and condensing the matrices is managed by the powerful indirect addressing of report positions with report lines and report columns.

5.6 Statistics and their Graphic Presentation

The graphic presentation of the results of statistical analyses is very instructive. A large insurance company makes extensive use of this feature available within the planning language ITS/73.

REFERENCES

1. Burwick, H. "ITS/73, An application oriented programming language for reporting and planning, Basic Language Elements." Aachen: GMI technical publication, 1975.

2. Burwick, H. "ITS/73, An application oriented programming language for reporting and planning, Advanced Language Elements." Aachen: GMI technical publication, 1976.

3. Burwick, H. "DMS/77, Ein anwendungsorientiertes System zur Verwaltung von Daten." Aachen: GMI technische Veröffentlichung, 1977.

4. Burwick, H. "GOGOL, Eine Programmiersprache zur Verarbeitung von Dateien." Aachen: GMI technische Veröffentlichung, 1978.

5. Gershefski, G.W. "Corporate Models—The State of the Art." *Management Science* 16 (1970): B303-B312.

6. Tilemann, T., H. Roden, W. Emde and H.P. Klütsch. "Betriebswirtschaftliche Analyse- und Planungssoftware: Struktur von Angebot und Nachfrage in der Bundesrepublik Deutschland." BIFOA—Forschungsbericht 77/2, Köln, 1977.

II MODELING METHODOLOGY

Chairman: Heiner Müller-Merbach

The basic purpose of methodological research is to provide methods. Hence, this section on "Modeling Methodology" has to deal with methods of model design.

There are two basic questions which have to be answered by methods of model design (as well as by methods in any other design field):

—What is the content of the method? What is its coverage? What are the elements or components of the modeling process?

—What is the procedural structure or order of the modeling process? How shall the process be organized? How to cope with the interdependencies between the elements or components of the process?

There is much literature on both questions. And nobody would expect that the three following papers would deal with all the single methodological aspects of modeling or provide complete methods of modeling, described in detail. Instead, *single* aspects of modeling will be discussed. They have to do, in particular, with recommendations to overcome the difficulties of model acceptance by means of a greater emphasis on the user's participation. The recommendations are quite different though.

R.J. Welke: "Planning Model Data Management—Issues and Alternatives"

Welke reports on his experience with a family services agency. Its typical problem was to assess the (particularly) financial consequences of alternative actions. Thus, the questions are of the "what if..." type. To answer these questions, a model was developed, based on an attribute/time-series matrix, where the time-series consist of a historic and speculative part (past and future).

Welke put particular consideration on the user: Who is the user? What are his information needs? What are the data to be provided by the model and by the user? How will or should he interact with the model? This is in correspondence with Churchman who suggests to put the implementation question first, i.e., to start with the needs of the users.

F. Rosenkranz: "Implementation and Design Problems of Corporate Simulation and Planning Systems"

As in Welke's paper, Rosenkranz paid particular attention to the implementation problem, emphasizing the participation of the model user in the model design process. He recommends this participation particularly for corporate models.

His means of incorporating the model user in the model design process is a Corporate Simulation and Planning System (CSPS) in the sense of a language supervisor program. He recommends the use of CSPS to design Corporate Simulation and Planning Models (CSPM).

Wolfgang Schuler: "An Information System on Models for Information and Documentation—A Concept"

Quite different from those of Welke and Rosenkranz is the recommendation of Schuler. He suggests to design an information system on models. All the existing models (in general or with respect to certain problem areas) should be collected and stored in centralized files. These files should be available for any interested user. He will have the advantage of choosing from the existing models rather than to develop new models as the consequence of limited information.

Schuler did not discuss the level of abstraction of the models stored in this information system. The questions of model and data maintenance remain open.

9. A Data-Centered, User-Evolutionary Approach to the Development of Planning Support Systems

by Richard J. Welke

1 DEVELOPMENT STRATEGIES AND DESIGN APPROACHES

1.1 A Situational View of Planning Support System Development

There is no one best way of developing and implementing information systems in general or planning information systems in particular. A cursory reading of the papers presented in this volume should serve to confirm this statement. See also [16; 32]. Rather, the would-be analyst is faced with a number of *situational factors* associated with the organization, the clients and the eventual users, their processes and tasks and various time, cost and experience constraints. A proper assessment of these factors should identify and influence development choices such as the role the analyst takes vis-à-vis the users, the overall design paradigm adopted and the form of the eventual support system and its interface with the user.

A summarization of what these factors are and how they should influence the analyst's thinking and behaviour regarding development and implementation will be left to the editors of this volume. At some point, however, the analyst must decide whether he is assisting in the development of support systems for *processes* or *individuals* (i.e., for planning or for planners). Further, it must be decided whether an all encompassing (synoptic) [3, p. 364] design is to be developed or an evolutionary approach tied to the evolving needs and understanding of the support system users. Situational factors will determine which of the four development strategies (process-synoptic, individual-synoptic, process-evolutionary, individual-evolutionary), or others, should be chosen. In this paper we will explore the implications of adopting one of these approaches in the context of planning systems. Before outlining the proposed development strategy, however, a few words seem appropriate regarding what is meant by planning in general, and current approaches to computer support of planning in particular.

1.2 Planning and its Support

Planning is with respect to something. Without loss of generality, we refer to that someting as an object system. Statically, an object system is a bounded collection of elements possessing properties and inter-related by structure. Dynamically, an object system co-processes time-sequences (trajectories) of external action realizations (events) and internal actions which result in changes to internal element property (outcome) trajectories and external consequence trajectories. The scope of the object system is reduced to more manageable proportions by considering *aspects* of it; that is, only selected elements, properties, structural relations, events, actions, outcomes and consequences. These may be organizationally sanctioned (e.g., financial accounting) or more commonly, those implicit in an individual's perception of the object system.

Based upon the preceding descriptions we define *planning* as:

> A process, comprised of a set of tasks, engaged in by one or a group of individuals acting collectively or separately, which given or assuming a "scenario" of future uncontrolled events produce a description of one or more (i.e., contingent) future outcome/consequence trajectories, and/or one or more internal action trajectories necessary to arrive at points along the future outcome/consequence trajectory.

The *components* of a planning process (formal or informal) derived from this view of planning become:

1.   Implicit or explicit identification of the object system in terms of the aspects of it to be planned for.
2.   Knowledge or assumption of the external event scenario.
3.   A basis for describing a future "state", i.e., selected properties of the outcome/consequence trajectory.
4.   A basis for differentiating and judging (in a good-bad, desirable-acceptable-unsatisfactory sense) between alternative future states.
5.   A means of exerting control over the future states by actions taken.
6.   A method for inferring future states from a knowledge of past and anticipated events, "aspected" object system dynamics, past and present internal property trajectories and future (proposed) internal action trajectories—a form of *predictive model*.

These components, of themselves, do not constitute a planning approach or methodology. Rather, it is in the deployment, sequencing, details and execution of the components, the object system aspect(s) considered and the mode of planning (reactive or proactive) that give rise to the diversity of planning approaches and methodologies.

There are many possibilities for formal support of each of the planning components above [1; 2; 3]. The component receiving the majority of the attention from a data processing viewpoint has been the predictive (planning model) component. While much of this "model-centred" development activity has been of a one-off, in-house nature, increasingly planning model "languages" have been developed to assist in the construction of such models. In a survey conducted by the author, seventy-four such languages were uncovered;* other papers in this volume suggest others, undoubtedly there are many more.

The existence of such languages provides a strong impetus for adopting a model-centred approach to DP support of the planning activity [28; 29; 30]. This approach, while appropriate in some circumstances, needs to be critically examined.

1.3 The Data-Centred, User-Evolutionary Approach: An Overview

As suggested in the first section, an analysis of situational factors should indicate whether a process-synoptic, individual-synoptic, process-evolutionary or individual-evolutionary is the preferred development strategy. In this paper we focus on the "user-evolutionary approach". By *user-oriented approach* we intend an approach in which individuals as idiosyncratic personalities with distinct cognitive styles (hereafter called *users*) are assisted with their planning tasks by a combination of improved data, data manipulation and supporting models. These tasks may be as limited as providing single property forecasts or as broad as formulating organization-wide scenarios and assessing their financial, operational and market consequences. With the user-oriented approach the user is the initial focus of the development effort. This is in contrast to the *process approach* in which the planning process are the basis for design. The *evolutionary approach* [9; 23; 31] intends that the support system for an individual evolves as the user's interest, need and understanding requires. This is in contrast to a more synoptic approach in

---

* The model/simulators eventually surveyed included those given in the Association of Time-sharing Users Application Directory on Financial Modelling languages: (1) AIDS, (2) AUTOPLAN, (3) AUTOTAB, (4) BBL, (5) BUDPLAN, (6) CALLPLAN, (7) CHI: PROJECT—SPREAD, (8) CUFFS, (9) CYPHERTAB, (10) DATAFORM, (11) EMS, (12) EXPRESS, (13) FACTS, (14) FAL II, (15) FAMS, (16) FCS, (17) FINANCE, (18) FINANCIAL REPORTING, (19) FINSIM, (20) FISCAL, (21) FLARES, (22) FML, (23) FORESIGHT, (24) FPS, (25) FRSS, (26) GPOS I & II, (27) IFPS, (28) INFOTAB, (29) KASH, (30) KEYDATA: A/P General Ledger—Financial Reporting, (31) LSFIL, (32) MARS, (33) MODSIM, (34) MORTGAGE, (35) OLSFMS, (36) OPTIBANK, (37) ORACLE, (38) PAUS, (39) PROBE, (40) PROBE, (41) PROFORMA, (42) PROPHIT, (43) QUICK, (44) RAPS II, (45) REPORT, (46) SIMPLAN, (47) SPECTRUM, (48) TSAM, (49) TYMTAB, (50) VALUELINE: Corporate Planning Model, (51) XSIM, to the extent they were documented in that directory. More detailed information (manuals) were obtained for (5), (24), (23), (26) and (46). From DATAPRO Reports, additional modelling languages were added to the list as: (52) ADSIM, (53) BRP, (54) Business Analysis/BASIC, (55) COFS, (56) DATABANK, (57) FIPAC, (58) FOCUS, (59) FP/70, (60) GUESS, (61) GVM, (63) IBM: APL/FPS, (64) MINI-PLAN, (65) MUFU1-Basic Financial Planning, (66) MUFU16-Corporate Feasibility Analysis Program, (67) Performance Planning and Control System, (68) PILOTE, (69) PROALF, (70) Sensitivity Analysis Model, (71) Technical Economics: Optimization of Long-range Planning, and examined to the level of detail afforded by the DATAPRO reports. In addition, detailed manuals were obtained and examined on the following languages not mentioned above: (72) CAPS, (73) PLANCODE and (74) PSG.

which the users support needs are *anticipated* and the planning system is put into place reflecting the anticipated use.

In the development of a planning support system one more decision needs to be taken—that of the *design approach* which "centers" the development effort as well as providing a (eventual) basis for integration among individuals/tasks. It would appear that there are at least two choices: model-centred and data-centred [19, p. 60]. The *model-centred approach* [7; 18; 28], discussed briefly in the preceding section, takes as its design approach the development of a model (or suite of integratable models) to assist planners/planning. Such an approach does not negate the need for data storage and manipulation; rather, it is subsumed in the model itself and accessible through the model.

The *data-centred approach* [14; 34] deals explicitly with the data/user interface without the necessity for an intervening model. Furthermore, when such models are needed, they can be radically different in their form (as GPSS is different from Systems Dynamics/DYNAMO) from one user to the next. It is concerned, in the first instance, with providing a manipulable data base suitable for users engaged in planning tasks. It is the data base, not a common model, which provides integration.

We do not feel that the choice of a development strategy and design approach are independent. In particular we feel that the user-evolutionary approach is best served by a data-centered design approach. There are several reasons for this. First, the individual users, in their first encounter with formal planning support, may not be prepared for the mental leap to an externalized formal model. Attempts to implement such a model in these cases can produce a number of dysfunctional consequences, varying from distrust and non-use to unwarranted "blind faith" trust and improper/erroneous use. An evolutionary approach permits users to progress at their own pace in terms of an externalized understanding of the planning task in which they are involved. Such externalizations and their inclusion in the formal planning support system may at first be trivial indeed, evolving over time to a better user understanding and, perhaps, attendant planning models.

A second reason for adopting a data centered design approach in the context of a user-evolutionary development strategy is that it permits the integration of individual planning task results without resorting to a *common* model or modelling language (and hence common object system view). That this is important stems from the consideration that users will have their own views of selected aspects of the object system for which they are responsible in terms of the assumed planning tasks. A planning model or language, by its nature, also possesses an object system view as regards elements, structure and dynamics. A common model or language implies a common view, which may be suitable to some, grudgingly acceptable to others, and unsuitable for the remainder of users.

1.4 Applicability of the Data-Centered User-Evolutionary Approach

There are many circumstances in which a development strategy other than user-evolutionary and/or design approach other than data-centered may be more appropriate. A typical situation is that of a limited number of planners in a corporate planning staff for whom a common view is probable and familiarity with formal planning tools is likely. In this situation a process-oriented, synoptic strategy may be more suitable, using a model-centered design approach. There are, however, numerous cases where an organization or organizational unit is faced with the necessity to initiate formal planning without benefit of a planning staff. It is in these situations that we believe a data-centered user-evolutionary approach has merit.

Because of the nature of the evolutionary approach, one cannot provide a concise normative description of the product to be produced. This is to be generated by the users. However, it is possible to detail the proposed data-centered approach and to describe the manner in which the evolution strategy might proceed. These remarks are based upon some work done with a local family services agency and the lessons learned from attempting to develop a planning model for them.

In the next part we examine some details of the data-centered approach. In the final part we consider how the user-evolutionary approach could be staged to provide an integrated outcome without recourse to a formal planning model.

2 DETAILED CONSIDERATIONS IN THE DATA-CENTERED DESIGN APPROACH

2.1 The Matrix Approach to Planning Data Management

Regardless of whether one is attempting to provide modest data support to a planning task or constructing an elaborate planning model or language, the need for providing a means for organizing and managing the underlying data becomes quickly apparent. The analyst/user is faced with trajectory data (i.e., time-series) for each of the variables (element properties, event, outcome, consequence, etc.) within their planning view. These time-series must be maintained in the traditional sense of creating, adding, deleting, updating, storing and retrieving individual time-series. However, one must add to this a number of additional data management capabilities not generally required or present in traditional DP applications. Among these are: alternative value sets for the same time-series variables (associated with alternative external event scenarios), maintaining correct time orientations between past (historic), current and future (speculative) components of the time-series, and the provision for individual data item insertion, deletion alteration, push-up and push-down.

The simpler the data structure adopted, the easier the above tasks become. One of the simplest is that of the data matrix. Its application to planning data has each time-series represented by a row of the matrix, each column a time interval. The popularity of such a data structure is apparent if one examines the underlying data model in any of the planning languages cited previously [see footnote 1, also: 21; 34]. There is also a certain logical appeal to such a view, appearing as it were, as a "spread sheet" to the user.

Despite this appeal, there are several drawbacks to the adoption of the matrix view as the basis for a data-centered design approach (and, as an underlying data model for the model-centered approach). Primary among these is the necessity to think in terms of a single "time step" (i.e., time interval size or period) for all of the time-series contained in the matrix. While such a constraint may not be binding in many cases (such as aggregated accounting data), there are many more cases where unnecessary artificiality is introduced by the uni-time step.

Consider, for example, a single planning variable: employee expense. If the time step elected is monthly and the labour expense is bi-weekly, what would normally be viewed as a constant value (until raises occur), appears as a cyclic value in the appropriate monthly partitioned time-series. If, on the other hand, the time-step utilized is bi-weekly, then monthly salary expense must be artificially partitioned and, in so doing, appear cyclical in a bi-weekly partitioned time-series. Similar remarks apply in terms of days in weeks (i.e., the number of working days are affected by holidays, cyclical production levels, etc.), weeks and months related to quarters, and so forth.

In supporting processes (as distinct from individuals) the arbitrary or artificial partitioning of time-series might not arise as an issue. However, if we take a user-oriented view towards development, the desirability of supporting users with a data representation which is more natural and efficient from the user manipulation viewpoint becomes a concern. Returning to the example of employee expense let us assume a user, as part of the planning task for which he is responsible, must, at some point, extend the time-series from the "historical past" to the "speculative future". Under the simplest of scenarios all that must be done is a straight extrapolation. Assuming a non-growth situation this should be very easy (i.e., the same bi-weekly pay for each bi-weekly interval). However, partitioning by month makes the extrapolation more difficult, requiring both extrapolation and interpolation. The issue is not whether the user could do this but rather *why* he should do it.

As a final comment on the concept of time-series we note that many time-varying values of concern to planners have no natural period to them at all. Consider annual salaries. At some time-point, these values will experience a step increase (or decrease) as a result of raises. The time-point at which these occur varies from year to year for many organizations. One can, of course, apply an artificial partitioning to force a periodicity on the annual salary as one must do employing a matrix approach. All this serves to do is unnecessarily increase the amount of data that must be examined and managed by the user. Once again this is not a process issue but it is, we believe, a user issue.

Another "user-oriented" consideration when adopting the matrix representation of time-series data is the inherent lack of data structure for between-variable associations. Each row in the matrix represents a variable (item) associated with some entity (e.g., product, product aggregate, employee, employee aggregate,

128

etc.) To provide even a modest amount of user-oriented data manipulation, one would expect to be able to associate entity types with their time varying properties (the row items). Yet the rows provide nothing more than a simple list and hence no associative relations except by physical grouping. This can, of course, be overcome by striking separate matrices, representing in effect, two-dimensional (time and property) relational tuples for each "logical" item collection. That becomes the "tip" of a relational data base "iceberg". This is á considerable departure from the simplicity of matrixed data storage.

To summarize, we detect two inadequacies in the prevailing matrix approach to data representation for planning. First, there is the forced periodicity on time-varying planning variables which may have either a different "natural" period (as seen by the user) or no period at all (aperiodic). Secondly, there is the inherent inability to form user-logical (infological) [22] associations between row items and the infological entity to which they are associated, to assist in the manipulation of the time-varying planning variables by the user. In the next section we suggest one plausible data description which overcomes these problems.

2.2 An Alternative Approach to Planning Model Data Representation

To consolidate the previous discussion we reassert that the basic element of data to be described and managed in a planning environment is the time trajectory of user identified element properties, i.e., time-series. We identified two types of time-series which we will term "periodic" and "aperiodic". A periodic time-series is one in which the validity of each of its values is associated with regular, pre-definable intervals. An alternative way of saying this is that a user can describe, in advance, a *calendar* of time points defining the intervals against which the values of time-series are associated. By explicitly incorporating the concept of a calendar into the data representation of time-series we have the facility to provide a generalized representation of periodic time-series without being tied to a particular interval size; each time-series is instead "linked" to one of a number of stored calendars. Thus, if a particular user perceives that the variables of interest to him change on either a weekly, bi-weekly, every tenth business day, monthly, on the twentieth day of each month, etc., he could establish calendars representing each of these periods and then establish and subsequently manipulate the time-series with respect to the appropriate calendar. In this manner the user would no longer need to insert redundant data, interpolate to fit artificial intervals or be faced with the artificially induced periodicity of data when attempting to extrapolate. Furthermore, the calendars themselves can now be manipulated to reflect hypothesized events affecting period size (e.g., long work week, strikes, changes in year-end closing) without having to re-adjust all of the associated data.

The aperiodic time-series has no regular periodicity and hence no calendar. Its treatment consists of maintaining a «time, value» pair for each entry in the time-series. By this convention, time-varying values which change (or are observed to change) at infrequent and irregular intervals, can be accommodated without forcing periodicity on the values. There are *two types* of aperiodic interval values, each requiring a slightly different treatment. *Accumulation* values are established by defining the upper (inclusive) bound of the time interval by the paired time-mark in the «time, value» pair. The lower (exclusive) bound of the accumulation interval is obtained from the preceding «time, value» pair. The value represents the total accumulated value over the interval. The application of this type of aperiodic time-series would be to situations where observation occurrences are random or irregular, either in the ''real-world'' or as output from event-list type simulators.

Rate values are the second type of interval value associated with the aperiodic time-series treatment. For this type, the time-mark of the «time, value» pair defines the (inclusive) *lower* bound of the interval. A subsequent «time, value» pair (if any) closes the preceding interval and asserts the value which is valid until yet another «time, value» pair closes that interval. By using this convention, the user needs to establish only one such pair for the time-series as long as the rate does not change. Because rate is with respect to a time interval, to provide maximum flexibility the rate can be assigned to a calendar to permit a more flexible definition of what is meant by say, ''month'' in units/month.

The next aspect of planning data time-series to be considered is the split between *historic-current* values, i.e., all those values which are factually known, and the *speculative* values, i.e., those values which constitute the presumed future based upon some particular speculative scenario. Whereas there is only one historical component, there can be a number of different speculative components, each distinguished by a particular scenario number.

A further refinement to the speculative component is that each value can be represented as a single value or as a random variable. The random variable can in turn be represented either in continuous or discrete form. For the continuous random variable, the approximating distribution is designated as parametric information at the beginning of the speculative component; each ''value'' is then, in fact, an n-tuple where n is the number of parameters necessary to specify the distribution. For discrete random variables, an $N \times 2$ array is associated with each ''value'' of the time-series; the first component being the value, the second being the probability associated with it.

Having considered the basic level of data to be described and managed—the time-series—we briefly consider the inter-relationships which should be permitted to exist between them. As previously discussed, each time-series represents a property of some element (object, activity) or event (environmental or internal) of the users perceived object system. Thus, it should be possible for the user to associate the various time-series with their related system elements or event-types (hereafter called *entities*) for purposes of retrieval and manipulation, as well as appending non-varying data which may prove helpful in displaying/reporting and/or modelling. To accomplish this we suggest the capability to establish entity descriptions. Each entity description is viewed as having one or more identifiers, one or more alphameric descriptions and none, one or more additional constants. These entity descriptions are, in turn, linked to the time-series segments described previously.

130

One can, of course, extend the notion of inter-relationships to the entities them-selves in a hierarchical or network form. At this juncture we move directly into the area of logical data structures as addressed by the voluminous data base litera-ture [24].

This brings us to considerations of the physical implementation of the proposed data structure. Neglecting the possibilities of inter-entity relationships we see no particular difficulties in implementing the proposed data structure using any lan-guage which supports random access (direct) file organizations. With the wide availability of data base management systems for micro-computers to large main frames, the necessity for one-off implementations of the proposed planning struc-ture should, however, be questioned.

A final question concerning whether the type of flexibility associated with the proposed data structure is really necessary; might it not in fact overwhelm the ini-tial user? As to whether it is necessary we can only say that the proposed data structure was suggested by unsuccessful attempts to develop a data-centered, user-evolutionary approach for the previously mentioned family-services agency using the matrix approach. This need was subsequently reinforced by private conversations with planning groups at several large corporations who had rejected a number of formal planning languages because of the simplistic (and cumber-some) data matrix representation.

Regarding the problem of overwhelming the initial user, we view this as a problem of proper implementation. Flexibility, of itself, should not provide a stumbling block to the user. Flexibility, badly implemented can. IBM's job con-trol language is often cited as such a failure. In our view the proposed structure permits the user to express the time-series values in any one of several ways that might be most natural to him. More importantly it permits a more natural ma-nipulation of the data once stored.

2.3 The Data Manager

Having provided for a flexible data structure, which forms the core of the data-centered approach, it is necessary to provide a facility to interface the data with the user for purposes of maintenance and manipulation. Just as we attempted to anticipate the various ways in which time-series data might be viewed in order to derive a flexible data structure, the development of an interface requires a similar type of analysis to anticipate eventual needs and provide flexibility with respect to access and usage. We have partitioned the interface requirements into the follow-ing categories:

1. Input and update of historical components
    1.1 By individuals
    1.2 By file maintenance programs
2. Input and update of speculative components
    2.1 By individuals
    2.2 By transference from other files

It is beyond the scope of this paper to take up each of these interfaces in great detail. Instead, we will suggest some general guidelines which might be followed.

First, in each of three input/output categories we highlight the need to provide the user (as defined in previous parts of this paper) with a direct interface to the data. The type of functional capability needed for each of the three categories as well as the form of dialogue and display most appropriate for user can be partially anticipated by studying the work of others [26; 34]. In the final analysis, however, it appears that either a participatory approach to the specification of the necessary interface and/or an evolutionary approach to its specification as needs arise must be considered as an explicit component of the development and implementation of this aspect of the interface.*

A second requirement is that the data be accessible to a variety of programs. For the case where a DBMS has been used, this requirement is partially fulfilled through the DML (data manipulation language)/sub-schema interface. There are a number of situations, however, where this approach cannot be adopted (e.g., no DBMS, no DML for the language being used—particularly various simulation languages). A general strategy that can be followed, is to provide standardized record formats for each of the various time-series types such that they can be, at a minimum, produced as ASCII files to an output media (either at a terminal— floppy disc, casette, etc., or via the systems secondary storage) and re-entered to the planning data system by an input program designed specifically for this purpose. Without this facility, the ability to use existing programs and models as well as external data sources which might be available from commercial time-sharing services, is unnecessarily limited.

A final requirement is to provide formated output in the form of reports. We take up this aspect of the data manager interface in the next section.

2.4 A "Calendarizer" and Report Generator Extension to the Data Manager

We have taken issue with the use of the data matrix approach as the *underlying* data structure. We must, however, acknowledge that there are a number of reasons for wishing to have time-series data conform to specific time intervals:

* One such approach was presented by J.C. Chambers of Xerox in a paper presented at the TIMS/ORSA conference in Atlanta, Georgia. the approach involved using two separate groups (a user group and a technical group) to determine the types of support procedures they felt would be useful in developing a planning model. Each group, in effect, formed a dialectic against which a "Hegelian"-like synthesis was performed to arrive at the initial design. It was reported that his approach produced good results.

132

1. To produce monthly, quarterly and other fixed interval reports.
2. To simplify pro forma report modelling and presentation.
3. To use various difference equation based modelling techniques and languages which depend upon a fixed time interval.

To provide for this regularity, we propose that a *calendarizing routine* be provided which is capable of providing matrixed data with a pre-specified time increment. The user would designate which time-series in the planning data base are to be used for which rows and to indicate the desired calendar to be used for the columns. The calendarizer routine will then perform the necessary mathematical interpolations to fit the natural (as stored) time-series to the artificial partitions specified for the desired matrix. Provisions should also be made for the data manager to label and store the generated matrices.

With the capability to produce matrixed data, we turn our attention to the production of reports utilizing this data. While it may occasionally be the case that reports are to be produced directly from the data as stored in the planning data base or as matrixed by the calendarizer, it will more often be the situation that the desired report will contain aggregations and time-lagged transformations of this data to produce the desired "pro forma" reports.

The report generator should provide two types of capabilities:

1. To provide data formatting and the insertion of constant data (e.g., field descriptions, titles).
2. To provide simple (deterministic) transformation to produce the required output variables.

These capabilities, as many readers may realize, are provided for, in large part, by the multitude of planning languages cited earlier. They can, with slightly more work, be accomplished by the use of standard report generators and/or using one-off application programs, without the necessity for incurring the expense of planning languages (where this is a factor).

In this section we have attempted to outline the requirements for a data-centered approach to planning. We have argued for a more flexible storage of the underlying time-series so that a more natural interface between the user and the data is possible. We recognized that there are different types of time-series (periodic, a-periodic) associated with differing time-steps (calendars) having different components (historic, speculative) containing values which can differ with respect to their content (accumulation, rate) and certainty (deterministic, random variable). We have suggested that access to and manipulation of these basic time-series should be through a separate and distinct data manager providing both individual user interfaces as well as program/file interfaces. Finally, we acknowledged the need for providing matrixed (i.e., time-regularized) data for purposes which include difference-equation-like modelling and (pro forma) report generation. In this regard we indicated the need for a "calendarizer" routine and a report generator as *adjuncts* to the planning data manager.

For those installations which have at their disposal a data base management system with query facilities and a report generator and/or planning language, the implementation of a dat-centered approach along the lines suggested here will require a change in thinking more than any specific major software modules (with the exception of the calendarizer). For installations with more modest resources, we believe the approach outlined in sufficiently modular as to permit its implementation on very small systems.

3 A USER-EVOLUTIONARY APPROACH TO PLANNING MODEL DEVELOPMENT

There are numerous ways in which formal planning support systems can and are developed in organizations. At one end of the continuum is the process-synoptic approach in which a group of planning consultants and/or systems analysts develop a sophisticated computer based planning model which is then turned over for use by those engaged in the planning process. Middle-points on the continuum take a more incremental approach to the implementation of a model and recognize the need for increased user participation in its construction.

At the other end of the continuum is what is termed the user-evolutionary approach to development. The basic tenet of this approach is that we take as the focal point of development the individuals involved in developing a plan. Each individual is to be supported as his/her needs and understanding dictate. The development of the planning support system *evolves* as the users needs and understanding permit it to evolve. There is no underlying normative model to which the user must be directed in this approach.

The reader may argue, and correctly so, that the user-evolutionary approach may be tenable for specific individuals having particular planning problems but does not guarantee the co-ordination of results necessary to provide organization-wide planning. It is perhaps this concern which motivates the model-centered approach discussed previously. We argue that by taking a data-centered approach, it is possible to retain the benefits of a user-evolutionary approach while providing the nucleus for co-ordination through the data manager. In the following sections we outline a three-stage user-oriented development strategy for providing, on the one hand, a centralised plan, while on the other hand permitting an evolutionary approach to the users/participants in the planning process.

3.1 Stage I—User Speculation

For the centralised aspect of the proposed approach, we adopt the pro forma financial reports as a matter of convenience. In fact, any pro forma report which can be constructed from known historical and projected data, requiring computation, but *not judgement*, is equally suitable. We note that the difference between standard historical reports and a pro forma report is, of course, the use of speculative data in the report preparation. We label the input speculation trajectories

134

which provide the basis for the pro forma reports as "primary aggregate time-series", or PATS. From the standpoint of the pro forma report, the users are generally viewed as those using the report output, or primary users. The PATS, however, must be obtained from somewhere. In a model-centered, process-synoptic approach, these speculations would be obtained from internal predictive procedures. With the user-evolutionary, data-centered approach, we explicitly introduce the concept of the "secondary user" as the initial "black-box" provisioner of these PATS. The concept of primary user and secondary user are introduced in an article by Bostrom and Heinen [8] which goes on to examine the relationship between the analyst and primary/secondary user in the context of implementation failures.

Specifically, a central planning system kernel is established using the report generator to formulate the mechanics of the pro forma report, which in turn obtains the PATS from the data manager outlined in the previous part of this paper. The provision of the PATS is delegated to a group of secondary users of the planning system. Typically, these secondary users of the central planning system will be chosen based upon their knowledge of the organizational aspect associated with the particular PATS. These secondary users become the external predictive models of the central planning system.

We now turn our attention to the secondary users. In the first stage we require nothing more than the secondary user to make ad hoc, informal judgements to produce the speculative components of the PATS delegated to him. These are then entered in any acceptable form using the data manager described in the previous part. The calendarizer and report generator then take over to produce the pro forma planning report required by the primary user. This completes stage I.

We now examine what has been accomplished in stage I. First, we have a "planning model" with high face validity as it automatically performs nothing more than is currently done preparing a historical version of the report, i.e., it is a clerical system. Secondly, we have initiated user participation in the planning process with a minimum of formal demands. Third, we generate a formal record of speculations which can be compared to subsequent actuals to provide feedback to the "user-speculators". Finally, and most importantly, the user (not the analyst) is required to think about how the speculative values are to be derived. This increasingly conscious recognition by the user of future outcomes as related to external event scenarios, past and current operations and other factors is an important precursor to the next stage.

3.2   Stage II—The Transition from Secondary User to Primary User

In the first stage, the secondary user is an individual faced with a prediction task. We now consider providing more formal support to these individuals through the same data manager. We begin by noting that there are five levels of support:

1. leave the user as a black-box processor
2. improve the user/data-manager interface by providing (additional) com-

mands, tailored to the user, to facilitate the manipulation and extrapolation of the PATS

3. provide additional information support to assist the user in developing the speculations

4. develop an information-model (DSS) support system [17]

5. supplant the user with an "equivalent" model.

There are many factors which might dictate the level of support chosen. In keeping with the user-evolutionary approach of this paper we take as the major factors: need, use and time. The first stage is designed to instigate need by providing feedback to the user regarding his inputs and to initiate the externalization of judgement. With this as a base, the next step is to work with the users to provide an improved interface with the data manager. This can proceed in several directions, depending upon the cognitive style of the user and the complexity of the speculation task he is faced with [6; 11]. For some users the initial need will be to provide level 2 support while further judgemental experience is gained in formulating speculative values. For others, the need will be to provide supporting formal information (through the data manager) to improve their internal black-box speculations. Yet others may wish to develop a combination information-model (decision) support system. It is beyond the scope of this paper to provide a detailed framework as to which level of support is appropriate and which techniques are appropriate for its implementation. These issues are, in part, addressed by other papers in this book [5].

Focusing briefly on the modelling aspect, we note that it is important to adopt a modelling methodology which is consistent with the users perception of the object system dynamics and the type of mapping desired. For some, a black-box, regression-derived model may be most suitable. For others a more detailed representation using a simulation methodology may be preferred. Here again, there are a number of choices, from the "continuous-time" system dynamics model [10; 12] to the discrete-time transaction driven simulators such as GPSS [13; 25; 35]. By adopting the data-centered approach outlined in the previous section, it is possible to allow different modelling methodologies to be adopted for different users while still achieving the necessary integration.

To summarize, the purpose of stage II is to permit each user to become an independent primary user of the planning system. We propose that the formal support evolve according to the users needs and learning rather than being imposed.

3.3 Stage III (and beyond)—Refinements to the Centralized Planning System

There are a number of refinements to the centralized "planning model" which have not as yet been addressed.

Among these are the introduction of constrained optimization models and risk analysis [15; 20; 27]. We believe that these refinements are best introduced after some experience and knowledge has been gained in stage II, particularly from working with the secondary users. Furthermore, such refinements are as potentially applicable to the secondary user's modelling efforts as they are to the primary users. The important point, to us, is that such refinements should be introduced as part of a natural evolution of user (primary and secondary) understanding.

4 CONCLUSION

In this paper we have attempted to combine two concepts of planning model development: a data-centered approach to design and a user-evolutionary approach to development which, if combined, form the basis of a workable strategy for developing integrated planning models without recourse to the far more common model-centered, process-synoptic approach. We have attempted to point out the shortcomings of the model-centered approach in contrast to the data-centered strategy and to outline a strategy using the data-centered approach which will permit a user-evolutionary development of an *integrated* planning model. We believe that such an approach, if used, should provide an acceptable compromise between those who view the main concern of formal planning to be the development of a central model/report and those who feel the major concern must be user involvement in an active, learning sense if implementation failures are to be reduced or prevented.

REFERENCES

1. Ackoff, R.L. *A Concept of Corporate Planning*. New York: Wiley-Interscience, 1970.

2. Ansoff, H.I. "The State of Practice in Planning Systems." *Sloan Management Review* 18 (Winter, 1977): 1-24.

3. Argenti, J. *Systematic Corporate Planning*. London: Thomas Nelson and Sons, 1974.

4. Argyris, C. "Single-loop and Double-loop Models in Research on Decision Making." *Administrative Science Quarterly* 21 (September, 1976).

5. Baumgartner, T., T.R. Burns, P. DeVille, and L.D. Meeker. "A Systems Model of Conflict and Change in Planning Systems with Multi-Level, Multiple Objective Evaluation and Decision-Making." *General Systems* 20 (1975): 167-83.

6. Benbasat, I. and R.N. Taylor. "The Impact of Cognitive Styles on Information Systems Design." *MIS Quarterly* (June 1978): 43-54.

7. Boulden, J.B. "Instant Modelling." in *Corporate Simulation Models*, edited by A.N. Schrieber, 1970, pp. 578-99.

8. Bostrom, R.P. and J.S. Heinen. "MIS Problems and Failures: A Socio-Technical Perspective; Part I: The Causes." *MIS Quarterly* 1 (September 1977): 17-32.

9. Courbon, J.C., J. Grajeur and J. Tolovi. "L'approche Evolutive Dans la Mise en Place des Systèmes Interactifs d'Aide à la Décision." *IAE Working Paper 78.02*, University of Grenoble, January 1978.

10. Coyle, R.G. *Management Systems Dynamics*. London: J. Wiley, 1977.

11. DeWaele, M. "Managerial Style and the Design of Decision Aids." *OMEGA* 16 (1978): 5-13.

12. Forrester, J. *Industrial Dynamics*. M.I.T. Press, 1961.

13. Gordon, G. *System Simulation*. Prentice-Hall, 1969.

14. Hamilton, W.F. and M.A. Moses. "A Computer-Based Corporate Planning System." *Management Science* 21 (1974): 148-59.

15. Hamilton, W.F. and M.A. Moses. "An Optimization Model for Corporate Strategic Planning." *Operations Research* 21 (May-June 1973).

16. Hayes, R.H. and R.L. Nolan. "What Kind of Corporate Modeling Functions Best?" *Harvard Business Review* (May/June 1974): 102-12.

17. Keen, P.G.W. and M.S. Scott Morton. *Decision Support Systems: An Organizational Perspective*. Addison-Wesley, 1978.

18. Kingston, P.L. "Concepts of Financial Models." *IBM Systems Journal* 21 (1973): 113-25.

19. Kirsch, W. and H.K. Klein. *Management-Informats-Systeme 1*. Kohlhammer, Urban-Taschenbücher, 1977.

20. Krouse, C.G. "Model for Aggregate Financial Planning." *Management Science* 18 (1972): B555-66.

21. Lande, H.F. "Planning-Data Systems." *IBM Systems Journal* 12 (1973): 145-60.

22. Langefors, B. and B. Sundgren. *Information Systems Architecture*. New York: Petrocelli/Charter, 1975.

23. Lucas, H.C. "The Evolution of an Information System: From Key-Man to Every Man." *Sloan Management Review* 19 (Winter 1978): 39-52.

24. Martin, J. *Principles of Database Management Systems*. New Jersey: Prentice-Hall, 1976.

25. McKenney, J.L. "The Roles of Simulation Models in Planning." in *Corporate Simulation Models*, edited by A.N. Schreiber, 1970, pp. 600-13.

26. Meador, C.L. and D.N. Ness. "Decision Support Systems: An Application to Corporate Planning." *Sloan Management Review* 15 (Winter 1974): 51-68.

27. Moses, M.A. "Implementation of Analytical Planning Systems." *Management Science* 21 (1975): 1133-43.

28. Naylor, T.H. "A Conceptual Framework for Corporate Modeling and the Results of a Survey of Current Practice." *Operational Research Quarterly* 27 (1976): 671-82.

29. Naylor, T.H. "The Future of Corporate Planning Models." *Managerial Planning* (March/April 1976): 1-10.

30. Naylor, T.H. and H. Schauvland. "A Survey of Users of Corporate Planning Models." *Management Science* 22 (1976): 927-37.

31. Ness, D.N. "Interactive Systems, Theories of Design." in *Joint Wharton/ONR Conference on Interactive Information and Decision Support Systems*. The Wharton School, University of Pennsylvania (November 1975).

32. Nutt, P. "An Experimental Comparison of the Effectiveness of Three Planning Methods." *Management Science* 23 (1977): 499-511.

33. Schreiber, A.N. (ed.). *Corporate Simulation Models*. Seattle: University of Washington Printing Plant, 1970.

34. Sprague, R.H. "System Support for a Financial Planning Model." *Management Accounting* 53 (June 1972): 29-34.

35. Welke, R.J. *A Conceptual Framework and Methodology for Describing and Evaluating Alternative Information Systems from a Managerial Perspective*. Ann Arbor: Xerox University Microfilms, 1976.

10. Implementation and Design Problems of Corporate Simulation and Planning Systems*

by Friedrich Rosenkranz

1 INTRODUCTION

Corporate simulation and planning models (CSPMs) are employed for the description and planning of a firm's activities in the areas of finance, marketing, and production. CSPMs are generally coded for a computer. Whereas originally higher level problem oriented programming languages were used, more recently corporate simulation and planning systems (CSPSs) were designed and applied for this purpose.

In general a CSPS consists of a *language supervisor program* which is coded in a general purpose or assembler language. It controls a number of ready made building blocks which allow access to a model's data-base and which perform user defined calculations with ready made methods using sometimes ready made submodels. With more recently developed systems additional logic, methods, and models may either be programmed with the CSPS's special purpose language itself or a general purpose language.

Ten years have elapsed since the first reports on CSPMs appeared in the literature and today a great variety of published case studies, surveys, and theoretical inquiries are available on the subject. They show that such planning models may be used for various combinations of environmental settings, organizations, users, and planning tasks. However, some of the original expectations were only partially fulfilled. The degree to which sophisticated management science and econometric methods are used is limited to a few applications, especially within larger organizations [8; 13; 21; 25; 29; 45; 46; 47; 51]. The typical CSPM may be better described as a plan and budget generator and evaluator. Marketing and production activities are very often expressed in purely financial terms, and the integration of different functional or organizational models is more the exception than the rule. CSPMs most frequently support short to middle-range planning activities, whereas strategic tasks in the predominant number of cases seem to be supported by either isolated submodels, e.g., for project planning, or by simple data-base evaluations.

The meaning of *implemented and successful models* in implementation research is by

---

* Parts of this paper are based on chapters 2.8 and 3.6 of F. Rosenkranz *An Introduction to Corporate Modeling,* Durham, N.C.: Duke University Press, 1979.

Table 1. Implementation Statistics

Type of Model	User	1970-1977 Number of Models Developed	1978 Number of Implemented Models	Difficulties Encountered
1. *Financial Planning and Budgeting Models* —deterministic —simulation, exploration —batch, interactive —COMOS [9], PL/I	controler head of planning head of finance corporation division subsidiary	7	5	—missing user commitment —relevant financial data not easily available —tendency to use models for reporting instead of planning purposes
2. *Econometric Marketing Models for Sales, Marginal Income Simulation, Manpower Planning* —deterministic, stochastic (mainly use of expected values and variances) —media-mix analysis, sales, and manpower forecasting, planning, simulation —batch, interactive —COMOS	heads of —marketing —market-research —logistics management development corporation division	7	4 (1 special investigation)	—communication problems for statistical results —organizational discontinuity —instable regression results due to multicollinearity, measurement errors, and latent variables
3. *Subjectively Parametrized Marketing Models with Marginal Income Simulation* —deterministic —'What IF' simulations —batch, interactive —COMOS, FORTRAN	head of marketing research division	4	1 (2 special investigations)	—validation very difficult —too much time required from the user's side —instabilities in team and organizational structure

4.	*Integrated Corporate Models* —deterministic, stochastic —econometric analysis, linear programming, experimental designs —batch —COMOS, PL/I, CSMP, FORTRAN	head of planning division	3	0.5	—missing user participation —coordination problems between user departments —communication problems modeling methodology —financial data not suitable for long range planning purposes
5.	*Investment Model* —detederministic, stochastic —different investment criteria, sensitivity analysis, risk analysis, decision tree analysis —batch —FORTRAN	controler used by all divisions	1	0.75	—communication problems for statistical results, risk and decision tree analysis not used on a regular basis
6.	*Portfolio Selection Model* —deterministic —net present worth calculation with (0,1) programming —batch —FORTRAN	head of planning division	1	0	—only small number of projects remained after consideration of ongoing projects, legal and environmental restrictions. Manual selection with multiple criteria more appropriate.

no means unique and a variety of instrumental variables are used to render the degree of implementation and success accessible to qualitative and quantitative empirical research. For example, the number of models used for more than two years may be employed as an implementation variable and a percentage success perceived and estimated either by MS/OR personnel or the user/client as a success indicator [48].

The literature supplies a number of longitudinal and cross-sectional studies as well as surveys which indicate factors that block or favour implementation and success of CSPMs in particular [24; 19; 42] or Operations Research/Management Science (OR/MS) models in general [5; 20]. Also within CIBA-GEIGY three CSPMs were abandoned after their construction had already reached quite a mature state [45; 46]. All these studies indicate that the impact of technical model and CSPS characteristics can not be evaluated in isolation from personal, organizational, and behavioural characteristics of a corporate modeling project.

Table 1 supplies an example for this observation. It represents implementation statistics of planning models constructed and used at CIBA-GEIGY. The first column briefly characterizes the main application area, the nature, and mode of operation of the models. The difficulties cited in the last column were perceived by OR/MS personnel who in most cases served as model builders and intermediaries to the user/client indicated in the second column.

It should be noted that the indicated failures to implement integrated corporate models and a portfolio-selection model were partially due to the fact that the corresponding projects were undertaken during the missionary phase of the OR/MS group [5, pp. 80-81]. Organizationally the group is within the planning and control function of the company which has proven to be a good position for financial planning applications. The content of OR-methodology and model success were subjectively assessed for a number of the models indicated. The level of sophistication, notably of group two models, was not found to be inversely proportional to the implementation rate and the success of the models. The users/clients of the models described in Table 1 were not systematically interviewed. However, missing flexibility, a too ''scientific'' approach, and a too large organizational distance were mentioned in a number of instances.

It is not possible to draw any general inferences from the given examples. Nevertheless, they indicate that the effect of software choice on the implementation and the success of CSPMs is often not a direct one and deserves a situational discussion. This will be attempted after a brief description and classification of types of models and CSPSs existing today has been given. For a more detailed discussion the reader is referred to [46].

2 LANGUAGES, SYSTEMS, AND OPERATION

The literature on corporate modeling contains a number of references, notably by Hamilton and Moses [25], which describe how different functional submodels in the areas of finance, marketing, and production as well as different modeling activities [44] may be supported computationally in an integrated fashion. Some of the more recent developments of CSPSs by computer manufacturers [16; 31], consultants [15; 50], and ourselves [6; 9; 46] exhibit a similar trend. However, surveys made by Grinyer et al. [22; 23] on the use of financial planning models employed in the UK in 1973 and by Naylor and Schauland [42] on the types of models used by American companies in 1975 reveal, first, that so far the integrated approach seems to be more the exception than the rule; secondly, that in Europe CSPSs seem relatively to be used more frequently than in the US, where the predominant number of models is still coded in and controlled by FORTRAN. Also in the UK in 1973 an approximately equal number of corporate financial models were coded in general purpose languages and constructed using a CSPS. Looking at this result one should certainly bear in mind that more flexible CSPSs have been available since only about four to six years ago and that the construction of most of the models which were evaluated by Grinyer, Wooller and Naylor was started some three to five years earlier [22]. At present the number of models supported by a CSPS should be much higher. The fact that of the order of fifty different systems are known today indicates a large and competitive software market.

CSPSs were developed for a number of reasons:

1. Scientific languages such as FORTRAN, APL, and to a certain extent PL/I provide execution efficiency, good documentation, and debuging facilities. However, models programmed in such a language are generally difficult to conceive for a user who has little background in programming or data processing. The identification of a user or intermediary with his model tends to increase if he is able to understand, change, and run it. Consequently, corporate modeling systems want to enable the model operators to construct their own models as far as possible. Certain technical disadvantages are accepted under these circumstances.

2. Also more technically oriented model builders may profit from the use of a CSPS. They are more problem oriented and possess commands which allow the
—automatic reading from or writing to external files and an automatic storage allocation,
—the parameter controlled specification of output reports,
—the invocation of completely integrated modeling software to either perform frequently encountered planning calculations (e.g., extrapolation, interpolation, growth-rates, financial ratios) or econometric and management science methods. Sometimes the systems comprise a model bank containing standard forecasting and financial models,
—the coding of English-like programs with a high degree of modularity, readability, and transparency.

143

Using these aids model builders may code, test, and debug models in a shorter time and are able to concentrate more on modeling and implementation than on data processing activities.

CSPMs are operated in conversational mode on time-shared computers or in batch, or remote-batch mode. Recent years have seen an increasing use of conversational systems and surveys indicating that more than fifty percent of the CSPMs known today are run in conversational mode [22; 42]. This goes hand in hand with the use of corporate modeling systems, since many are installed on bureaux time shared computers. Also conversational programming languages, like APL, are used more often on either in-house or bureaux computers. Since mostly technical reasons speak in favour of APL, this fact has reduced the urgency of the call for user oriented CSPSs and stressed the importance of the intermediary between model and end-user.

Altogether the choice of appropriate computer support for a corporate modeling project must be determined by
—the planning problem to be solved,
—the type of user, intermediary, and model builder,
—the available computing facilities.

Extending a classification originally due to Grinyer and Wooller [22, pp. 86-108], Figure 1 distinguishes several types of CSPMs according to the given computer support. A more detailed discussion is given in the sequel.

2.1 Ready-made Models

Such models possess a structure which is not specifically designed for a particular company. Examples are general models and corresponding programs for
—balance sheet calculations,
—investment analysis using standardized
  —discounted cash flow methods,
  —internal rate of return calculations,
—routine trend or smoothing forecasting.

These models do not depend on special planning, accounting, or controlling conventions of a company.

Because of their fixed and unspecific structure ready-made models are often purchased from computer manufacturers or consultants. Most often they are programmed in a scientific language, such as FORTRAN, or even Assembler language. The user is familiar with the model and its general logic. Therefore, it is not necessary that he knows the program or is able to change it. From a programming point of view one may thus concentrate on execution efficiency. Ready-made models may be operated on an in-house computer or at a service bureau. Especially in the latter case the model tends to be run in conversational mode using teletype terminals and a time-shared computer.

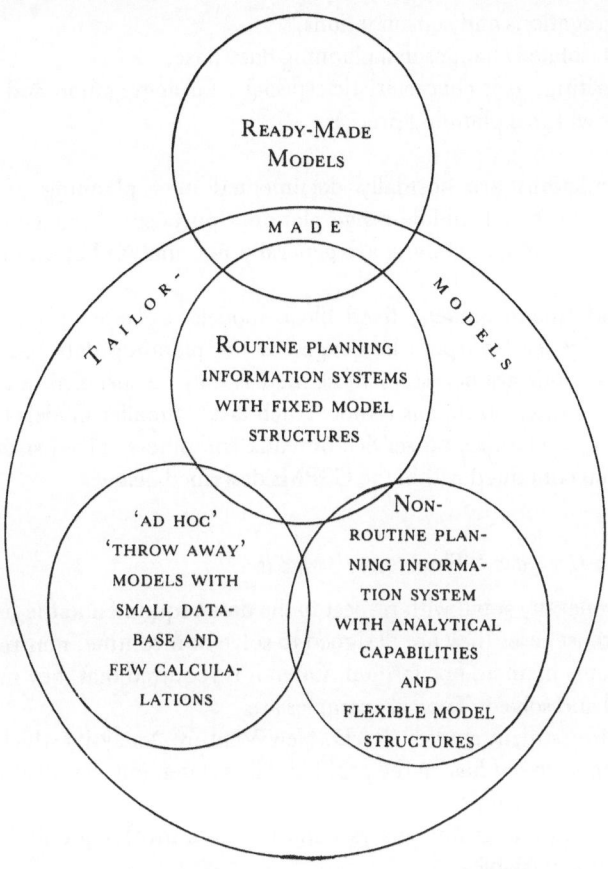

Figure 1. Different types of corporate models

2.2 Tailor-made Models

Tailor-made Models incorporate a logic which is specific for a particular company and is not transferable to others without difficulties.

2.2.1 Fixed Structure Models

Fixed structure, tailor-made models consist of fixed blocks of submodels, programs or dialogues which perform specific planning jobs. In general, they do not need to be flexible, because changes in their structure are only in rare instances necessary. The user does not need to understand their detailed logic, because the models only automate routine and regular plan calculations, such as

—plan aggregations and consolidations,

—effects of isolated changes in a planning data-base,

—report writing, as is characteristic especially for aggregation and consolidation activities within a planning process.

These calculations are normally documented in a planning and controlling manual for short and middle-range planning purposes. Management decisions and an environmental analysis are generally not analyzed or simulated by such models.

Like ready-made models, fixed block models are often programmed using scientific or general purpose languages. If the planning data-base is large and many calculations are necessary these models may be specified in conversational mode and are often started as remote batch tasks. Smaller models tend to be run interactively, sometimes on service bureaux computers. Fixed structure submodels are often contained within the CSPMs described below.

2.2.2 "Ad Hoc" and "Throw Away" Models

They are generally small with respect to the data required and the programs to be coded. In most cases they are designed to solve non-routine, non-repetitive planning problems in an ad hoc fashion. Often it is required that they may be quickly formulated and solved. Typical examples are

—isolated investment studies (R&D, New Venture Analysis) which show the effects an investment has on the profit and loss statement as well as the balance of an organizational unit,

—econometric product line analysis and forecasts involving only few exogenous and decision variables,

—income margin simulations for a small number of products.

Besides the speed of information and computing such applications frequently require that

—the user, or his intermediary, formulates and understands the model himself. Among other reasons, this is the case, because it would often take too long to obtain the appropriate data processing and management science support,

—modeling methods and software are easily and flexibly available.

These requirements may to a large extent be fulfilled by the available on-line CSPSs [12; 17; 30]. Such systems are again either installed in-house or on a service bureau computer. Usually they include a special purpose simulation and planning language, a simple data-base management system, and a ready-made modeling software.

2.2.3 Models Based on Planning Information Systems with Analytical Capabilities

Some of the CIBA-GEIGY applications belong to this class of tailor-made models [45; 46]. Their data-base may be large and is in most cases kept on external storage devices, mainly disks. The model structure may contain up to several thousand equations, although these are in most cases of a very straightforward nature. Simple and more sophisticated modeling tools are required at the same time.

Like the CSPSs mentioned above, planning information systems with analytical capabilities include a simulation language, a data-base management system, and integrated modeling software needed for marketing analysis and forecasting, financial analysis, and resource allocation. The command and simulation language allows the communication with the user and a coordinated use of the database and the method as well as model banks. The components described are designed for small and large models and are further developed than for the packages cited above. They require larger computing systems, good user documentation, explicit error messages, diagnostics, and debuging aids [15; 50; 9; 6; 16 and 40]. Models based on planning information systems with analytical capabilities serve both ad hoc and regular planning activities. The systems must therefore be very flexible to fulfil very heterogenous requirements, e.g., interlanguage communication facilities are needed to code efficient fixed structure models, dialogue programs may be required to interactively specify econometric models, finally, the system may call for interactive programming and execution. As a consequence, it should be possible to operate models in conversational, remote batch, and batch mode.

The planning environment and personal, organizational, as well as behavioural factors define design requirements and problems for both CSPMs and their software support. Mainly this complex will be dealt with in the following section.

3 ORGANIZATION, TASK STRUCTURE, AND PLANNING PROCESS

The planning and controlling process and system of a firm frequently generate the basis for CSPMs. The formalized model uses numerical methods which may be available from a CSPS to process data and assumptions. The latter may, for example, be expressed in equations and logical relationships which describe the development of model variables according to "mental planning models" the user has already had previously.

It is well known that planning activities have a different content for various planning tasks. Some contain a large proportion of programmable elements, others are unique, extremely complex, and rely mainly on intuition as well as mental planning activities. The nature, but also the importance and urgency of a planning task are factors influencing the choice of models and software. For example, one finds that in a certain area the sophistication of planning models increases proportionally with the complexity of the task structure. However, often this does not hold for ill-structured problems in the strategic planning area: the complexity has increased beyond a threshold and the sophistication employed decreases with increasing complexity of the planning task. Also, organizational factors influence the type of model and software used: planning philosophies, technologies, and resources are different for alternative organizational units. As a consequence, planning information systems with analytical capabilities are mostly chosen or developed by larger firms, whereas middle sized firms have a tendency to subscribe to on-line packages for ad hoc modeling. Marketing departments are more likely to employ statistical models and software, finance departments are more inclined to choose planning software which enable them to effectively perform tabular calculations and reporting tasks. These and similar observations are largely self-explanatory. They do not supply much new insights into a discussion of how far planning activity may be supported by a CSPS.

Most authors agree that a CSPM should be compatible with, and its use integrated into the planning and controlling system and proces. Both should use the same definitions and hypotheses and serve the same ends. Otherwise there is a danger of duplication of planning work or the distortion of planning information.

Several authors [4; 7, pp. 237-40; 26; 36; 37; 53] have distinguished different types of planning systems and processes. Today most larger industrial companies have implemented two to three types of planning: liquidity and operations oriented short-term planning and budgeting, profit oriented middle-range or tactical planning, and profit potential oriented strategic planning [3; 18]. Finally, some firms have started to implement systems for survival and adaptability oriented strategic management [4]. These developments evolved in several steps over the last twenty years and reflect the changes in the external and internal environment of the firm, the state of the planning philosophy as well as technology, and the computer sciences.

These planning systems usually comprise all the three *bottom up, top down* and *ad hoc planning elements*. Normally the content, activities, and time schedules connected with these elements are formalized in a planning and controlling procedure. Different activities may call for alternative CSPS support.

3.1 Bottom Up

With bottom-up planning activities the information about strategies, action programs, and the continuing business are formulated by the operational units of a company. This is usually done on a regular basis, i.e., once a year or a quarter, in fixed form employing a large proportion of non-monetary information such as market share and volume of sales. The information is aggregated level by level and compared with controls until it reaches the top of the organizational hierarchy. During this process not only the degree of detail, but also the content of the information changes: with decreasing detail and proportional to the hierarchical level purely financial information becomes of increasing importance.

Bottom up activities may be supported by ready-made models, fixed block tailor-made models, and models employing a planning information base with analytical capabilities. It depends on the stability of the environment and organization whether the first two supply sufficient flexibility. Very often CSPMs that

148

only automate manual planning activitis have degenerated into bottom up report generators. This difficulty has been noted for some of the CIBA-GEIGY financial models in Table 1.

Historically bottom up activities created the "first generation" planning procedure of many firms between the mid-1950s and mid-1960s. They were originally supported by computer-based planning information systems which were mainly report and history oriented. Rigid file structures and commercial programming languages like COBOL or RPG were employed. At this stage the model support of the planning process was largely missing and consisted only of data aggregations, comparisons, and consolidations. Sometimes the operational units were supported by isolated planning aids, such as production planning and scheduling systems.

The missing information feedback and confrontation of alternative value systems, objectives, and plans across organizational levels of a firm as well as progresses in computer technology lead to the introduction of top down planning activities.

3.2 Top Down and Bottom Up

The bottom up reporting oriented procedure was complemented by a more specific top down procedure and activities as is indicated in Figure 2.

On the top management level, supported by staff functions, stylistic objectives and headquarter strategies [55; 36] are formulated. They are based on an environmental analysis and an analysis of strengths and weaknesses with respect to functional, product, and geographically oriented activities of the firm. A project oriented strategic planning process deals with particular business opportunities and dangers. The definition of business objectives, the environmental analysis and the strategic planning process create an information base which is explained to such organizational units as planning subsidiaries, divisions or functional groups (Figure 2). Quantitative objectives like ROI, ROA, EPS, debt/equity ratios and productivity figures are defined and negotiated. Often the use of index performance ratios is institutionalized [52; 43; 34]. This input is used by the divisions, subsidiaries, and functional groups for a middle-term planning process which consists of decomposed planning activities. The result is fed back to the top by a stage-by-stage bottom up process. It is centrally aggregated and consolidated. The results are used as a basis for discussions and more accurate negotiations about middle-term financial, production, and marketing objectives. The information and consensus thus generated is then fed into a short-term planning and budgeting process. It is carried out on the lower operational levels, but is again centrally consolidated and approved. Both the information generated by the middle-term and short-term planning process is employed for control purposes and to trigger corrective actions by the upper organizational levels.

Compared to the purely bottom up systems the combined approach possesses definite advantages: it is more problem and task oriented. Because of its feedback nature the assumptions, goals and objectives of adjacent organizational units are

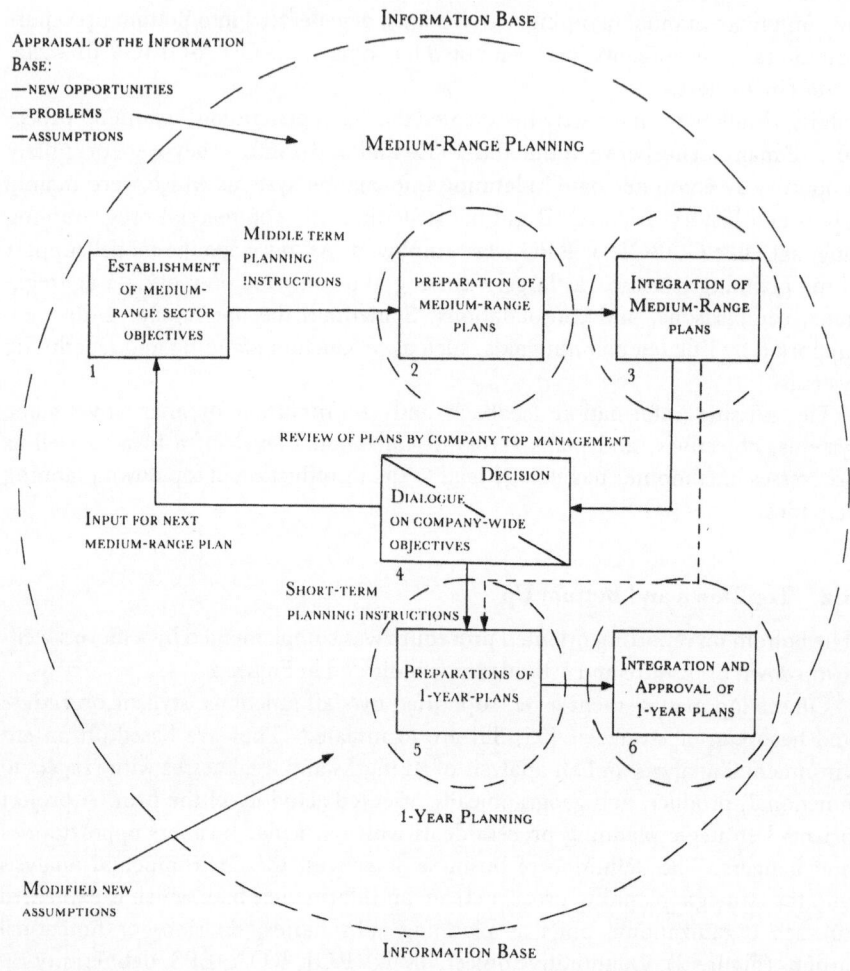

INFORMATION BASE

APPRAISAL OF THE INFORMATION
BASE:
—NEW OPPORTUNITIES
—PROBLEMS
—ASSUMPTIONS

MEDIUM-RANGE PLANNING

MIDDLE TERM
PLANNING
INSTRUCTIONS

| ESTABLISHMENT OF MEDIUM-RANGE SECTOR OBJECTIVES 1 | PREPARATION OF MEDIUM-RANGE PLANS 2 | INTEGRATION OF MEDIUM-RANGE PLANS 3 |

REVIEW OF PLANS BY COMPANY TOP MANAGEMENT

DECISION
DIALOGUE ON COMPANY-WIDE OBJECTIVES
4

INPUT FOR NEXT
MEDIUM-RANGE PLAN

SHORT-TERM
PLANNING INSTRUCTIONS

| PREPARATIONS OF 1-YEAR-PLANS 5 | INTEGRATION AND APPROVAL OF 1-YEAR PLANS 6 |

1-YEAR PLANNING

MODIFIED NEW
ASSUMPTIONS

INFORMATION BASE

Figure 2. Combination of top down and bottom up planning activities

150

·confronted with each other. Sikora notes that "... corporate planning may be conceived as a game for which the formalized planning procedure defines the rules" [49, p. 284, author's translation]. The planning dialogue thus reduces the distortion of planning information, increases opportunities for participation and gives more responsibility and motivation to the planners at different levels. While bottom up systems were report oriented, top down/bottom up or second generation systems are conceptually more dialogue and decision oriented.

It seems as if most corporate models known today support especially the middle-range and short-range planning activities encircled in Figure 2 [22; 42]. The reduction of clerical work so achieved and the possibilities of calculating alternative plans and scenarios in a shorter time represent substantial progress and allow the approximate evaluation·of alternative states of uncertainty and management decisions.

Not only changes in planning philosophy, but also the progress in the computer sciences has made these developments possible. Planning file structures and database management systems have become more flexible. The development of general purpose programming languages like PL/I or special purpose CSPSs facilitated the design and use of more scientifically oriented planning tools.

Notably systems for ad hoc planning purposes and planning data-bases with analytical capabilities enabled planning personnel to participate more directly in the model building process.

Several disadvantages connected with the use of the combined systems described above were identified more recently: they are often criticized for generating too detailed planning information at too high costs. Some critics argue that planners in different organizational units are absorbed too much by the collection and processing of routine information as is needed for input to the middle-range and short-range planning process [4; 53]. Since calendar deadlines have to be met, they often have not enough time to deal with planning problems met in the areas of strategic management and planning. The response to environmental changes and turbulences is too slow for certain markets, firms and organizational units. In addition the potential to support the strategic management and planning process, and also the dialogue phase of the middle-range planning process is by far not exploited.

As a consequence some firms are currently attempting to increase the flexibility and content of manual and computer-assisted planning activities. Additional formalized but ad hoc activities are introduced to cope with the flexibility problem. This already has or will create additional design requirements for the supporting CSPSs.

3.3 Ad Hoc

The further developed planning systems still incorporate a middle-range and short-range planning process which contains the activities shown in Figure 2. They are still performed on a regular basis, but in contrast to first and second generation systems there is a tendency to decentralize, call for less detail, and frequently adapt the formulation of planning requirements. As a consequence, the amount and type of planning information to be collected may vary strongly between different organizational units and from planning cycle to planning cycle.

The ideal of such a "third generation system" is a continuously ongoing and adaptive planning process [1]. The results of the middle-range and short-range planning process may be conceived of as snapshots from it. Planning units are expected to maintain permanently updated information bases. They contain not only expected plans, but also optimistic, pessimistic, and contingency plans.

The middle-range and short-range planning processes again obtain their input from an ad hoc and strategic planning process. This process tends to be irregular, of varying content, and both project and task oriented. It incorporates an environmental analysis, strategic management to plan the organizational adaptation of the firm to a changing environment, and typically a business portfolio planning process [27; 28].

Planning teams for the strategic and ad hoc planning process have more often something like a matrix structure, instead of the strictly hierarchical compositions of functional or divisional planning teams observed for bottom up and top down activities. This tends to simultaneously involve planners who define and set objectives and targets, people who are responsible for their operational achievement and others who directly perform project work. The increased participation of several hierarchical, organizational and functional levels in the planning process is supposed to further decrease the distortion of planning information. Several companies discuss systems of financial incentives to be tied to performance measures in order to avoid the famous "hockey stick effect" of extrapolative planning. Others plan and introduce new organizational structures. A company like Texas Instruments has institutionalized dual organizational structures. One structure is operation oriented, the other is planning oriented and for example distinguishes the levels of goal setting, objectives formulation, strategic and tactical planning [34[. Planning for both structures is computer-assisted. One may expect the evolution of still other organizational structures.

3.4 Computer Support of Third Generation Systems

CSPMs have to support the regular bottom up or top down activities mainly in the planning activities which are encircled in Figure 2. Both models and the supporting CSPSs should fulfil the following requirements:

—The data-base and the model structures must posses different levels of aggregation and hierarchical structures which are a picture of the true operationally and planning oriented organizational structures. It should be possible to flexibly choose and change the level of detail according to the planning task and the wishes of the user.

—It should be possible to decentralize both the data-base and model structures. Users on different organizational levels should be enabled to use models and data (e.g., local or consolidated) which they are authorized to employ for their planning. This may fulfil information needs of planners and speed up the dialogue and negotiation phase of the planning process.

—The models should supply an automatic interface between different organizational levels. The structure of the interface should allow for bottom up calculations, disaggregations for target definitions, and top down calculations.

—The language and software of the CSPS should permit and facilitate the formulation of models which may either run in "What If"/bottom up mode or "What to do to Achieve"/top down mode.

—The dialogue and negotiation phase of the planning process should on request be supported by dialogue programs which as a minimum allow for easy mutations, editing, and retrieval of planning data,

—The supporting corporate simulation and planning system (CSPS) should incorporate the means to easily deal with large numbers of tabular data, e.g., balances, profit and loss statements, financial key figures, sales, and production reports. It should be possible to efficiently treat tree-structures of tabular data as are typically encountered with hierarchical organizational structures.

Additional requirements have to be fulfilled for the support of strategic and ad hoc planning activities:

—It must be possible to quickly assemble, change, and delete models that describe the aspects of a certain strategy, project, or environmental scenario.

—The system must possess integration capabilities. It must be possible to easily link models to environmental data-bases or to specify assumptions about the development of a company's environment. A user should also be able to combine the model based ad hoc planning process with regular middle-range and short-range planning process in order to show an overall picture, and the influence which certain projects or developments have on an organizational unit or the company as a whole.

—The system must be "user-oriented". Ad hoc planning teams will be composed of members from several organizational units and hierarchical levels. This calls for modeling systems which support or guide users with different backgrounds, i.e., users not having a background in quantitative methods and data processing, and also modellers who want to do statistical analysis, forecasting or even resource allocation using management science techniques.

The requirements formulated above are not easy to fulfil by a single CSPS. However, what has been described as a planning information system with analytical capabilities comes closest to the ideal. So far these CSPSs are centralized systems. Although this solution may be technically and intellectually very appealing, practical reasons, such as costs, security, availability, and manageability often speak against it. As a consequence many firms use several of the CSPSs described simulteneously.

Developments of the computer sciences will also in the future have a strong impact on planning technology and CSPS design. The storage and processing costs connected with a model of any type will continue to sharply decrease. Computer and telecommunication networks, intelligent terminals, and front-end computers allow a better support of the planning dialogue as well as decentralized and distributed modeling efforts. The future will probably bring the development of CSPSs for this purpose. The demand for external information and macro-models has caused a number of private firms to offer support. The problem with such services is not their technical linkage to CSPMs, but their organizational implementation [32], the definition of an interface between internal and external models as well as between in-house and out-of-house modeling activities. Some firms construct their CSPMs out-of-house using one of the available communication and computer networks, others buy external information and forecasts on tape or use terminals to load such information directly into their in-house CSPS. Still other firms start to construct in-house strategic and competitive data-bases [35]. These developments will continue in the future.

While technical support of third generation systems does not seem to be the constraining factor on further developments and implementation, the modeling side is likely to be more difficult [38, pp. 18-22; 53, p. 453]. At the present state of the art it is not entirely clear how far the support of planning activities by formalized models and the computer may go. Rosenkranz [46] has tried to describe possibilities for CSPS support for some twenty different planning activities [10; 11; 38]. While the potential in the area of short and middle-range planning is rather obvious, the support of activities in the area of strategic planning and management by other than data inquiry, retrieval and edition is difficult to assess. One may in principle design interactive strategic planning systems which supply adaptive guidance tailored to the qualification of the user and the complexity of the planning or modeling task. But the development of such systems will not be general enough before the contents of these activities are better classified, structured, and formalized. In addition, one has to take into consideration that planning tasks may remain unique, ill-structured and dynamic. A third generation planning system is intended "to learn" and to adapt to new requirements. To a certain extent this counteracts the possibilities of model integration for different types of planning and alternative organizational units. Although one might be able to deduce the properties of models which may be used under these circumstances, not much is known yet about the adaptation and integration problem.

4 PERSONAL AND BEHAVIOURAL ASPECTS

A number of surveys and reports indicate that CSPMs are often used on a rather high management level [42; 22, pp. 139-53]. Research on the implementation of management science and operations research models in general is still in its initial phase. Although there is no doubt that a large number of non-technical factors are responsible for the success or failure of a model, it is yet not possible to state the nature and relative importance of these factors. Since implementation research itself influences the type of model to be selected and the implementation strategy to be adopted, it will always be difficult to make such statements in this dynamic environment. Nevertheless, all surveys and reports agree that top management

154

support is a very important organizational and, concerning the work undertaken by project teams, also decisive behavioural factor. Among other factors this may explain the relatively high acceptance especially financial CSPMs have found compared to other types of management science models.

The survey undertaken by Grinyer and Wooller [22, p. 17] indicates that corporate modeling project work is mainly carried out by operations researchers, accountants, and financial analysts, as well as data processing personnel. Such team members are organizationally very often within the control and finance department of a company and two to four organizational levels below the user or sponsor level.

4.1 Team Structure and Software Choice

In such a team structure users and model builders tend to have a different age, educational background, objectives, cognitive characteristics, and value systems. Hall notes that "... plans are developed by managers who are responsible for performing multiple tasks under continuous time pressure. In this situation there is a limited ability or incentive to explore in detail the consequences of a range of alternative decisions or the consequences of a range of alternative future environments" [24, p. 34]. In addition a number of authors have noted top managements dislike of formal planning activities and preference for mental models [41, p. 107; 54].

Due to their organizational status and their background the situation of the model builders in the OR/MS area is different. Hall sees the following factors endangering especially the implementation of strategic planning models: "... because of their isolation, modellers fail to capture many important facets of the strategy formulation process in their model.... Those facets generally missed are the qualitative, skill and politically oriented factors which dominate the actual strategy formulation process within all firms. ... The modellers view their tasks as one of 'getting something running', since they will be evaluated on the basis of this 'end' product. The result is a model—often mathematically sophisticated— which is inadequate and is consequently unutilized by general managers in their decision analysis" [24, p. 38].

More recent research and our own experience [46] have shown that the ideal of bringing the top executive directly to the computers, an information system, or model has so far only in rare instances been achieved [2; 39]. Typically top executives or users have problems which they describe to staff personnel who then work together with the model builders on the description and solution. Functionally either the staff members or the model builders play the role of so-called "chauffeurs" or intermediaries: they perform the model runs and supply them to the user. At the same time they are "exegists, confidents, crusaders, and teachers" [33, p. 11].

Practitioners have found that especially the team combination of an analytically thinking *planning diplomat* or intermediary, e.g., a younger executive or staff member having the potential to reach the presidential level within, say, five years, and

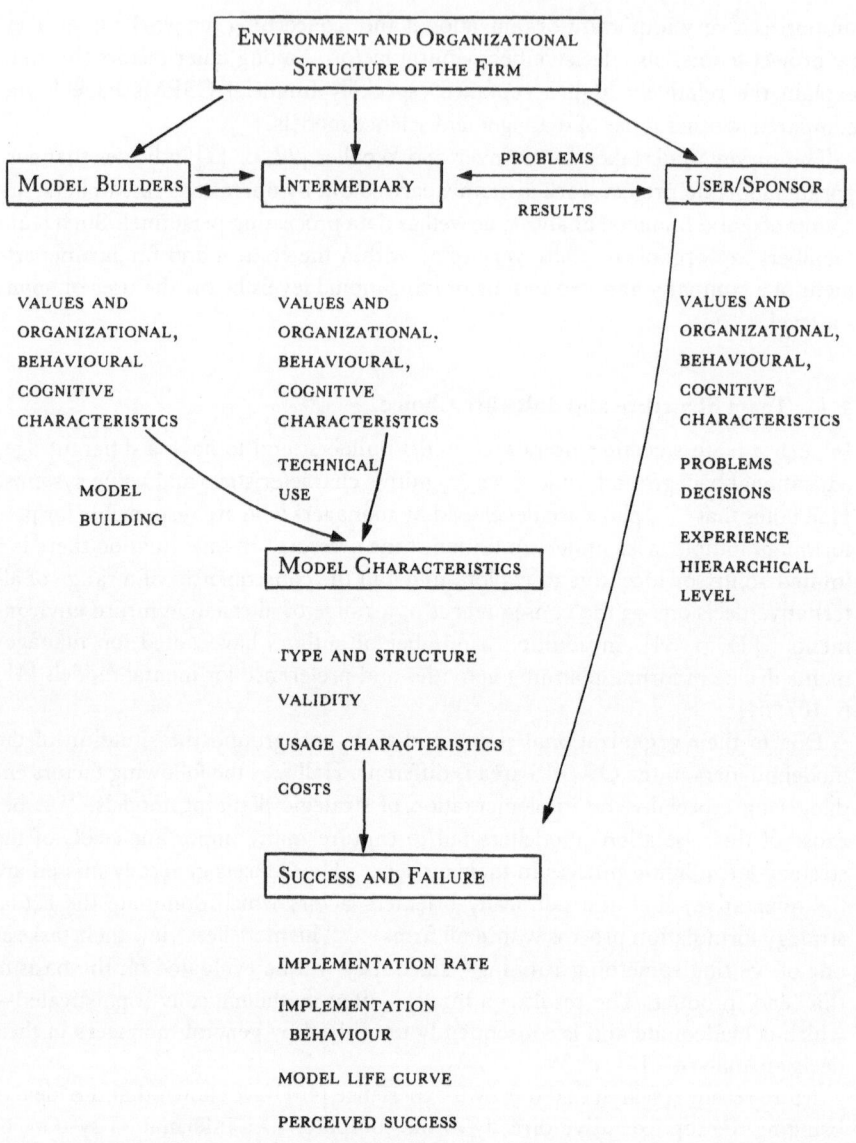

Figure 3. Factors and relations influencing success of model

the *hungry analyst*, i.e., a quantitatively educated economist/management scientist who at the same time is a risk taker and eager for recognition of his technical skills and professional work, are a strong success indicator for CSPMs. Figure 3 visualizes how these relations may influence the type of model to be built and its implementation and success. Further relations must often be considered if external consultants play the role of "pioneers", agents of change, and model builders in a corporate modeling team.

In any case, the structure shown incorporates a number of so-called "manager-model" interface problems:

—Goals, objectives, and problems of the end-user have to be understood by the model builders and intermediaries.

—The structure, limitations, and results of a model must be explained to the end-user [14].

Although the choice and design of a CSPS affects these problems, its importance should not be overestimated: with the exception of financing decisions and on-line screen presentations for curious executives the choice and design of a CSPS is not a question of top management concern. Apart from economic and technical considerations it is mainly determined by the cognitive characteristics, education, and function of model builders or intermediaries. Experience suggests that technically very different solutions may be implemented successfully, examples being:

—an APL based financial CSPM programmed by a mathematician, the results being interpreted by an economist,

—an entirely PL/I programmed model using a traditional financial information system and fast batch operation,

—a financial CSPM programmed by the economist/intermediary himself using one of the available CSPSs.

4.2 Market Interpretation of Software Choice

It should be noted that a competitive situation within a firm may influence the choice or design of a CSPS.

In many cases the user/sponsor may be viewed as a monopolist asking for planning information and offering time, recognition, and career advancement opportunities. On the supply side there will not be much competition, if both intermediaries and model builders are the client's direct subordinates. In this case the latter will probably exhibit a tendency to decide as short-term cost and time minimizers with given user requirements. However, also internal staff personnel, an OR/MS group in another department, or an external consultant may compete for a contract. The choice of software will quite likely be connected to the expected payoffs: an OR/MS group will not try to eliminate itself, but in time to become a supply-monopolist. Finally, the consultant will try to maximize a weighted sum of material and immaterial rewards often including the circumvention of internal OR/MS groups and the purchase or lease of his CSPS. Advertisements which have been published more recently clearly support this observation of market competition and price formation.

4.3 Dynamics and Relations

Bean, et al. have argued that implementation and success of OR/MS projects should also be viewed as a dynamic phenomenon depending on the life cycle of the OR/MS activities or the model builder function within the firm [5, pp. 80-81]. They distinguish the stages of prebirth, the missionary stage, the stages of organizational development and deprofessionalization, the reprofessionalization stage, and, finally, the stages of maturity and diffusion. A generalization of their taxonomy would include other developments as well.

A first example are stages due to intermediary/planning diplomat promotion. Whereas he might be model and methodology oriented at the beginning of a corporate modeling project, he might end up being purely output oriented after his promotion. This may influence the type of acceptance and model development. In addition one should realize that like any product a CSPM possesses a life cycle from market introduction to technical obsolescence. OR/MS and the intermediaries may develop alternative strategies to manage the model over its life cycle. The software choice may be part of a penetration, development, or diversification strategy. Last, but not least, it should be considered that the variety of planning software available to support CSPM design and implementation has greatly increased over the last ten years.

Figure 4 shows these developments (the hard and software developments being viewed cumulatively), and by sliding the time axes shown against each other one may obtain quite different constellations and choices of software. For example, during the missionary stage of the model builders there might be a preference for totally integrated CSPMs and their own software development. This would not conflict with a result and output oriented intermediary if modeling results are obtained quickly enough (which historically was very often not the case). Alternatively, the model builders might decide on the lease or purchase of a simple on-line package for ad hoc applications if they are in the stage of organizational development and the intermediary does not threaten to usurp the model formulation and coding. There are a great number of other constellations and it does not seem to be possible to predict a unique trend of team functioning or software choice.

5 CONCLUSIONS

Empirical evidence shows that CSPSs may be used for the construction and use of corporate simulation and planning models. CSPSs involve the user or his intermediary more directly in the modeling process. Because of their special purpose design they are also economically interesting for more technically oriented model builders.

Planning systems existing today consist of bottom up, top down and ad hoc elements. While the planning activities contained in the first two groups may partially be automated and supported by corporate models, the potential of CSPSs for the support of their integrated use during the dialogue phases of the planning process is as yet largely unexploited. The same is true for the strategic planning ac-

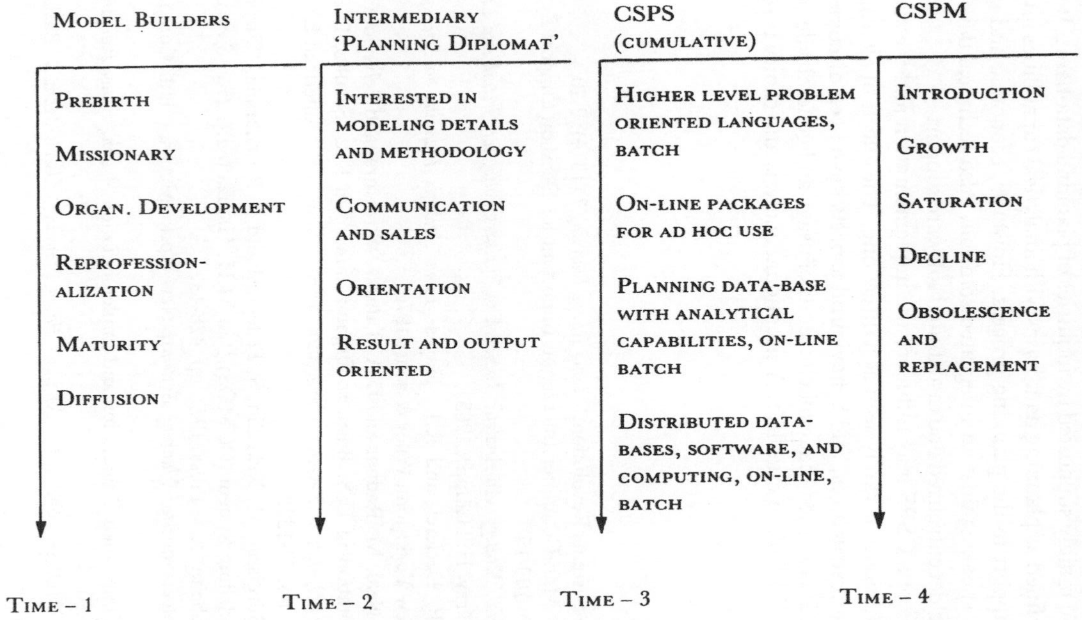

Figure 4. Corporate modeling life cycles

MODEL BUILDERS	INTERMEDIARY 'PLANNING DIPLOMAT'	CSPS (CUMULATIVE)	CSPM
PREBIRTH	INTERESTED IN MODELING DETAILS AND METHODOLOGY	HIGHER LEVEL PROBLEM ORIENTED LANGUAGES, BATCH	INTRODUCTION
MISSIONARY	COMMUNICATION AND SALES	ON-LINE PACKAGES FOR AD HOC USE	GROWTH
ORGAN. DEVELOPMENT	ORIENTATION	PLANNING DATA-BASE WITH ANALYTICAL CAPABILITIES, ON-LINE BATCH	SATURATION
REPROFESSIONALIZATION	RESULT AND OUTPUT ORIENTED	DISTRIBUTED DATA-BASES, SOFTWARE, AND COMPUTING, ON-LINE, BATCH	DECLINE
MATURITY			OBSOLESCENCE AND REPLACEMENT
DIFFUSION			

TIME – 1 TIME – 2 TIME – 3 TIME – 4

tivities which so far are mainly supported by inquiries of planning data-bases. It is argued that CSPSs defined as planning data-bases with analytical capabilities give the best integrated support to the planning process. However, economic and situational factors may speak against an integrated solution. Also technical developments may lead to a decentralized and distributed software support.

Although the choice of a CSPS may influence the implementation and the success of CSPMs, this influence is rarely seen as a direct one. The effects of alternative organizations, team structures, and behavioural aspects have been discussed in a dynamic context. It is argued that explicit trends of usage and general rules of software decisions are difficult to establish. A situational analysis and choice is recommended.

REFERENCES

1. Ackoff, R.L. "The Systems Revolution." *Long Range Planning* 7 (1974): 2-20.

2. Alter, St. "Why is Man-Computer Interaction Important for Decision Support Systems." *Interfaces* 7 (1977): 109-15.

3. Ansoff, H.I. *Corporate Strategy: An Analytic Approach to Business Policy for Growth and Expansion.* New York: McGraw Hill Comp., 1965.

4. Ansoff, H.I., R.P. Declerck and R.L. Hayes. *From Strategic Planning to Strategic Management.* London, New York: John Wiley & Sons, 1976.

5. Bean, A.S., R.D. Neal, M. Radnor and D.A. Tansik. "Structural and Behavioural Correlates of Implementation in U.S. Business Organizations." in R.L. Schultz, D.P. Slevin (eds.) *Implementing Operations Research/Management Science.* New York: American Elsevier Publ. Comp., 1975, pp. 77-132.

6. Boissaye, E., R. Bürgisser, H. Kränzlin, S. Pellegrini and F. Rosenkranz. "Structure of a Corporate Modelling System (COMOS)." in M.H. Hamza (ed.). *Proc. Sympos. SIMULATION '77.* Anaheim: Acta Press, 1977, pp. 428-432.

7. Boulden, J.B. *Computer-assisted Planning Systems.* New York: McGraw Hill Comp., 1975.

8. Chandler, W.J. "Plans, their Preparation and Implementation." *Long Range Planning* 11 (December 1978): 14-20.

9. CIBA-GEIGY, *COMOS—A System for Computer Based Planning, User's Manual.* Basle, January 1978.

10. Cohen, K.L. and R.M. Cyert. "Strategy: Formulation, Implementation, and Monitoring." *Journal of Business* 46 (1973): 349-67.

11. Cohen, K.L. "The Bank Strategic Planning Process and the Use of Management Science Models." in Th.H. Naylor (ed.) *The Politics of Corporate Planning and Modelling.* Oxford (Ohio): Planning Executives Institute, 1977, pp. VIII, 1-31.

12. Control Data Corp. *CALL/370: PROPHIT II Reference Manual.* Form No. 65-2640, San Diego: Service Bureau Company, 1974.

13. Davis, B.E., G.J. Caccapolo and M.A. Chaudry. "Economic Planning Model for American Telegraph Company." *The Bell Journal of Economics and Management Science* 4 (1973): 29-56.

14. Doktor, R.H. and W.F. Hamilton. "Cognitive Style and the Acceptance of Management Science Recommendations." *Management Science* 19 (1973): 884-94.

15. Dynamics Ass. *XSIM a Reference Manual*. Cambridge, Mass., January 1977.

16. Esprester, A.C. "Die Entwicklung einer Methodenbank und einer Methodenbank-sprache." *Angewandte Informatik—Applied Informatics* 20 (1978): 203-06.

17. Execucom. *Interactice Financial Planning System User's Manual*. Austin, Texas: Execucom Systems Corporation, 1976.

18. Gälweiler, A. "Unternehmenssicherung und strategische Planung." *Schmalenbachs Zeitschrift für betriebswirtschaftliche Forschung* 8 (June 1976): 362-79.

19. Goldie, J.H. "Simulation and Irritation." in A.N. Schrieber (ed.) *Corporate Simulation Models*. Seattle: University of Washington Press, 1970, special Appendix.

20. Gössler, R. *Operations Research-Praxis*. Wiesbaden: Gabler Verlag, 1974.

21. Graham, D.A. "Congruent Planning and Organization Systems in a Multi-Industry Corporation. Case Study: R.J. Reynolds Industries, Inc." in Th. H. Naylor (ed.) *The Politics of Corporate Planning and Modelling*. Oxford (Ohio): Planning Executives Institute, 1977, pp. XIV-1-16.

22. Grinyer, P.H. and J. Wooller. *Corporate Models Today*. The Institute of Chartered Accountants in England and Wales, Moorgate Place, London EC2R 6EQ, 1975.

23. Grinyer, P.H., J. Wooller and Ch. D. Batt. "Some Tentative Findings on Corporate Financial Simulation Models." *Operational Research Quarterly* 25 (1974): 149-67.

24. Hall, W.K. "Strategic Planning Models: Are Top Managers Really Finding them Useful?" *Journal of Business Policy* 3 (1973): 33-42.

25. Hamilton, W.F. and M.A. Moses. "A Computer-Based Corporate Planning System." *Management Science* 21 (October 1974): 148-59.

26. Hayes, R.H. and R.L. Nolan, "What Kind of Corporate Modeling Functions Best." *Harvard Business Review* (May-June 1974).

27. Henderson, B.D. *Construction of a Business Strategy*. Series on Corporate Strategy, Boston: The Boston Consulting Group, 1971.

28. Hinterhuber, H.H. *Strategische Unternehmensführung*. Berlin, New York: De Gruyter, 1977.

29. Holloway, C., G.T. Jones. "Planning at Gulf—a Case Study." *Long Range Planning* (April 1975): 27-45.

30. IBM (UK) Ltd. "Applications System—Modelling." *Users Guide London*, June 1975.

31. IBM (France) Ltd. "System 370 Planning, Control and Decision Evaluation System (PLANCODE/S)." *OS/VS Program Reference Manual*. IBM France, July 1975.

32. Keegan, W.J. "Multinational Scanning: A Study of Information Sources Utilized by Headquarters Executives in Multinational Companies." *Administr. Science Quarterly* 19 (1974): 411-21.

33. Keen, P.G.W. " 'Interactive' Computer Systems for Managers: A Modest Proposal." *Sloan Management Review* (Fall 1976): 1-17.

34. Knight, C. "Business Planning at Texas Instruments." presentation given at the IBM Education Center Europe, "AMF Advanced Management and Financial Applications." La Hulpe (Belgium), October 17-19, 1977.

35. King, W.R. and D.I. Cleland. "Information for More Effective Strategic Planning." *Long Range Planning* (February 1977): 59-64.

36. Lorange, P. and R.F. Vancil. "How to Design a Strategic Planning System." *Harvard Business Review* (September-October 1976): 75-81.

37. Lorange, P. "A Framework for Strategic Planning in Multinational Corporations." *Long Range Planning* 9 (June 1976): 30-37.

38. Lorange, P. and J.F. Rockart. "A Framework for the Use of Computer-Based Models in the Planning Process." Working Paper WP 860-76, Alfred P. Sloan School of Management, Cambridge, Mass., June 1976.

39. Meador, Ch.L. and D.N. Ness. "Decision Support Systems: An Application to Corporate Planning." *Sloan Management Review* (Winter 1974): 51-68.

40. Mertens, P., W. Neuwirth and W. Schmitt. "Verknüpfung von Daten- und Methodenbanken, dargestellt am Beispiel der Analyse von Marktforschungsdaten." in H.D. Plötzeneder (ed.) *Computer Assisted Corporate Planning,* Lectures and Tutorials, Vol. 1. Stuttgart, Chicago: Science Research Ass./Munich: R. Oldenbourg, 1977, pp. 291-331.

41. Mintzberg, H. "Managerial Work: An Analysis from Observation." *Management Science* 18 (October 1971): B97-B110.

42. Naylor, Th.H. and H. Schauland. "A Survey of Users of Corporate Planning Models." *Management Science* 22 (1976): 927-36.

43. Reichmann, Th. and L. Lachnit. "Planung, Steuerung und Kontrolle mit Hilfe von Kennzahlen." *Schmalenbachs Zeitschrift für betriebswirtschaflichte Forschung* 28 (1976): 705-23.

44. Rosenkranz, F. and S. Pellegrini. "Corporate Modelling: Methodology and Computer-Based Model Design Procedure." *Applied Informatics—Angewandte Informatik* 18 (1976): 259-67.

45. Rosenkranz, F. "Status and Future Use of Corporate Planning and Simulation Models: Case Studies and Conclusions." in H.D. Plötzeneder (ed.) *Computer Assisted Corporate Planning,* Lectures and Tutorials, Vol. 1. Stuttgart, Chicago: Science Research Ass./ Munich: R. Oldenbourg, 1977, pp. 143-79.

46. Rosenkranz, F. *An Introduction to Corporate Modelling.* Durham, N.C.: Duke University Press, 1979.

47. Schober, F. "Interactive Simulation Models in Planning." in A. Blaser and C. Hackl (eds.) *Interactive Systems.* Lecture Notes in Computer Science, Vol. 49. Berlin, Heidelberg, New York: Springer Verlag, pp. 341-60.

48. Schultz, R.L. and D.P. Slevin. *Implementing Operations Research/Management Science.* New York: American Elsevier Publ. Comp., 1975.

49. Sikora, K. "Systemkonzeption für die computergestützte Unternehmungsplanung in der zusammensetzenden Industrie." *Die Betriebswirtschaft* 37 (1977): 283-97.

50. Social Systems Inc. *SIMPLAN—Command Descriptions.* Chapel Hill, N.C., June 1976.

51. Springer, C.H. "Strategic Management in General Electric." Presentation Operations Research Society of America, Milwaukee, Wisconsin, 9 May 1973.

52. Staehle, W.H. *Kennzahlen und Kennzahlensysteme als Mittel der Organisation und Führung von Unternehmen.* Wiesbaden: Verlag Th. Gabler, 1969.

53. Szyperski, N., K. Sikora and J. Wondracek. "Entwicklungstendenzen computergestützter Unternehmungsplanung. in H.D. Plötzeneder (ed.) *Computer Assisted Corporate Planning,* SRA Lecturs and Tutorials. Stuttgart, Chicago: Science Research Ass./Munich: R. Oldenbourg, 1977, pp. 453-93.

54. Taylor, R.N. "Psychological Aspects of Planning." *Long Range Planning* (April 1976): 66-74.

55. Vancil, R.F. "Strategy Formulation in Complex Organizations." *Sloan Management Review* (Winter 1976): 1-17.

162

11. An Information System on Planning Models: A General Concept

by Wolfgang Schuler

1 OBJECTIVES, NECESSITY, GOALS

For the purpose of planning, design, operation and further development appropriate formalized models are necessary and have been designed.* The number of formalized models which have been designed to support the planning process is steadily growing as becomes obvious by a brief glance in OR-Abstracts of journals and other sources [1; 7, p. 235]. Unfortunately, most of these models are, however, seldom applied although they were originally designed for practical use and not for theoretical purposes [6].

This dilemma can be explained, among other things, by information problems about the models indicating the *necessity* of a special information system:

—Lacking transparency for the great number of models offered; only a small number of surveys, synopses and registers are available.

—Access to these documents is very difficult; therefore the acquisition of literature is troublesome.

—Models are described in an incomplete, inconsistent and biased form and mostly appear in various (different) sources; descriptions are of different standards and too extensive in depth and volume.

—Descriptions lack consistent terminology and clearness.

—There is no judgement or evaluation of the models since the number of institutions dealing with these aspects is too small and in most cases the criteria necessary are not available. Methodological or other theoretical aspects of models are not considered adequately; for planning models, see [2; 3; 4].

—There is no uniform systematic scheme for the description of models which could reflect their essential characteristics and thus support their comparison and their evaluation.

—The exchange of information and experience among designers and users of models is insufficient.

Any information system on formalized models should contribute to avoiding the difficulties described above. In order to achieve this aim the following *objectives* should be considered:

—standardized description of the models concerning content and methodology,

---

* See also the contributions of F. Rosenkranz, T. Tilemann and R.J. Welke in this volume.

—a systematic recording of models at present available or in the course of development,

—information on concrete application of models, comments and judgements,

—a presentation of different models for one problem that facilitates their comparison,

—the indication of links and networking possibilities with other models,

—reference to appropriate models for certain problems, to exhaustive literature on each model with access possibilities, and to current research activities for models,

—referral to experts and institutions dealing with models, who are able to give sufficient information,

—compilation of central catalogues and periodical surveys on models, of lists, surveys or synopses on models in any form.

If these objectives were fulfilled they could be particularly useful for achieving the following *benefits*:

—reducing search efforts and preparation of data by eliminating all redundant information,

—supporting a standardized presentation of models,

—avoiding duplicate work in the design of models,

—presenting a survey on the models offered, on the state of the art of modelling techniques, aids for the use of models and for the comparison with models,

—the propagation and announcement of models and their designer respectively users,

—setting up direct information channels between designers and users of models,

—revealing deficiencies; for instance, the lack of models on certain issues or the insufficiency of models and methods available. The findings could be helpful for current research on models,

—the provision with and selection of models according to problem areas. It could be necessary, for instance, in extremely important cases, to sort out models with computer programmes already operating, in order to incorporate them in a model bank.

2 PROBLEMATIC NATURE OF MODELS: DEFINITION, PROCESS OF MODEL DESIGN

The core of an information system on models is a file containing the data on models. For the acquisition of models and as a basis for their evaluation it is necessary to have an appropriate framework, the characteristics of which allow the descriptions of the models. The essential characteristics which have to be considered in describing a model partially result from the concept of the model and the process of model design. I will try to give a brief summary of these aspects.

We set out from the idea of the broadest possible definition of a model M as representation of a real, material or imaginary system or process (model object, original O): an object M (object, material or imaginary system, process) is considered as a model if there are any analogies between M and an other object O which allow certain conclusions with regard to O.

The model is, however, not a complete representation but reflects certain aspects of the system which are selected according to the purpose and objectives the model is designed for. The model design process always leads to an abstraction from the inessential system characteristics, i.e., to a reduction of complexity. Aspects which are to be considered in the model are selected according to the interpretation of those persons participating in the model design (model subject). These subjective components, which from the beginning are attached to the model, determine, among other things, the limits of its applicability. From the view of cybernetics, the *general model concept* can be regarded according to Klaus as a three digit relation between subject S, object O, and model M. Consequently, it is not possible to simply talk of the model, but a model is always determined by its relations with the object of which it is a model and with the subject for whom it is a model [9, p. 143; 7, p. 158].

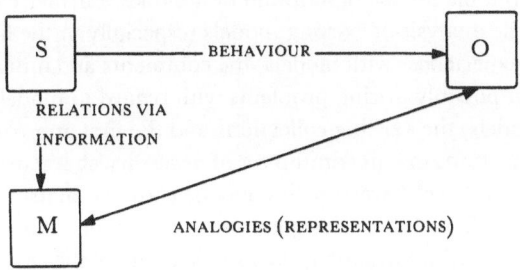

Figure 1. Cybernetic Model Relations [9].

Between subject S and model M there are relations via information which influence the S's behaviour towards the original O. What kind of information S gets (resp. wants to get) from the model depends upon S's aim and the intent of his behaviour towards O. Evaluation and application of a model thus depends essentially upon the relationships between S and M and between S and O. In the case of an information system on models, a model is generally conceived of as an aid for reproducing existing or imaginary objects. It serves to enlarge someone's knowledge and to present relations between cause and effect; dependencies which usually occur in reality are represented by a network of variables, if possible.

Other model characteristics result directly from the *process of model design* which, according to Brewer, can be subdivided into four steps [1, p. 18; 3]:
—definition of the problem, the intent, and objectives
—structural specification (structure of model),
—data acquisition and technical implementation of the model,
—validation.

165

The next steps are the application of the model and the interpretation of the results gained. These two steps are particularly important since the usefulness of a model is revealed only in the course of application. Those models especially designed for solving practical problems must be considered useless if they fail to be applied or turn out to be inappropriate. The results obtained by the model are in the course of their interpretation referred to the original real system represented by the model. The definition of the problem as well as the interpretation of the results are determined by the attitude and the objectives of the model subject (i.e., model designer, orderer of the model).

During the structural specification the most important variables and processes, the appropriate structure to represent the processes, and the kind of structure of relations among the variables and among the model components are determined.*

3 DESCRIPTIVE CHARACTERISTICS OF MODELS

The roughly indicated model qualities already determine the significant model characteristics to be used in a file for the description of a model. Further characteristics were obtained by the analysis of existing models (especially in the field of environmental planning), experiences with models, the comments and hints from experts, the examination of possibly arising problems with regard to models, the analysis of literature on models, the existing collections and the first approach towads a model typology. This leads to a maximum set of necessary characteristics, laid down in a list from which those characteristics may be chosen that are able to satisfy requirements of a specific file to be designed. Selective criteria, therefore, are the availability of the required information, the practicability of the characteristics and the collecting effort. For any application the potential users of the system should participate in this selection. The characteristics are appropriate for the description of nearly any type of model [10], which means for formalized models, like mathematical ones, as well as for more qualitative or even verbal models. The models may belong to a single technical field or may be interdisciplinary, for instance as it is in the case of environment or planning. The practicability of the characteristics has been tested with environmental planning models and has been thoroughly discussed by experts. In a previous paper these characteristics were explained and described separately [15]. In order to use a consistent terminology it is necessary to keep a list of term definitions and to complete it constantly.

---

* Other problems are described in the paper of H. Müller-Merbach: "Towards a Modeling Methodology" in this volume.

Table 1. Descriptive Characteristics of Models

1. Generalities About the Model

1.1 name of the model
1.2 persons who developed the model (experts)
1.3 institution where the model was/is developed
1.4 status of the model (planned - in work - finished/tested - applied)
1.5 publications on the model
1.6 referral statements
    —similar model (i.e., sub-model, general model, improvement)
    —research and development project (concerning the model)

2. Model Classification

2.1 subject heading/class (list of subject classes)
2.2 keywords, descriptors and combinations of them (keyword list, descriptor list, thesaurus)
2.3 model type (open list, classification in five classes)
    —general formal types (representation)
    —mixed types (objective, structure)
    —subject-oriented types
    —specific types (of a discipline)
    —methodological types
2.4 state variable classification
    —static, dynamic
    —deterministic, stochastic
    —quantitative, qualitative
    —open, closed
    —concept-based, data-based
    —linear, nonlinear
    —stable, instable

3. Subject and Objectives of the Model

3.1 modelled issue resp. system
3.2 purpose and objectives of the model
3.3 application fields (functional, temporal, spatial)
3.4 abstract (short description)
3.5 further developments
3.6 comments

4. Model Structure

4.1 theory
4.2 assumptions, hypotheses
4.3 submodels and their connections (interactions)
4.4 functional relationships
4.5 variables and parameters
4.6 validity domains of the variables and parameters (time, space, other variables)

5. Modelling Techniques

5.1 mathematical instruments
5.2 methods and procedures
5.3 EDP-usage, technical auxiliary means

6. Data and Results

6.1 input-data
6.2 availability and gathering of data
6.3 output-data
6.4 results and their interpretation

7. Statements on Success and Evaluation

7.1 validation test of the model
   —criterium of validity
   —test method used
   —degree of test precision
   —test data used
   —situation and test conditions
   —test results and protocols
7.2 applications
   —cases of application
   —possibilities of application
7.3 judgements, comments and critics concerning the model and its evaluation
   (informal description or referral to literature)
7.4 efforts (time, costs, manpower)
   —for development
   —for operation

This list consists of seven groups of characteristics which can be subdivided in three fields according to their content and the collecting effort they require. For it is neither possible nor sensible to record all the characteristics of a model at one time. The available documents mostly lack part of the necessary information and, therefore, further search is unavoidable. For this reason, it is advisable to collect the characteristics of each field separately, that means to proceed in three steps:

1. The first field comprises formal statements which are strongly formatted and includes the two characteristics groups "generalities about the model" and "model classification". They fulfil the purpose of formal model identification, model classification and its retrieval by means of keywords and a systematical listing of subject headings. They also serve the referral to publications, R&D projects and similar models. For that purpose the available documents are mostly sufficient.

   This first collecting stage should be carried out without delay in order to create the basis for the following two steps of information collection. The result is a referral file for models as a basis file which can be supplemented by the third characteristics group, namely "subject and objectives of the model".

2.   The second field relates to statements concerning content and method and comprises the characteristics groups 3 - 6:
—subject and objectives of the models (i.e., short description)
—model structure (i.e., variables, equations)
—modelling techniques (i.e., methods, EDP)
—data and results (input and output data)

These statements are less formatted and can often be written in full text. This applies particularly to the third characteristics group concerning subject and objectives, in which the model is described substantially and phenomenologically without having to use a specific model terminology; this description should be understandable even for users who are not model experts; whereas the methodological statements on model structure, modelling techniques as well as data and results are strongly subject-oriented. Both the substantial and methodological statements are difficult to ascertain and need further searching and inquiries. For this reason, special knowledge is necessary which only experts have. At this step it is absolutely essential to carry out a more profound and thorough evaluation of all documents available and to collaborate with the model designers.

3.   Characteristics group 7, "statements on success and evaluation" forms the third field. These statements enable the recording of users' and experts' experience with the model and, moreover, the description of and references to the results of validation tests and effort.
    The statements mainly refer to applications, comments and expert opinions. In contrast to the characteristics of the two previous fields, they cannot be recorded in one single step, but have to be collected and registered in the course of the operation of the data file. This requires a permanent exchange of information between file managers and model experts.
    The statements, however, help to evaluate a model. For it is important to know if and under what conditions a model has been tested or applied, whether it has proved useful and who can provide further information on it. The same applies to critical investigations, comments and references to problems and deficiencies of the models. In view of the fact, that a model functions as a representative of a real phenomenon, characteristics group 7 describes the empirical experiences, gained by experimentation with the model.

4   SYSTEM ORGANIZATION AND OPERATION

Besides the basis file for models, the information system consists of additional files which complete the information on models or improve the information exchange between the system and modelling experts (see Figure 2). In the models file, there can be references to these additional files which can be run separately as autonomous external files or be sub-files of an overall system assigned to other purposes than the models file. The informations recorded in these additional files are necessary for achieving the ends of the information system on models mentioned

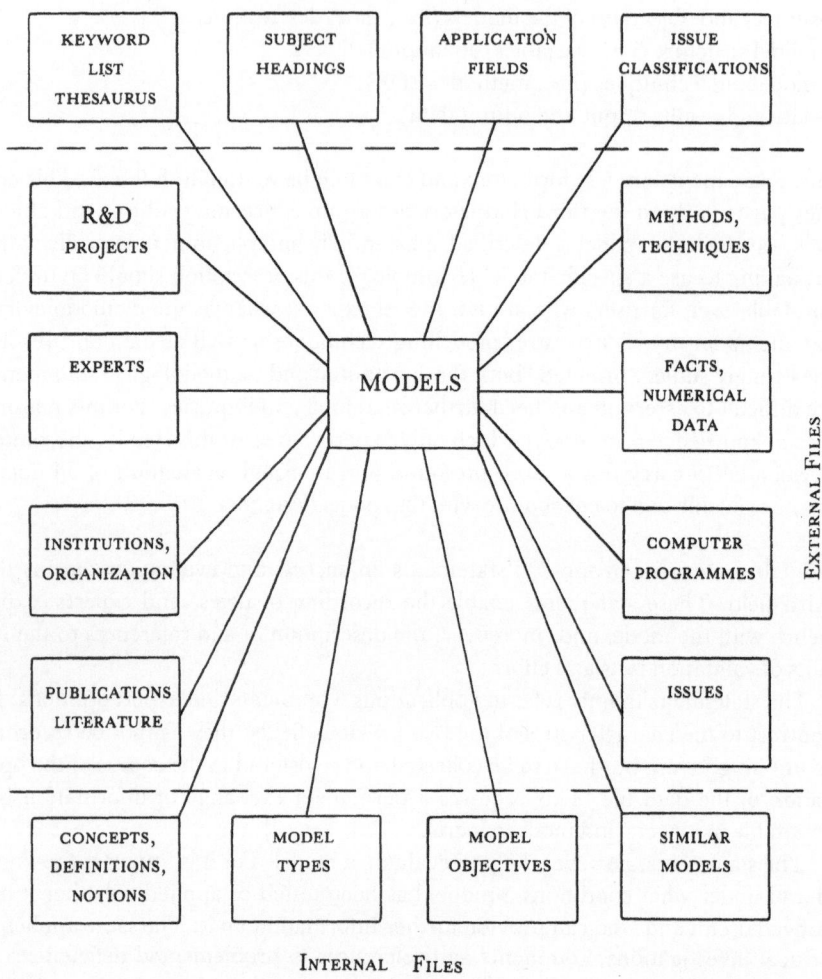

Figure 2. Connection of the Models File with External Files, Overall Classifications and Internal Relationships.

above. Moreover, it is reasonable to run separate files and to connect them with the models file which will simplify the collecting, recording and updating of the relevant data separately from the models file.

The additional files include statements on:
—R&D projects relating to models
—publications, literature sources on models
—methods and techniques
—experts on modelling issues
—institutions, organizations and establishments dealing with models
—model issues—organized in an issue based information system IBIS [11]
—facts, numerical data or data sources
—computer programs

The files relating to experts and institutions are useful for the gathering of documents and information as well as for communication purposes. The projects file broadly informs about current research and developments while the literature file provides references to more specific information on models. Both latter files can also be used for the search and registration of new models.

The methods and data files contain more methodological and data information. Since models and methods are two distinct concepts—though often confused—they constitute two distinct files. Just as it is possible to use several different methods for one model, a single method or technique can be applied to different models [12; 18]. The issue file (IBIS) allows the problem-oriented connection between the models and between the models and other files. As far as already implemented models are concerned, the programme file refers to the respective computer programmes.

In order to effectively run the models file, current statements on experts, institutions, literature and R&D projects are indispensable and should also be immediately available. That is the reason why the models file and the corresponding files should be run simultaneously. Such files are already either in operation or in preparation and their characteristic lists, recording rules and eventually existing data can be used.

The contents of the models file and the additional files is indexed for retrieval purposes by means of "overall" classifications. Thus, besides the direct connection by means of references, the models file is also indirectly connected with the additional files by means of systematical classifications by key-words (thesaurus), subject headings, application fields (i.e., geographically) and issues (according to the issue file).

Equally, an auxiliary file on concepts, definitions, and notions "internally" supplements the models file, which is also connected to a classification of model types and objectives being only significant for the models file. Similar models are connected by means of references; that is to say the models file is connected to itself. The internal classifications, like the "overall" classifications, contribute to link the models indirectly. Both classifications serve the model retrieval. Figure 2 shows all these possible connections.

The gathering of literature is very time-consuming and troublesome. It requires the aid and cooperation of modelling experts and has usually to be carried out in two or even more steps. As sources may be used:
—complete publications
—literature references, publication lists
—catalogues of R&D projects
—hints from experts (designers and applicants) and institutions as well as the annual reports of the latter
—congress reports, seminar reports (references to experts)
—existing modelbanks, indications of their managers and users.

The long-term objective should be an exhaustive recording or at least the improvement and completion of all the essential characteristics by the model designers themselves. By this procedure, which is at the same time an economical one, authentic model descriptions are gained. As far as new models were concerned all the experts interviewed up to now have agreed to this procedure. The creation and operation of a model file necessarily requires the collaboration of institutions and model experts. They have the best know-how on models, are the best suppliers of information and documentary sources and will at the same time be users of the information system. That is why information suppliers and system users have to be regarded as partners and not as two different groups. From the system theoretical point of view, they and the system managers are active parts of the overall information system. They can participate in collecting and recording information, in completing and up-dating files currently (by cost sharing). Other cooperative activities possible are to satisfy inquiries, to search for appropriate models, comments, evaluations, to complete and correct synopses and catalogues and to act as experts for other users.

5 SPECIAL MODEL FILES PROTOTYPES—PRESENT WORK

Each realistic application of the described concept for an information system about models determines a special selection of the characteristics list and the particular features of the system structure. Thus, special types of model files and information systems are created. The model file concept has been tested on the basis of natural scientific and *environmental models* being suitable for environmental planning and concerning various fields and problem areas [5; 14]. Furthermore, a reference file of these models has been realized as a computerized databank (MODAT), which is an integral part of the information and documentation system for environmental planning (UMPLIS) of the Federal Environmental Office, Berlin (*Umweltbundesamt*). For reference purposes no profound substantial model description is necessary; therefore, not all the descriptive characteristics have to be used, but only a reduced set corresponding to the first characteristics field (group 1 - 3) and the first information collection step. The data base is or will be connected with other UMPLIS files on environmental R&D projects [19], institutions, literature and special data [16]. The keywords and environmental subject headings used will be part of a planned overall classification for the whole UMPLIS system. As a first result, a reference catalogue of computer-aided environmental models (800 models, 1400 literature citations) has been published by the Federal Environmental Office [20]; it provides registers with keywords, model types, geographical application fields, model designers (persons) and modelling institutions in order to support retrieval functions.

Another application will be an information system on *models for information systems design and implementation* purposes, that is on models generally concerning information science. There are already various, mostly mathematical models representing the structure, function, organization of information systems or of their interrelations; serving to forecast the future development of information and documentation and to evaluate information policy decisions; OR-models for the operation of libraries, the management of information systems and data-bases, models of information transfer, structure and transformation of data, of data-banks, of costs, etc. These models shall be made retrievable and kept available for practical use for planning, development, implementation, operation and improvement of information systems. At the same time, a summarizing survey on the use and application possibilities of mathematical models in the field of information systems is envisaged. In a first stage, files on literature, experts and institutions as well as a test file on models is planned. The collection of literature and its indexing by substantial and methodological (model type) keywords has been started; first work on models typology and subject headings classification has begun, too.

At the same time a methods file is envisaged comprising not only the methods applied in the models but also the various, very different methods applied in the field of information systems, which partially originate in many disciplines, i.e., methods for user research and participation, for system planning and development, for evaluation of information services, for operation and management of information systems, indexing, retrieval and search methods, etc. As a first result of this work, a survey of literature on information systems models (and later on methods) will be presented to those interested, with various registers (keywords, subject headings, model types, experts, institutions) in order to encourage and motivate the potential system users.

REFERENCES

1. Brewer, G.D., F. Savage and M. Schubik. "The Literature of Gaming, Simulation and Model-Building—Index and Critical Abstracts." The Rand Corporation, Santa Monica, R-629 ARPA, June 1972.

2. Brewer, G.D. and O.P. Hall jr. "Policy Analysis by Computer Simulation—the Need for Appraisal." The Rand Corporation, Santa Monica, P-4893, Aug. 1972.

3. Brewer, G.D., *Politician Bureaucrats, and the Consultant—a Critique of Urban Problem Solving.* New York: Basis Books Inc., 1973.

4. Brewer, G.D. "Professionalism—the Need for Standards." *Interfaces* 4 (Nov. 1973): 20-27.

5. Bürstenbinder, J., H. Illing, and W. Schuler. "Aufbau einer Datei für Modelle—Analyse umweltrelevanter Modelle." Studiengruppe für Systemforschung e.V., Heidelberg, Zentrum für Zukunftsforschung e.V., Berlin, ZBZ-Bericht Nr. 41, Berlin-Heidelberg, Dec. 1975.

6. Data Resources Inc., Abt. Associates, Inc. "Federally Supported Mathematical Models—Survey and Analysis." Study for the US National Science Foundation. Washington: Gov. Printing Office, 1974.

7. Harbordt, S. *Computersimulation in den Sozialwissenschaften.* vol. 1 and 2. Hamburg: Rowolt Verlag, 1974.

8. Harbordt, S. "On the Methodological Evaluation of Simulation Studies." in H. Bossel, et al. (eds.) *The Systems Theory in the Social Science.* Basel and Stuttgart: Birkhäuser-Verlag, 1976, pp. 361-73.

9. Klaus, G. (ed.) *Wörterbuch der Kybernetik.* Frankfurt and Hamburg: Fischer-Bücherei, 1969.

10. Kornbluth, M. and D. Little. "The Nature of a Computer Simulation Model." *Technological Forecasting and Social Change* 9 (1976): 3-26.

11. Kunz, W. and H. Rittel. "Issues as elements of information systems." Working paper No. 131, Institute of Urban and Regional Development, University of California, Berkeley, July 1970.

12. Noltemeier, H. "Verknüpfungsprobleme: Modelle-Methoden-Daten." in H. Noltemeier (ed.) *Computerunterstützte Planungssysteme.* Würzburg: Physica-Verlag, 1976, p. 347.

13. Nowak, J. *Simulation und Stadtentwicklungsplanung.* Stuttgart: Kohlhammer-Verlag, 1973.

14. Schuler, W. "Informationssystem für Methoden und Modelle." *Analyse und Prognosen* 47 (Sept. 1976): 28.

15. Schuler, W. "Informationssystem für Modelle: Systemanalyse, Spezifikationen, Organisation." Studiengruppe für Systemforschung e.V., interner Forschungsbericht, Dec. 1976.

16. Seggelke, J. "Das Informations- und Dokumentationssystem Umwelt UMPLIS." Vortrag, Umweltbundesamt, Berlin, Sept. 1977. Published in: Gesellschaft für Mathematik und Datenverarbeitung mbH, Bonn, and Umweltbundesamt, Berlin (eds.) *Datenverarbeitung auf dem Umweltsektor.* Munich/Vienna: Oldenbourg, 1978, pp. 101-132.

17. Studiengruppe für Systemforschung e.V. (SfS). Jahresbericht 1976, Heidelberg, Sept. 1977.

18. Szyperski, N. and U. Winand. *Entscheidungstheorie.* Stuttgart: C.E. Poeschel, 1974, pp. 85-90.

19. Umweltbundesamt (ed.), UMPLIS—Umweltforschungskatalog '76 (UFOKAT '76). Berlin: E.-Schmidt-Verlag, 1976.

20. Umweltbundesamt (ed.) UMPLIS-Verzeichnis rechnergestützter Umweltmodelle. Berlin: E.-Schmidt-Verlag, 1978.

21. Will, H.J. "Model management systems." in E. Grochla and N. Szyperski (eds.). *Information Systems and Organizational Structure.* Berlin: de Gruyter, 1975, pp. 467-83.

III. TOOLS FOR MODEL IMPLEMENTATION

Chairmen: Norbert Szyperski,
Thilo Tilemann

The increasing application of decision support systems is being influenced both by the readiness of management to explain the calculable parts of their mental models and by the computational power of specialized data processing equipment. These factors contributed to a breakthrough of formal models in decision processes. The mathematical development of solution algorithms probably would not have been able to bring about this on its own.

Besides organizational and personal factors research on model implementation therefore has to integrate planning and data processing technologies suitable for the task to be supported. Related to these technologies two implementation problems can be distinguished:

1. the "implementation" of abstract (mathematical) model types into an individual application situation on the conceptual level and

2. the implementation of the individual model concept into an application program on the software level.

In a recent analysis of quantitative decision making Müller-Merbach stated that, compared to the perfection of existing mathematical algorithms and standardized programs (OR Technology), the state of the art of design and implementation methodologies (OR Methodology) is very poor.* Besides the model solution software (e.g., mathematical programming packages) we do find, however, a lot of software tools supporting model definition and representation.

The following session concentrates on this latter group of software tools, which not only aids model implementation on the software level, but should support model design on the conceptual level as well. The requirements these software tools have to fulfil depend on the intended design and solution type of a model (see Table 1).

Model design can be based on the one hand on (artificial) definitions, often reducing the design task to the more or less aggregated repetition of predefined structures. On the other hand, model design may have to yield specific representations of relevant real life phenomena. In addition, models of both types can be designed in order to consider decision margins, for example, by inequalities. In

---

* H. Müller-Merbach. "Quantitative Entscheidungsvorbereitung." *Die Betriebswirtschaft* 37 (1977): 11-24

Table 1. Types of Models

Solution Type Design Type	Simulation	Optimization
definitional	e.g., accounting	e.g., portfolio optimization
representational	e.g., waiting lines	e.g., production optimization

this case, a feasible solution of the model must be found by an optimization or satisfaction algorithm.

Since model implementation usually includes man-machine interaction, the computer operation mode too becomes an important factor. In this context it seems to be useful to analyze an interactive modelling approach and the state of the art of planning languages and matrix generators.

Dipl.-Kfm. Hermann Kampffmeyer: "Interactive-Modelling—Problems in Design and Practical Use"

Mr. Kampffmeyer described an adequate decision between time-sharing and batch processing as a prerequisite of a reasonable analyst computer interaction. Usually the following factors are critical for this decision: the way of input supply, the amount of data and parameter I/O, the ease of data modification and the ease of output interpretation.

Table 2. Use of Interactive Mode

Modelling Steps	Model Level		
	operational	tactical	strategic
data-base check/ creation	seldom	sometimes	sometimes
analysis	seldom	often	often
model choice and design	never	seldom	seldom
model test	sometimes	often	often
model use	sometimes	sometimes	often

In an analysis with Siemens AG several in-house users of the interactive mode have been related to seven modelling steps and to three model levels (see Table 2).

Following this sample interactive modelling seems to be less suitable for operational models, and there is a remarkable lack of interactive users in the model choice and design phases.

Prof.Dr. Joachim Griese: "User-Oriented Programming Languages—Tendencies of Development"

For the implementation of planning models an increasing number of planning languages (some 100) has been developed in the last ten years. Different definitions and generations of these languages, however, make it difficult to distinguish clear development trends. Against this background, Mr. Griese analyzed the hypothesis that planning languages do not have a future. Among his arguments were the higher flexibility of general languages, the lot of existing standard tools (e.g., for data management and documentation, and the insight that the programming phase is no longer the bottle-neck in systems development.

Kari Kallio: "On Designing LP Interface Structures"

Mr. Kallio distinguished four phases in the development of tools for the generation of linear programming models. A review of existing generators showed that they mainly use methods of the first three phases. Mr. Kallio presented his own fourth generation development performing not only data input into fixed structures but also data driven arrangement of arbitrary model structures. Main features are a CODASYL independent organization of a relational data-base and a model definition language with predicate calculus expressions.

An intensive discussion was stimulated mainly by two points: the sample of interactive computer users and the hypothesis on the future of planning languages.

—For the high frequency of interactive computer use on the tactical level the following explanation was suggested: most of the operational models concentrate on detailed extrapolations of the firms development and thus batch mode predominates. For the strategic level on the contrary a lot of ill-structured innovational problems tend to reduce the possibility to apply computerized models at all.

Regarding the different modelling steps the poor use of interactive computer aid in the model choice and design phases was further analyzed. The assumption that a lack of know-how to conduct reasonable dialogues may be responsible for these phenomena was supplemented by the aspect that modelling methodologies, being hard to conceive on principle, are still more difficult to be offered in a computerized form.

—Referring to planning languages it was pointed out that their future, too, largely depends on advances in modelling know-how. The intention of less serious language suppliers, to get managers to use terminals, has soon proven to be a fiction. The intended user, however, is not only the programmer. Assistants and analysts in planning departments are reasonable user alternatives. The discussion brought up a lot of arguments for the usefulness of planning languages. The programmers barrier to learning a second language and the large market shares of established general languages, however, will at least reduce the number of planning languages in the future. Less enthusiasm and more realism may be necessary.

12. Interactive Modelling: Problems in Design and Practical Use

by Hermann Kampffmeyer, Klaus-Dieter Steffen

1 INTERACTIVE MODELLING: A WAY OF GETTING BETTER ANSWERS MORE QUICKLY

For convenience, let us start with a situation which is still typical for the contemporary analyst who is involved in some modelling using the computer (Figure 1). He has a problem and works out a solution, phones a systems analyst in the data processing department and tells him what he wants him to do. The systems analyst will probably be busy this week, so they meet a week later and discuss the details of the problem.

Another seven days will pass until our analyst receives a phonecall requesting some more input on the problem, because now the program will be run. Two weeks later he gets the desired output, but, unfortunately, it turns out that there was some misunderstanding between them. Meanwhile four weeks have passed, our analyst has started working on some other matter, and so it again takes him some time to get back to the problem.

This example already indicates what interactive modelling will help to avoid: overhead costs which result due to a misfit between task and organizational framework. The advantages for the analyst communicating directly with the computer clearly are:

—He need not wait
—He need not explain
—He need not start more than once at the same point.

Furthermore, there is a second factor to be mentioned. In the outlined situation there is hardly any chance for our analyst to use his creativity. In an interactive mode his creativity will be stimulated: While analyzing something he sees the results, gets an idea and continues the analysis until coming up with a sufficient solution.

2 A FRAMEWORK FOR A REASONABLE USE OF THE INTERACTIVE APPROACH

Keeping in mind the situation of our analyst, it is of course true, that not every problem is suitable to be solved interactively. Especially because there are some other factors which have to be taken into account when talking about the benefits and problems of interactive modelling. A simple pragmatic model that considers

Figure 1. Interactive Modelling.

three dimensions will help to decide whether the interactive approach will be adequate or not (Figure 2).

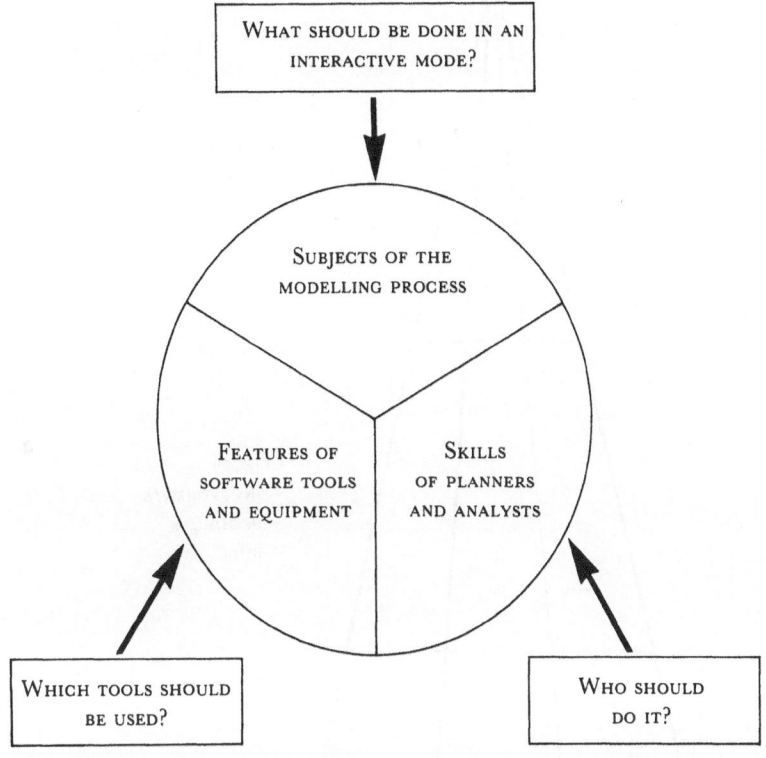

Figure 2. Factors of main importance for the benefits of interactive modelling.

3 MODELLING PROCESS AND PLANNING FUNCTIONS: WHEN TO RECOMMEND DIRECT COMMUNICATION WITH THE COMPUTER

In order to break down our framework to something more concrete for our concern within the modelling process, the management pyramid is a useful starting point (Figure 3).

As there are typical planning functions for each management level, we shall use them to give some examples of whether to use interactive or batch mode (section 3.2).

Before going ahead with the planning function itself, we have to break down the modelling process into steps and find criteria for the decision; to work interactively or not (section 3.1). In this section we assume that the planner has perfect tools and perfect knowledge. What we mean by that, we shall explain in following sections (sections 4 and 5).

THE MANAGEMENT LEVELS   THE MANAGEMENT PLANNING
FUNCTION IS RELATED TO:

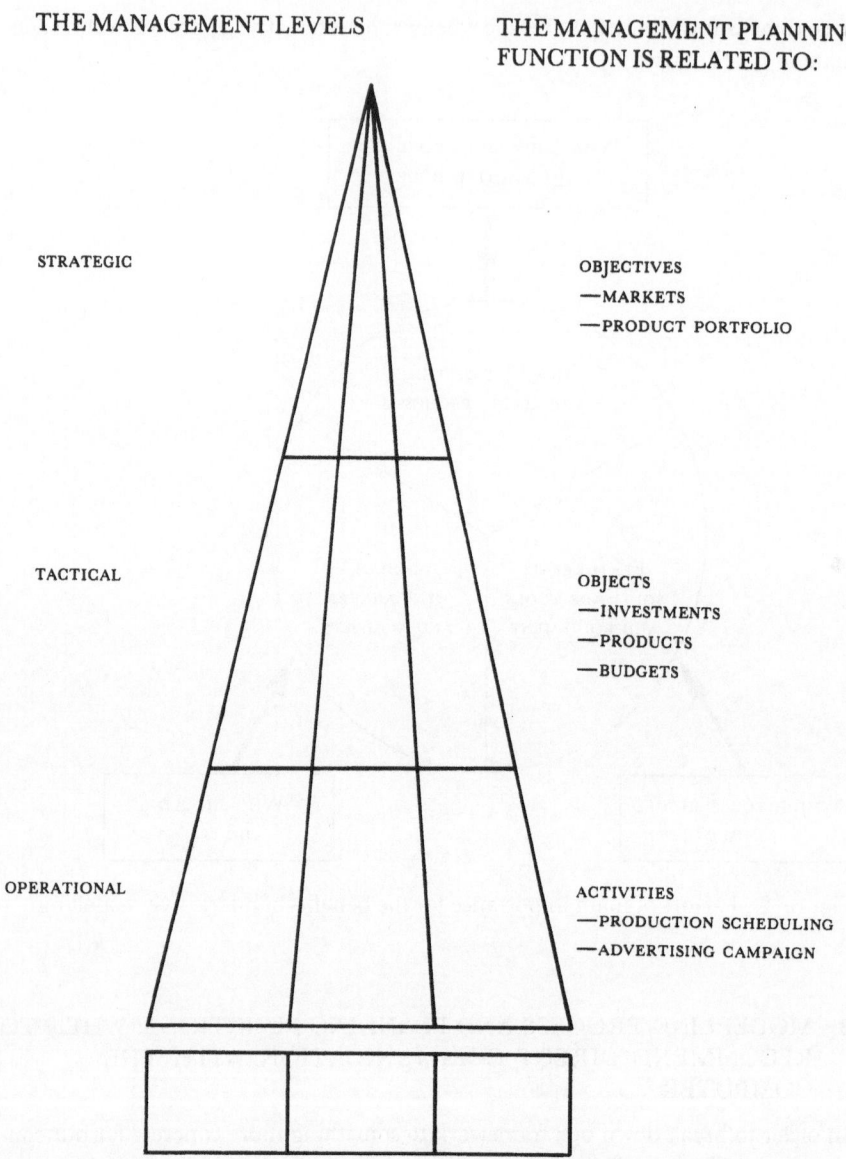

Figure 3.   Management Pyramid.

3.1 Steps in the Modelling Process

Having roughly outlined the main subjects of planning, we further have to detail the modelling process and divide it into steps. As we are considering only those *activities* related to the modelling process itself, it is sufficient for our purpose to use just five steps (Table 1).

Table 1. Steps in the Modelling Process

	management planning function according to the management level		
	operational level	tactical level	strategic level
data base check/creation			
analysis			
model design			
model test			
model use			

3.1.1 Data Base Check and Creation

We feel that the data base for the problem at hand is one of the most critical factors in the whole process, in that the data usually determine what questions can be answered by the model later on. At this early stage the flexibility of the model may already be restricted very seriously. If the data base has yet to be created, this possibly could mean great data processing efforts, because the amount of data has to be put into a more compact and suitable form. In any case, the data base created for the problem solving should contain all items and factors which can possibly be used as model items. Checking the data base in terms of the problem requirements therefore means a qualitative screening for important items or factors. Looking at our applications, we find that the most important criteria for the decision—interactive or batch mode—are:

—the way the data are available
  —in manual data bases,
  —in different EDP-files,
  —in a data-base system,
—the amount of data to be checked.

3.1.2 Analysis

We conceive the analysis phase as a further but more detailed screening of factors and items. Contrary to the data base check, the analysis will be quantitatively orientated, because one aims to know the critical factors from the quantitative point of view. The analysis phase is, of course, very much dependent on the complexity of the problem and one's knowledge of the data. If these factors are already known, there will be no need for further analysis. If these factors, however, are unknown, statistical methods like regression and correlation analyses may be used to get some idea about the importance of the factors. Grouping items by using frequency tables, cluster analysis and so on may further contribute to reduce the amount of data and concentrate modelling only on the important items.

For our decisions—working interactively or not—we found the following criteria to be important:

—amount of data to be processed
—possibility to validate the results at once, i.e., if the number of results is too big or the results are too complex, one will need to do some thinking at one's desk. In these cases working interactively is not very useful.

3.1.3 Model Design

When talking about models, we usually mean a formalized representation of the way we conceive the problem. On the one hand, the job will already be done by assigning variables (factors) to a regression model and perhaps doing some forecasting. On the other hand, model design could mean defining a system of submodels each containing lots of equations.

For the decision—interactive or batch mode—the following criteria might be useful:
—complexity of the problem
    —number of items to be used,
    —number of equations and their complexity,
    —single method or a sequence of methods (i.e., regression analysis, linear programming in one model),
    —one independent model or a class of dependent submodels,
—problem structure, i.e., whether it is poorly or well structured.

In our applications we found that in most cases model design is at the beginning purely desk work. One has to think to get a sufficiently formalized representation of a problem. Only models consisting of some simple equations or a single method (i.e., forecasting) can be designed conversationally.

3.1.4 Model Test

Today interactive programming has been proven to be a very economic means when testing software products for error detection and cleaning them immediately. The same holds true, in most cases, when testing models. Here we do not mean canned programs like a program that performs a regression analysis, but, for instance, a number of recursive equations. Model testing concerns the logical structure of the model. Think, for example, of a corporate planning model consisting of a production model, a marketing model and a financial model at the front end. First, we have to test each of these models interactively for logical consistency. Putting these models into a sequence, because the marketing and production model will generate some input for the financial model, we further test the aggregate interactively. This testing procedure will help to save much time and overhead. But sometimes there will be some problems in using the conversational mode:

—if the amount of minimal test data base is too big
—if the complexity of the model is too great, i.e., there is no possibility to decide at once whether the model is correct or not.

3.1.5 Model Use

Having outlined all the preliminary steps necessary before a model is ready for practical use, what are the main criteria which suggest running it interactively? First of all, it is the urgency of a solution to a problem. If there exists a very rigid time frame for coming up with some solution it is common practice to use the advantages of direct communication with the computer. Secondly, under more normal conditions, two factors directly impact the benefits of an interactive use:

—the ease of use of the model, and
—the amount of data to be processed.

While the latter factor is self-explanatory, the first one has to be further detailed:

—What are the preliminary steps and how many of them are necessary to supply the input data?
—What are the parameters and how many of them require the assignment of values before the model can be executed?
—Since it is common practice to use models for all kinds of "What-If" analysis, how easily can input data and parameters be modified for rerunning the model under different assumptions?
—Since the model generates some output, how easily and quickly can the results be interpreted by the user and possibly provide the input for another model?

3.2 Planning Functions According to Management Levels

Considering the management planning function according to management level let us start with the operational level.

3.2.1 Operational Level of Planning

Here we say that planning is *activity-oriented*. For example, think of a planner in a production department, who is responsible for integrating incoming orders into a weekly production schedule, whereby he must satisfy the usual constraints like manpower and machinery equipment. For this purpose he might use an algorithm telling him whether the existing production schedule is still feasible, when considering an additional order. Thus, he is directly concerned with the activities in the production shop.

To make some suggestions as to where the interactive mode may be reasonable, let us be more specific about this example. An algorithm is needed to aid the decision whether to accept an order or not. The data requirements are as follows:

—Total machine time available, the machine time each product requires, assembly time per product

—number of products per order, price and cost data per product.

Analyzing all these data on the single order level requires processing the whole data base which could take much time, and there will be no interaction between the computer and the user until the run is completed. That is batch work, of course. If the data base has already been broken down into smaller data pools, i.e., the utilization of the machines is already calculated and one is going to find out the critical machines, this possibly can be done interactively by using features of the planning tool to calculate frequency tables (see Table 2).

Table 2. Frequency Table of Machine Utilization.

	0-60	61-80	81-99	100	machine utilization (%)
Machine A					
•	•	•	•	•	
•	•	•	•	•	
•	•	•	•	•	
Machine X			•		

number of time periods, where machine X was employed between 81% and 100%

In the model design stage, one considers the alternative types of models to employ. In our example, it will not be so easy to do it interactively. Interactively we will test the models to validate them, to change them and to get a better fit between the model and reality. In our example:

—One looks for extreme orders according to prices, delivery dates, etc., and checks the model results.
—One further uses historical orders to check the model behaviour for plausibility, i.e., which orders does the model accept, which orders should better be refused, or the opposite. Here a first check might be done interactively. A systematic check should be done at your desk.
—The use of the model should be conversational, because there are only some data for each order. The solution is urgent and quite easy; accept the order or not. For the activity level our example clearly is an exception. Most models on this level are working with a rather large amount of data and have a lot of output data.

We resume our considerations in Table 3.

Table 3. Use of Interactive Mode in Planning: Operational Level

Modelling Step	Use of Interactive Mode	Comment
data base check	seldom	amount of data is rather large
analysis	seldom	amount of data is rather large
model design	never	many data, great complexity of the problems
model test	sometimes	often the minimal test data base will be rather big
model use	sometimes	often there are too many results to handle them interactively, i.e., job-shop scheduling

3.2.2 Tactical Level of Planning

Continuing with the tactical level we want to introduce the term "object" as a synonym for projects, organizational units, product groups and so on. Think of a manager whose job is to balance product group plans with a profit center performance plan. The product groups are considered as objects as is the profit center. The time horizon for this kind of planning usually lies between two and five years and one has to break down given overall performance measures like revenues and costs to annual figures and other specific items. Because in the beginning of that process both plans are worked out independently, they have to be adjusted to each other in the end, so that both plans are feasible. This process is a typical interactive one, because the models are run under different assumptions. If the amount of data is quite easy to handle the interactive mode is recommended for getting immediate results for various types of "What-If" and "What-to-do-to-achieve" questions. Also, it should be possible for the user to access directly data of the operational level for further use and analysis. The adequate mode again is based on the amount of data to be processed.

We believe, that in addition to the problem itself the planning system impacts the way the computer is used. Analysts in a centralized planning department frequently lack the details of the problem (i.e., why did certain products perform very poorly?). This fact restricts their work to a more formal one, such as testing models interactively and executing them.

For those stages in the modelling process which still require a detailed knowledge of the problem, i.e., for the interpretation of the results, one still needs experts of the respective departments such as Sales, Finance, and so on.

Taking into account our applications within the Siemens AG on this level, we come to the conclusions in Table 4.

Table 4. Use of Interactive Mode in Planning: Tactical Level

Modelling Step	Use of Interactive Mode	Comment
data base check/creation	sometimes	for products and investments there should be no problem; for corporate planning models there are, because of the large amount of data and different data bases for the input data
analysis	often	in most cases there are no problems
model design	better not	the models are seldom easy enough to design them without mathematical desk work
model test	often	no problems
mode use	sometimes	for products and investments no problem, for corporate planning there are often too many input parameters required and too many results to decide at once

3.2.3 Strategic Level of Planning

Planning at the level of objectives is concerned with the evaluation of long range strategies which refer to new markets, new technologies, product-portfolios and financing. Here, the following factors will be considered: volume of the market, market growth, competitors, market shares, how much growth can one afford, policy on dividends and financing, etc.

The most important but also most difficult step at the strategic level is to find reliable data and to create a sufficient data base for conducting various types of analysis. This usually requires much data processing effort using the batch mode. A software package, which aims to support these activities, should possess good facilities to retrieve data from activity and object related data bases. For the analysis stage various methods—pragmatic and mathematical ones—are useful, their usage mode, again, should depend on the amount of data to be processed. On the other hand modelling seems to be a mainly interactive-oriented matter, since the number of new data, which are generated, for instance, by projection methods, is quite small.

We believe, that it is good practice to employ "What-If" models interactively for strategy evaluation and forecasting, since a satisfying solution often is based on the creativity of the model user.

On this planning level interactive use of the computer facilities will be most useful (see Table 5).

Table 5. Use of Interactive Mode in Planning: Strategic Level

Modelling Step	Use of Interactive Mode	Comment
data base check/creation	sometimes	because of the sometimes large amount of data for cost-structure analysis
analysis	often	no problems
model design	seldom	the models are seldom easy enough
model test	very often	very useful
model use	very often	creativity

4 PLANNERS AND ANALYSTS: WHAT MUST BE THEIR ABILITIES?

First of all, the analyst or the manager who is doing some interactive modelling, should know his problem and the data base by heart. He has to be able to check the results immediately and interpret them, e.g., for a reasonable modification of the model parameters. Furthermore he needs to know the mechanics of the methods he is employing and he should have the ability to formalize his problems. Last but not least, he needs some basic knowledge referring to the equipment he is

189

using and what to do in certain critical situations, e.g., when the computer system or the line breaks down.

5 SOFTWARE TOOLS

Today we can observe a strong tendency towards planning and modelling packages for the problems we have considered so far. There may be around seventy packages available at the market, ranging from simple financial report generators to more complex packages with econometric features. Check lists have been worked out which consider many critical factors for the design of a model and the design of entire planning systems.

For the successful interactive use of a model there exist a few main criteria which heavily impact the adequacy for conversational use and which have to be met by planning languages (Figure 4):

—The planning language must be highly flexible to be adapted to the user's problem environment.
—The planning language must be easy to learn for someone having no programming background (Table 6).

Table 6. Easy to learn

Data structure
application-oriented concept for easy access of data

                   t i m e

items

Data entry
—free format
—mask controlled

Language design
—user-oriented naming of the commands
—user-defined symbolic names

Default options
—options which not directly relate to the problem are put into effect for the whole session, e.g., display functions

Help options
—at every level of the system alternative choices can be displayed

Choices for controlling the run
—input requests are under control of the program

A Planning Language Has to Fit:

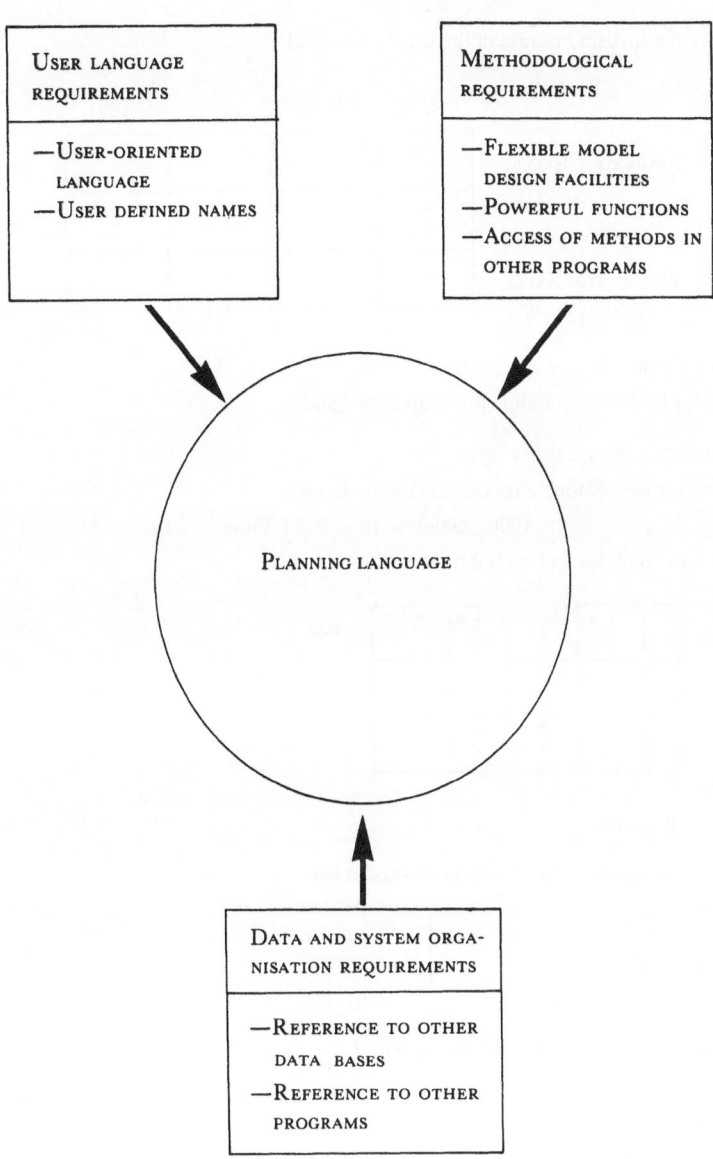

Figure 4.

Table 7. Ease of Use

Data
—access of data using names of the user's own field

	I/78	II/78	....	IV/80
PRODUCT 1 SALES				
	:	:	....	:
PRODUCT X SALES				

Language design
—default parameters for allowing short commands

Model definition and calculation logic
—text editor for defining a model and modifying it
$$1000 \quad Sales = 10 + 0,3 * Time$$
—automatic repetition of calculations

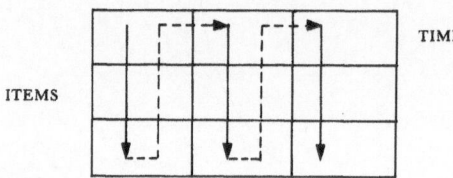

—built-in-functions

Powerful analysis functions at the command language level
Example: RESULT

Table File = abc

Functions for special purposes of the user's own field
e.g., depreciation methods
        investment algorithm

Definition of user functions

Facilities for policy simulation
—"What-to-do-to-achieve" function
—"What-if" function

Report-facilities for a quick and readable data display
—paging function
—graphical display function

—The effort to define and to solve a problem must be small (Table 7).

—Changing the model or some of the parameters must be very easy for the user.

—The results must be presented in a very clear and readable form.

These requirements, of course, are not new, but they are basic for a reasonable interactive use.

From the point of view of a software manufacturer this means much investment into a planning language, which will possess these features to meet the requirements of an interactive situation.

Having the choice to use the adequate mode for each modelling step, one further comment should be made about the hardware equipment. Besides a TV-screen for the interactive mode we recommend a remote-batch-printer unit to execute jobs and to have immediate access to results after the jobs are completed. When there is no such unit we recommend at least a hardcopy device. Everybody who has done some interactive modelling knows about the situation where one comes to a point where it is recommendable to continue work at one's desk based on the most recent results.

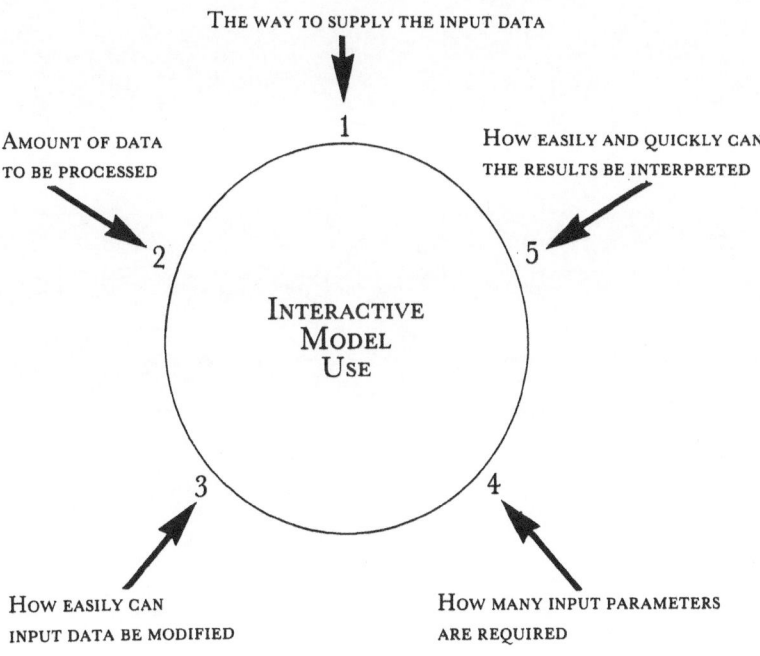

Figure 5. Critical Factors for Interactive Model Use.

6 CONCLUSION

We have shown that interactive work may help saving overhead costs and enforce creativity. But there are three essential factors which determine the success of the interactive modelling approach (Figure 2).

—The size of the problem in terms of its data and parameter requirements, its complexity and results (Figure 5).

—The planners and analysts with their knowledge about the subject, planning methods and data processing equipment.

—The software tool in terms of the effort to learn and handle it and its functional facilities.

In an ideal sense all these factors have to fit perfectly, but this seldom is the case.

Given that the subject is well suited for the interactive approach, two critical factors still remain: the skills of planners and analysts and the software tool. One can, of course, argue, that people can be trained and the software tools be improved to meet the requirements. But this will cost time and money.

Often the idea of the interactive modelling approach is a very attractive one, but we recommend to thoroughly consider the critical factors and check whether the requirements are met.

13. User-Oriented Programming Languages—Tendencies of Development

by Joachim Griese

1 INTRODUCTION

In this symposium we talk about computer-based planning systems. Here—we can argue—"programming languages" mean planning languages, and "user-oriented" points out a special objective of these languages. But who is the user? Is the user the programmer who implements a computer-based planning system using a planning language? Or is the manager the user who uses the implemented planning system? Or is the manager the programmer, meaning it is not necessary to raise the question? We will talk about both, the manager and the programmer and I think it is not a tendency of development but a fact that they are not the same person.

To get an impression of what planning languages are, we mention the features a typical planning language has or should have.

Discussing the tendencies of development we point out the different approaches to planning languages and try to say something about the changing role of planning languages within the implementation process of computer-based planning systems.

2 FEATURES OF PLANNING LANGUAGES

Naylor [7] names eight basic elements which one must consider in designing a planning and modeling system:
—planning system,
—management information system,
—modeling system,
—forecasting system,
—econometric modeling,
—user orientation of the system,
—system availability,
—software system.

The planning system may consist of financial planning models, for instance, income statements and balance sheets; marketing planning models, for instance forecasting models and econometric marketing models; production planning

195

models, for instance minimum cost production planning; and consolidated corporate planning models.

The management information system consists of a data base with internal and external data, a data base management system with access control to protect the planning information, and a report generator. This is the first feature a planning language should have: to manage elements of a data base and to output them in a flexible manner.

The modeling system must be able to support the implementation of recursive models, simultaneous models, logical models, riks analysis, and optimization techniques. Within the forecasting system a variety of forecasting tools, for instance, exponential smoothing, adaptive forecasting, Box-Jenkins techniques, should be available. Econometric modeling involves a four-step methodology, model specification, parameter estimation, validation, and policy simulation. The second feature a planning language should have is the ability to formulate the various model building approaches.

The third feature is a user orientation; that means a planning language should be easy to learn, easy to work with, and open-ended to permit the user to write his own subroutines.

The fourth feature of a planning language is availability, interactively or in batch mode, either on a user's inhouse computer or on an outside service bureau.

The software system will be discussed in the following section. Let us summarize the features of a planning language:
—manage and output the elements of a data base,
—formulate the various model building approaches,
—easy to learn, easy to work with, open-ended,
—interactive/batch mode, inhouse/service bureau.

3 GENERATIONS OF PLANNING LANGUAGES

Rosenkranz [10] states three to four generations of planning languages:
—problem oriented languages like FORTRAN or PL/1,
—report generators and financial "dialects",
—special purpose languages that allow the modeling in the marketing and financial area,
—special purpose languages that in addition allow the modeling in the production area.

In the beginning of computer-based planning systems problem oriented languages were used.Gershefski [3] found in a survey he made in 1969 that fifty percent of the nearly one hundred computerized planning models used FORTRAN, twenty percent COBOL, four percent PL/1 and two percent DYNAMO, a special-purpose language to formulate industrial-dynamics-models.

Rosenkranz [10] supposes that the first planning language was PSG 1 (Planning System Generator; [6]) published in 1968. Naylor and Schauland [8] made a survey in 1974 and report that fifty percent of the existing models in 213 firms were programmed in FORTRAN, eight percent in COBOL, five percent in PL/1, four percent in APL, two percent in Assembler, and one percent in DYNAMO. Twenty-six percent of the models were programmed in one of the over forty available planning and budgeting languages in 1974. Grinyer and Wooller [5] got information from fifty companies in Great Britain; fifty percent of them were using the problem oriented languages in their computer-based planning system and thirty-six percent were using planning languages. Tilemann et al. [4] reported in 1976 that seventy percent of eighty medium sized companies in the FRG used problem oriented languages and twenty-three percent planning languages to program their planning models.

In 1976 Naylor [7] states that nearly fifty planning and modeling packages are on the market; today the number may be about sixty. Tilemann [13] reviews thirty-nine planning languages.

Naylor and Schauland [8, p. 932] argue that the planning languages tend to be much more user (management) oriented than scientific languages such as FORTRAN, APL, and PL/1. In the early 1970s planning systems analysts had the idea that the manager would directly communicate with the computer formulating his planning model via a planning language and execute it, for instance, sitting at a display terminal [12; 9].

The distinction between problem oriented languages (first generation) and planning languages as special purpose languages for computer-based planning systems is clear. It is also understandable that within the planning language there are simpler ones (report generators) and more complex ones. Naylor [7] estimates that two-thirds of the nearly fifty planning and modeling packages in 1976 were primarily report generators. We follow Rosenkranz in distinguishing a second and third generation.

To give an impression of how to work with a planning language we give an example from the planning language SIMPLAN [11]. The inputs made by the user are in lower case:

The user wants to work with the following data:

| Year | Product A | | Product B | | Advertising |
	sales	price	sales	price	
1970	8.500	130	6.200	69	10.000
1971	10.100	132	7.600	69	11.000
1972	10.200	135	7.600	73	11.200
1973	10.900	135	7.700	75	11.500
1974	12.200	138	9.300	75	12.500
1975	14.000	140	10.000	80	13.500
1976	15.000	140	10.700	80	14.000
1977	15.500	140	11.000	80	14.200

The user enters the data at the terminal:

MARKETING
time 1970-1977

TIME RANGE RESET TO 1970-1977
MARKETING
enter asales, aprice, adv

ASALES:
(8 VALUES)
8500 10100 10200 10900 12200 14000 15000 15500

APRICE:
(8 VALUES)
130 132 135 138 140 140 140

ADV:
(8 VALUES)
10000 11000 11200 11500 12500 13500 14000 14200

MARKETING
enter bsales, bprice

BSALES:
(8 VALUES)
6200 7600 7600 7700 9300 10000 10700 11000

BPRICE:
(8 VALUES)
69 69 73 75 75 80 80 80

MARKETING
mean asales bsales adv

VARIABLE	MEAN	MEDIAN	STANDARD DEVIATION
ASALES	12050.0000	11550.0000	2386.9436
BSALES	8762.5000	8500.0000	1619.3650
ADV	12237.5000	12000.0000	1448.2207

The user wants to do a regression analysis with asales as dependent variable and aprice, bsales and adv as independent variables:

MARKETING
estimate asales aprice bsales adv

LEAST SQUARES REGRESSION

ESTIMATED EQUATIONS:
ASALES = $-154.6632*$APRICE $-0.3889*$BSALES $+2.4518*$ADV $+6522.4609$

198

INDEPENDENT VARIABLES	ESTIMATED COEFFICIENT	STANDARD ERROR
APRICE	– 154.6632	28.88203
BSALES	– 0.3889	0.17188
ADV	2.4518	0.21678
CON	6522.4609	3039.12549

R-SQUARED = 0.9995
R-SQUARES ADJUSTED FOR DEGREES OF FREEDOM = 0.9987
NUMBER OF OBSERVATIONS = 8
DEGREES OF FREEDOM FOR T-TEST = 4
STANDARD ERROR = 75.7053
F-STATISTIC (3, 4) = 2649.5698
DURBIN-WATSON STATISTIC = 1.14298

MARKETING
store pmodel 1

After storing the regression analysis with asales as dependent variable, the user repeats the procedure for bsales:

MARKETING
estimate bsales bprice asalesadv

LEAST SQUARES REGRESSION

ESTIMATED EQUATION IS:
BSALES = – 113.0904*BPRICE – 0.3702*ASALES + 2.0443*ADV
         – 3297.2979

INDEPENDENT VARIABLES	ESTIMATED COEFFICIENT	STANDARD ERROR
BPRICE	– 113.09042	15.54946
ASALES	– 0.37024	0.13297
ADV	2.04430	0.23038
CON	– 3297.29785	1166.79858

R-SQUARED = 0.9994
R-SQUARED ADJUSTED FOR DEGREES OF FREEDOM = 0.9989
NUMBER OF OBSERVATIONS = 8
DEGREES OF FREEDOM FOR T-TEST = 4
STANDARD ERROR = 58.1430
F-STATISTIC (3, 4) = 2067.1929
DURBIN-WATSON STATISTIC = 2.3735

MARKETING
store pmodel 2

The user wants to see the two equations:

MARKETING
edit pmodel

EDIT
list
1 ASALES = − 154.66324*APRICE − 0.3889*BSALES + 2.4518*ADV
        + 6522.4609
2 BSALES = − 113.0904*BPRICE − 0.3702*ASALES + 2.0443*ADV
        − 3297.2979

EDIT
end

The two equations model is a simultaneous system of linear equations. The user solves the model by giving a guess for the initial value of bsales:

MARKETING
simul bsales 8500

MARKETING
solve pmodel

MODEL PMODEL IS A SIMULTANEOUS SYSTEM

TIME	PMODEL ASALES	APRICE	BSALES	BPRICE	ADV
1970	8540.43	130.00	6180.81	69.00	10000.00
1971	10116.96	132.00	7641.47	69.00	11000.00
1972	10165.60	135.00	7579.96	73.00	11200.00
1973	10850.63	135.00	7713.48	75.00	11500.00
1974	12245.16	138.00	9241.51	75.00	12500.00
1975	14075.64	140.00	10042.71	80.00	13500.00
1976	15043.30	140.00	10706.63	80.00	14000.00
1977	15431.80	140.00	10971.66	80.00	14200.00

The user wants to forecast asales and bsales for 1978-1983:

MARKETING
time 1978-1983

TIME RANGE RESET TO 1978-1983
MARKETING
enter bprice, adv, aprice

BPRICE:
(6 VALUES)
85 85 85 90 90 90

ADV:
(6 VALUES)
14500 15000 15500 16000 16500 17000

APRICE:
(6 VALUES)
145 145 145 150 150 150

MARKETING
simul bsales 11000

MARKETING
solve pmodel

MODEL PMODEL   IS A SIMULTANEOUS SYSTEM

	PMODEL				
TIME	ASALES	APRICE	BSALES	BPRICE	ADV
1978	15366.73	145.00	11043.59	85.00	14500.00
1979	16332.83	145.00	11708.09	85.00	15000.00
1980	17300.65	145.00	12371.95	85.00	15500.00
1981	17624.30	150.00	12708.84	90.00	16000.00
1982	18590.18	150.00	13373.41	90.00	16500.00
1983	19558.00	150.00	14037.27	90.00	17000.00

The user may repeat these procedures changing the data for instance for adv.

4 TENDENCIES OF DEVELOPMENT

What has changed since the early 1970s, when analysts believed that managers would program and execute computer-based planning systems?

It was a pitfall to assume that managers program their own models. In [1] the answer to the question "do managers actually become hands-on users of computers to aid them in their problem solving and decision making?" is a resounding "No".

But what about our user-oriented languages if the manager is not the user? Is the user-oriented design accepted by the skilled manager too, or does he re turn to the more flexible problem-oriented programming languages?

Let us accept for a moment the hypothesis that planning languages do not have a future, because people who program computer-based planning systems prefer using a general problem-oriented programming language, and look for arguments which can support this hypothesis:

—general problem-oriented languages offer a greater flexibility to build and program planning models. Grinyer and Batt [4] report that in a company the decision was made for FORTRAN because an American planning language did not employ English accounting conventions.

—In a student course at our university we installed PLANCODE/S, a planning language developed by IBM. The students had a course in PLANCODE and were qualified PL/1 programmers. The one group had to program some reports in PLANCODE, the other group programmed the same task in PL/1. There was no significant difference in programming and testing time, but the PLANCODE group was very unhappy because of the limitations of the planning language.

—there are a lot of standard tools like data base management systems or teleprocessing monitors you can combine with general problem-oriented languages to support the implementation of planning models.

—the programming phase is not the bottleneck in systems planning it was five years ago; the programming process is now going to be well organized and has more technical support, for instance, interactive programming and testing.

—projects of computer-based planning systems are short ones (for instance, less than a year; compare [3] and [4]) and therefore a possible advantage in programming more quickly using a planning language does not save a large absolute amount of time and money.

—computer-assisted documentation systems begin to work in practice; what about the documentation feature of a planning language?

—what shall we do with our planning language if hardware and/or system software, for instance, the operating system, is going to be changed?

I am sure that many of us who develop, sell or use a planning language can tell us the advantages of planning languages.

The point I want to make is that there is no clear tendency of a growing use of planning languages. The objective in designing these languages was to help the manager; this objective is not realistic.

5 FINAL REMARKS

But what about the manager? We had in mind to help him in his planning process by giving him a planning language. Also if the manager himself does not use the computer-based model his assistant probably will use it; therefore, we have to design a user interface. The user interface, for instance, a list of commands offered as a menu at the display screen, is a feature of planning languages in a few cases; in general it is not. This interface can be realized by a general problem-oriented language, too. It seems to me that in this area a lot of theoretical and empirical research (compare [2]) has to be done.

REFERENCES

1. Canning Publications, Inc. "APL and Decision Support Systems." *EDP Analyzer* 14 (1976): 5.

2. Gerrity, T.P. "The design of man-machine decision systems." Unpublished Ph.D. thesis, Massachussetts Institute of Technology, 1970.

3. Gershefski, G.W. "Corporate Models—The State of the Art." *Management Science* 16 (1970): B303-B312.

4. Grinyer, P.H. and C.D. Batt. "Some Tentative Findings on Corporate Financial Simulation Models." *Operational Research Quarterly* 25 (1974): 149-67.

5. Grinyer, O.H. and J. Wooller. "Computer Models for Corporate Planning." *Long Range Planning* 8 (1) (1975): 14-25.

6. Lande, H.F. et al. *Planning Systems Generator*. Share Library Program Np 360 D-15.6.002. New York, 1968.

7. Naylor, T.H. "Elements of a planning and modeling system." *Proceedings of the National Computer Conference*, 1976, pp. 1017-26.

8. Naylor, T.H. and H. Schauland. "A Survey of Users of Corporate Planning Models." *Management Science* 22 (1976): 927-37.

9. Rölle, H. "Man-Machine Decision System statt MIS Management Informationssysteme—konzeptioneller Rahmen und gegenwärtige Anwendung." *adl-Nachrichten* 66 (1971): 10-16.

10. Rosenkranz, F. *An Introduction to Corporate Modeling.* Basel, 1974 (especially pp. 398-450).

11. Social Systems, Inc. *SIMPLAN: Marketing.* Version July 1974.

12. Tilemann, T. *Planungssprachen—Abgrenzung und Analyse ihrer Einsatzmöglichkeiten in entscheidungsorientierten Informationssystemen.* BIFOA-Arbeitsbericht 72/14. Cologne, 1972.

13. Tilemann, T. "Zum Entwicklungsstand von Programmiersprachen für betriebswirtschaftliche Planungsaufgaben." *Angewandte Informatik* 19 (1977): 375-79.

14. Tilemann, T. et al. *Betriebswirtschaftliche Analyse- und Planungssoftware. Struktur von Angebot und Nachfrage in der Bundesrepublik Deutschland.* BIFOA-Forschungsbericht 77/2. Cologne, 1977.

14. On Designing LP Interface Structures

by Kari Kallio

Relational data management has since about 1970 been a subject of an increasing interest in computer science. Here relational concepts are applied to matrix generation. LP-matrix and input data tables are regarded as mathematical sets and LP-matrix definition—or a generator program—is given as *predicate calculus expressions*.

1 CONCEPTS AND NOTATIONS

Given sets D_1, D_2, ..., D_n (not necessarily distinct), a relation R is a set of n-tuples each of which has its first element from D_1, second element from D_2, etc. More concisely, R is a subset of the Cartesian product $D_1 \times D_2 ... \times D_n$. The sets D_1 are called domains. The number n is called the degree of R, and the number of tuples in R is called its cardinality. Relations of degree 1 are often called unary, degree 2 binary, degree 3 ternary, and degree n n-ary. A relation can be represented as a table in which each row represents a tuple. Each tuple may occur only once in the table. When a relation is represented as a table, its degree is the number of columns and its cardinality its number of rows.

In the tabular representation of a relation, it is customary to name the table and to name each column, e.g.:

MATRIX	ROW	COLUMN	VALUE
	RPROD01	CPROC14	.274
	RPROD23	CPROC05	.365
	RPROD23	CPROC07	.532
	.	.	.
	.	.	.

The columns of the table are called attributes. It is important to distinguish between attributes and domains. For example, in the MATRIX relation ROW and COLUMN are attributes, which are both based on the same domain: the set of possible variable names.

A column or a set of columns whose values uniquely identify a row of a relation is called a candidate key—or simply a key—of the relation. In the MATRIX relation the key consists of the ROW and COLUMN columns. A relation can have more than one key and then it is customary to designate one of the keys as the primary key. A relation represented as a table is usually denoted by the table name which is followed by the column names enclosed in parentheses, where the primary key columns are in bold type, e.g.:

MATRIX (**ROW, COLUMN,** VALUE).

A projection of a relation is a relation which has been derived from the first one by dropping columns and removing resulting multiple occurrences of the same row. In this paper projections are denoted by inserting asterisks for the dropped columns, e.g.:

MATRIX (ROW,*,*)

is a unary relation of the matrix row names. We also use the same name for a relation and for an element inclusion predicate, i.e.:

R(x) is   TRUE if x « R and
           FALSE otherwise,

and also:

R(x,*) is   TRUE if for some c (x,c) « R and
            FALSE otherwise.

"For some" is used for existential and "for all" for universal quantifiers and "not" is used for negation. Character strings are given in italics, while "&" is used as a concatenation operator for joining character strings, e.g., $X \& Y = XY$.

2   LP MATRIX AS A RELATION

Here we represent in a relational form the information found in most LP-package input files. The representation is general, not oriented towards any special LP package, but is in no way unique. The rhs and ranges vectors are considered as columns and the column upper-, lower- and fixed-bound vectors as rows. Our relations are

ROWS (**ROW**, ROW-TYPE)
COLUMNS (**COL**, COL-TYPE)
MATRIX (**ROW, COL,** VAL).

where

ROW   = matrix row names (character string)
COL   = matrix column names (character string)
VAL   = matrix element values (number)
COL-TYPE   = matrix column types (character string)
ROW-TYPE   = matrix row types (character string).

For normal matrices—generalized upper bounding, separable programming and possible other special operating modes are not considered—possible row types are:

206

EQ, LE, GE, FR	= in the usual meaning
BUP	= upper-bound row
BLO	= lower-bound row
BFX	= fixed-bound row

and the possible column types are:

CV	= continuous column
BV	= binary column
IV	= integer column
RHS	= rhs-column
RNG	= ranges-column.

The extension of the possible types to special operating modes is not difficult.

3 THE CASE MODEL

Our case model is a profit maximizing production model where
—products and semiproducts are made from semiproducts and raw materials,
—the production uses a number of limited processing capabilities, which can to some extent be increased by overtime working and
—markets for products and availability of raw materials are limited.

The structure of the model is given in Figure 1. The basic relations—input data tables—are:

> RECEIPT (**PROD, USED-MAT,** MAT-USE)
> PROD-PROC (**PROD, PROC,** PROC-USE)
> PRODUCT (**PROD**, PRICE, MARKET-LIM)
> RAWMAT (**RMT**, COST, AVAIL-LIM)
> PROCESS (**PROC**, COST-NORM, CAP-NORM, COST-OVRT, CAP-OVRT),

where

RECEIPT	= table of raw material and semiproduct usages for products
PROD-PROC	= table of process usages for products
PRODUCT	= product vector with price and market limit attributes
RAWMAT	= raw material vector with cost and availability attributes
PROCESS	= process vector with cost and capacity attributes
PROD	= product code
PROC	= process code
RMT	= raw material code
USED-MAT	= product or raw material code
MAT-USE	= usage of material USED-MAT in production of product PROD (unit/unit)

207

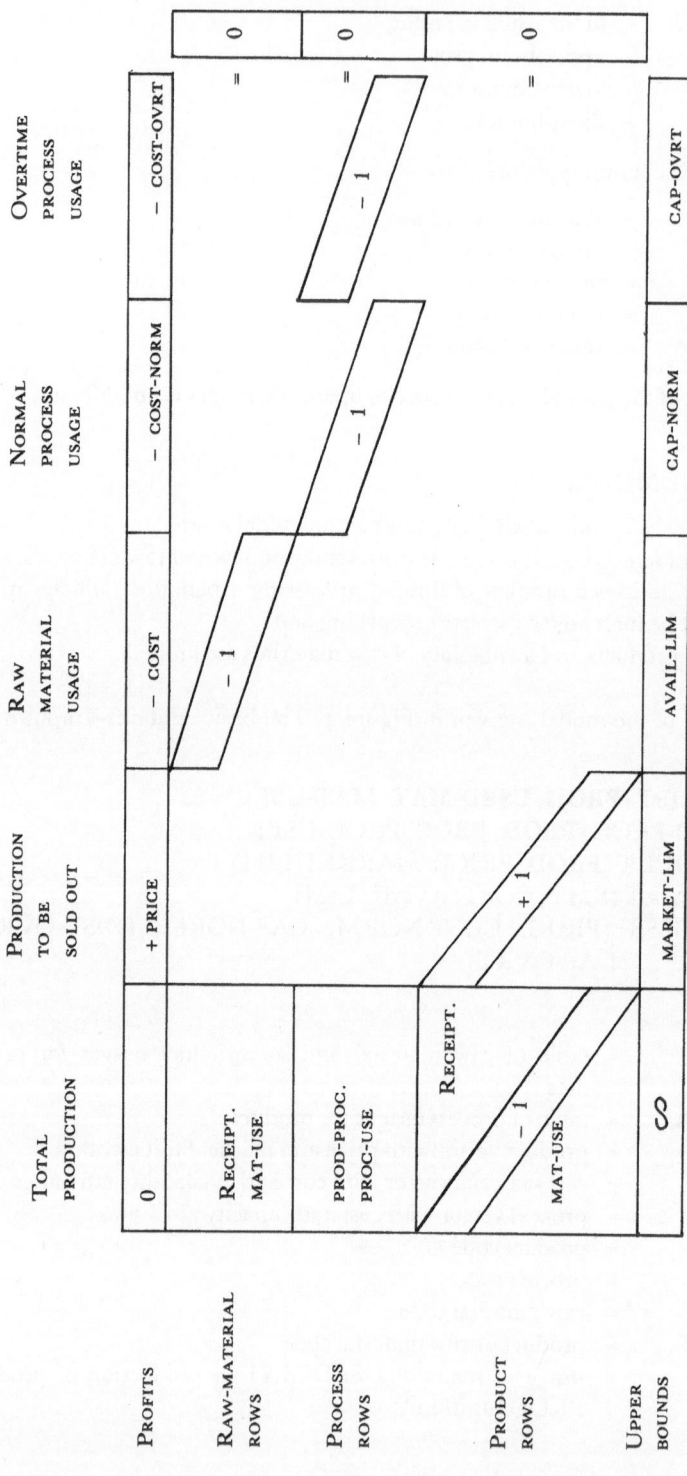

Figure 1. The Case Model

PROC-USE   = usage of process **PROC** in production of product **PROD** (unit/unit)
PRICE   = unit selling price of a product
MARKET-LIM   = market upper limit for selling a product
COST   = unit cost of raw material
AVAIL-LIM   = upper limit of raw material availability
COST-NORM, COST-OVRT, CAP-NORM and CAP-OVRT are normal and overtime costs and capacities of a process.

In our LP-matrix the general variable naming rule is: the ordinary variable names will begin with R for rows and C for columns, which are followed by material or process codes—we suppose a unique coding.

A process and a product each need two columns in the matrix, which must be identified by the name coding. The normal process usage and total production columns are denoted by appending a '1' at the end of the basic name. The overtime process usage and the sold production columns are denoted by appending a '2' at the end of the basic name. For example, the column "amount of product P1234 sold out" is coded as 'CP12342', which can also be represented as C & $P1234$ & 2.

4 THE LP-MATRIX DEFINITION

The LP-matrix is defined by a number of predicate definitions because of notational reasons. According to our earlier convention, we may think of a predicate as denoting a relation with the same name.

We suppose, that the model user supplies a list—a unary relation—P(**PROD**) of products to be included in the model. Our fist task is to enlarge P to list PRODS (**PROD**), which includes also all semiproducts used in the production.

(1) PRODS(x) = P(x) or (RECEIPT(x,*,*) and for some y
$$\text{(PRODS(y) and RECEIPT(y,x,*)))}$$

Because of the finite length of the production path, the recursive definition of PRODS can be evaluated in a finite number of steps. Also lists of raw materials and processes in production of PRODS are needed.

(2) RAWS(x) = for some y (PRODS(y) and not PRODS(x) and
$$\text{RECEIPT(y,x,*))}$$

(3) PROCS(x) = for some y (PRODS(y) and PROD-PROC(y,x,*))

Raw material rows × total production columns:

(4) SUB1(R&x, C&y&1,v) = PRODS(y) and RAWS(x) and RECEIPT (y,x,v)

Processing rows × total production columns:

(5) SUB2(R&x, C&y&1,v) = PRODS(y) and PROCS(x) and
$$\text{PROD-PROC(y,x,v)}$$

Production rows × total production columns:

(6) SUB3(R&x, C&y&1,v) = PRODS(x) and PRODS(y) and
$$(\text{RECEIPT}(y,x,v)$$
$$\text{or } (x = y \text{ and } v = -1))$$

Production rows × sold production columns:

(7) SUB4(R&x, C&y&2,v) = v = 1 and (PRODS(x) and x = y)

All diagonal − 1 matrices:

(8) SUB5(R&x, C&y,v) = v = − 1 and
$$((\text{RAWS}(x) \text{ and } y = x)$$
$$\text{or } (\text{PROCS}(x) \text{ and}$$
$$(y = x\&1 \text{ or } y = x\&2)))$$

Object vector:

(9) PROF(C&x,v) = (RAWS(x) and RAWMAT(x, − v,*))
$$\text{or for some } y$$
$$(\text{PROCS}(y) \text{ and}$$
$$(x = y\&1 \text{ and } \text{PROCESS}(y, -v,^*,^*,^*))$$
$$\text{or } (x = y\&2 \text{ and } \text{PROCESS}(y,^*,^*, -v,^*)))$$
$$\text{or for some } y$$
$$(x = y\&2 \text{ and}$$
$$(\text{PRODS}(y) \text{ and } \text{PRODUCT}(y, v, {}^*)))$$

Upper bound vector BND is defined analogously to PROF. We decide that default value for rhs element is 0 and default type for column type is CV and we do not need the COLUMNS relation at all.

The main matrix definition:

(10) MATRIX (r,c,v) = SUB1(r,c,v) or SUB2(r,c,v) or SUB3 (r,c,v) or
$$\text{SUB4 (r,c,v) or SUB5(r,c,v)}$$
$$\text{or } (r = PROFIT \text{ and } \text{PROF}(c,v))$$
$$\text{or } (r = UPPERBND \text{ and } \text{BND}(c,v))$$

The row information:

(11) ROWS(r,t) = t = EQ and for some y
$$(r = R\&y \text{ and } (\text{PRODS}(y) \text{ or } \text{PROCS}(y) \text{ or } \text{RAWS}(y)))$$
$$\text{or } (r = PROFIT \text{ and } t = FR)$$
$$\text{or } (r = UPPERBND \text{ and } t = BUP)$$

5 COMPUTER IMPLEMENTATION

Basically the significance of the presented method of matrix generation does not entirely depend on whether it is implemented or not as a programming language.

210

As a notation only it can serve as an exact and concise documentation of a model and as an interface between the modeller and the matrix generator programmer.

A model structuring can be made by submatrix definitions, which further can be mapped one-to-one to generator program modules.

Some of the existing relational data manipulation languages are almost capable of performing the desired tasks—extended by the concatenation operator and with their own syntaces. Efficiency is another question because the relational systems have not been optimized for manipulation of large sparse matrices.

If the implementation is not based on any existing high-level relational system, the basic tools needed are:

—an intelligent optimizer to transform the relational definitions to efficient access paths and operation sequences, and

—an efficient binary-ternary relational storage system for vectors and large sparse matrices.

In addition we should be able to define and reference virtual matrices, i.e., only a definition or a pointer structure is physically stored; values are stored in data tables or in actual—physical—submatrices.

The LP-matrix definition could be evaluated either by an interpretive system or could be translated to executable code. In the second case we could speak of a matrix generator generator.

C.
Working Group:
Organizational Aspects
of Systems Design
and Implementation

I. PARTICIPATIVE SYSTEM DESIGN

Chairman: Michael J. Ginzberg*

The title of this session was Participative System Design (PSD). All three papers presented deal with this general topic, though the specific areas addressed differ substantially. Professor Mumford presents the general arguments for PSD, and then describes a particular approach she has used (''Consensus Design'') and the problems and advantages associated with it. Mr. Clausen presents a framework for understanding PSD from the viewpoints of different actors—computer specialists, sociotechnicians, and system users. He then differentiates the sociotechnical approach to PSD (common in the U.K. and the U.S.A.) from the labor union approach to PSD (an approach that is emerging in the Scandinavian countries). Mr. Podger focuses on a narrower question: what tools can be developed to foster user participation in system design? The answer he suggests is a general purpose, high-level language with a structure based on the potential user's professional role.

This note attempts to summarize the discussion of these three papers. As the recording of this discussion was accomplished with pencil and paper (rather than with audio equipment), it is impossible to provide a verbatim transcript. Thus, I have attempted to summarize the comments and discussion by incorporating them into an overview of PSD.

Many people participated in the discussion of these papers. While I cannot acknowledge separately the contribution of each person, I want to point out that the content of this note is in large measure the result of their joint contributions.

WHAT IS PARTICIPATIVE SYSTEM DESIGN?

PSD can be best understood if we contrast it with conventional system design. The conventional approach to system design can be characterized as:

1. change minimizing,
2. technology focused, and
3. controlled exclusively by the systems analyst.

In conventional design the user is passive and the analyst active. The analyst:

1. interviews users to document their stated needs,

* I want to acknowledge with thanks the help of Dipl.-Kfm. Hartwig Garmers in recording and summarizing the discussion which is the basis for this note.

215

2. examines the existing system of information flows in the area of concern, and
3. prescribes a new system of information flows which, in theory, efficiently meets the stated needs.

The user's only role is to respond to the analyst's questions, and, of course, to use the new system.

Advocates of participative design call for a redistribution of tasks between user and analyst, for the user to play a more active role in the design process. At a minimum this means that users must have an opportunity to review and comment on the design before it becomes final. Some (e.g., Lucas [5]) have dubbed this "pseudo-participation", and argue that users must actually design their own systems in a true participative design process. The authors of the three papers presented at this session clearly hold this view; but they differ on where they would draw the boundaries of the necessary group of participants.

Beyond the issue of task distribution, most advocates of participative design differentiate it, at least by implication, from conventional design in another respect. They see the system development process as a change effort which impacts not only the technological system of the organization, but its human system as well [1; 3; 4]. Thus, they are concerned with changes on both of these dimensions; rather than trying to minimize change, they try to deal with it.

WHY PARTICIPATIVE DESIGN?

The fundamental impetus for a participative approach to systems design is that conventional design has not always worked. Following the conventional approach has resulted in systems which:

1. did not truly meet the organization's needs;
2. had to be modified substantially before they could be used;
3. were rejected, sabotaged, or otherwise defeated by their users; or
4. were never used at all.

True, this did not happen in every case; but it happened often enough to cause many people to question the conventional process of design.

The advocates of participative design cite a number of benefits to be gained from this approach. Among these are:

1. greater commitment on the part of the user to the new system and to the changes that will be necessary to make it work;
2. better understanding by the user of the system and its use, making successful use more likely; and
3. better access to the user's knowledge and understanding of the problem, leading to a better solution.

216

Each of these claims points to a system that should be more readily accepted by the users, and should better meet the organization's needs. These might be termed the pragmatic arguments for participative design. Recently, another argument for user participation in design has been advanced. This argument, the ethical argument for participation, states that individuals have a right to influence their working situations; and, since an information system has a great impact on the conditions of work, system users should play a significant role in its design. In the Scandinavian countries, this ethical basis for participative design has become the law.

Mumford, Clausen, and Podger are all advocates of PSD, and their papers stress its advantages. During the discussion, however, Harold Sackman raised some potential disadvantages or dangers of PSD.

First, a participative approach may result in a longer elapsed time for system design than would a conventional approach. Mumford countered that there is no evidence to support this contention. Other PSD advocates argued that even were it true, the other advantages would likely outweigh the additional time required.

A second danger raised was the threat of mediocrity in design; i.e., users do not have sufficient skills to design good systems. In response it was suggested that users need not design in a vacuum, without the help of a system analyst. Rather, the *choices* must be left to the users. Further, the PSD advocates argue that the additional issues and dilemmas that users are likely to raise during design will result in superior designs, not mediocre ones.

Third, PSD may result in polarizing, fragmenting, and politicizing the user group. This threat was not disputed, and it was agreed that skilled organizational development practitioners, facilitators of change, must be included in the design team.

A final threat was that of manipulation—either of individual participants or of the entire process through selection of the "right" participants. Again, this threat was not disputed, and all agreed it must be watched for and steps taken to prevent it. It was also pointed out that this problem is likely to be most serious in the case of planning systems.

In summary, numerous arguments can be raised in favor of PSD, but it is clearly not without problems. We will return to some of those problems in the final section of this note. But first, we should consider how user participation in design can be achieved.

MECHANISMS FOR USER PARTICIPATION

There are a great many potential patterns of user participation in design. Hence, a considerable number of mechanisms for involving users in the design process have been proposed. One of the first methods to be used was feedback to the user as the design progressed. As was stated before, this is not true participation; yet, it is still widely used—e.g., the formal sign-off procedures between the stages of many structured development methodologies.

One step beyond simple feedback are the notions of user liaisons and steering committees. In the case of the liaison, the bulk of the design work is done by the analyst (or a team of analysts), but there is also a user formally responsible for monitoring the development process and providing the user group's input to it. Steering committees composed of users can perform in an oversight capacity, but again the analysts do the principal design work. Mumford's "Consultative Design" falls into this group. However, none of these approaches reach the goal of having users design their own systems.

The next logical step is to have a design team composed of users and analysts, preferably with a user as its head. This approach assures significant contact between users and analysts, but does not guarantee that users will play a major role in design. The task divisions among team members may cast the users in the role of input providers and design reviewers. Mumford's "Representative Design" fits this description, and discussion focused on some problems associated with this approach (and similar ones). One of the questions raised was how much representation is enough? Further, how do you assure that all factions, including minorities, are represented? Clearly, one solution is to appoint the representatives to the design group; but, this raises the problem of manipulation by the person doing the appointing. Mumford prefers structuring the rules of election to assure representation of all factions.

Another question raised concerns the handling of conflicts that are likely to arise when multiple factions are involved in system design. It was agreed that it would be rare to find a solution favored by one hundred percent of the user group (or their representatives). Indeed, it was suggested that if more than fifty percent of the group favor a solution, it should probably be implemented. Effective techniques for dealing with the remaining fifty percent, however, were not discussed.

Other techniques go even farther toward involving the user in the design process. Mumford advocates an approach she calls "Consensus Design", in which *all* users are actively involved in design. Lucas and Plimpton describe a variant of this—a "town meeting" format during which users and other interested parties took a tentative system design and completely revised it [6]. Obviously, the issue of conflict resolution is again important in this type of approach.

Additional mechanisms for gaining user involvement have also been proposed. Boland describes an experiment using a "learning model" approach to design, in which users and analysts temporarily reverse roles [2]. Podger proposed the use of appropriately structured high-level languages as a vehicle for participative design, and ultimately autonomous design (i.e., design by the user without any analyst involvement). Discussion of this proposal centered on whether such languages could eliminate the need to worry about PSD by eliminating the need for system analysts. Generally, the discussants did not believe this would be the case. Indeed, it was pointed out that other similar languages (e.g., SPSS, COGO, etc.) have not eliminated the need for analysts. Rather, they have provided users with better mechanisms for problem formulation. Developments along the lines of Podger's or Boland's work are likely to blur the distinction between users and analysts, as each is recognized as a specialist whose contribution is necessary to the design process. However, it is unlikely that either role will be eliminated.

UNRESOLVED QUESTIONS

We have seen that there are numerous arguments for user participation in design as well as multiple ways to achieve it. Nonetheless, there are still many questions about participative design which need to be answered. For one, there is little conclusive evidence of the value of participative design. The advocates point to instances where conventional design methods have failed, and claim that a participative approach would have succeeded. Indeed, Clausen's presentation began in just this fashion. However, asserting that something is so does not prove it. Indeed, Boland performed a direct comparison of participative and conventional design [2]; and, while he was able to conclude that the systems designed in the participative manner were qualitatively *different* from those designed conventionally, he was unable to conclude that systems developed in a participative fashion would necessarily be better.

Even if we were able to prove that participative design results in better systems, we would still have to ask what method (or methods) for achieving user participation is best. Participation is costly, both in time and money. Generally, the more participative the method, the higher the cost. Thus, we would like to know what are the most effective methods of participation? and how much participation is enough? A closely related question arose during the discussion: Is PSD equally effective for all types of systems, clerical versus managerial, operational versus planning? The experience with PSD is almost entirely at the bottom, operational level of the firm. Thus, little is known about how it would work at the managerial level, e.g., for the development of planning systems.

User participation in design can open an organization to problems it has not previously dealt with. The goals and objectives of users, systems analysts, and managers are likely to differ. When users are kept outside of the design process, these conflicts can be hidden. However, in a truly open design process, these conflicts will be exposed. Dealing openly with these goal conflicts, some of which may not be easily resolvable, adds a new dimension to system design and creates the need for a new set of tools. Whether adequate tools to support PSD currently exist was a point on which the PSD advocates did not agree. Mumford contends that they do. Clausen, however, does not believe that the needed tools are yet available to support either the sociotechnical or the labor union approach to PSD. Further, he contends that this will be more of a problem as the group participating in the design process widens (i.e., as the general public becomes involved).

Finally, there remains the question of how PSD will evolve. Which of the possible techniques for involving users will become dominant is one side of the question. But, there is also the question of national differences in the direction PSD will take. In most Western countries, the sociotechnical systems approach is likely to remain the basis for PSD development. In the Scandinavian countries, however, the model is more likely to be political, relating to the distribution of power and influence in society. How this approach will affect what systems are developed as well as how they are developed remains to be seen.

Clearly, participative system design is an approach which has many advocates and for which numerous benefits are claimed. It is not, however, without its problems (real or potential), and many questions about it remain unanswered. The three papers presented in this session begin to answer some of these questions and help to identify others.

REFERENCES

1. Bjorn-Andersen, Niels and Bo L.T. Hedberg. "Designing Information Systems in an Organizational Perspective." *TIMS Studies in the Management Sciences* 5 (1977): 125-42.

2. Boland, Richard J., Jr. "The Process and Product of System Design." *Management Science* 24 (9) (1978): 887-98.

3. Bostrom, Robert P. and J. Stephen Heinen. "MIS Problems and Failures: A Socio-Technical Perspective, Part I: The Causes." *MIS Quarterly* 1(3) (1977): 17-32.

4. Bostrom, Robert P. and J. Stephen Heinen. "MIS Problems and Failures: A Socio-Technical Perspective, Part II: The Application of Socio-Technical Theory." *MIS Quarterly* 1(4) (1977): 11-28.

5. Lucas, Henry C., Jr. *The Analysis, Design and Implementation of Information Systems*. New York: McGraw-Hill, 1976.

6. Lucas, Henry C., Jr., and Rodney B. Plimpton. "Technical Consulting in a Grass Roots, Action Oriented Organization." *Sloan Management Review* 14(1) (1972): 17-36.

15. Consensus Systems Design: An Evaluation of this Approach

by Enid Mumford

1 INTRODUCTION

There are many strategies which one group can use to ensure the compliance or cooperation of another. There is compliance through deference, because a group knows its place; or through trust because there is confidence that the right thing will be done. There is compliance through understanding which comes from good communication. There is compliance through negotiation and through shared control and participation in decisions. Which of these strategies is used in an organisation will be determined by values, expediency and power. The author of this paper has been associated for the past five years with a number of industrial and commercial organisations which have been willing to try the third of these strategies and to involve users in the design of their own computer systems. At the same time she has been working with two colleagues, John Hawgood of the University of Durham and Frank Land of the London School of Economics, developing a set of simple tools and techniques which assists users who are not professional systems designers to acquire the competences necessary for them to assume a design role. These tools and techniques are described in another paper [6] and here she will concentrate on discussing the pros and cons of a particular participative approach that she calls Consensus Design.

2 PARTICIPATIVE SYSTEMS DESIGN: ITS RATIONALE

Participative systems design means handing responsibility for the design of a new work system to the employees who eventually will have to operate it. Its acceptance as an efficient and ethical approach appears to be growing as the values of Western society become more democratic. There are four principal arguments for the use of such an approach when new computer systems are being designed. These are, first, an argument based on values which states that people have a moral right to control their own destinies and that this applies as much in the work situation as elsewhere [4]. In many countries, including Britain, this philosophy is now part of the policy of the main political parties, although there is still argument over how it shall be achieved. The second is an expediency argument and states that activities are ultimately controlled by those who perform them, and that people who do not have a say in decisions may decide to repeal the decisions of others as soon as those others leave the scene [2; 8]. The third relates to the location of knowledge and states that the experts on operational factors such as task design are the people who do the jobs [1]. The fourth argument is that involvement acts as a motivator and will lead to more productivity and efficiency [9]. Those managers and trade unions who support this kind of participation probably do so for mixed motives which may include some or all of the above. However, from the employee's point of view it is the consequences of a participative philosophy for his own work and work situation that are important rather than the motives that lie behind the enthusiasm of either side in industry to subscribe to it.

3 PARTICIPATIVE SYSTEMS DESIGN: DIFFERENT APPROACHES

Participation in systems design can take a number of different forms and the author calls the three approaches which she has used "Consultative" Design, "Representative" Design and "Consensus" Design. Each approach requires a higher level of participation than the last and their development has been the result of an evolution of thinking and practice. To date the author has used participative design methods in five organisations as follows: Consultative Design in the first, Representative Design in the next two and Consensus Design in the last two. Consultative Design leaves the bulk of design decisions with the traditional systems design group, although the objectives they set and the eventual form the system takes is greatly influenced by the needs, particularly the job satisfaction needs, of the user department. With this approach the technical system design group will make considerable efforts to diagnose accurately what kind of new system will give the user, including here subordinates and supervisors, a more satisfying and efficient work environment. In the engineering firm where the author adopted this approach she made a diagnosis of job satisfaction needs using both questionnaires and small group discussions. This information was then fed to the systems design team. At the same time users were given responsibility for identifying efficiency problems in the department, which the computer could help correct. The systems designers then attempted to produce a design solution that catered for both job satisfaction and efficiency needs. To increase job satisfaction a great deal of thought was given to the enrichment of user jobs. When the system was revealed to the clerks in the user department their response was that it was a good system, but that they in the meantime had thought of a better one in which the department was organised into a number of autonomous groups. It was the users own solution that was finally implemented and the author realised that by consulting with users in this way a learning process had taken place which had enabled the clerks to acquire the skills to formulate their own solution. She believed that this learning process could be assisted and formalised.

Her next two organisations provided an opportunity to do this. In the first of these, a California Life Insurance Company, she was priviliged to work with Professor Louis Davis of the University of California, Los Angeles, helping a group of insurance clerks to design a new structure of work into which a computer sys-

222

tem was to be embedded. In the second, an international bank, a group of clerks were given the responsibility of designing a new, more motivating and satisfying, work structure for a foreign exchange department, with a new on-line real-time computer system acting as the catalyst. In both of these situations a number of clerks representing all grades and functions in their departments were formed into a design group. The task of this "representative" group was to design a computer-based system of work which improved both job satisfaction and efficiency. Through this approach, staff in the department were able to exert a major influence over the design of the system. The technical systems designers concentrated on keeping the technical part of the system flexible enough to accept the form of work organization decided on by the user design group. In the bank this was a number of autonomous groups with each group assuming responsibility for all the activities associated with buying and selling a particular currency.

In the last two organisations, an engineering and a chemical company, the participative design approach was taken to a higher level, again using the consensus approach of attempting to involve all staff in the user department continuously throughout the systems design process. In the engineering firm a representative design group of eight people was formed from the user department and the computer department systems analysts. This was selected by management although in the author's view it should have been democratically elected. In the chemical plant, where a word processing system was to be introduced, the design group consisted of all the secretaries in a management services department, a group of six. The user department in the engineering firm was concerned with the processing and paying of suppliers invoices and had a staff of fifty. This design group not only had to come up with a new form of work organisation for the department, incorporating the use of a computer, it also had to feedback its ideas to departmental colleagues on the form this new work system should take, and allow the final decision to be taken by the department as a whole. In order to do this the design group required the same information on job satisfaction and efficiency needs as the consultative and representative design groups, and the same job design skills. But in addition it needed communication and consultation skills so that it could keep constantly and effectively in touch with the views of all clerks in the department. Experience to date suggests that the latter skills are more difficult to acquire than the former.

4 PROCEDURES FOR CONSENSUS DESIGN

As Consensus Design embraces Representative and Consultative Design the participative structure for its successful use will be described here and no further reference will be made to the other two approaches. The first and most essential step is to get the agreement of management and clerks in the user department to a consensus design approach. Departmental management must be enthusiastic rather than merely acceptive as to some extent they are handing over their own design role to their subordinates. Once management has agreed, the proposition is discussed with the clerks in small groups and it is their decision whether the approach shall be tried. The next step is to set up two participative structures, a design group and a steering group. Ideally a design group should be elected by all clerks in the department, although at the same time it must also represent the different grades, functions, age groups and sexes in the department. The technical systems designers will also be members of the design group and the departmental manager should have the option of joining it if he wishes to. This design group is likely to have two major problems: one, of ensuring the interest and sanction of top management and the trade unions; two, of not producing design solutions that are unacceptable to the organisation because they conflict with some important aspect of company policy. The answer to these problems is the creation of a steering group. In the engineering firm this consisted of the senior manager responsible for the user department, the head of management services, the chairman of the trade union branch, the systems manager responsible for the user computer system, the factory medical officer, the author and, at a later stage the clerk who acted as the chairman of the design group. The Steering Group had two important roles: one of giving the Design Group support and encouragement, the second of acting as an arbitrator if the Design Group was uncertain whether a particular design solution would conflict with the company policy. In the event the Steering Group never imposed any constraints on the Design Group. Their message was always "You design the best system from your point of view and we will support you".

Once the Design Group and the Steering Group were in existence the Design Group's first task was the diagnosis of efficiency and job satisfaction needs. Two techniques were used for doing this. The first was "variance analysis" in which system weaknesses are identified through noting where the actual behaviour of a system deviates from the desired behaviour. All staff in the department were involved in this analysis as they were all experts of those aspects of the work of the department where problems occurred. The second technique was "job satisfaction analysis" using questionnaires, in which a theory developed by Mumford was used as the framework for measurement [3]. The information collected as a result of these efficiency and job satisfaction diagnoses was then fed back to all staff in the department and discussed in small groups. This was done to check its accuracy and to establish improvement priorities. The benefit assessment approach [6] was not used in this study although it will shortly be used in the chemical plant design exercise. Once objectives had been set and priorities established the Design Group began to formulate alternative sociotechnical designs. The first of these was to split the department up into a number of autonomous groups with each group looking after the accounts of a group of suppliers. This would enable the clerks to become multiskilled, give them more control over their work and provide opportunities for problem solving which did not exist with the present functional organisation of work. This solution was reported back to the clerks but met with considerable hostility from a group of senior clerks who saw the opportunity for all clerks to be multiskilled as threatening their status. A second alternative design was then prepared with improvement being focussed on enriching the most routine jobs. The clerks rejected this on the basis that it did not greatly improve on the present organisation of work. The third alternative, and the one that was eventually accepted, was a compromise. The majority of clerks in the department were to be organized in autonomous groups and provided with the opportunity of increasing their grade and salary as they became expert in all the tasks for which the groups were responsible. A small specialist group would be created to meet the needs of the senior clerks who had indicated that joining an autonomous group would reduce their status. In addition a service group would be created with responsibility for a number of routine tasks such as photocopying, filing and handling the mail. This service group was a response to the request of a number of older clerks in the department who said they wished to do routine work and did not want the stress of becoming members of multiskilled autonomous groups.

These three alternative designs were presented to the Steering Group by the Design Group members themselves. At this stage they had all been carefully documented and their advantages and disadvantages thought through in detail. The Steering Group was most impressed by the competence of the Design Group and somewhat amazed that a group of clerks could do such an excellent design job. They indicated that any of the three design solutions would be acceptable to them, although they preferred the first or the third. The three solutions were then presented in detail to the staff of the user department at a meeting chaired by the Chairman of the Trade Union Branch. They were voted on and it was agreed that the third solution should be implemented.

Although a decision had been taken, the Design Group's task was by no means over. They now had to specify the selected solution in considerable detail and develop a the framework for the new autonomous group structure. They also had to consider a strategy for implementation which would include training and the physical layout of the reorganised department. They also had to work with the technical systems designers and decide how the clerks would interact with the new computer terminals. This system has now been implemented and is working successfully. Details of the complete design are provided in [5].

5   PROBLEMS OF USING A CONSENSUS DESIGN APPROACH

All strategies for change have their own problems and Consensus Design is no exception. Those discussed below are derived from the author's experience and more skilled change consultants might find them easier to avoid:

5.1   Trust

It must not be assumed that because a group of office or shop floor workers agree to participate in a Consensus Design approach this means that they are convinced of management's good intentions. In the engineering firm suspicion of management's motives in permitting this unusual degree of democracy continued for some time. It required many statements from management that they had no evil intent for trust to be established.

5.2 Election versus Selection of the Design Group

The author strongly believes that if a Consensus Design approach is used the Design Group should be democratically elected. In the engineering firm management was worried that an election would lead to the recruitment of the most militant clerks in the department to the Design Group. They therefore preferred to select the group themselves. Although this produced an admirable representation of the different interests in the department, for a long time the Design Group were seen as management "blue eyes" and this affected their relationships with their clerical colleagues.

5.3 Conflicts of Interest

It cannot be assumed that a group of clerks, although they work on similar jobs in the same department, will all have the same interests or favour the same design solution. With a Consensus Design approach these conflicts of interest will quickly surface and will have to be discussed and negotiated. This is not an easy task for a Design Group.

5.4 Stress

A Design Group formed from a group of clerical or shop floor workers has "no place to hide". Whereas a professional group of technical systems designers can return to their own department when relationships become difficult, a Consensus Design Group must continue to work side by side with its colleagues during the design process. As this inevitably has its conflict periods they are likely to experience stress from time to time and this is something they will not be used to.

5.5 Communication and Consultation

In order to avoid some of the problems of 5.3 and 5.4, Design Groups need to have some skills in communication and consultation. In the author's experience it is more difficult to transfer such skills to the Design Group than it is to give them design expertise.

5.6 The Role of Professional Systems Designers

With a Consensus Design approach the role of the professional systems designer is greatly altered. Instead of being a "designer" in the traditional sense he becomes a consultant to the Design Group. Some systems designers may regard this change of role as a threat to their authority and status.

226

5.7   The Role of the Departmental Manager

If the departmental manager decides not to become a member of the design group because he believes that his presence will have an inhibiting effect on discussion, then he must always be kept in touch with what is taking place. He must also approve the solution that is eventually chosen by his department.

5.8   Rapidly Changing Technology

Whereas there are no serious difficulties in assisting a Design Group to acquire the skills necessary to design their own work situation in association with an established technology, difficulties increase when this technology is developing very rapidly. The author is experiencing this problem at present with the word-processing project in the chemical company. It is clear that word processing is a transitory technology that will soon be replaced by general purpose terminals as part of a move towards the electronic office. At this moment in time it is very difficult to visualise the consequences of the electronic office for clerks and therefore to design a satisfying work situation.

6   ADVANTAGES OF USING A CONSENSUS DESIGN APPROACH

Although Consensus Design has its problems the author believes that its advantages greatly outweigh these. She sees these advantages as the following.

6.1   Values

The approach fits well with the current ideology on the need for participation and industrial democracy.

6.2   Commitment

The system that emerges from the design process will be seen by the user department as very much its own system. Employees will have identified their own problems and arrived at their own solution. In doing this they will have been assisted to create a good technical solution by the computer professionals whose focus of attention will be how the department can receive the most help from computer back up. A good human solution will emerge from the knowledge and skills of the Design Group.

6.3   Knowledge

The practical exercise of analysis and design should provide all users with a high level of knowledge of departmental problems and an awareness of how a new organisation of tasks and responsibilities, together with the use of a computer or a new level of computer technology, can assist these.

6.4 Job Satisfaction

This should improve because the user group has identified its own job satisfaction needs and created its own job satisfaction solution. A word of warning is required here, however. In the author's experience a well-designed human solution can be damaged through poor implementation, particularly when the regrading of jobs is involved. Also in a user department with a high labour turnover and interacting with a rapidly changing labour market, the job satisfaction needs of one group of employees may not be the same as those of the group that replaces them.

6.5 Efficiency

Again efficiency should improve because the group with the most detailed knowledge of work problems has been responsible for their analysis and solution. In the engineering firm the Design Group said that it was not until they were involved in the design exercise that they understood both how their department *did* work and how it *should* have worked. These newly-acquired analyses and design skills can be used to monitor the new work system and make corrections when new problems occur.

6.6 Integration

A well-functioning organisation will have succeeded in integrating four important variables. These are technology, tasks, human needs and organisational objectives. The design and use of technology needs to create a set of tasks that people are motivated to perform efficiently. In turn the way these tasks are structured must assist employees to achieve job satisfaction, and the interaction between technology, tasks and human needs must positively assist the organisation to achieve its goals. The practice of the past has been to attempt to use technology to assist the organisation to achieve its goals through an approach to efficiency based on tighter controls and a routinisation of work. Human needs for job satisfaction and the influence of task structure on job satisfaction and motivation were ignored. Consensus Design helps to integrate all four variables.

7   TRAINING, MONITORING AND DEVELOPMENT

Success with Consensus Design does not come about of its own accord and in the author's experience the transfer of design skills to the user can be assisted by a formal training programme. When a new design group is formed its members are given a two-day course which includes discussion of the concept of job satisfaction, and instruction in how to carry out a "variance analysis" and to measure job satisfaction. They are then required to undertake a practical exercise in socio-technical systems design, with the computer professionals in the group focussing on identifying technical needs and solutions and the users doing the same for human needs and solutions. This and other similar exercises will shortly be published [7]. This exercise has the function of communicating to the Design Group that there are alternative ways of designing work systems and analytical tools that can help the design process. Real learning only occurs when the Design Group begins to design its own system, however. Because of this learning requirement, most systems designs will take at least six months. The Design Group cannot easily acquire the necessary skills in a shorter period of time.

Once the new system is designed and implemented its success has to be monitored. A test of its efficiency can be made by examining the earlier list of variances and checking that these have either been eliminated or made more easy to control, without the introduction of major new variances. Job satisfaction improvement can be measured by using the job satisfaction diagnostic tool once again and checking that the "fit" between what employees are seeking from their work and the work situation and what they are receiving has now improved.

An important final point is that systems design and development can never stop. Job satisfaction needs and expectations are not static but change constantly as new employees enter the labour force or the expectations of existing employees increase. Similarly a work system only remains efficient so long as it enables a department or organisation to cope successfully with its external environment. In these days of rapid change this environment is likely to be very dynamic. Any system therefore needs to be constantly montiored to ensure that it continues to meet efficiency and job-satisfaction needs and to be adjusted if it is not doing so.

8 CONCLUSIONS

To sum up, the advantages of a participative approach to systems design based on *consensus* decisions can be said to be the following:

From the author's value position it is morally right. Employees should be involved in the design of their own work situations.

From management's point of view it is advantageous because the result is an efficient system and a satisfied work force.

From the employees' point of view it is advantageous because they are able to create a system that meets their efficiency and job-satisfaction needs.

From the organisation's point of view it is advantageous because the result is a system that has positive relationships between its technical, human and administrative parts and is therefore a viable system.

REFERENCES

1. Edstrom, A. and L. Nauges. "The Implementation of Computer Based Information Systems under Varying Structural Conditions." Paper presented to Altorg Conference, Gothenburg, May 1974.

2. Hedberg, B., P. Nystrom and W. Starbuck. "Camping on See-Saws, Prescription for a Self-Designing Organization." *Administrative Science Quarterly* 21 (1) (1976): 41-62.

3. Mumford, E. "Job Satisfaction: A Method of Analysis." *Personnel Review*. 1 (3) (1972): 48-87.

4. Mumford, E. "Human Values and the Introduction of Technical Change." in Moneta (ed.) *Information Technology*. Proceedings of the 3rd Jerusalem Conference on Information Technology. North Holland, 1978.

5. Mumford, E. and D. Henshall. *A Participative Approach to Computer Systems Design*. Associated Business Press, 1979.

6. Mumford, E., F. Land, and J. Hawgood. "A Participative Approach to the Design of Computer Systems." *Impact of Science on Society* 28(3) (1978): 235-253.

7. Mumford, E. and M. Weir. *Computer Systems in Work Design: The Ethics Method*. Associated Business Press, 1979.

8. Nystrom, P.C. "Resisters, Adaptors and Innovators: On the Implementation of Managerial Goal Setting Systems." Working Paper, University of Wisconsin, Milwaukee, 1975.

9. White, J.K. and R.A. Ruh. "The Effects of Personal Values on the Relationship between Participation and Job Attitudes." *Administrative Science Quarterly* 18(4) (1973): 295-333.

16. Concepts and Experiences with Participative Design Approaches

by Hasse Clausen

1 A PRACTICAL EXAMPLE

"Involving Users Causes Conflicts" versus "Exclusion of Users Causes Conflicts"?

In 1972 an agreement was made between the various organisations which have some relation to the library world in Denmark about developing an information system for all libraries in Denmark. The Librarian's Union and Kommunedata (the central computer for the municipalities and counties) were both among the organisations party to this agreement.

The system development went on in quite a normal way until 1975 when suddenly the librarians in several libraries got interested in the ongoing work.

In 1977, after five years' work, the project—FAUST—was stopped.

The idea of the system evolved in the first few years of the 1970s: the computer system should be able to produce the catalogue of the books. Almost all people having contact with the library sector approved of the idea, which slowly grew into a proposal for a nationwide system able to take care of book-lending control. This proposal was discussed in 1972 by about two hundred people from the libraries; it was decided to start the project.

A project organisation was formed with computer specialists, representatives from the central organisations and a few representatives from the libraries—all these holding leading positions in the libraries. This organisation worked for almost two years without any serious outside interruptions. The project team came up with a proposal for a system solution at the beginning of 1975. At this time the project team found that it would be a good idea to present the proposal to the librarians around the country with the aim of getting comments and then make minor adjustments. It was decided to start by publishing a series of newsletters called FAUST-Information and to arrange meetings with librarians in various places in the country. This decision turned out to be the beginning of the end of the project FAUST. The information given initiated a great deal of activity among the librarians. Local FAUST-groups were formed in various libraries, and the material given by the project group was studied carefully by the librarians. At the meetings there was great interest in discussing the purpose of the project, to the great surprise of the specialists who thought they should discuss the proposal.

The librarians were interested in influencing the project while the specialists were interested in getting comments on their proposal.

The following year a debate went on in the librarians' magazine and in the newspapers with contributions for and against the FAUST-project. This debate ended with a petition of signatures demanding a halt to the project. About one-third of all librarians supported this demand and signed the protest. In the summer of 1977 the project was officially stopped.

It was characteristic that the computer specialists reacted to the librarians' actions by being offended. They really thought that they had done a good job, and now they needed the librarians' comments on the elaborated system proposal. It was inadmissible to question the purpose of the system, since an agreement had been made three years earlier, and the specialists had worked on the basis of this decision.

The specialists considered the librarians as reservoirs of knowledge who could be used in the system development process, but they had never thought about the problem that these reservoirs might want influence. From the specialists' point of view the involvement of the users caused a conflict "which was not fair".

On the other hand the librarians had a lot of objections to the system when they found out what some of the consequences would be if the system was implemented on the basis of the system proposal. The librarians thought that the proposal was absolutely unusable, and that a lot of changes were necessary. Many of the problems could have been avoided if the librarians had not been excluded from the system development.

2   WHY PARTICIPATION?

The above-mentioned example illustrates two different but essential ways of considering the question of user participation in the system development process. From the computer specialists' point of view it is necessary to involve the end-users in the system development process, first of all because these people are to be part of the system. The system cannot function unless the people using the system accept the system. Secondly the users need to be involved because they are resources of knowledge, but they are expected to accept the bounds of the system concept.

From the employee's point of view, participation is a question of getting influence in the system design process, not only on specific details but on the system as a whole.

Both groups are interested in the problem area "user involvement in the system design process", but obviously they have been motivated in different ways.

2.1   The Computer Specialists' Point of View

EDP has been used for a period of only about twenty to thirty years in most of the Western countries. In this short period the application of the technique has undergone radical changes as the technique was developed. It is essential to note that the technique has been used to support three different system types: technical systems, formalised administrative systems, and information systems. It is also essential to note that the system design process for these three system types are very different in nature. A great difference exists between the first two system types and the third. In the case of technical systems, it is a matter of construction of a well-defined system where the bounds of the system are under control. Usually, it is possible for the constructor to survey and control the problems connected with the design process. In the case of administrative systems, I would postulate that the question of constructing a system is a question of accomplishing a translation process and not a system design process.

The computer specialists' perception of the system concept, and the problems connected with the system design process, are very closely connected with the experience the computer specialists have from working with these two kinds of systems.

The information system is in many ways different from the two just mentioned in spite of many similarities. First of all, the information system is not formalised or controllable, as was the case for the two other system types. This is due to the way in which the human being is expected to interact with the system. The unpredictability of the human being is going to be an important factor in the system design process. It is a factor with which the computer specialist has no experience. Most often specialists will apply the system concepts and methods which were used on the two other kinds of systems. This could lead to two ways of solving the problems of designing information systems. One way is to ignore the existence of human factors. This is for instance the case with the IBM Class-System, a production and planning system in which the atoms in the system are machine groups. On the other hand, the specialists could try to solve the problem by making a model of the human being and then try to get the real human being to act in accordance with this model. This can be seen in many of the supermarket systems where the terminals are provided with light-panels to help the cashiers perform the activities in a special sequence.

In other words, human beings are objects—system resources in the specialists' view.

A last and radical proposal for solving the problems concerning the human factor in computer systems is simply to eliminate the worker, i.e., to automate the whole system. Newspaper systems are examples of this.

2.2   The Workers' Point of View

The workers' interest in the use and development of computer systems is also influenced by and different for the various kinds of system types. Interest among workers appeared at the same time as the development of information systems began. There are of course a lot of parameters which account for this growth of interest, but I think two of these are of special importance, namely, technical progress and the tradition for and improvement of democratization at the working places. It is important to note that the application of computer systems has provided a bridge between blue-collar and white-collar workers, because the white-collar workers are now being confronted with the consequences of the second industrial revolution. They are now being affected in the same way as the blue-collar workers were decades ago.

In the Scandinavian countries this democratization process has resulted in workers' representation on the boards of enterprises, agreements which give the workers greater influence on their own situation at work, etc. The application of computers has not supported these activities; on the contrary, it has counteracted these drives. The fact that the application of computer systems has had a lot of consequences for the working situation of almost all workers in these countries must give rise to some reactions from the union side. But first of all, the activities of the unions must be seen as part of the activities to get more influence in a broad sense.

Therefore, from the workers' point of view, computer systems are only a special—but a very important—technique over which the workers must get influence if they want to have any influence at all in their working situation.

It will be from these two different points of view that various activities will be initiated in connection with the problems of user participation in the system design process.

2.3   Some Proposals for Participation Solutions

A proposal for organising the users' participation related to the system design process will of course be influenced by the viewpoint from which the problem is contemplated. Therefore, I will continue to distinguish between the above-mentioned two different viewpoints, even though I am aware that in most practical situations, participation of users will be a combination.

3 SOCIO-TECHNIQUE IN THE HANDS OF COMPUTER SPECIALISTS

It is not quite fair to the socio-technicians to intimate that they have the computer specialists' viewpoint as described above. The reason why I want to mention the socio-technique at this time is, however, the fact that the methods are suitable for the computer specialists' objectives. Unfortunately, the computer specialists are apt to misinterpret the socio-technique by emphasizing the word technique too much.

I mention two examples from Denmark which will illustrate how computer specialists tend to solve the problem of user participation.

SYSKON (system construction) is a method which has developed from the background of practical experience with the construction of computer-based systems in the 1960s. It could in many ways be compared with PORGI although it is smaller. In this method it is stated that it is important to show consideration for the users of the system. Therefore, it is advisable to let the various users be represented in the development process and to help the system specialists to find out who should be represented in the different phases the project has to go through. And it is advisable to make a matrix in two dimensions with the different groups of personnel in one dimension and the phases in the other dimension. Then you plot into this matrix the importance of the participation of the different groups in

234

the different phases. That is almost all. In this case we see that it is the computer specialists who are responsible for decisions about who should participate in what, and secondly, we see the desire to quantify the need for users to participate.

Kommunedata has been inspired by all the problems of showing considerations for the social aspects of implementing computer systems. Therefore, a fundamental systems development method has been worked out which should satisfy the social objectives. This is done by recommending the use of the model in Figure 1.

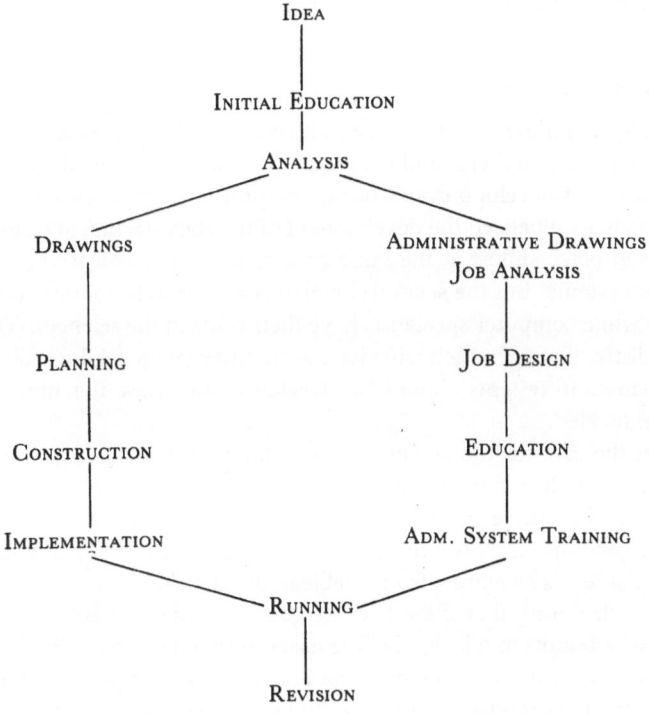

Figure 1. Phase Model.

Unfortunately, it has not been possible for Kommunedata to describe the contents of the so-called social phases. But even if it had done so, the model suffers from the fact that it is made on the premisses of the computer specialist. The employees are expected to accept the system idea, the employees and the specialists should be taught some common methods (only technical methods are mentioned) and they have to accept that the system developing process is cut up in small pieces.

Even when the users have agreed to participate on the conditions of the computer specialists as expressed in this model, it has proved to be very difficult for the users to get real influence in the system work. The reason for this can be explained primarily by the fact that the methods used are those used by the specialists and the time pressure under which the system work is carried out.

None of the above-mentioned activities met the employees' requirement for real influence in the system design process.

3.1 Socio-technique

First of all, it is important to notice that sociotechnique is an area developed by organisational researchers, and consequently it is not specifically connected with the problems of developing and using computer systems. Of course the use of computers has influenced the development of the socio-technical research area, as it has taken place almost at the same time as the expansion in the area of using computer systems. But the socio-technician is very closely connected with the humanities while computer specialists have their roots in the sciences. This is an important distinction because it will give rise to different viewpoints concerning how the information systems should be developed and how the human problems should be tackled.

As was the case for the evolution of computer systems, it is possible to divide the evolution of the socio-technical research related to the problems of employees' participation into three generations. This is done by Max Elden in [1]. He named the three generations "Sleeping Bag", "Tool Kit" and "Do-It-Yourself Workshops". Table 1 is an extract from a table in this article.

It is worth noting that there is quite good accordance between the computer specialists' attempts to take hold of the users' problems and the Sleeping Bag strategy. But even in this case the different scientific starting points will imply rather different practical solutions. Anyway, there is a gap between the computer specialists' methods of solution and the third generation, the Do-It-Yourself Workshop strategy.

4 THE ACTIVITIES OF THE UNIONS

During the last several years there have been a lot of activities among the employees in the Scandinavian countries. Strikes have occurred because of the implementation of some computer systems.

Some of the most well-known results are probably the data agreements which have been made between the Norwegian TUC and the employers. These agreements tend to regulate the employees' influence and participation in the system design process. Though this result is the most visible and could be directly connected with the system design process, it is only one of several activities to help the unions to get influence in the use and development of computer systems. The goal

236

Table 1. The Three "Generations"

	1st Generation "Sleeping Bag"	2nd Generation "Tool Kit"	3rd Generation "Do-It-Yourself Workshops"
Period	1964-1967	1968/69-early 1970s	From early 1970s
Aim	Demonstrate feasible alternative forms of organization (e.g., autonomous workgroups) in industrial organizations	Diffuse alternative organization forms (e.g., to democratize organization structure) beyond industrial work places (foreman's role, wage systems plus non-industrial applications	Diffuse a way of working—"participative design" (i.e., to democratize organization change processes)
Way of working	Researcher works for labor-management committee which sanctions/supports his work: Researcher analyses, recommends changes, and manages implementation/evaluation	Researcher works under labour-management committee but more directly and cooperatively with workers affected: Researcher analyses but employees participate in developing recommendations and take responsibility for implementing and evaluating	Employee redesign teams analyze own organization and, in workshops together with redesign teams from other organizations and researchers, help to develop recommendations, implement and evaluate
Researcher Role	Expert	Consultant	Co-learner

for the unions is to get influence on the total system; that means the total activities of the enterprises.

The unions in the Scandinavian countries have several activities going on in connection with the problems of computers. These can be grouped in the following way: research, education, activating members, documents, and political influence.

4.1 Research Activities

The aim of these activities is to procure knowledge which could be used to influence progress in accordance with the interest of the members of the union. NJMF, DEMOS, and DUE are the names of the projects started by and managed by the TUC in Norway, Sweden, and Denmark. All these projects are based on a negotiation strategy, which means that they are pure union projects and are not accomplished in cooperation with employers. Furthermore, they deal primarily with the problems of getting influence in the development and use of the computer systems.

In Denmark these projects constitute only a minor part of the research activities initiated by the unions. Thus, for example, the TUC in Denmark has formed a Research Council of the Union and they have initiated quite a lot of research projects.

4.2 Educational Activities

It is important for the union that the experience from the research projects is communicated to the members of the union. Educational activities are used to serve this purpose but, further, it has turned out to be necessary to educate the members of the union so that they are able to participate in the activities within the research projects. So there are two kinds of educational activities which are of importance to the union, the formalised general courses and the activities closely connected with a special research project.

4.3 Activating the Members

The above-mentioned research projects are all carried out as action-research projects. This means that the project should be formed by the researchers and the people in the work places jointly. The reason for this is that it is only possible for the members of the union to get influence in single computer systems if they themselves are able to bring different kinds of acts into effect and carry them through. In the individual work place it should be the local union which is responsible for the kind of influence the workers will have in an actual situation. This is a very important point in the strategy of the union—the results should be usable for the workers in the work places.

4.4 Documents

By these activities I mean the introduction of documents which somehow will regulate the other activities. This would typically be documents like data-agree-
ments or laws concerning working conditions. These documents could either arise
as a result of the other activities mentioned or they can support the workers' possibilities for realizing different kinds of acts.

4.5 Political Influence

The question of the extent to which the union and the workers should have influence on their own working situation and thereby on the politics of the individual
organisation is by nature closely connected with and dependent on the political
climate in the country. Is there general acceptance of the union as an organisation
which represents the workers' interests against the employers'?, is it accepted that
the workers should have influence in their own working conditions?, etc.

The acts which will be possible for the unions will be dependent on this political
climate and different political acts will influence these possibilities; laws concerning the labour market are an example of an area in which it is important for
the union to have political influence. The Swedish *Medbestemmelsesloven* (Participation in Decision Making Act) is an example of a law which will influence the
possibilities of worker participation in the system design process.

5 SOME CONSEQUENCES OF TAKING THE PARTICIPATION PROBLEM SERIOUSLY IN CONNECTION WITH THE SYSTEM DESIGN PROCESS

I believe in the necessity of taking the participation problem seriously in the years
to come, even though there are a lot of obstacles to overcome before the system
design process in general will be based on a participation strategy. I expect that
the system design process will be influenced by ongoing socio-technical activities
and activities within the unions. But I want to point out that there will be essential
differences between a system design process based on a socio-technical strategy
and a system design process based on a union strategy.

It is my expectation that if you want to base development strategy on the idea of
participation it will be necessary to change the traditional way of designing
computer systems in the following problem areas: the purpose of the project, the
steering of the project, the participants, the working area, working methods and
the role of the specialist.

On the other hand it is not unabiguous how these changes should be. As examples which can illustrate the two different kinds of strategies I will refer to two
Norwegian research projects.

The socio-technical project has been carried through in a sub-branch of a Norwegian bank. This project has mainly followed a Do-It-Yourself Workshop strategy.

The union project is the NJMF project. This project was initiated by the Norwegian Iron and Metal Trade Union. The project took place within the local trade union in four different factories; it was the first of its kind in the Scandinavian countries. These two projects are not comparable in all senses but they are typical of the two kinds of activities dealt with in this paper. They may be compared with respect to the following problem areas.

5.1 The Purpose of the Project

Today nearly all computer systems are developed to accomplish rationalization. This purpose is normally expected to be achieved by the setting and fulfilling of some technical and economic goals.

Both the union and the socio-technical strategy imply that social goals should also be established. So far there is accordance between the two kinds of strategy, but the socio-technician does not question the overall purpose of the system and this might be the case in a union strategy. The reasons for this are the differences in the overall purpose of the two kinds of strategies. The socio-technician wants to make better systems and better working conditions, while the union strategy is based on the overall purpose of strengthening the union and thereby making better working conditions.

5.2 Steering of the Project

Today the system design process is steered by the employers and the computer specialists, the latter normally through technical requirements.

The socio-technician is questioning the steering of the computer specialists.

Within a union strategy it is important that the local trade union has resources of its own. Furthermore, a union strategy will normally be based on a negotiation strategy, which means negotiations will play an important role in the design process.

5.3 The Participants

The employees will normally be consulted by the computer specialists several times in the system development process. Both the unions and the socio-technical strategy agree that it is necessary to involve the employees in a much more active way, but the socio-technical strategy accepts the employers' right to choose who should be the participants in the project. In the union strategy it is a demand that the unions have the right to choose the participants.

5.4 The Working Area

Both strategies demand that in addition to technical and economic problems, social problems like working environments, working conditions and contact between employees should also be taken into account.

Compared with the situation today, some of the major changes would be that it will be necessary to take the environments into consideration at the start of the system design process. Furthermore, this process will be open-ended, which means the design process will be infinite.

5.5 The Working Methods

Most design work in connection with the construction of computer systems is based on the use of phase-model, and it is often the case that time limits determine the amount of work in the project.

These conditions have to be changed if design work is to be based on a participative strategy. In both strategies the employees are going to participate; that means they should have the time to discuss the problems connected with the project, which is very time-consuming.

Furthermore, it should be possible to raise any problem which the employees find to be important, at any time.

It will be necessary to develop and use different kinds of methods and techniques in design work. This is especially important in connection with description, documentation and analysis of the system. Unfortunately, there is a great lack of methods and techniques which are usable by the employees. On this last point a disagreement between the unions and the socio-technical strategy exists.

5.6 The Role of the Specialists

Both strategies expect the specialists to be in a consultant function but they differ on the question of the neutrality of the specialists. In the union strategy it is necessary for the specialists to choose a side in the conflict, whereas in a socio-technical strategy he could be neutral.

6 SUMMARY

The progress towards employees' participation in the system design process will continue. How this participation will take place is primarily dependent on the computer specialists' need for cooperation with the employees and the demands introduced by the unions. The socio-technical arguments and proposals introduced by the socio-technicians will only play a secondary role, and will only be used to the extent that these could be used by one of the former groups.

It will be necessary to make quite a lot of changes in the system design process, as it is known today. What kind of changes, how and when these will take place, are dependent on the power and influence of the different interest groups. In connection with this the attitudes among specialists as well as among the employees and employers play an important role; changes will probably not occur until attitudes are changed. This implies that the political climate in countries will influence the degree of participation in the design process; therefore it will be the case that the concept of participation will have different meanings in different countries.

However, it could be the case that the problem of user participation in the system design process wil be totally irrelevant within a period of five, ten or twenty years because of progress in computer science.

REFERENCES

1. Elden, M. "Three Generations of Work Democracy experiments in Norway—Beyond Classical Socio-Technical Systems Analysis." to appear in C.L. Cooper and E. Mumford (eds.) *The Quality of Working Life: The European Experiment.*

2. Hoeyer, R. *Teknologisk Forandring og Organisasjonsutvikling.* (Norwegian)

3. Nygaard, K. and O.T. Bergo. *Planleggning, styring og databehandling.* Tiden Norsk Forlag. (Norwegian)

Most of the literature about the projects mentioned is written in the Scandinavian languages, so instead of giving the pertaining references, I will list the addresses for these projects.

DEMOS: Box 5606, 114 86 Stockholm, Sweden.

DUE: Datalogisk afdeling, Ny Munkegade, 8000 Aarhus C, Denmark.

Norsk Regnecentral: Forskningsveien 1B, Oslo 3, Norway.

17. High Level Languages—A Basis for Participative Design

by D.N. Podger

1 INTRODUCTION

This paper sketches a theoretical development in the field of systems design, indicates how a new design method relates to it and briefly demonstrates the method by showing how a design solution to a particular practical problem can be derived. The example solution itself is of some intrinsic interest in that it is claimed to be a general purpose small business accounting language, potentially executable on very low-cost equipment.

This general purpose language, which is one of the end results of the research, provides a basis for the participative design of computer accounting systems for small organisations in that it provides a view of accounting that can readily be shared by an analyst and a businessman. One may go further and claim that, for a well-educated accountant, the language provides the capability of autonomous design. We will return to this latter claim at the conclusion of this paper.

2 THE SETTING

In the space of this paper it is not possible to provide a detailed account of the developing society within which the research was done. Suffice to say, however, that the environment of Papua New Guinea, a newly independent nation now going through the process of seeking economic independence, is one of great variety as to the various forms its businesses take and of great speed of change as these businesses develop.

3 ROLE CENTERED SYSTEMS DESIGN

Amidst the flux of events that constitute the setting for our problem, the role of the accountant stands out as the possible anchoring point since his procedures may be observed not to change as rapidly as the organisations. Could the process of designing a system commence with this role?

We know that systems definition is always job or role definition as well; if a system is designed and built up primarily on data analysis and on systems requirements then the jobs or roles that emerge from this design process will only accidentally be suitable. The proposal here is to reverse the usual order of systems analysis and commence with an analysis of the role of the accountant. It is important to distinguish this proposal from quite commonly, but more generally expressed concerns about the users of computer systems. Depending on the point of view taken in the current debate about users, he is to be consulted on schedule, or must participate in the whole design process, or must himself design his own system with minimal interference from experts. This respect, however implemented, for diversity in user needs, user environments and user views has been valuable in shifting the focus of systems design away from the machine and has made it to some extent more responsive to human requirements. But there is perhaps some danger in this very process, particularly if such a contingent view of the user tended to deny that there may be more constant patterns beneath the shifting ones that make up his visible behavioural surface.

4   THE NATURE OF CHANGE

This paper proposes the existence of the above patterns and seeks to describe them. Behaviour within any procedural system is viewed as always being subject to *differential* rates of change over time. A procedural or information processing system, whatever else it may be, is at least both a social system and a theoretical system. There is, in the case of accountants, a recognizable community of professionals and their staffs who perform the various procedures of their profession, informed by a more or less systematic body of knowledge. There is correspondence between the two systems in that the more senior the professional, the more fundamental the knowledge area he utilises. Social and theoretical systems have both

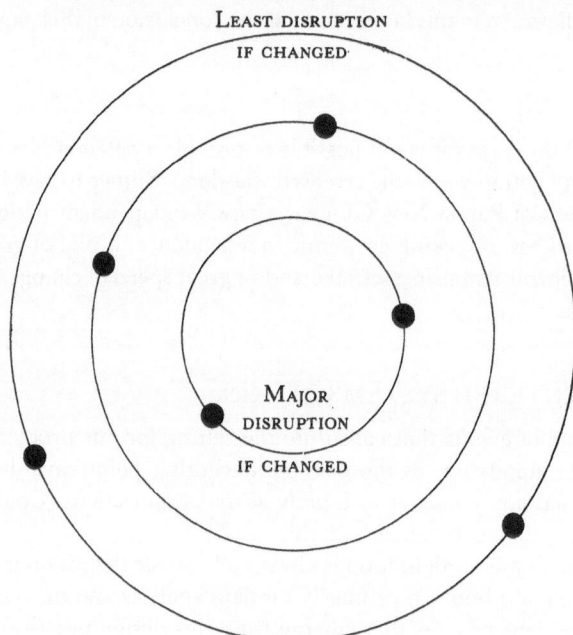

Figure 1. Maslow's model of a social system

separately been described in the way proposed, that is, as subject to differential rates of change. Maslow (quoted in [11]) has pictured a social system as a ring structure where the periphery is made up of those elements whose change would require least disruption of the system as a whole. The nucleus, on the other hand, consists of those elements whose change would entail a reorganization of the whole system. The concept occurs again in Quine's [10] and in Kuhn's [5] treatment of structure in bodies of scientific knowledge and in Epstein's analysis of social networks [2]. Quine describes an ordering of the elements in these bodies which is based on the extent to which other elements depend upon them. It can be argued that such ordering is a nucleus-centred web of related dependencies. Popper's autobiography concludes with the view that that objective world which is the systematic outcome of all human thought, problem solving and theorizing (termed World 3) has a deep nucleus containing such ultimate values as truth [5]. Kuhn argues for a corresponding ranking of change incidents in such a schema, ranging from ''puzzle-solving'' through ''paradigm change'' to wholesale upsets within ''disciplinary matrices''.

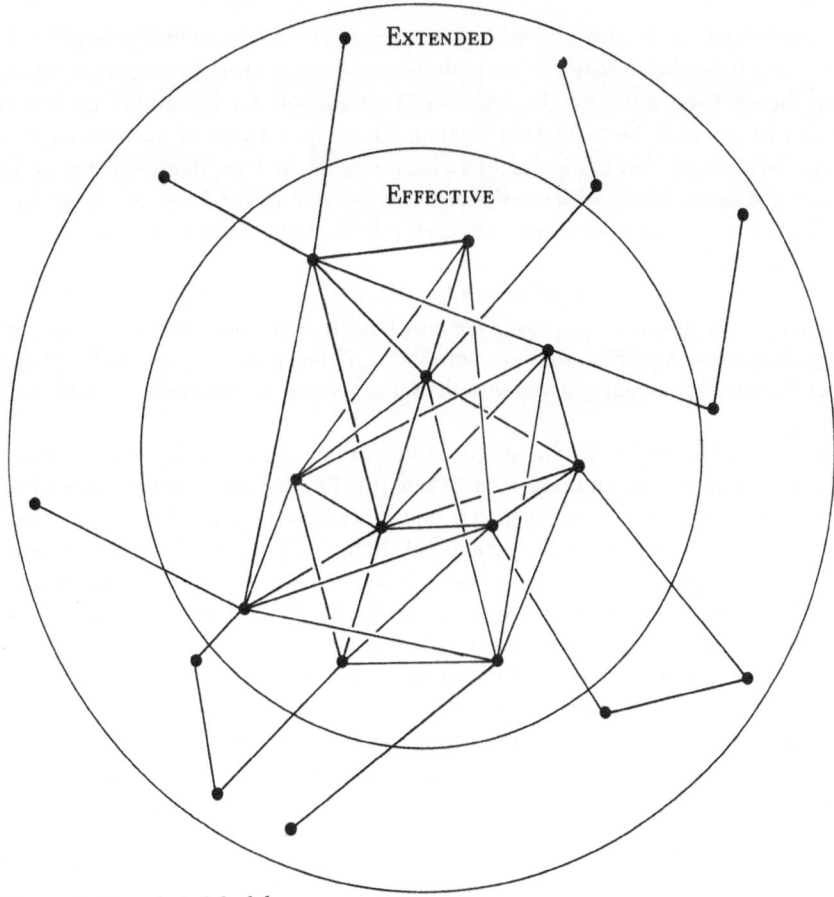

Figure 2. Epstein's Model

245

Integral to all these models is the notion that the occurrence of change complies with the schema, being rare at the nucleus and frequent at the periphery.

Kelly [4], in his theory of personal constructs, built a general theory of psychology out of the notion that a person can be viewed as a theory builder who, during his lifetime, puts together hierarchies of dichotomous constructs, construing experience through them. Again, patterns of dependency form and link together as assemblages of constructs which will undergo differential rates of change, corresponding, perhaps, to Morris's three aspects of the person, "routine", "ritual" and "drama" [6], according as to where the change process occurs in relation to the construct nucleus. Different kinds of learning are suggested by such a perspective on the person. Bateson provides a generally consistent view with his Learning I (simple accomulation), Learning II (structural change) and Learning III, the last being rare and revolutionary in effect [1]. Finally, we may note that for social, theoretical and personal systems, the deeper the change the longer it takes.

5 ROLE MAPS

Every procedural system can be seen as a related set of roles. The nucleus-centred view of a procedural system from both its social and knowledge structure aspects can therefore be extended through to roles, each role having a nucleus-centred map within which the role task is located. The map is a view of the object system with the point of view being that of a given role; its nucleus, though, is not necessarily the given task and its periphery may be well beyond the task boundary. Shifting our attention to the person, each role incumbent can be viewed as being in possession of this same nucleus or nuclei-centered map. Through this map, the incumbent construes and elaborates his job role and, more specifically, his particular job requirements, or task. We now have a view, then, of external roles integrally possessing differential rates of change, *fitting*, more or less, similarly organized internal personal systems with the same general characteristic of differential change.

It is possible to expand this simple model to take up a number of related concepts such as values, interests and beliefs [8]. One of the major utilities of the model that has so far been sketched is that it predicts the general location, the order of incidence and the likely duration of change in procedural systems. As such it assists designers and users in the selection of the nexus of an information system, those processes which they may make the backbone of their system and those they should make either more or less flexible, that is, alterable on one of a number of time scales, depending on the assumed lifetime of the system. The model as a whole can be argued for, criticized and related, as we have seen above, to other models. But, because it also generates predictions concerning the performance of a procedural system, the model is, to this degree, capable of being tested.

6 THE ACCOUNTING MAP

The hypothesized, descriptive model which has thus far been built up only in general terms is now applied to develop the concept of the role of an accountant.

The procedural system of accounting is extensive and relatively stable even though it is at present experiencing the extensive "drama" of the inflation accounting debate. The accountant's role map may be approached through an examination of the accounting process.

At the boundaries of this process are the various reactive transaction-raising processes. Invoices are raised, receipts written, pay slips distributed. Information collected from these boundary activities flows inwards through successive processes of summarization. As one moves from the periphery towards the centre, activity becomes more proactive. Debtors' statements are distributed and late payers pursued, inventory balances are checked and replenishment orders placed. Transactions still penetrate but their volume is much reduced; the occasional bad debt is written off, an asset is sold.

At the centre the information flow has lost much of the environmentally adaptive character it had at the periphery; invoice formats vary considerably, balance sheets do not. The processes have lost, to some degree, the characteristic of arbitrariness, the requirement that strings of activities should follow each other in a rigid sequence. Discretion as to the placement of processes in time has also increased and alternative actions must be weighed, as when investment decisions are required. Interrelationships are generally more complex; what improves profits may or may not adversely affect cash flow and vice versa.

In the analysis the above somewhat discursive account is organized using the more abstract concepts of connections and connectedness. These are, respectively, the associations between process elements and the extent to which these associations are drawn together into nets of association or assemblages. There are a great variety of associations or connections and they can be categorized according to what relationship pertains between element and elements or between assemblage and assemblage. A nonexhaustive list follows, with examples:

Table 1. Connections of Process Elements

x subsumes y	An example of a ledger is a debtors' ledger
x may precede y	Sequential preparation of an invoice
x must precede y	Key the fields before releasing the record
x looks like y	Credit notes are "mirror images" of invoices
x has the same effect as y	Journal entries used instead of a credit note

Connectedness, then, is the measure of the sum of all the possible relations within a given set of elements in the accounting process.

With these preliminaries attended to, the hypotheses can be set out:

1.   The accounting process is a network of elements and assemblages exhibiting high connectedness at its centre or nucleus and diminishing connectedness as its periphery is approached. A particular pattern of connectedness is termed a configuration. (A close visual analogy is the road network of a city but it is an analogy only and breaks down on the next point).

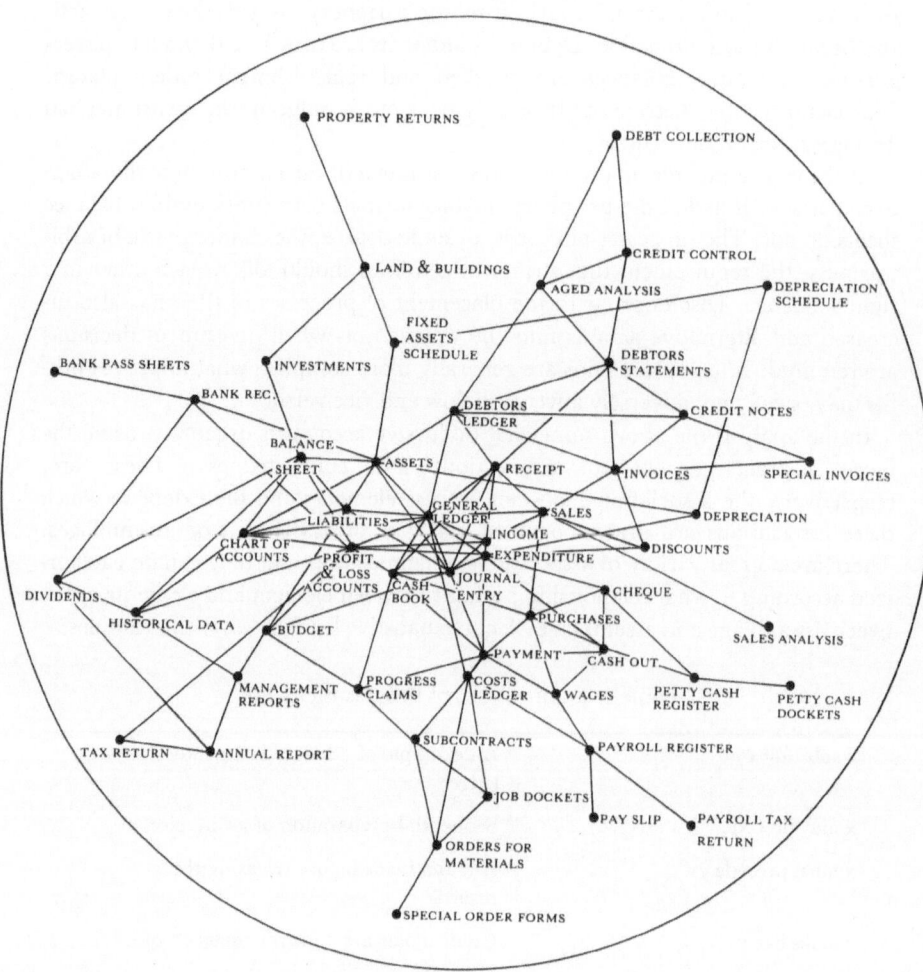

Figure 3. Accounting process network

2. The frequency of occurrence of a given event is inversely related to the connectedness of that part of the accounting process impacted.

3. The scheduling latitude of an event is inversely related to its frequency of occurrence.

4. The change rate incidence within the process is high at the periphery and low at the nucleus.

Table 2. Connectedness/Frequency

Connectedness / Frequency	Low connectedness	High connectedness
High frequency	Satisfaction from speed and accuracy	Boredom
Low frequency	Frustration	Satisfaction in the exercise of skill and judgement

5. The cycle time for an event at the periphery is shorter than the cycle time for a nucleus event. The time span of discretion for an event is similarly related.

6. Value and affect tend to attach to map areas of high connectedness. Change at the periphery is accomplished rapidly and is termed routine adjustment. Change at the nucleus is "drama", following John Morris [2], and is more drawn out in time.

7. Value and configuration consensus within the community of accountants is highest at the role map nucleus.

8. Map elements at the nucleus are dichotomous constructs: Debit/credit, entry/reversal, asset/liability, payment/receipt, sale/purchase—all are dichotomous map elements.

7 APPLYING THE MODEL TO SYSTEMS DESIGN

It is not possible in this short paper to proceed rigorously from model to systems criteria, but some isolated insights can be described:

1. A budget change transaction is rare, and our model suggests that it should have, therefore, a "connected" format. It should therefore look like a journal entry. How often is this true in computer systems? Budget change is often a file maintenance transaction with a highly arbitrary format driven by the data structure of the file to be revised. It thus makes more sense in the analyst's map than it does in the accountant's.

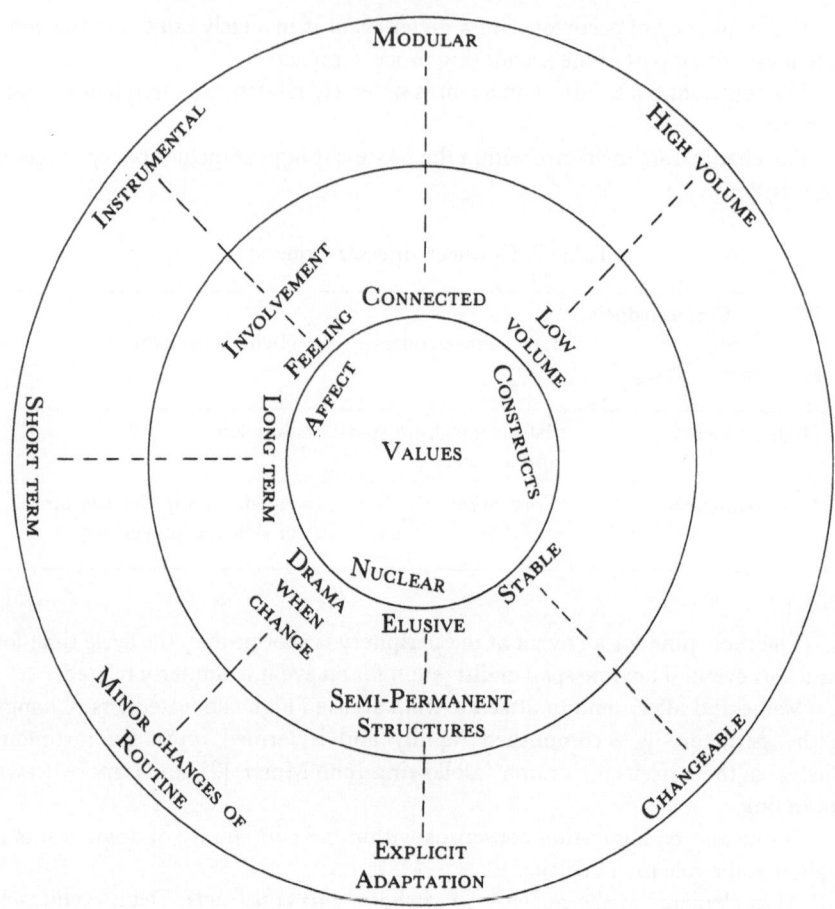

Figure 4. The role map model

2. Every transaction exchanged between a system and an accountant is discourse. The adaptive, peripheral structure of this discourse will change often; input formats for high use invoices will change frequently and from firm to firm, but every transaction *will* be posted somewhere, according to a dichtomous schema; and this deeper structure will change very infrequently. Thus we could safely predict on this basis that such systems as matrix or triadic accounting would have little chance of success. The core of our solution would therefore incorporate double entry ledgers while, at some distance, out from this core there would be a transformation process which translated arbitrarily formatted high volume data into a standard form before it was posted to the ledger.

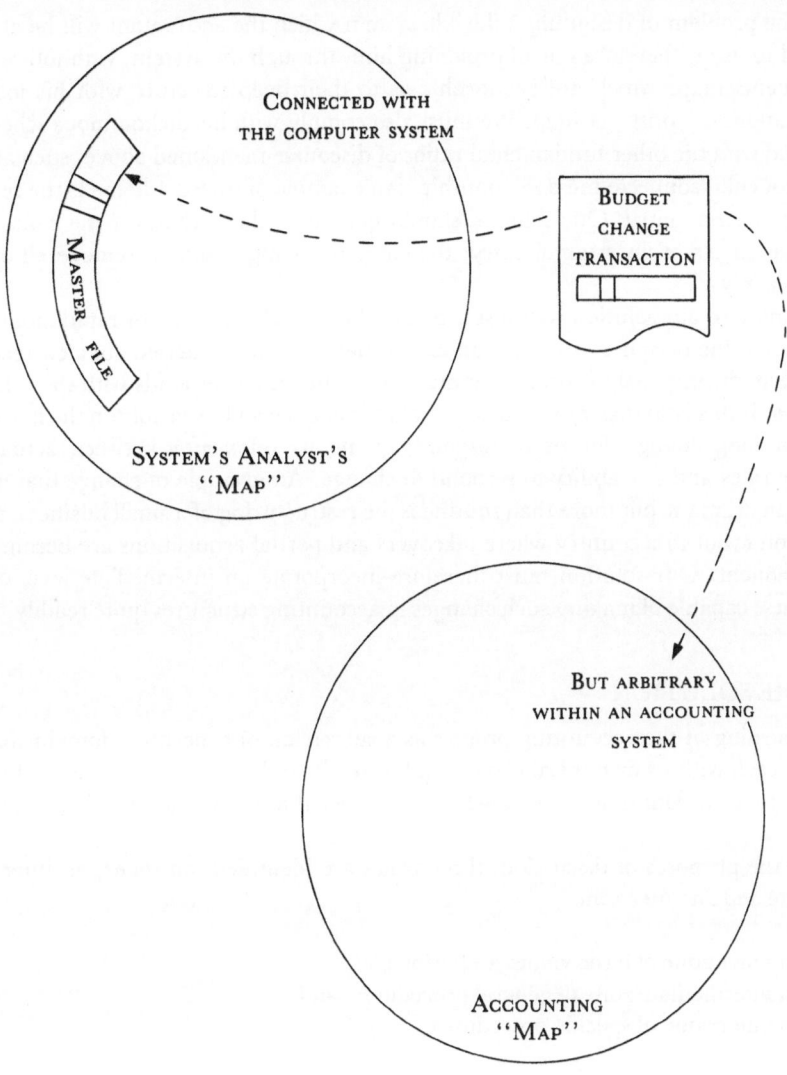

Figure 5. The budget change transaction

3.   The problem of designing a flexible system which the accountant will be attracted to use is therefore one of providing him, through the system, with job requirements maps which are isomorphic as to their deep structure with his job expectations or construct map. We must also comply with his dichotomous schema, and with the other fundamental ratios of discourse mentioned above, such as the frequency/connectedness relationship. An example of such a schema is the reversing journal entry. Our solution should guarantee that, whatever the consequential effects of an original entry, the entry reversing it should remove all of them cleanly.

4.   Built into our solution we must provide a high level language for rapid modifications at the periphery, but we can *assume* that, if we have carried out a correct transform during analysis, our computer system nexus corresponds with the role nucleus. If this is so then any clouds of dramatic change will be visible on the horizon for long enough for us to respond; giving us *synchronism* between actual change rates and our ability to respond to change. An example of change that is less than dramatic but more than routine is the restructuring of a small business, a common event in a country where takeovers and partial acquisitions are becoming frequent. Our solution must therefore incorporate an intermediate level of discourse capable of making such changes in accounting structures quite readily.

8   THE SOLUTION

A construing of the accounting process as a succession of concentric domains or zones, each with its own inertia level, leads directly to the notion that a computer language for accounting should itself be constructed according to the same schema.

For the purposes of discussion, three zones are identified: an inner, an intermediate and an outer zone.

1.   an inner zone of basic values and principles;
2.   an intermediate zone of general procedures; and
3.   an outer zone of specific procedures.

The operative computer software that is to function in each of these three zones may be typified as follows:

8.1   Inner Zone

This is the stable nucleus of the software which implements those elements of the accounting process that have the highest inertia, the highest resistance to change. In all accounting systems, for instance, input transactions are eventually posted to a ledger. The structure of these ledgers and the details of the posting action are variable but there is no doubt as to the basic process. It follows, then, that one of the capabilities of inner zone software would be the application of transactions to a ledger. No more than this *general* updating capability is nuclear, however. The software which fills in the missing details is located in the intermediate or outer zone.

Another example of inner zone software rests on the observed fact that ledgers which have been updated for a given accounting period are invariably reported on. Whether this reporting takes the particular form of a set of debtors statements or of a balance sheet or of a set of pay envelopes is in this setting immaterial. Inner zone software, software that implements only the invariant, basic processes of accounting, would provide a *general* report preparation capability and leave it up to intermediate or outer zone software to specify report content and format details.

Other candidates for inclusion in the nuclear software would be the double-entry principle and the software implications of the fact that all organizations with the rudiments of an accounting system possess a chart of accounts. Each particular organization has its own internal structure which the chart of accounts reflects but the generalized characteristic of possessing such a chart in some shape or form is common to all organizations. Inner zone software would therefore, to be consistent with this, implement a generalized capability to endow serviced organizations with a varying chart of accounts.

A further basic characteristic of accounting is that it is an information reduction process. The mass of information in the transaction flow is first reduced to the information contained at the subsidiary ledger level. At this level particular customer account balances are available and also much detail as to sales by product or area and the like. Further reduction generates the nominal and general ledger accounts and the end product of even further information compression is the balance sheet and summary cashflow statements. General mechanisms to accomplish this reduction process without detailing its particular structure clearly belong in the inner zone.

Another obvious characteristic of the accounting process is the extensive use of dichotomies. The debit/credit, payment/receipt, purchase/sale, prepayment/accrual opposites are a long way from the mythical dichotomies of Lévi-Strauss but they do, when taken together, provide most of the constructs that structure the actions of book-keeping. Because of this consistent structure it is possible to take any commercial voucher, of no matter what format, and reduce it to a set of postings that together sum to zero. That is, there is an underlying general form to which all accounting transactions can be reduced. A general capability to handle the posting of these ''primitive'' documents is therefore a part of inner zone software, whereas the mechanisms that convert particular vouchers to the underlying form are intermediate or outer zone in character.

8.2 Intermediate Zone

This is the zone of accounting which is subject to occasional change. Changes in the following gross features of an accounting system are examples:

1. the introduction of a new firm, as when an existing firm is split or a new one commenced or acquired;

2.   a change in the ledger structure of an existing firm so that the upward posting flow from subsidiary ledgers through the balance sheet requires revision;

3.   the introduction of a new family of transactions and balances, as when budgeting is introduced into a firm's books of account for the first time;

4.   the rearrangement of a company's managerial structure, as when branch accountability is introduced to replace a fully centralised system; and

5.   a major rearrangement of the accounts production schedule; as when weekly reporting is introduced in place of monthly, or subsidiary ledger statements are produced at altered points in time in the accounting calendar, requiring widespread office reorganization.

Where inner zone software implements only the basic principles of accounting by providing generalised capabilities, intermediate zone software must provide the means of expression of the above changes in accounting structure and a means of executing gross accounting processes. Thus, inner zone software may be written to provide a generalised capability to process changing charts-of-account but intermediate zone software permits the definition of specific charts and their execution. Intermediate zone software therefore has an external representation to the language user but inner software does not. This representation provides the user with a syntax and a range of expressions and functions using which he may describe a given accounting structure. Whether he will construct an adequate structure, one that will be well suited to a given organization, is itself a complex question, but one for which the syntax can only provide scope. How the syntax is actually used is a matter of skill and judgement, which a mere syntax cannot provide.

8.3   Outer Zone

This is the zone which is subject to high change rates. Changes in the fine detail of an accounting system are examples:

1.   credit limit checking is to be introduced for selected debtors;

2.   a record of the date of last purchase is now to be kept for all customers;

3.   a new invoice format is to be introduced to speed up the processing of credit sales at the counter;

4.   the accountant requires a new report that projects end-of-year results from a combination of actual-to-date, budget and historical data already on file; and

5.   a new, trial petty cash system is to be introduced in one department while the old system is retained in the remaining departments—transaction formats for the new cash dockets are required.

The syntax range required to cope with such detailed matters as the above is necessarily considerable. Particular data fields, their disposition in input and output formats, and their precise manipulation in very particular calculation routines are all involved. Outer zone software must therefore provide the user with this same texture of syntax or the language will not meet obvious performance requirements. A characteristic of the outer zone of the accounting process rescues the user, however, from any extensive use of this language level. This is the low value of the "knock-on" factor at the role map periphery. Whereas changes in the intermediate zone are pervasive in effect, this is not the case for changes in the outer zone. Examination of the above five examples will demonstrate that the logic required to execute each of them is relatively self contained and not entangled with other processes. This characteristic of outer zone processes strongly suggests that the syntax required to define them should be modular, since the processes themselves are relatively independent and poorly connected with other processes. The role map theory can be used in this general way to indicate where modularization of a system will be effective.

9   A LANGUAGE DESIGN

The above sketch has used a scatter of examples to typify the division of accounting processes into three zones. The criteria for the classifications are the hypothesized characteristics of the role map model. Where, for instance, a process has a high frequency, is relatively arbitrary in its construction in relation to basic accounting principles, is subject to frequent and rapid alteration and is concerned with the recording of an event at the periphery of an organization (a sale, for example) then there is no doubt that we are dealing with an outer zone process. Major processes, such as the posting of a ledger, are not so simply classified but must be analysed. Any particular instance of a major process can be shown to be a "piece of pie", that is, to consist of components from each of the three zones. Firstly, posting a ledger applies the basic principle that transactions are invariably subjected to information reduction, secondly, the posting process proceeds according to the structure of a given chart-of-accounts and, lastly, every posting process contains its relatively isolated, micro-actions such as the calculation of a particular interest charge. A ledger updating computer program which was an undifferentiated mixture of processes from all these three zones could be predicted to require a substantial maintenance investment throughout its lifetime. Even "modularised" programs would suffer if the module boundaries were drawn to some schema which left a mixture of processes (by zone) within each module.

In the proposed computer software, however, three levels of change event are recognized, corresponding to the three zones:

1.   changes to outer zone processes: effected by writing or changing discrete modules using a syntax capable of manipulating data at the detail level;

2.   changes to intermediate zone processes: effected by writing or changing descriptions of the accounting structure using a syntax that minimises the use of detail level logic by providing constructs, familiar to an accountant: ORGANIZATION, LEDGER, CHART, etc; and

3. changes to inner zone processes: effected by altering the basic software that implements the accounting language.

The purpose of such carefully defined divisions is to achieve a synchronism with the time scale of external events. Thus, frequently occurring change events are themselves of short duration and user expectations consistent with the user role map will be that the change process to implement them within a computer system will also be of short duration. A variation to some basic capability or principle of accounting, on the other hand, will be recognized as a "drama" by the user because of its high inertia within his own experience (an inertia compounded out of mutually reinforcing psychological, social and rational factors) and the *time* to effect a profound change will be more likely to be available, being sanctioned by the user's own view of his procedural environment.

As well as providing appropriate syntaxes for the *specification* of accounting systems, a computer accounting language must also provide a means for the day-to-day operation of each system. If this is not done then some conventional job control language must be used and there will be an arbitrary division of processing into the running of one program after another—a division that makes no particular sense within an accounting role map. Also, an opportunity will have been lost to provide within the syntax of the operating language a means to the acceptance and understanding of the systems design syntaxes. Arranging the syntax of the operating language so that it grounds those who use it in the basic expression structures of the rest of the language is one means towards providing the "graded" language needed to facilitate learning by experience on the part of its users.

Incorporating the requirements of day-to-day running within the proposed computer accounting language has the further advantage of concealing the details of machine-oriented processes, such as data security procedures, from the user. For instance, files such as the index sequential, data base files that are unavoidably involved in a system of the proposed complexity require periodic reorganization to maintain processing efficiency and, like all computer files, periodic copying to allow recovery from machine breakdown. Neither of these activities is particularly well related to conventional accounting processes, but they can be arranged to occur automatically whenever another more accounting-oriented activity is triggered by the user. By these means the user can be kept within the environs of one syntax and each experience he has with his syntax has a place in his model of what is going on.

The solution proposed takes the form of a very high-level language (SBAL) embedded in a host lower-level language, a decision table processor which follows the syntax of FTL6—a program product marketed by the U.K. National Computing Centre [7]. The run time environment of any SBAL (Small Business Accounting Language) system is conceived as being contained within SBAL itself rather than being controlled by any conventional job control language. Indeed, if the theoretical model is correct, such languages are failures in discourse terms. Also, many data control and all file security procedures are placed under SBAL control, with the aim of making a "total environment language".

The data structure solution is a modification of conventional files. The master file consists of variable content, virtual records and is able to contain every ledger type within the one file through the use of table-driven charts-of-account. The chart-of-accounts of a business, in model terms, is *not* at the nucleus; thus it cannot be at the system nexus within SBAL. SBAL also provides a "recharting" feature which permits a business to be redefined under a new identifier and for the live data in the old structure to be transformed and transmitted into the new structure.

9.1 SBAL Syntax

As indicated above, SBAL contains a number of discourse sets.

1. Run directives
These directives control the operation of a computer with an established SBAL system. Examples: *INPUT, *POST, *CLOSE, *REPRINT. SBAL checks the intent of these directives and can *RERUN also, automatically reinstating earlier ledger versions.

2. Run control
These directives activate file security measures. Examples: *ARCHIVE, *CYCLE, *DUMP. SBAL knows when different security measures must be taken and prompts when they are neglected.

3. Transaction data
As stated in the discussion of the model, the exchange of transaction data between user and SBAL is viewed as a discourse set. SBAL provides for fully variable input formats so that the proposed frequency/connectedness ratios can be observed.

4. Report generation
The FTL6 compiler contains a powerful report generator which can be accessed since SBAL is embedded in an FTL6 compiler. Fully variable output formats are thereby provided.

5. Systems directives
These directives describe and change accounting structure. Examples: *SYSTEM, *PEOPLE, *ORGANIZATIONS, *LEDGERS, *CHARTS, *TRANSACTIONS. These latter directives define a business or a set of businesses. Then, a second set of system directives (*ACCEPT, *BLOCK, *SELECT, *STREAM, *SCHEDULE) describe the required behaviour of the structure. In Michael Jackson's terminology, the above definitional directives describe entities and the second set describes the processing actions of these entities [3].

6. Rechart directives
These directives affect the restructuring of a business. Examples: *MAP, *TRANSFORM, *FREEZE.

Each of these discourse sets is intended for the different participants in an SBAL system. The accountant's main set is the *transaction data* and its structure is established and modulated by other discourse sets, such as the systems directives.

257

Thus the pressing requirements of a particular accountant can be met first and then, as he becomes accustomed to SBAL, other language features can be made visible to him on a response-to-need basis.

9.2 SBAL Feasibility

SBAL, of course, is as yet purely a design solution of which only some elements have been programmed. Within Papua New Guinea, spare computing capacity is available and the development agencies are relatively insensitive to machine throughput costs. In a stricter environment SBAL is targeted on low cost auxiliary storage devices in the 20m to 60m characters area and low-cost CPU's with stores of 32K to 64K bytes. The target machine for the present programming effort is the microcomputer-based PDP 11/03 from DEC.

10 CONCLUSION

SBAL is hopefully much more than just another procedural language; it is put forward, as stated earlier, as a "total environment language". Looking at it as such one can then ask what kind of environment it provides. This paper has, in effect, argued that it offers a *learning* environment, one in which the user may explore a variety of solutions to his problems, expressing each solution in a syntax that is immune from all but revolutions in accounting theory. The syntax is a *graded* one so that the learning process is smooth, and the syntax is itself a coherent and connected assemblage built on a nucleus/periphery scheme so that, if the theory is in reasonable accord with reality, a comfortable fit is provided for its user and it will be viewed by him as merely an extension of his own powers as he comes to identify with and value his new capability and freedom. I propose that this may be the emerging business of small systems design; the construction of deep structures, syntaxes that function as coherent and growing user environments, in consistent and dynamic relation to the changing procedural and sociocultural context. Returning to the concept of autonomous design described at the outset of this paper, it can be seen that such a high level language could be an important tool. If the language structure replicates the deep structure of the profession within which it is to be used then it will "fit" and become an easy means to the expression of systems designs that stay within that profession's ambit. At the least such a language would be a basis for participative design and at most a tool for autonomous design.

REFERENCES

1. Bateson, G. *Steps to an Ecology of Mind.* London: Paladin, 1973.
2. Epstein, A.L. "The Network and Urban Social Organization." *Rhodes-Livingstone Institute Journal* (June 1961).
3. Jackson, M.A. *Structural Design of the Information System.* Michael Jackson Systems Limited, 1977.

258

4. Kelly, G.A. *A Theory of Personality.* New York: Norton, 1963. (first pub. 1955).

5. Kuhn, T. *The Structure of Scientific Revolutions.* Chicago: The University of Chicago Press, 1970 (2nd ed.).

6. Morris, J. "Three Aspects of the Person in Social Life." in R. Ruddock (ed.) *Six Approaches to the Person*, Chapter 4. London: Routledge and Kegan Paul, 1972.

7. National Computing Centre (NCC). *FTL6 Reference Manual for ICL 1900 and 2903.* Manchester: NCC, 1976.

8. Podger, D.N. "Computer Systems Design in a Developing Country: Human Factors." Unpublished Ph.D. thesis, 1978, The Papua New Guinea University of Technology.

9. Popper, K. *Unended Quest: An Intellectual Autobiography.* Glasgow: Fontana, 1976 (revised ed.).

10. Quine, W.V.O. *Methods of Logic.* Henry Holt, 1960, p. 13.

11. Schon, D.A. *Beyond the Stable State.* London: Temple Smith, 1971.

II. EVALUATION OF SYSTEMS
Chairman: F.F. Land

The session was devoted to the problem of evaluating the costs and benefits from systems change.

Two major evaluation problems were identified:

1. The problem of estimating the costs and benefits of a proposed systems change in order to be able to make a rational investment decision.
2. The problem of assessing the costs and in particular the benefits accruing from the change once it had been implemented, and how to isolate the effects of the systems change from all the other changes which may have affected the organisation in the same period.

A common theme for all three speakers was the role played in actual achievement by behavioural rather than technical factors.

Domsch: "Application of Utility Analysis in Systems Development"

Michel Domsch reported on empirical research in the use of cost/benefit analysis techniques for the evaluation of alternative information systems design. The empirical research was followed by an analytical study of utility analysis methods.

The empirical research took the form of a pilot study of a number of computer-based information systems which had employed cost-benefit analysis prior to systems development.

Costing exercises carried out after implementation suggested a negative cost-benefit ratio in about seventy-five percent of the investments. This result appeared to be caused by:

1. Delays in starting the project development—average of eight months late.
2. The project took longer to complete than had been scheduled—average thirty percent longer.
3. The development required more resources than had been anticipated—average fifty percent more.

Since these deviations threw doubt on the cost/benefit methods employed, the researchers attempted to analyse the causes of the variances. The study found that variances were due in part to inadequate use of cost/benefit analysis together with inaccurate estimates (poor performance standards?), and inadequate information. However, the statistical analysis suggested that only fifty percent of the variances could be explained that way. Could the variances be due to failures in "motivation" where motivation is expressed as a measure of the support for the systems change by all involved in the relevant information systems? The study indicated two factors of importance in achieving "motivation".

1. The extent to which the interest groups are involved in the cost/benefit evaluation and investment decision.
2. The extent to which the interest groups' own goals are attainable by the systems change.

Despite some difference in the different organisations sampled the result of further empirical work·indicated that the "motivating" factors were absent or only poorly represented. Positive attitutes on the other hand were associated with higher interest group integration and goal achievement. This result led to the formulation of an optimum integration strategy which would lead to the highest "motivation" but could be offset by higher costs or low achievement in that the development process takes longer, and because conflicting interest group goals might have to be resolved through compromise.

DISCUSSION

The subsequent discussion focussed on the difficulty of determining "costs" and "benefits". Costs comprised both costs of development and the costs incurred by the interest groups. The latter are often particularly difficult to define.

Questions were asked about the changing relation between costs and benefit during the development process. It was pointed out that the use of the method was intended for the planning phase of the cycle.

Swanson: "The Evaluation of an Information System Development"

Burton Swanson drew attention to the importance of an existing information systems growth and enhancement and focussed on the evaluation of already implemented systems.

He suggested that three interrelated activities have to be performed in the evaluation processes.

1. *Activity Analysis*—concerns itself with a measure of the systems productivities. It looks in particular at the measurement of input and its transformation into output. Swanson illustrates the problem of measuring output information. Information can be viewed from many perspectives:
—*physical units*—number of reports, number of report pages

—syntactic units—number of characters, number of words

—semantic units—number of sentences

—pragmatic units—perception of value of information by the receiver of the output. Measurement becomes more problematic and less precise with each category.

A second aspect of activity analysis is the measurement of the allocation of resources.

2. *Possibility Analysis* seeks to establish that which is technologically possible, whether achieved or not. It is an attempt to:

a. identify the more efficient points within the technological possibilities provided by the system.

b. assess the output capabilities of the system, for example, by examining alternative job mixes.

c. assess the possibility and capability of alternative technologies including the process of transition from the given technology to the alternative technology.

3. *Utility Analysis* attempts to value information as perceived by the consumer of the information. But different users may value the same information differently, and the ultimate value is determined by how the use of the information by its consumer serves the organisational purpose. This involves the search for appropriate measures of performance.

Swanson suggested the use of periodic surveys by means of questionnaires and interviews as a means of establishing utilities.

To choose a preferred information system, alternatives have to be evaluated in a way which reflects productivity, alternative possibilities and the transition to them, and information utility. Thus the interaction of the three types of analysis has to be considered.

DISCUSSION

The discussion focussed on the need to distinguish between job satisfaction as a measure of performance and participation in systems design, which is a technique for systems development.

The question was raised—why are there so few good methods of evaluation. It was suggested that the "selling interests" of the hardware vendors dominated the evaluation and development processes.

Seibt: "User and Specialist Evaluation in Systems Development"

Dietrich Seibt first sketched an "ideal" evaluation method based on a process of goal definition, in which all goals are valued with respect to each other. An estimate was made of the extent to which alternative designs are likely to achieve the goal targets and the alternatives ranked in relation to this achievement. A score is calculated by multiplying the ranking of the alternative systems by the goal value. The best system is the one which gives the highest overall score.

The speaker drew attention to the need to differentiate between three basic levels of goal definition and evaluation. Each represented a different perception of the systems function and purpose.

1. The top or senior management concerned itself with global decisions—whether to initiate a systems change or not—and global goals, expressed in broad categories such as profit targets, productivity targets, product quality targets, cash targets, etc. Some of these are expressed in financial terms, but others in strictly organisational terms such as "improve social image of organisation", "increase ability of organisation to respond to external events".

2. Level of operational management. This level concerns itself with alternative operational strategies. Goals are expressed in forms such as "improved speed of order processing", or "decrease the resources needed to complete a process", or social objectives such as "increase job satisfaction in the purchase order function".

3. Level of information systems designers and implementors. At this level the goals concern themselves with decisions related to the design and implementation of the system. Goals are expressed in terms of detailed design considerations—output formats and media, input and data capture requirements, timing schedules, use of storage, flexibility capabilities and so on.

In theory the three levels are linked. The goals of the second level are derived from the goals of the first level and determine the third level goals. In practice, communication and "perspective" difficulties can cause failure of the three levels of goals to be properly connected. Each level has its own values and priorities and this affects the perception of their own goals and colours their view of the goals from the other levels.

DISCUSSION

The discussion concerned itself with the problem of the mismatch of goals between the three levels of goals identified by the speaker.

18. Effectiveness Measurement of Computer-Based Information Systems through Cost-Benefit Analysis: Empirical Research and Perspectives

by Michel Domsch

1 PROBLEM DEFINITION AND INITIAL SITUATION

1.1 Delimitation of the Subject and Procedure

Cost-benefit analyses are decision-making tools for evaluating individual or alternative courses of action. They are intended to prepare, objectify, and clarify decisions. In such analyses, the data of all ascertainable negative and positive consequences, that is, costs and benefits of an action, are collected, quantified—if possible—and compared. The purpose of this comparison is to measure the effectiveness of an action or to weigh the effectiveness levels of alternative actions against each other with respect to predetermined objectives. In this connection, we are not concerned with a definite method or theory, but with a specific type of analytical method, that is, a mode of thought within the above framework.

It is not the purpose of this paper to discuss the entire cost-benefit complex in a general and comprehensive manner. Instead, our attention will be focused on the following points:

1. The results of empirical research in the form of a pilot study followed by an analytical study are the central theme of this paper. These investigations have been conducted from the point of view of an external management consultant.

2. The cost-benefit analyses under consideration were confined to investment decisions or, more precisely, investments in computer-based information systems. The reason why management consultants are particularly interested in this subject is obvious. Clients often have to carry out system investments at a fixed price within a definite period of time. As a rule, the sales talk and the calculation of the fixed price require cost-benefit analyses for alternative system investments. Such analyses are, therefore, of vital importance in the planning or even the pre-planning phase.

3. The reasons for demanding special attention to be given to the so-called "motivation factor" in the application of cost-benefit analyses are as follows: The motivation factor helps to improve the measurement of the effectiveness of system investments. In addition, it is of topical interest with respect to the current discus-

sions on the concretion on the rights of various interest groups, especially employees and their representatives, to participate in the development and operation of computer-based information systems.

1.2 Present State of the Discussion on Cost-Benefit Analyses

The evaluation of computer-based information systems under cost-benefit aspects has been a subject of discussion for many years, both in the scientific world and in practice. The literature on this subject is abundant. The present state of the discussion may be characterized as follows:

1. As a rule, it is economic standards that are applied to the evaluations. This is in accordance with the economy-of-effort principle included in the statement of objectives. Interdisciplinary approaches have so far been given priority in the scientific field. In practice, however, they are mostly not considered explicitly.

2. Benefits are seldom expressed in monetary terms as direct quantification is often impossible. Sometimes an attempt is made to reach an indirect quantification (for example, by scores) through qualitative statements and by means of transformation and translation rules (for example, utility analysis). Sometimes only lists of arguments with qualitative information on benefits in the form of key words are presented. This information is often not even included in the cost-benefit analysis, and is thus used only as something like an alibi.

3. A considerable amount of research activities in the field of business administration is focused on determining the value and price of individual information. In this connection, detailed and sometimes theoretically highly sophisticated information-cost and information-benefit computations are conceived and information optima calculated. A direct transfer of this individual approach to the evaluation of complex information systems is often neither possible nor reasonable because of the large amount of information and the phenomenon of "joint information".

4. It is assumed that the interest group "management", which receives the decision-making information from the interest group "planning", is of primary importance for decisions on system investments. Therefore, the cost-benefit analyses—as far as their method and contents are concerned—are conceived accordingly.

5. In practice, the attention is focused on hardware and software issues which are closely related to organizational problems. Recently, however, legal aspects have also been more and more discussed, which is due, for example, to the German Labor-Management Relations Act and the data privacy legislation.

In practice, this confronts both the management consultant and the investor with a number of problems regarding the application of cost-benefit analyses to the evaluation of system investments. Some aspects will be dealt with in the following.

2 PILOT STUDY ON SYSTEM INVESTMENTS

2.1 Scope of the Pilot Study

From 1974 to 1977, an empirical research was done in the form of a pilot study. The central theme of this study was the problem of cost-benefit analysis from the point of view of a management consultant. A total of fifty-two systems have been investigated. However, a subset of only sixteen systems is of actual interest within the scope of this symposium. The number of actually relevant systems is shown in Figure 1.

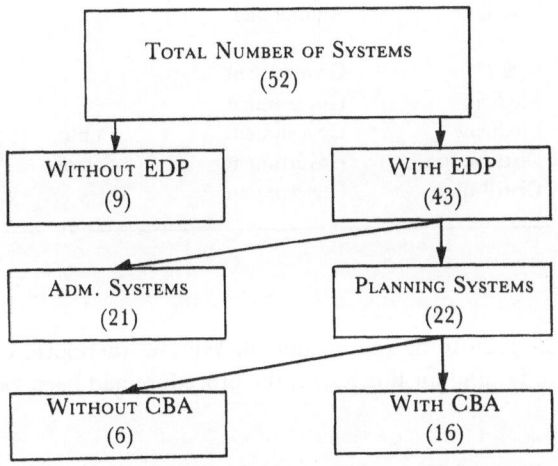

Figure 1. Number of Relevant Systems (CBA Cost-Benefit Analysis).

To this subset the following conditions apply:

1. All systems are computer-based.
2. All systems include, among others, planning factors.
3. For all systems the companies had conducted cost-benefit analysis prior to system development and operation.

Table 1 shows the structure of this subset classified by application, branch, and sector.

Table 1. Details about the Systems

No.	Application	Branch	Sector
1	Accounting	Consumer	
2	Accounting	Consumer	
3	Accounting	Consumer	
4	Marketing	Printing	
5	Production	Steel	Private
6	Personnel	Automobile	Sector
7	Personnel	Automobile	
8	Personnel	Insurance	
9	Personnel	Computer	
10	R & D	Oil	
11	R & D	Automobile	
12	R & D	Government	
13	Medicine	Government	
14	Medicine	Government	Public
15	Distribution	Government	Sector
16	Distribution	Government	

This sample does not claim to be representative. We are, therefore, only concerned with a pilot study, and for this reason the procedure had been very pragmatic:

1. From the point of view of management consulting, there had been no interest in an extensive research project. For this reason, neither time nor funds were available for a detailed representative survey.

2. Despite great efforts on our part, many system investors were not very cooperative in supplying information to external persons. Some data were too inaccurate or simply wrong. Therefore, mainly such systems have been included in the study for which management consulting services had been used within the scope of system investments.

3. A similar study in the field of ''System-Based Quantitative Personnel Planning'' showed that the results of a pilot study deviated only slightly from those of a far more extensive study.

2.2 Results of the Pilot Study

Postcosting performed after the implementation of the system investments has shown a negative cost-benefit ratio for about 75 percent of the investments (Table 2).

Table 2. Analysis of Cost and Benefit

Criterion	1st Group	2nd Group	total
Cost-Benefit Analysis	no	yes	—
Number of Systems	6	16	22
Results:			
C > B	5	12	17
B > C	1	4	5

17 out of 22 = 77% "unprofitable"
5 out of 22 = 23% "profitable"

This result is due mainly to the following factors:

1. The development phase started later than scheduled.
2. The development lasted longer than scheduled.
3. The development was more expensive than expected.

The development phase started about four months earlier and up to eighteen (on an average, eight) months later than scheduled. The actual implementation times deviated from those estimated in the cost-benefit analysis between – 20 percent and + 60 percent (on an average + 30 percent). In the development phase, the maximum cost underrun amounted to 30 percent and the maximum cost overrun was 80 percent (on an average, 50 percent). Comparatively large deviations were found for systems Nos. 6 through 12. The monetary benefit determined in the operating phase for eight systems was between 20 percent lower and 100 percent higher than that estimated in the planning phase; the operating costs were exceeded by an average of 20 percent. Table 3 shows the results in detail.

This, however, casts doubt on the effectivness of some of the system investments based on cost-benefit analyses. For, in view of such deviation, the question is whether wrong decisions had been preprogrammed and whether the cost-benefit analyses had been at all relevant:

a. with respect to their concept, that is, methodically, and
b. with respect to their significance in concrete cases, that is, in contents.

Subsequent to the pilot study, it has therefore been attempted to analyze the causes of the great differences between the estimated and the actual results. The analysis was of interest, on the one hand, because of its scientific nature and, on the other hand, because the persons responsible for system implementation, and

Table 3. Controlling the Development/Implementation

No.	Start of Dev. and Implementation (Diff. in months)	Time of Dev. and Implementation (Diff. in percentage)	Cost of Dev. and Implementation (Diff. in percentage)
1	− 4	20	40
2	—	− 10	− 30
3	− 1	20	40
4	7	—	30
5	8	− 20	− 10
6	16	50	80
7	18	50	70
8	9	50	70
9	10	50	60
10	6	40	50
11	8	50	70
12	9	30	60
13	8	60	80
14	14	30	70
15	14	40	70
16	6	20	50
Mean	8	30	50

the system investors, were interested in the causes. The special position of an external consultant has already been mentioned. In this connection, cost-benefit analyses are of vital importance as a tool for sales and for pricing, particularly in the case of fixed-price projects.

3 ANALYTICAL STUDY FOR EVALUATING SYSTEM INVESTMENTS

3.1 Cost and Benefit Evaluation Factors

In the analysis of the causes under discussion, we have used the following approach: The effectiveness SI of a system investment of the type i with respect to the point of time t may be expressed as a function of the cost K_{it} and the benefit N_{it}. For a system alternative, in general, this may be written as follows:

$$SI_{it} = f(K_{it}, N_{it}) \tag{1}$$

Within the scope of the analytical study, especially the following partly interrelated evaluation factors have been identified as relevant, that is, cost- and/or benefit-effective parameters:

A_{it} = initial condition/present situation
V_{it} = application factor/information need
S_{it} = system factor/hardware—software
E_{it} = environmental factor/external effects
M_{it} = motivation factor

Thus we have:

$$K_{it} = f(A_{it}, V_{it}, S_{it}, E_{it}, M_{it}) \tag{2}$$

$$N_{it} = f(A_{it}, V_{it}, S_{it}, E_{it}, M_{it}) \tag{3}$$

and, using Equation (1), we obtain

$$SI_{it} = f(A_{it}, V_{it}, S_{it}, E_{it}, M_{it}) \tag{4}$$

The hatched areas in Figure 2 indicate to what extent the above evaluation factors were considered in the examined cost-benefit analyses for system investments.

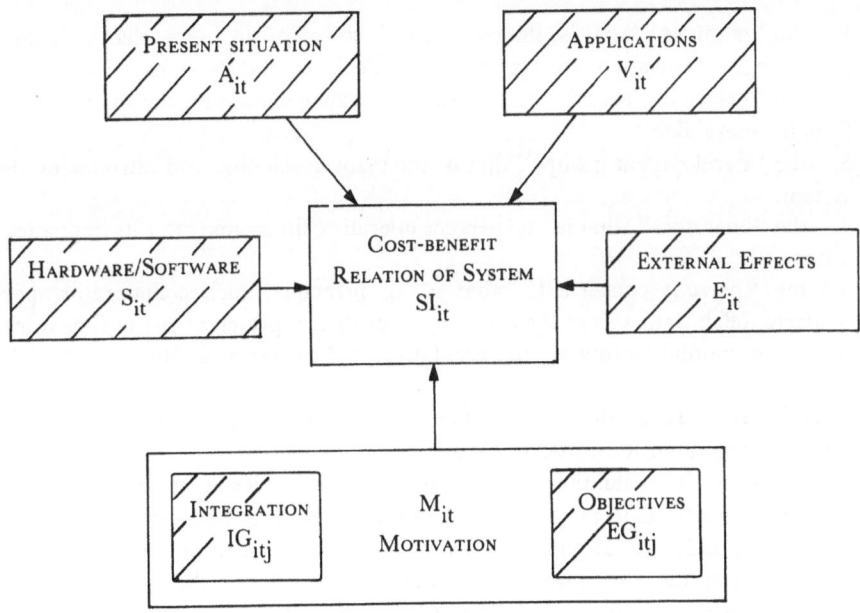

Figure 2. Relevant Evaluation Factors.

Some of the deviations were caused by the evaluation factors A_{it}, V_{it}, S_{it}, and—to a certain extent—E_{it}. The main reasons were too inaccurate estimates, too small an information basis, and inadequate application of the tool of cost-benefit analysis. In addition, system modifications had been introduced which were taken into account only in the development phase and not included in the original cost-benefit analysis. However, an average of only 50 percent of the deviations could thus be explained. It therefore seemed advisable to consider the evaluation factor "motivation factor" (M_{it}) in more detail; it had been taken into account in the cost-benefit analyses only in passing or ignored completely.

3.2 The Motivation Factor as an Evaluation Factor

If cost-benefit analyses are conducted on the basis of the economy-of-effort principle only from the point of view of the interest group "management", the following aspect gaining more and more significance in practice is underestimated: Costs and benefits depend largely on the direct or indirect influence exerted on system development and operation by different interest groups. It is true that, de jure, the top management plays an important role with respect to the system investments under study. However, de facto and de jure—for example, in accordance with the German Labor-Management Relations Act—particularly the following internal groups of the company have to be taken into account:

1. the "planners", that is, the team (collaborators of the users, electronic data processing, organization, etc.) preparing the decision on the system investment;
2. the "decision-makers", that is, the top management and the management from the users' fields;
3. the "development group", that is, the team developing and introducing the system;
4. the "operators", that is, the persons operating the system after its implementation;
5. the "persons concerned", that is, in principle, each collaborator, particularly collaborators from the users' fields or their representatives such as works council, economic committee, representatives of the executives, etc.

In addition, there are the external interest groups (for example, customers, suppliers, public authorities, stockholders, etc.).

In general, the evaluation or rating of the system investment varies, and it is not constant with respect to time. The resulting rating matrix is shown in Table 4.

From a purely formal point of view, the top management or their representatives decide on the system investment. In fact, however, it is the overall decision-making process, the implementation of the system investment selected, and system operation which must be considered, taking into account the participation of, or the influence exerted by, the above interest groups. Within the scope of the empirical research study, we have found that—because of the one-sided orientation towards a single interest group (in particular, the top management)—any resist-

Table 4. Rating Matrix

Phase Group	Planning	Decision	Development	Implementa- tion	Run
Planning Group					
Decision Group					
Development Group					
Operator					
Persons con- cerned/Client System/Em- ployees					
External Groups					

ance to adaptation, lack of willingness to work, lack of satisfaction, the fear for one's livelihood, possible sabotage during system development and operation as well as, on the other hand, increased cooperation of the different interest groups and thus essential cost- and benefit-effective evaluation factors had been ignored in the cost-benefit analyses. These characteristics must therefore be included in the "motivation factor" (M_{it}).

The magnitude of this factor depends largely on two parameters:

1. level of integration (IG_{itj}), that is, the extent to which the respective interest group of the type j participated in the individual phases (t) of the system investment of the type i;

2. level of objective attainment (ZG_{itj}), that is, the extent to which the objectives of the respective interest group of the type j will probably be realized, from the point of view of this interest group, through the system investment of the type i at the point of time t.

Thus we have:

$$M_{it} = f(IG_{itj}, ZG_{itj}) \tag{5}$$

and, using Equations (1) through (4), we obtain:

$$SI_{it} = f(A_{it} \dots E_{it}, IG_{itj}, ZG_{itj}) \tag{6}$$

273

3.3 The Summary Case History Method as an Analytical Method

The sixteen system investments under discussion have been observed from 1974 to 1977. It has, however, been impossible for an external consultant to make a detailed survey and collect quantified individual data. For this reason, it has been deemed necessary to use a summary case history method instead of an analytical procedure. The three questions shown in the simplified questionnaire (Figure 3) were put to each interest group at the start of each new phase.

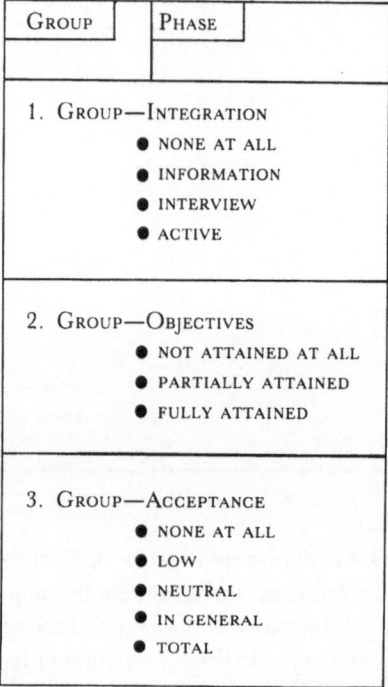

Figure 3. Questionnaire.

The resulting three answers in each matrix square of the rating matrix (Table 4) refer to the following factors:

1. level of integration,
2. level of objective attainment,
3. motivation for system investment.

3.4 Results of the Analytical Study

It has turned out that, in the case of multiple observations within a group, the results are not always identical. The variation is, however, small so that it may be neglected in this connection.

The following is a summary of some results of the analytical study:

1.   Point of Time of Cost-Benefit Analysis

For almost all systems investigated, a cost-benefit analysis was conducted only in the planning phase.

2.   Participation in the Cost-Benefit Analysis

In general, only the interest groups "planners" and "decision-makers" participated in the cost-benefit analysis.

3.   Participation in the Realization of the System
Investment with Respect to Time

The groups participated in accordance with the "traditional" procedure, that is, the group of "persons concerned" did mostly not participate until the implementation phase. In general, employees' representatives participated, if at all, prior to the development phase, but after the cost-benefit analysis.

4.   Level of Objective Attainment with Respect to Time

The results were not uniform. The answers changed with respect to time and varied among the groups. We have, however, found a clear tendency that the groups Nos. 1 through 4 considered their objectives attained to a greater extent than did the group of "persons concerned".

5.   The Acceptance of (Motivation for) the System
Investments with Respect to Time

In this case, we have observed the same effect as for the previous factor: The rating changed with respect to time within the same interest group and it varied among the groups at the same point of time. The resulting rating graph is plotted in Figure 4. Again, the negative tendency prevails in the group of "persons concerned".

Although some of the results obtained are not clear, the essential results relating to the group of "persons concerned" can be given in abstract form as shown in Figure 5. The tendency of all system investments studied may thus be expressed as follows:

1.   The positive attitude towards the system investment increases as the level of integration increases.

2.   The positive attitude towards the system investment increases as the level of objective attainment increases.

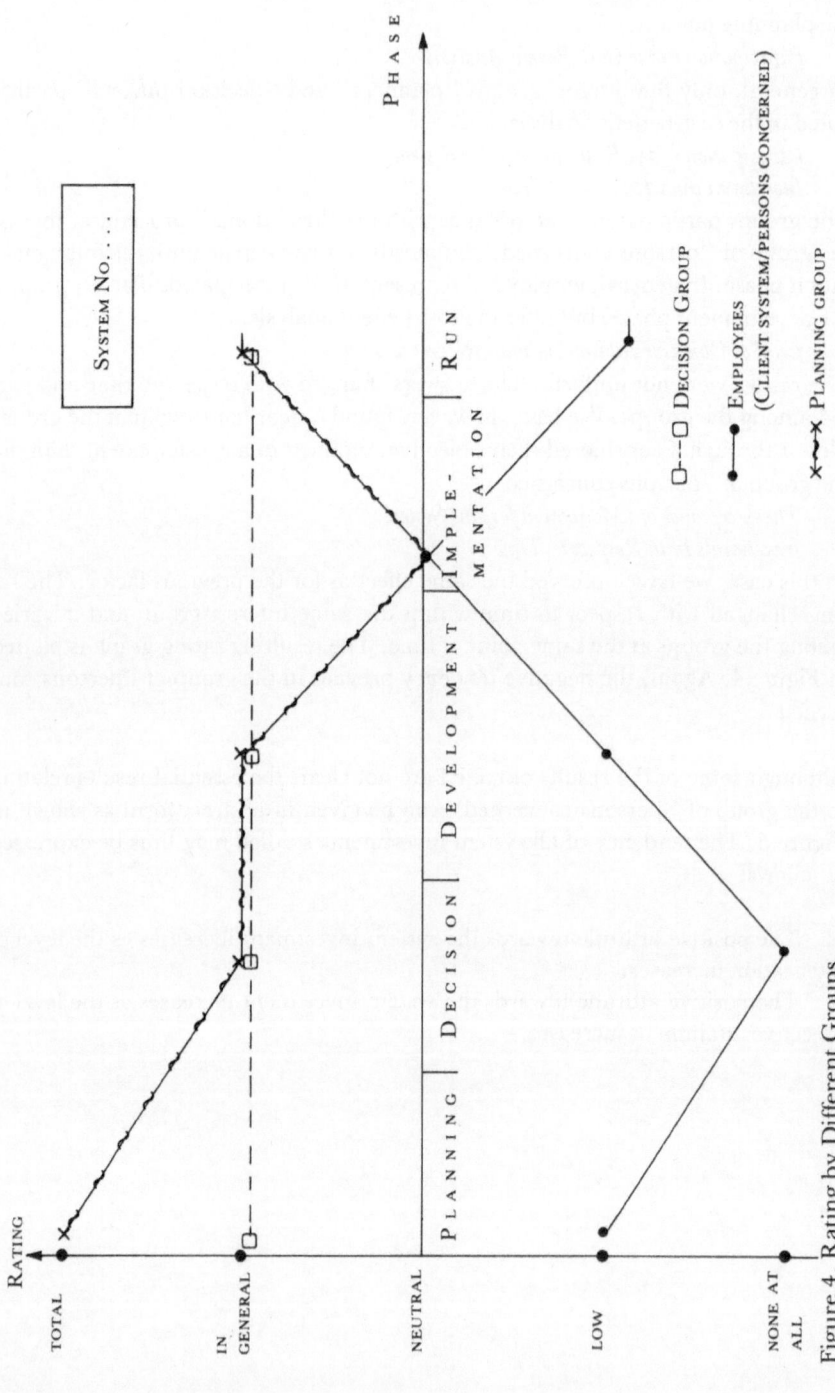

Figure 4. Rating by Different Groups.

SYSTEM NO. . . . .

□---□ DECISION GROUP

●——● EMPLOYEES
(CLIENT SYSTEM/PERSONS CONCERNED)

✕——✕ PLANNING GROUP

PHASE

PLANNING | DECISION | DEVELOPMENT | IMPLE-MENTATION | RUN

RATING

TOTAL

IN GENERAL

NEUTRAL

LOW

NONE AT ALL

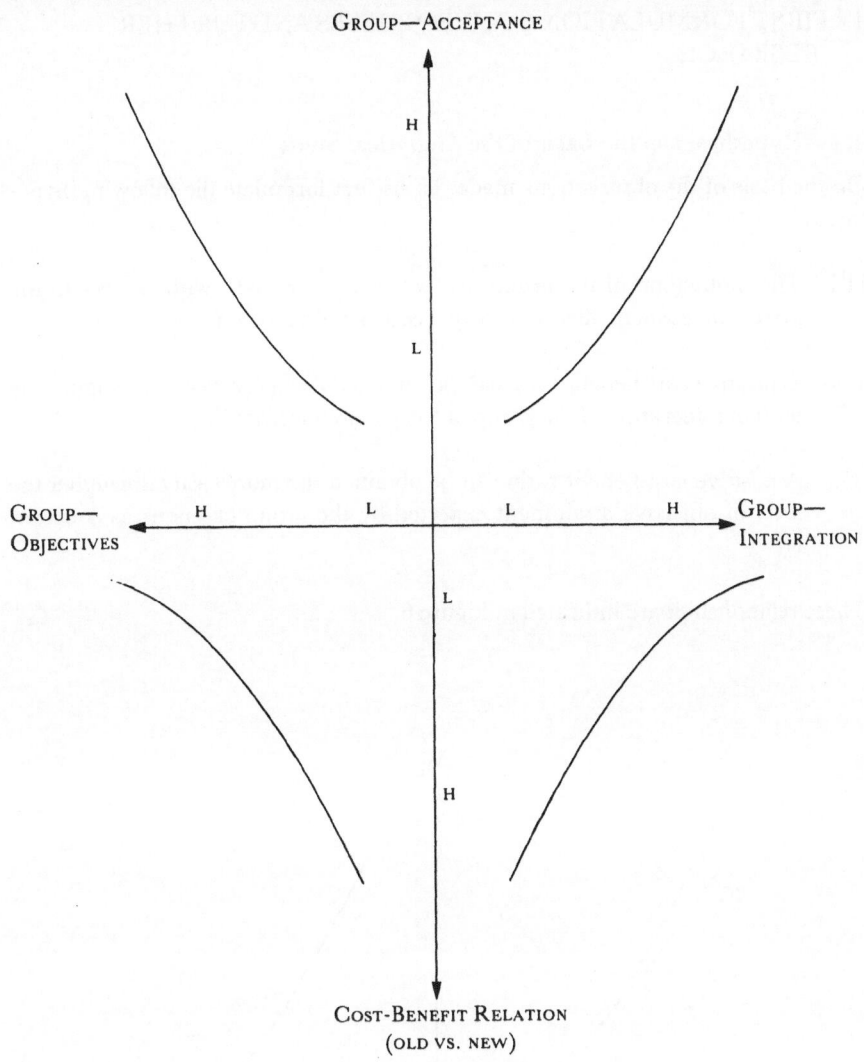

Figure 5. Influence of Different Factors upon Cost-Benefit Relation.

4 FIRST FORMULATION OF HYPOTHESES AND FURTHER RESEARCH

4.1 Hypotheses on the Basis of the Analytical Study

On the basis of the observations made, let us first formulate the following hypotheses:

H 1   The motivation of the group of "persons concerned" with respect to the system investment affects the actual cost-benefit relation.

H 2   A positive cost-benefit ratio can be obtained the more easily the higher the level of integration of the group of "persons concerned".

H3   A positive cost-benefit ratio can be obtained the more easily the higher the level of objective attainment expected by the group of "persons concerned".

These relationships are indicated in Figure 6.

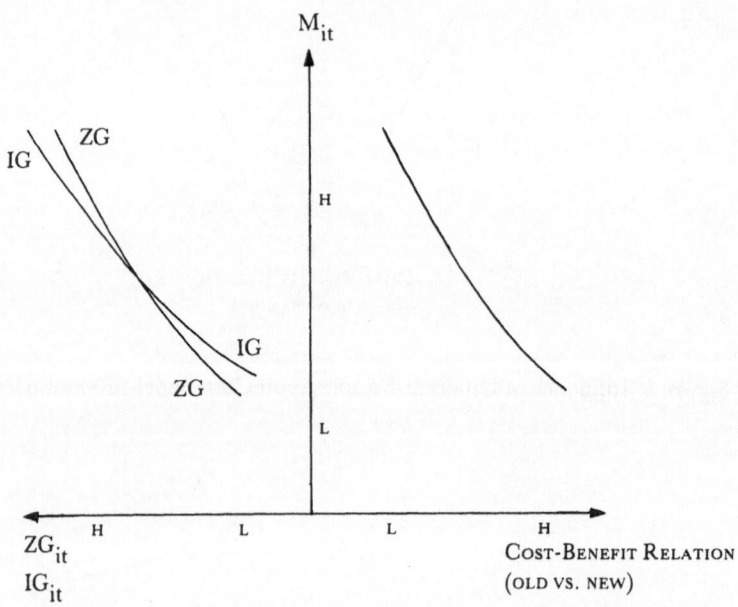

Figure 6. Influence of Motivation Factor upon Cost-Benefit Relation.

The hypothesis H 2 (and hence also H 3) is of special topical interest, as the type and amount of participation of employees' representatives in the development and operation of computer-based information systems are increasingly being discussed. It is true that rights of participation have already been established in the German Labor-Management Relations Act; they have, however, not yet been reinforced concrete. In particular the Metal Workers' Union has recently made demands for co-determination and participation with respect to computer-based information systems, and model agreements have already been made. Thus, from the employers' point of view, the question of an "optimum integration strategy in the sense of participative approaches" arises.

4.2   The "Optimum Integration Strategy"

For determining an optimum integration strategy, let us proceed from the following assumptions:

1.   In participative approaches, both economic ("traditional" employers' objectives) and social objectives have to be considered. The latter are relevant particularly with regard to the group of "persons concerned". For this purpose, Maslow's hierarchy of basic needs is sufficient as a conceptual model (Figure 7).
2.   Depending on the present situation, the value of objective attainment will, from the point of view of the group of "persons concerned", increase or decrease through the system investment (estimated result). The cost will decrease or in-

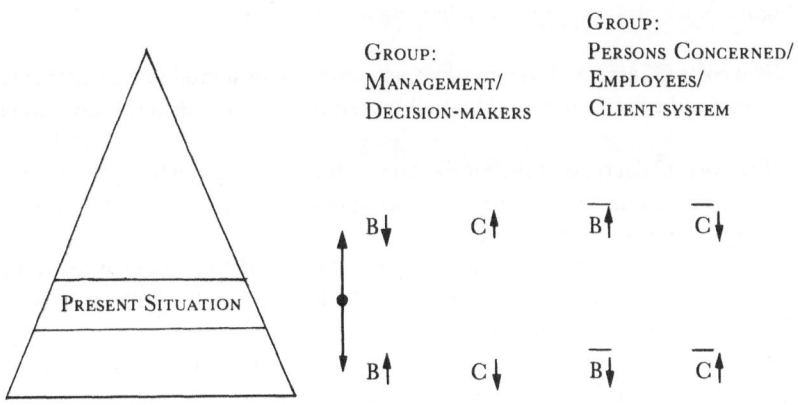

Figure 7. Influence of Change upon Cost and Benefit.

crease as a function of the level of integration and thus as a function of the possibility of attaining one's own objectives. This is shown in Figure 7.

3. The opposite effect may, however, occur from the "management's" point of view; this is because a high level of objective attainment on the part of the "persons concerned" may result in higher costs owing to additional investments (supported, for example, by arguments for humanization of working conditions). Similarly, a low benefit may be obtained by reducing rationalization efforts. This tendency is also indicated in Figure 7.

For example, the above effects have recently been observed with respect to the rationalization efforts made in the printing industry.

Thus, from an overall point of view, the hypotheses H 2 and H 3 cannot be valid in general. As described above, opposite effects may occur with regard to costs and benefits. Figure 8 shows the problem of an optimum integration strategy in the form of a rough graph.

The exact formulation of the question is as follows:

—To what extent and
—in which phase (planning, decision, development, implementation, run) shall
—the individual interest groups (planners, decision-makers, development group, operators, persons concerned, external groups) participate, from a cost-benefit point of view,
—in the implementation of computer-based systems
—so that, from an overall point of view with regard to economic and social objectives, an optimum result can be guaranteed?

In Figure 8, we proceed from the following assumptions:

1. The costs C increase if the motivation factor is considered to a greater extent, for example, through higher additional investments or longer resolution processes.

2. The costs $\overline{C}$ decrease if the motivation factor is considered to a greater extent, for example, because of less resistance being offered to the system investment by the group of "persons concerned".

3. The benefit $\overline{B}$ to the group of "persons concerned" increases if the motivation factor is considered to a greater extent, as the group believes that it will reach a higher level of objective attainment.

4. The benefit B to the system investors decreases if the motivation factor is considered to a greater extent, as the group cannot realize its objectives to a full extent. On the contrary, the participative approach forces the group to make compromises with respect to its objectives.

Figure 9 shows the optimum value of the motivation factor, M_{opt}, from an overall point of view. The related optimum level of integration IG_{opt} and the optimum level of objective attainment ZG_{opt} can be derived from M_{opt}.

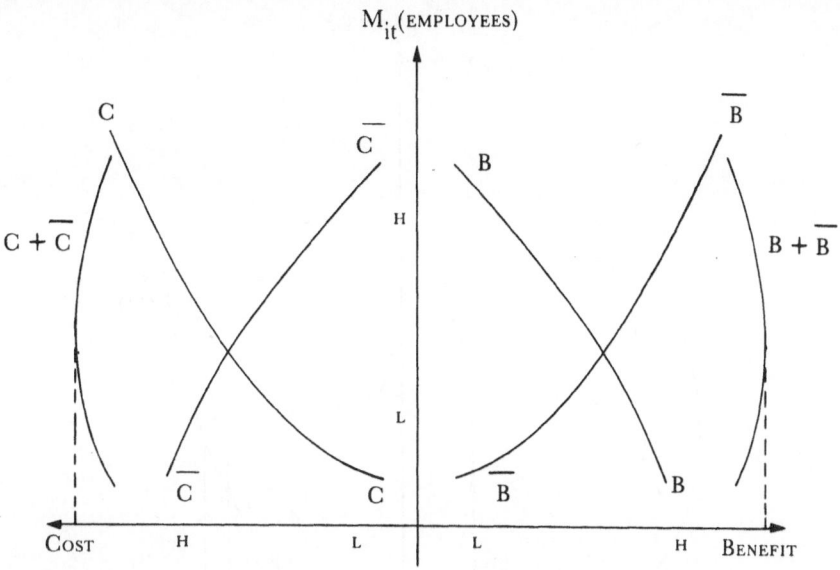

Figure 8. Defining the 'Cost Maximum' and the 'Benefit Optimum'.

5 SUMMARY

Cost-benefit analyses can be used as decision-making tools for evaluating computer-based system investments. Empirical research (pilot study) has, however, shown that, contrary to original planning, a positive cost-benefit ratio was achieved only in few cases after system implementation. Additional investigations (analytical study) have revealed that insufficient consideration of the "motivation factor" is one of the reasons for this. The motivation factor indicates to what extent the individual interest groups participate in the system investment and to what extent they consider their objectives realized through the system investment.

The analysis has shown that the group of "persons concerned" was not considered sufficiently and that this was the main reason for a negative cost-benefit ratio.

This leads to the question of the "optimum level of integration in a participative approach". It is of topical interest as participation in the planning of computer-based systems is being more and more often demanded, especially on the part of labor unions.

Finally, an abstract example shows how the optimum level of integration could be derived from an overall point of view. The statements must still be verified and concretized by further research.

281

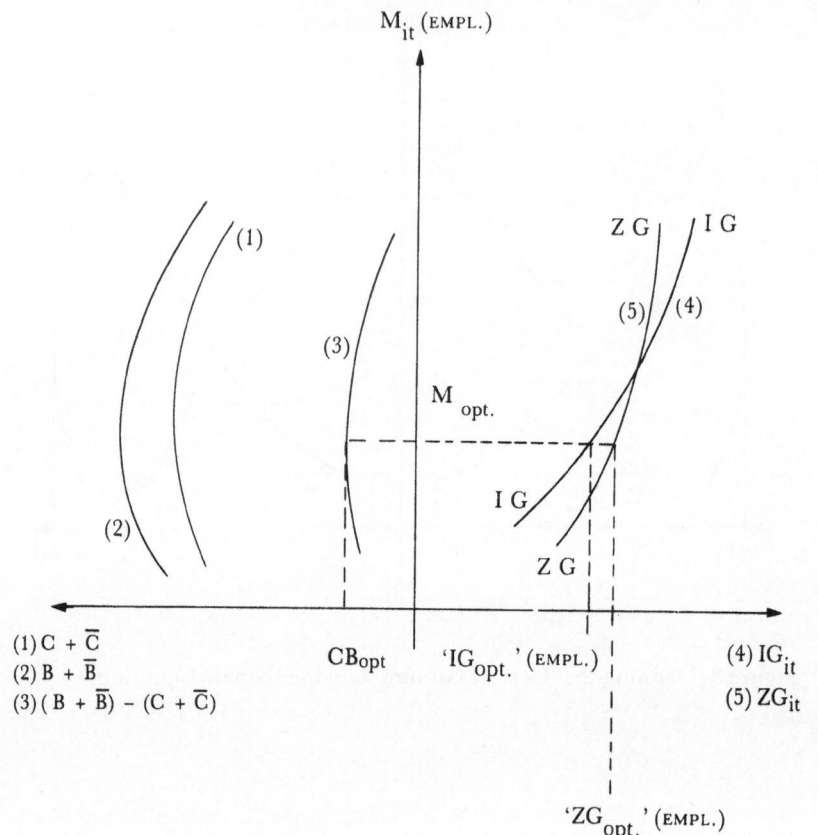

Figure 9. Defining the "Cost-Benefit Optimum" (CB_opt) for "Management Participation".

REFERENCES

1. Böhnisch, W. "Personale Innovationswiderstände." in E. Gaugler (ed.) *Handwörterbuch des Personalwesens*. Stuttgart, 1975., col. 1046-61.

2. Böhnisch, W. *Personale Widerstände bei der Durchsetzung von Innovationen*. Stuttgart, 1978.

3. Domsch, M. "Interdisziplinäre Kosten-Nutzen-Analysen bei Investitionsentscheidungen." in H. Albach and H. Simon. *Investitionstheorie und Investitionspolitik privater und öffentlicher Unternehmen*. Wiesbaden, 1976, pp. 65-96.

4. Dyson, R.G. "Participation in Planning—A Study of Two Organizations in The Netherlands." *Long Range Planning* 11 (1978): pp. 61-69.

5. Esser, W.-M. and W. Kirsch. *Einführung von Planungs- und Informationssystemen—Ein empirischer Vergleich*. Munich, 1978.

6. Gabele, E. "Das Management von Neuerungen." *Zeitschrift für betriebswissenschaftliche Forschung* 30 (1978): 194-226.

7. Gaitanides, M. and B. Gottschalk. "Zur 'rechtzeitigen' Unterrichtung des Betriebsrates von Planungsvorhaben (§ 90 Betriebsverfassungsgesetz)." *Angewandte Planung* 2 (1978): 22-28.

8. Grochla, E. (ed.) *Die Wirtschaftlichkeit automatisierter Datenverarbeitungssysteme*. Wiesbaden, 1970.

9. Hempel, J. and A. Kehler. *Probleme der Kosten-Nutzen-Analyse für Informationssysteme in öffentlichen Verwaltungen*. Pullach b. Munich, 1974.

10. Horváth, P., H. Kargl and H. Müller-Merbach (eds.) *Controlling und automatisierte Datenverarbeitung*. Wiesbaden, 1975.

11. IBM Deutschland GmbH (ed.) "Datenverarbeitung—Gewinnquelle des Unternehmens. Nutzenanalyse als Basis einer Wirtschaftlichkeitsrechnung für Datenverarbeitungsanlagen." IBM Form GE 12-1307-02, o.O., 1976.

12. IG Metall Vorstandsverwaltung, Abt. Automation (ed.) *Rationalisierung durch Bildschirmsysteme*. Frankfurt/M., 1977.

13. IG Metall Vorstandsverwaltung, Abt. Automation und Technologie (ed.) *Computergestützte Personalinformationssysteme*. Frankfurt/M., 1977.

14. Mumford, E. *The Participative Design of Computer Systems*. London, 1978.

15. Obermeier, G. Nutzen-Kosten-Analyse zur Gestaltung computergestützter Informationssysteme. Munich, 1977.

16. Paul, G. *Bedürfnisberücksichtigung durch Mitbestimmung*. Munich, 1977.

17. Siemens AG (ed.) "Wirtschaftlichkeit von DV-Verfahren. Eine Entscheidungshilfe" (author: K. Riepl), in *Siemens-Schriftenreihe data praxis*. Munich o.J. (Best.-Nr. D 10/1048).

17. Watson, W. "Resistance to Change." in W.G. Bennis, K.D. Benne and R. Chin (eds.) *The Planning of Change*, 2nd ed. New York, 1969, pp. 488-98.

19. Zangemeister, C. *Nutzwertanalyse in der Systemtechnik: Eine Methodik zur multidimensionalen Bewertung von Projektalternativen*, 3rd ed. Munich, 1973.

19. User and Specialist Evaluations in System Development

by Dietrich Seibt

1 PROCESSES OF GOAL DEFINITION AND EVALUATION TO START SYSTEM DEVELOPMENT

Traditional approaches to the process of analysis, design and implementation of computer-based information systems start with activities such as:
—problem definition
—requirements specification
—feasibility study, etc.

One of the assumptions of these traditional approaches is that a number of detailed goals, which are compatible with or which are derived from the broad aims of an organization, can be—better: *must* be—specified at the beginning of system development and give the guidelines for all further activities.

A second assumption is that "the user" will be able to formulate these detailed goals. He has to give:
1. a list of functional specifications for the new system;
2. restrictions or targets (e.g., monetary, time, organizational, technological, etc.) for the system development process
to system analysts and designers, who then take "control" of system development and construct the "best" system.

As Figure 1 shows, processes of goal definition and evaluation at the beginning of system development are by no means simple processes. They comprise a lot of very complicated activities requiring systematic consideration of different aspects, factors or variables. Their complexity increases with the number of users and professional system designers who are participating in them. We find very strong suggestions that users should be dominant in defining *their* goals and objectives, but we find very few comments on the difficulties which will arise in connection with this task. Recommendations to overcome the difficulties are rudimentary.
—User A has not the same interests as user B concerning the same future system to be developed, especially if A and B belong to different departments (of the same organization).
—In the ideal case users know their "problems" well enough to formulate them, but in most cases they have only diffuse perceptions of the technological alternatives to solve them. This is especially true in the field of rapidly evolving information and communication technologies.
—Most users don't have sufficient knowledge about the conditions and conse-

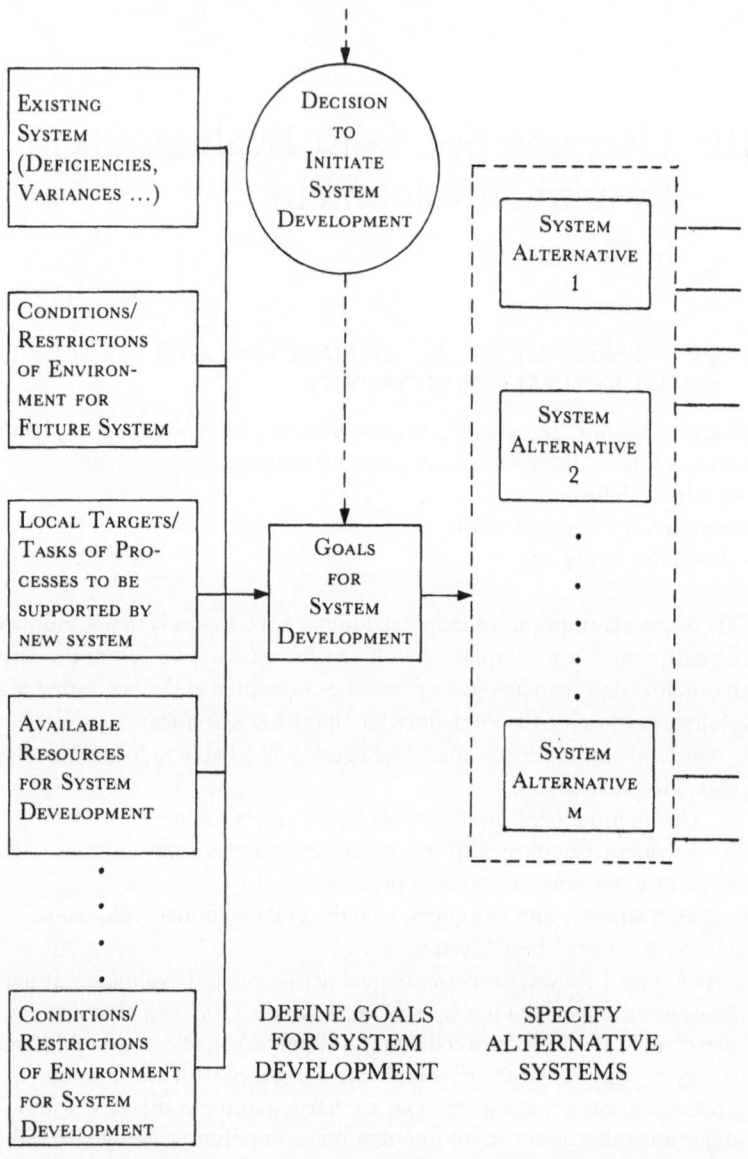

Figure 1. Processes of goal definition and evaluation at the start of system development.

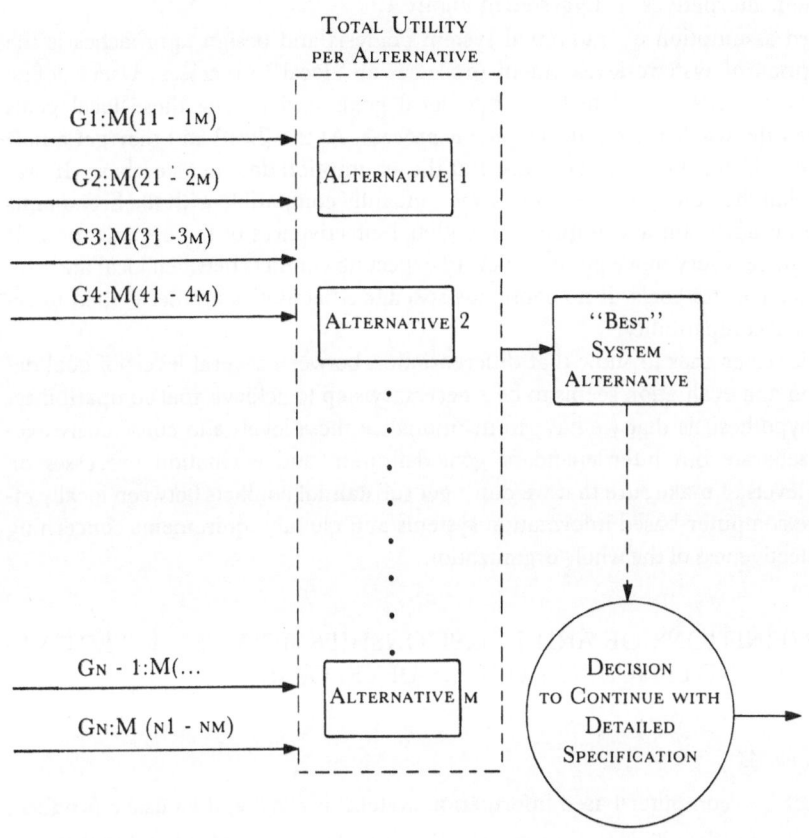

SCORE EACH
ALTERNATIVE
IN MEETING
EACH GOAL
(INCL. WEIGHT-
ING OF EACH
GOAL)

FIND A RANK-
ING ORDER OF
SYSTEM
ALTERNATIVES
(INCL. MULTIPLYING
GOAL-WEIGHTS
BY CORRESPONDING
GOAL MEASURES AND
AGGREGAT PER
ALTERNATIVE)

SELECT SYSTEM
ALTERNATIVE
WITH HIGHEST
TOTAL UTILITY

quences (e.g., organizational, behavioral, etc.) of different technological alternatives. On the other hand this knowledge is urgently needed for the tasks of goal definition, formulation of system alternatives and selection of the "best" system alternatives as suggested in Figure 1.

A third assumption of traditional system analysis and design approaches is the perception of system development processes as "local" processes. Users define *their* local needs, translate them into local goals and pursue these local goals through the whole system development process. At the (best) end they get a new system, which achieves these goals. But the assumption does not stop here. It pretends that the new system is at the same time fully compatible with the broad aims of the organization and improves the global effectiveness of the organization. It seems to be a very naive point of view to expect no conflicts between local and global effectiveness goals, if no conscious specialized activities are performed to secure goal compatibility.

This paper tries to show that differentiation between several levels of goal definition and evaluation seems to be a necessary step to achieve goal compatibility. The hypothesis is that we have to institionalize these levels and consciously execute separate but interdependant goal definition and evaluation processes on these levels to make sure that we don't get substantial conflicts between locally effective computer-based information systems and global requirements concerning the effectiveness of the whole organization.

2 DEFINITIONS OF AND RELATIONSHIPS BETWEEN EFFECTIVENESS AND EFFICIENCY OF CBIS-DEVELOPMENT

Definition A:

A CBIS (= computer-based information system) is *effective*, if its usage produces planned improvements (e.g., increases of output) of the process(es) supported by the CBIS. The degree of system effectiveness can be measured by comparing planned improvements with actual improvements achieved with the system.

Definition B:

A CBIS is *efficient*, if its usage produces planned improvements (e.g., increases of output) of the process(es) supported by the CBIS *with "minimal" (SIMON) input of resources*. The degree of system efficiency can be measured by comparing "minimal" input of resources with actual input of resources.

Consideration of both definitions A and B shows that a CBIS, which is efficient, necessarily has to be effective too, but not vice versa. The main problem with system efficiency is that usually nobody knows, what marks the "minimal" input of resources at the start of system usage. But in many cases there is a chance to increase the efficiency of a CBIS by systematic experiments during the first periods of usage.

Definition C:

The process of developing a CBIS is *effective*, if planned design goals are achieved. The degree of system development effectiveness can be measured by comparing planned design goals in terms of planned outputs, functions, results, effects, etc. with actual outputs, functions, etc., of the system developed.

Definition D:

The process of developing a CBIS is *efficient* if planned design goals are achieved with "minimal" input of resources. The degree of system development efficiency can be measured by comparing "minimal" input of resources with actual input of resources.

Consideration of both definitions C and D shows that a system development process, which is effective, is not necessarily efficient. The main problem with efficiency of system development in the area of CBIS: usually development of a specific system for a specific environment is a unique process in the same sense as the system is unique. Both cannot be repeated. Therefore "minimal" input of resources cannot be determined by experiments.

Another important point: the notion of an effective/efficient CBIS is separated from the notion of effective/efficient CBIS-development. This coincides with observations in reality. You may achieve a high degree of effectiveness in developing a specific CBIS (= achieve all or nearly all design goals), but at the same time produce a system which shows only a low degree of effectiveness during its usage. On the other side: a CBIS which is highly effective during its usage may be the result of a system development process, which has reached only a low degree of effectiveness because of the differences between planned and achieved design goals.

It is one of the main problems of system development to make sure that there is a 1:1-correspondence between system design goals (applied in definition C) and improvements/advantages expected by the usage of the new system (applied in definition A). This might be only a small problem, if the system designer/implementer is the future user of the system himself. But this problem increases immensely if the activities of system design, implementation and usage are spread over many persons or groups with different interests and backgrounds. The larger the number of people participating in or concerned with these activities, the larger the number of objectives and expectations which are pursued by them, the higher the difficulties and the costs to integrate them, i.e., to agree on one set of common goals which are binding all those participating in system design, implementation and usage. Which tools are available to obtain such common binding goals? There is one very simple answer to this question:

Communication is the basis for all integration, adjustment and synchronizing procedures.

3 DIFFERENT LEVELS OF GOAL DEFINITION AND EVALUATION

Figure 2 provides an idealized view of several goal definition and evaluation processes, which have to be performed before and during the process of CBIS-development. In many cases system specialists feel responsible only for level 3: specification of technical (hardware, software), organizational, economic requirements to the new CBIS which are needed for sysem design decisions, i.e., for specification of system alternatives and for detailed system plans. System specialists not seldom presume that the various departments of an organization have defined local goals, which are derived from or at least compatible with the broad/global aims of the organization. They don't recognize that

a.   evaluation/limitation of those global aims or local goals, which can and should be supported by a new CBIS,

b.   translation of those aims/goals into concrete design goals, which should be achieved during system development

are very difficult tasks. For both kinds of tasks special know-how is needed, which includes clear understanding of what can be reached by a CBIS. This know-how usually is available after a long period of system usage but not at the start of system development.

CBIS development is a very complex process which often reveals a lot of problems which have been hitherto unknown. We are not in the position to presume clearly formulated global aims and local goals at the start of this process. At least the first phases of design and implementation should be organized in such a manner that participating users and system specialists can perform learning processes and goal specification processes in parallel. Professional system designers should consider themselves primarily as supporters of learning processes in the first phase of system development.

Evaluation processes appear in combination with definition/specification of goals (left side of Figure 2) and in combination with measurement of results of system development and system usage (right side of Figure 2). Principally the same criteria/factors/variables/measures, which are applied to specify/define the goals, are to be used for measurement and evaluation of goal achievement. But as Figure 2 shows, it is important to distinguish between at least three levels of goals for CBIS-development.

The next section shows some goal-examples for each level. The examples should clarify and verify the idea of differentiation between these levels.

4 EXAMPLES OF GOALS BELONGING TO DIFFERENT LEVELS

System design goals (as goals in general) must have certain elements, to be operational, e.g., elements specifying:

—content,

—extent,

—aspiration level,

—time constraints.

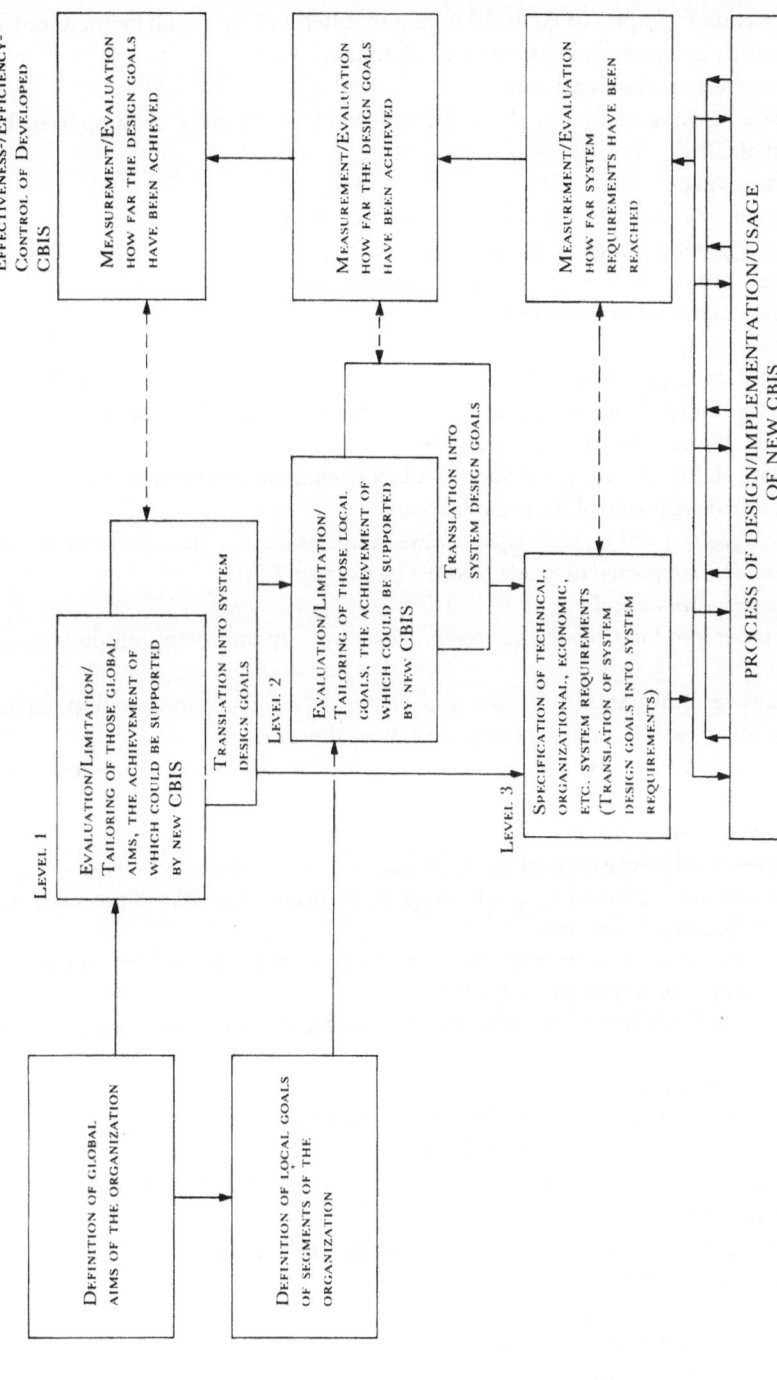

Figure 2. Different Levels of Goal Definition and Evaluation before, during and after CBIS Development

291

In this section examples of goals belonging to different levels shall be mentioned, which mostly comprise only expressions of content.

Three levels are differentiated:

a. *Global organizational aims,* the achievement of which *could* be supported by usage of of CBIS:

—realize savings,

—reduce/minimize costs (e.g., cost of personnel, material),

—increase profit (e.g., of certain products),

—increase productivity (e.g., of a production system),

—increase market share/revenues,

—increase cash,

—increase strategic potentialities,

—increase ability of the organization to respond/react to external events,

—decrease fluctuation-rate of employees,

—increase ability of the organization to adapt to changing environment,

—improve social image of the organization.

b. *Local goals of one or some organizational units/departments,* the achievement of which *could* be supported or made possible by usage of CBIS:

1. *process-oriented goals:*

—improve products/results of user-process (e.g., by improving product quality),

—improve information basis for user-process (e.g., more information; information, which is more precise and/or more topical),

—standardize/simplify user-process (e.g., concerning inputs, outputs, schedules, etc.),

—speed up user-process,

—decrease/minimize costs of user-process,

—increase realiability of user-process (e.g., by decreasing risks of mistakes and disturbances of user-process),

—improve coordination between user-process and "neighbour"-processes which are not supported by CBIS),

—increase flexibility of user-process concerning responses to unexpected external events.

2. *user-oriented goals:*

—decrease quantity of (routine) tasks to be fulfilled,

—increase quality of tasks be ful-filled,

—decrease degree of dependence on tasks which precede or follow the task supported by new system,

—increase the possibility for the user to display initiative and creativity,

—increase scope for own decisions,

—increase span of control,

—increase recognition/social status,

—increase job security,

—increase income,

—increase chances for promotion.

c. *System requirements,* here concerning hardware/software components of a CBIS:

—functions (content, scope, methodological basis),
—output (content, forms/formats, media),
—input (content, formats, media, source),
—timing/schedules (of functions, input, output),
—execution times/response times/access times, etc.,
—action-mode (on-line, off-line),
—kinds/amounts of functional processors (hardware/software); degree of centralization/decentralization,
—kinds/amounts of storage required for input, functions, output,
—kinds/amounts of input/output units, control units, etc., required,
—data protection facilities and data security mechanisms,
—reliability requirements,
—flexibility requirements, e.g., concerning externally induced changes.

Combinations and pronunciations of these goals belonging to different levels or layers vary between organizations and between system development processes. The same is true for the relationships between goals belonging to different levels. Even if you find in reality very similar CBIS-development cases concerning defined system requirements, you have to expect different combinations and pronunciations of local goals and global aims, from which system requirements have been derived. On the other side not all system requirements can be derived from afore-defined goals and aims. In many cases the necessary formulation of certain system requirements corresponding to the possibilities of a certain technology induces the search for or the selection between alternative possible goals, which could be achieved by the new system. Figure 3 gives an overview of possible relationships between:

—global aims,
—process-oriented local goals,
—user-oriented local goals,
—system requirements.

Types of relationships are not specified. One type could be "is derived from", another type could be "delivers variables for specification". In considering these examples of relationships, it will become clear that differentiation between 3-4 levels of aims/goals/requirements leads to very crude results. The overview (Figure 3) could easily demonstrate a lot of empirically proven relationships between the items of each single column. But at the same time one could induce differentiation between a much larger number of goal levels in order to avoid special types of relationships which cannot be expressed with such a crude model.

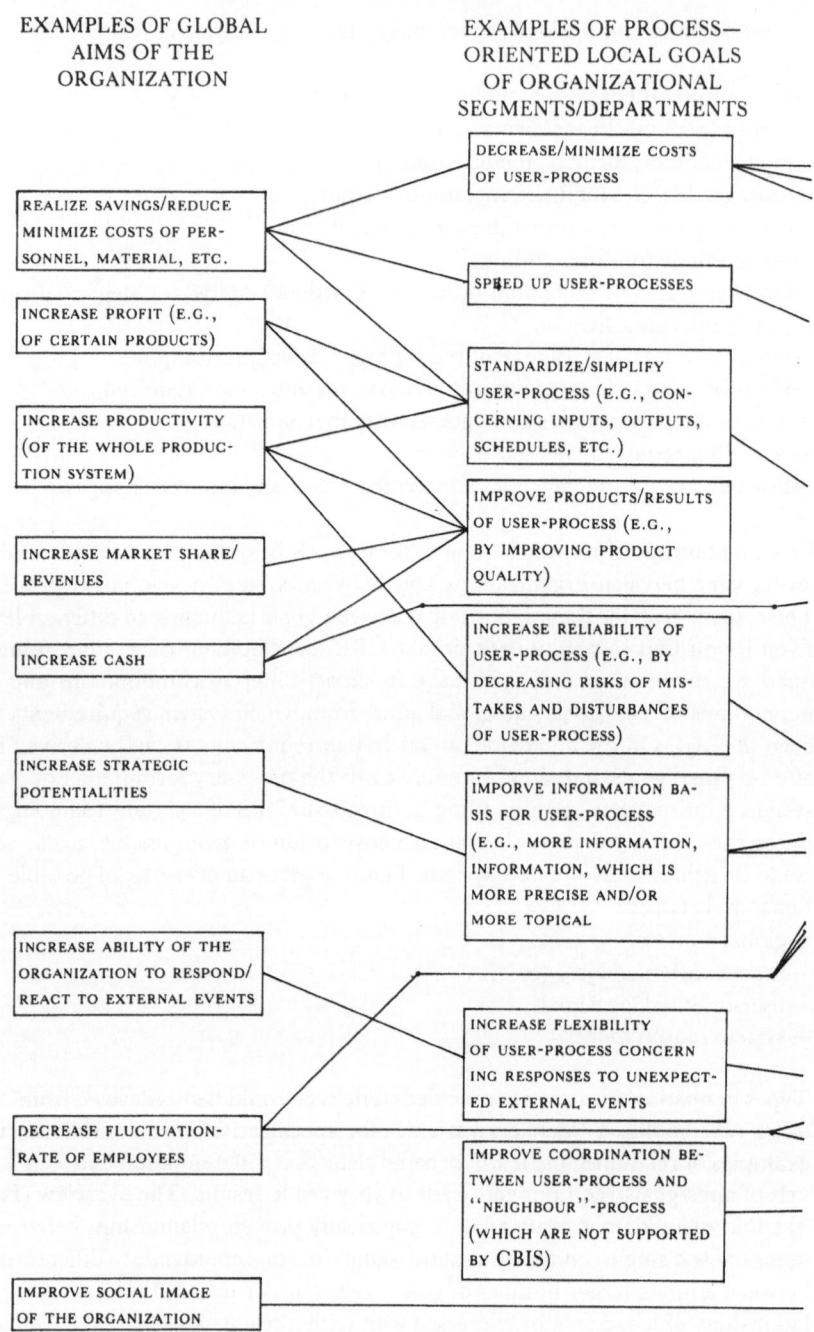

EXAMPLES OF GLOBAL
AIMS OF THE
ORGANIZATION

EXAMPLES OF PROCESS—
ORIENTED LOCAL GOALS
OF ORGANIZATIONAL
SEGMENTS/DEPARTMENTS

DECREASE/MINIMIZE COSTS
OF USER-PROCESS

REALIZE SAVINGS/REDUCE
MINIMIZE COSTS OF PER-
SONNEL, MATERIAL, ETC.

SPEED UP USER-PROCESSES

INCREASE PROFIT (E.G.,
OF CERTAIN PRODUCTS)

STANDARDIZE/SIMPLIFY
USER-PROCESS (E.G., CON-
CERNING INPUTS, OUTPUTS,
SCHEDULES, ETC.)

INCREASE PRODUCTIVITY
(OF THE WHOLE PRODUC-
TION SYSTEM)

IMPROVE PRODUCTS/RESULTS
OF USER-PROCESS (E.G.,
BY IMPROVING PRODUCT
QUALITY)

INCREASE MARKET SHARE/
REVENUES

INCREASE RELIABILITY OF
USER-PROCESS (E.G., BY
DECREASING RISKS OF MIS-
TAKES AND DISTURBANCES
OF USER-PROCESS)

INCREASE CASH

INCREASE STRATEGIC
POTENTIALITIES

IMPORVE INFORMATION BA-
SIS FOR USER-PROCESS
(E.G., MORE INFORMATION,
INFORMATION, WHICH IS
MORE PRECISE AND/OR
MORE TOPICAL

INCREASE ABILITY OF THE
ORGANIZATION TO RESPOND/
REACT TO EXTERNAL EVENTS

INCREASE FLEXIBILITY
OF USER-PROCESS CONCERN
ING RESPONSES TO UNEXPECT-
ED EXTERNAL EVENTS

DECREASE FLUCTUATION-
RATE OF EMPLOYEES

IMPROVE COORDINATION BE-
TWEEN USER-PROCESS AND
"NEIGHBOUR"-PROCESS
(WHICH ARE NOT SUPPORTED
BY CBIS)

IMPROVE SOCIAL IMAGE
OF THE ORGANIZATION

Figure 3. Examples of Goals belonging to Different Levels and Examples of Relationships between these Goals

294

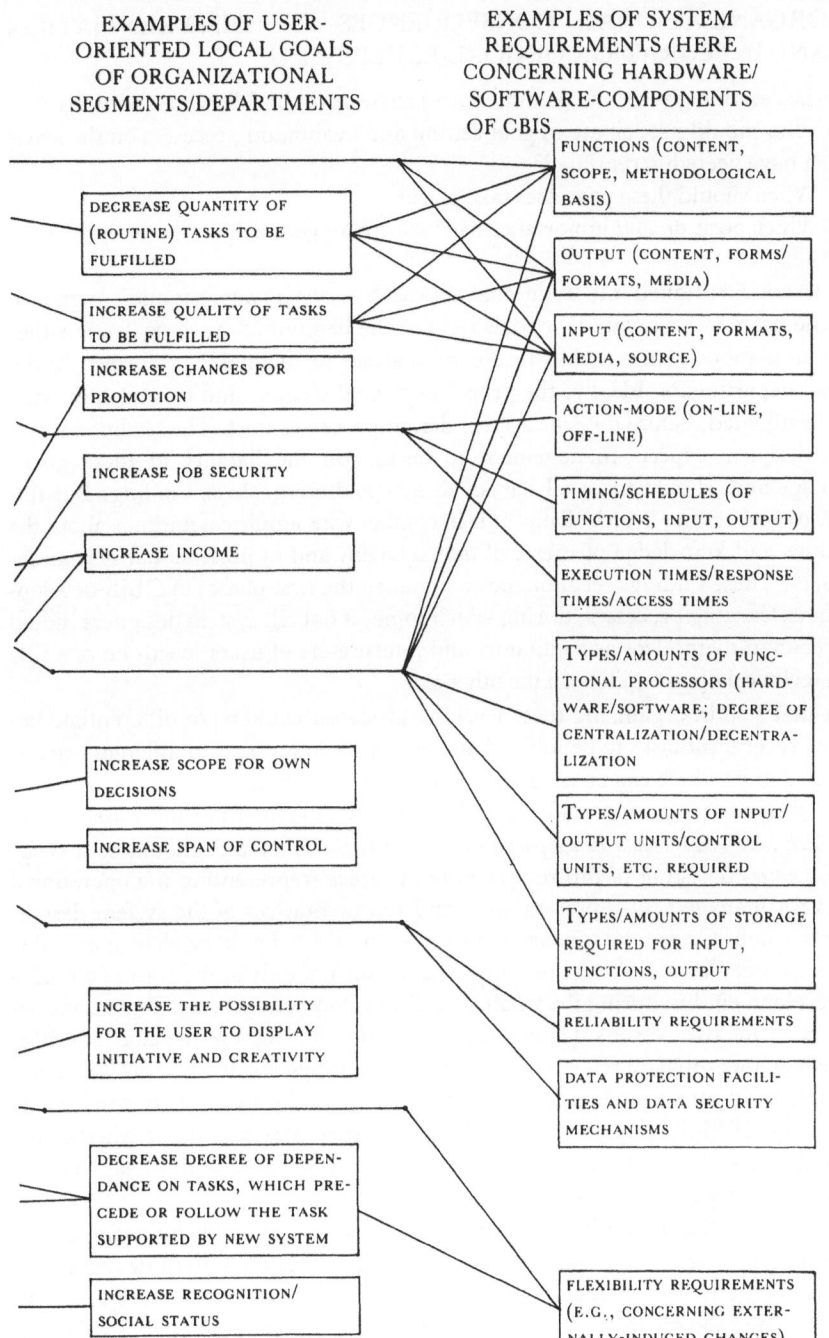

EXAMPLES OF USER-
ORIENTED LOCAL GOALS
OF ORGANIZATIONAL
SEGMENTS/DEPARTMENTS

EXAMPLES OF SYSTEM
REQUIREMENTS (HERE
CONCERNING HARDWARE/
SOFTWARE-COMPONENTS
OF CBIS

FUNCTIONS (CONTENT, SCOPE, METHODOLOGICAL BASIS)

DECREASE QUANTITY OF (ROUTINE) TASKS TO BE FULFILLED

OUTPUT (CONTENT, FORMS/ FORMATS, MEDIA)

INCREASE QUALITY OF TASKS TO BE FULFILLED

INPUT (CONTENT, FORMATS, MEDIA, SOURCE)

INCREASE CHANCES FOR PROMOTION

ACTION-MODE (ON-LINE, OFF-LINE)

INCREASE JOB SECURITY

TIMING/SCHEDULES (OF FUNCTIONS, INPUT, OUTPUT)

INCREASE INCOME

EXECUTION TIMES/RESPONSE TIMES/ACCESS TIMES

TYPES/AMOUNTS OF FUNC- TIONAL PROCESSORS (HARD- WARE/SOFTWARE; DEGREE OF CENTRALIZATION/DECENTRA- LIZATION

INCREASE SCOPE FOR OWN DECISIONS

TYPES/AMOUNTS OF INPUT/ OUTPUT UNITS/CONTROL UNITS, ETC. REQUIRED

INCREASE SPAN OF CONTROL

TYPES/AMOUNTS OF STORAGE REQUIRED FOR INPUT, FUNCTIONS, OUTPUT

INCREASE THE POSSIBILITY FOR THE USER TO DISPLAY INITIATIVE AND CREATIVITY

RELIABILITY REQUIREMENTS

DATA PROTECTION FACILI- TIES AND DATA SECURITY MECHANISMS

DECREASE DEGREE OF DEPEN- DANCE ON TASKS, WHICH PRE- CEDE OR FOLLOW THE TASK SUPPORTED BY NEW SYSTEM

INCREASE RECOGNITION/ SOCIAL STATUS

FLEXIBILITY REQUIREMENTS (E.G., CONCERNING EXTER- NALLY-INDUCED CHANGES)

5 ORGANIZATIONAL CONSEQUENCES OF DIFFERENTIATION AND INTEGRATION OF GOAL-LEVELS

This last section gives some (rudimentary) answers to the following questions:

a.   Who should participate in goal-setting and evaluation processes on the levels which have been differentiated?

b.   When should these processes take place?

c.   Which position and importance has "control of goal-achievement"?

As already mentioned, the traditional approach of system analysis and design is to get the users to formulate *their* goals right at the beginning. Such goals are either set autonomously or stated as results of analyses or diagnoses performed in the users' departments. Ideally, the processes of goal setting, finding and specifying are terminated, before the true system design processes start. The traditional system designer expects management to decide on the liability of these goals. Management should force all parties to accept these goals as binding. But this view of goal setting is unrealistic. It is in conflict with empirical findings about the abilities and knowledge of users, of management and of professional system designers. These findings recommend to organize the first phases of CBIS-development as learning processes, during which some, if not all, system designers should understand themselves as facilitators and interpreters of users' needs on one side and technical opportunities on the other side.

A first step in organizing these learning processes could be to differentiate between several subtasks to be fulfilled and assign these subtasks to different organizational units which can be made responsible for the subtasks:

—Formation of a (temporary) organizational unit A responsible for *decisions about which local goals should be supported by the new CBIS*. This unit should be a *project committee* consisting of future system-(end) users (representing the operational level), management-representatives and representatives of the system designer's group. One of the management-representatives should be chairman of this committee. Unit A should perform evaluations not only at the start of a CBIS-development but during the whole system development process. This seems necessary for two reasons: (1) nobody has enough foresight at the start of CBIS-development that all relevant local goals, to be supported by the new CBIS, are considered and consciously determined; (2) periodically or at certain events during CBIS-development the project committee has to evaluate whether the goals set will be achievable by the new system or perhaps must be changed (compare Figure 2, right-hand side).

—Formation of a (temporary) organizational unit B responsible for *decisions about which system requirements should be specified* as objectives for system design activities. This unit should be a *project-team* consisting of future system-(end)users (representing the operational level) and professional system designers/implementators (including programmers). One of the end-users should be project-manager during all phases of system development except the programming and testing phase. Unit B has the (sub)task to translate the goals, which are output of the decisions of unit A, into system requirements. Unit B has to perform evaluations not only in connection with this translation-task but also during the whole process of CBIS-development. Permanent evaluations are necessary to determine whether system requirements are actually reached by the activities of the designers/implementators. On the other side: there will be a lot of occasions when the project-team has not enough information about (local) goals to be supported by new system and therefore is forced to ask the project-committee to be more precise and/or complete concerning these goals. Maybe such local goals have changed in the meantime.

—Formation of a (permanent) organizational unit C, responsible for *decisions about which global aims should be supported by the new CBIS,* but also by all CBIS which have been developed in the past or will be developed in the future. This unit should be a *steering committee* for all global decisions concerning the information services infrastructure of an organization, into which local CBIS must be embedded. The steering committee should be composed of at least one top management representative, management-representatives of all important user-areas (e.g., functions or regional units) and management representatives of the information services area. The top management representative should be chairman of this steering committee. At least it is important that this function of being chairman to the steering committee is considered as one of the top management functions.

Unit C should perform evaluations not only at the start of a larger CBIS-development program, e.g., when alternatives concerning priorities and budgets for several CBIS (as subsystems of a large integrated system) are to be prepared and selected. Unit C should be a standing institution, which is responsible primarily for the global control of CBIS—and infrastructure—effectiveness. There will be a lot of occasions when temporary project-committees have not enough information about global aims to be supported by new CBIS and therefore are forced to ask the steering committee to be more precise and/or complete concerning these global aims of an organization.

Figure 4 shows some relationships between the units A-C, which have been assigned to the aforementioned levels of goals and goal-setting. Figure 4 also shows some time-relations between the decisions (including evaluations) which might occur on the different levels. Many and complicated communication and coordination problems are connected with such an organizational structure. But these cannot be dealt with in such a short paper as this.

Only by conscious cooperation of organizational units like those recommended here, it will be possible to accomplish the difficult task of permanent goal-setting and evaluation processes necessary to produce systems, which are locally effective and at the same time improve the global effectiveness of an organization.

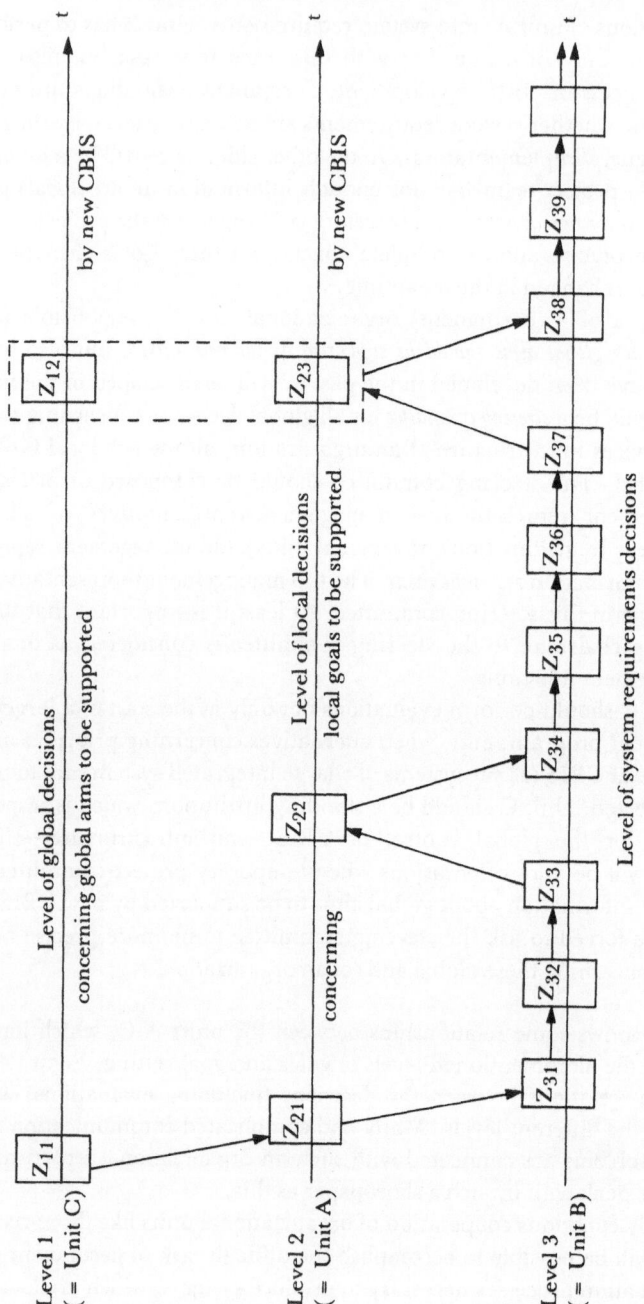

Figure 4. Relations between Activities (= Decisions) on different Levels of Goal Definition and Evaluation (Z_{nm} = decision points concerning goals and requirements; arrows between them mark time relations and other contextual dependencies.)

REFERENCES

1. Bildingmaier, J., and D.J.G. Schneider, "Ziele, Zielsysteme und Zielkonflikte," in E. Grochla and W. Wittmann (eds.), *Handwörterbuch der Betriebswirtschaft*, 4th ed., Vol. 3 (1976), Col. 4731-4740.

2. Björn-Andersen, N., and B. Hedberg, "Designing Information Systems in an Organizational Perspective," *TIMS-Studies in Management Science* (1977): 125-142.

3. Blaser, A., and E. Keppel, "Developing Business Application Systems—Can the User Do it?," in H.R. Hansen (ed.), *Entwicklungstendenzen der Systemanalyse*, Munich-Vienna, 1978, pp. 435-464.

4. Genkinger, P.F. (ed.), "Implementing 'Nutswertanalyse'," in A.B. Frielink (ed.), *Economics of Informatics*, Amsterdam-Oxford, 1975, pp. 129-143.

5. Ginzberg, M.J., "Implementation as a Process of Change: A Framework and Empirical Study," Sloan School Working Paper 797-75/CISR-13, M.I.T., July 1975.

6. Ginzberg, M.J., "A Detailed Look at Implementation Research," Sloan School Working Paper 753-74, M.I.T., June 1974.

7. Grün, O., "Zielbildung, Prozesse der," in E. Grochla and W. Wittmann (eds.), *Handwörterbuch der Betriebswirtschaft*, 4th ed., Vol. 3, 1976, col. 4719-4730.

8. Hamel, W., *Zieländerungen im Entscheidungsprozess*, Tübingen, 1974.

9. Hauschildt, J., "Zielbildung—ein heuristischer Prozess," *Zeitschrift für Betriebswirtschaft* 46(1976): 327-340.

10. Hawgood, J., "Quinquevalent Quantification of Computer Benefits," in A.B. Frielink (ed.), *Economics of Informatics*, Amsterdam-Oxford, 1975, pp. 171-180.

11. Hawgood, J., "Participative assessment of library benefits," *Drexel Library Quarterly* (July 1977).

12. Kolf, F, H.J. Oppelland, D. Seibt and N. Szyperski, "Instrumentarium zur organisatorischen Implementierung von rechnergestützten Informationssystemen," *Angewandte Informatik* 20(7) (1978): 299-310.

13. Kolf, F, H.J. Oppelland, D. Seibt and N. Szyperski, "Tools for Handling Human and Organizational Problems of Computer-Based Information Systems," in G. Bracci and P.C. Lockemann (eds.), *Information Systems Methodology*, Proceedings of the 2nd Conference of ECI, Berlin-Heidelberg-New York, pp. 82-119.

14. Land, F.F., "Evaluation of system goals in determining a decision strategy for a computer-based information system," *The Computer Journal* 19(4) (Nov. 1976): 290-294.

15. Mumford, E, F. Land and J. Hawgood, *A Participative Approach to Forward Planning and System Change (The ABACON Approach)*. Durham, England, 1978.

16. Obermeier, G., *Nutzen—Kosten—Analysen zur Gestaltung Computergestützter Informationssysteme*. Munich, 1977.

17. Schein, E.H., *Professional Education: Some New Directions*. New York, 1972.

18. Seibt, D., "Budgeting and Control of Information Systems Development," in A.B. Frielink (ed.), *Economics of Informatics*. Amsterdam, 1975, pp. 343-358.

19. Seibt, D., "Begriffliche Grundlagen der Evaluierung rechnergestützter Informationssysteme sowie ihrer Entwicklungsprozesse," Beitrag zur GI-Fachtagung "Begriffliche Grundlagen für rechnergestützte Informationssysteme," Weinheim, 1976 (manuscript).

20. Seibt, D., "Zielbildung für Sollkonzepte," in H.R. Hansen (ed.), *Entwicklungstendenzen der Systemanalyse*. Munich-Vienna, 1978, pp. 223-259.

21. Sorensen, R.E., and D.E. Zand, "Improving the Implementation of OR/MS-Models by Applying the Lewin-Schein-Theory of Change," in R.L. Schultz and D.P. Slevin (eds.), *Implementing Operations Research/Management Science*, New York-London-Amsterdam, 1975, pp. 217-236.

22. Szyperski, N., "Das Setzen von Zielen als primäre Aufgabe der Unternehmungsleitung," *Zeitschrift für Betriebswirtschaft* 41(10) (1971): 639-670.

23. Szyperski, N., and F. Kolf, "Integration der strategischen Informationssystem-Planung (SISP) in die Unternehmens-Entwicklungsplanung," in H.R. Hansen (ed.), *Entwicklungstendenzen der Systemanalyse*. Munich-Vienna, 1978, pp. 59-81.

24. Thelen, H.J. (ed.), "Die Integration von Planungs-, Ziel-, und Informationssystem zur Führung komplexer Projekte (2. Teil)," *Angewandte Planung* 3(1) (Feb. 1979): 30-36.

25. Zangemeister, Ch., "Measurement of Effectiveness of Computerized Information Systems from a Management Point of View through Utility Analysis," in A.B. Frielink (ed.), *Economics of Informatics*, Proceedings of the IBI-ICC-International Symposium, Mainz 1974, Amsterdam-Oxford, 1975, pp. 440-451.

20. The Evaluation of an Information System Implementation

by E. Burton Swanson

1 INTRODUCTION

Relatively little attention has been given in the literature to information systems already implemented. Understandably, the focus to date has been on the design, development, and implementation of new systems. Nevertheless, a substantial population of information systems now exists, and the "care and feeding" of these systems places substantial demands upon organizational resources. For example, recent survey results indicate that about fifty percent of an organization's applications systems and programming personnel time is devoted to the maintenance of existing application software [3].

The maintenance of existing information systems is seldom the routine activity it is often thought to be. Correcting faults in software occupies a relatively small percentage of staff time. The most substantial activity is the providing of enhancements of the system for its users [3]. In some cases, the providing of certain enhancements is formally recognized as redesign work, rather than maintenance, but this distinction does not alter the important reality: existing information systems tend to grow and evolve in terms of products and services provided their users. The effective management of this growth and evolution is thus the source of the need for a system evaluation.

The purpose of this paper is to briefly sketch and summarize the problem of evaluating an information system implementation, and to call attention to those aspects of the problem which are most troublesome, and/or offer promising research opportunities.

In sketching the problem, the paradigm of microeconomic theory will be loosely applied. From this point of view, it may be argued that three interrelated activities are necessary for the evaluation of an information system implementation:

1. activity analysis,
2. possibility analysis,
3. utility analysis.

As understood here, *activity analysis* seeks an answer to the question: what is the nature of the present information system implementation? *Possibility analysis* seeks an answer to the question: what alternative information system implementations are possible, technologically? *Utility analysis* seeks an answer to the question: what is the preferred information system implementation?

301

2 ACTIVITY ANALYSIS

The term "activity analysis" is borrowed from the economic theory of the firm, where an economic activity is understood to be "a particular way of combining inputs for the production of an output" [1]. This notion is sometimes formalized in an expression such as:

$$x_{ij} = a_{ij}q_j \qquad i = 1, ..., m$$
$$j = 1, ..., n$$

where x_{ij} represents the quantity of the i'th input allocated to the production of q_j, the quantity of the j'th output, and where a_{ij} may be understood as the quantity of the i'th input necessary to produce one unit of the j'th output.

The formalization of an economic activity need not be pursued further here. It is important only to note that the concept rests fundamentally on inputs and outputs which are enumerable and measurable.

Accordingly, an activity analysis of an information system demands that one be specific about inputs and outputs. Specification of inputs is not greatly different from that associated with other forms of production. Plant, equipment (e.g., computers, communication systems, storage media, software), and labor (e.g., clerical, systems analysis, programming) are typically involved.

It is in output specification that the greatest problem in the activity analysis of an information system arises. "Information" is commonly said to be the output of any information system, but the term has various interpretations, and the problem of useful specificity is a severe one. To illustrate, consider that information can be measured in terms of

1. physical units, e.g., number of reports, number of report pages;
2. syntactical units, e.g., number of characters, number of words;
3. semantic units, e.g., number of sentences, number of data;
4. pragmatic units, e.g., expected value of a communication; amount of belief change.

At the physical level, measurement is rather straight forward, but the notion of information is weak, having little connection to the purposes of the system. At the syntactical and semantic levels, the notion of information is more sophisticated, but measurement becomes somewhat more tenuous. At the pragmatic level, the notion of information achieves a direct connection with the user, but current measurement techniques remain imbedded in theories which have yet to be generally applied in information systems practice. On the whole, then, the problem of output specification is especially severe in the case of information systems, and this constitutes a significant barrier to effective activity analysis. At the same time, it presents a challenging research opportunity. (For a more extensive consideration of the problem, see Mason [4]).

A second aspect of activity analysis is the monitoring of the allocation of information system resources. In the case of computer system resources, the operating system may include a job accounting facility. In the case of personnel resources, some form of work activity reporting may be established. In both cases, it is necessary that information system activities be defined in terms of "jobs" and "operations", or the equivalent, to which the allocation of system resources can be made.

The completion of a job associated with an information system is sometimes taken as the "output" of the system, in lieu of the specification and measurement of actual information output.

Specification of information system inputs and outputs, together with resource allocation accounting systems, make possible the assessment of information system productivity, in terms of actual allocation decisions made. (The most notable research in this area is that of Kriebel [2]). However, the *possibilities* in resource allocation are not necessarily sufficiently explored. The exploration of these possibilities is regarded here as necessary for the evaluation of an information system implementation.

3 POSSIBILITY ANALYSIS

The term "possibility analysis" is adapted from the concept of the firm's production possibility set, which consists of "... the feasible input-output vectors as determined by the technology of the economy" [5]. Thus, while activity analysis of an information system provides a description of actual input-output combinations achieved, possibility analysis seeks to establish that which is technologically possible, whether achieved or not.

The technology of an information system consists of all the technical information about the combination of its inputs necessary for the production of its outputs. Particularly significant is the *production function* associated with this technology, which presupposes technical efficiency in production, and states the maximum output obtainable from every possible input combination [5].

Where current resource allocation is efficient, activity analysis will yield points lying within the production function of the system. In practice, however, most allocations are likely to be inefficient in some respect. Management seldom has the information necessary to make the most efficient choices. For example, the manager of a computer center, faced with the problem of scheduling a day's work, is not likely to know with assurance the most efficient schedule. Thus, an activity analysis of an information system will likely yield many points not lying within the production function.

The first task of possibility analysis, then, is to identify the more efficient points within the possibility set of the system. Continuing with the above example, suppose that management has employed several different schedules on alternative occasions in which a particular mix of jobs has been processed. A comparison of the total times required to process the job mix should enable the most efficient schedule to be identified. In such a fasion, the production function of the information system would be approximated.

A second task in possibility analysis is the assessment of output capacities.

Again, activity analysis may not yield such capacities for a significant range of output mixes, since current output mixes may be set within a rather narrow range. For example, a system supporting both batch processing and real-time inquiry might not yield data indicating the capacity of the system in terms of batch processing or real-time inquiry *only*.

The assessment of output capacities enables management to consider new possibilities in output mixes which may be provided the information system users.

Still another task in possibility analysis is the assessment of alternative technologies which may be employed by the information system. Such technologies involve the application of new or additional system resources, and provide for adjustments in the capacity of the system. A well-known example is the upgrading of computer equipment from one generation to the next, or from a smaller system to a larger system. An important aspect of possibility analysis, in this regard, is the establishment of the transition feasibility, given the current technology of the system.

The motivation for the consideration of alternative technologies, and for the adjustment of the capacity of the information system, is likely to stem from the desire to provide the users of the information system with new mixes of products and services. Such a desire may be based in a utility analysis of the current system.

4 UTILITY ANALYSIS

The term "utility analysis" is adapted from the economic theory of the consumer. The familiar postulate of rationality of this theory assumes that the consumer chooses among the alternatives available in such a manner that the satisfaction derived is as large as possible. Further, a utility function may be constructed which contains all the information pertaining to the satisfaction derived by the consumer from the various alternatives [1; 5].

The consumer may be regarded as the client of the economic system, i.e., the individual for whom the system exists. Similarly, we must identify the client of an information system, if we are to place a value on its performance. Since an information system is not typically organized as an economic system, it is not usually the case that its consumers constitute its client. Rather, as an instrument of the organization, the information system typically exists to serve organizational purposes. Thus, the utility analysis of an information system relates to organizational utility rather than consumer utility.

The assessment of organizational utility involves a search for an appropriate measure of performance of the information system. Multiple criteria may be involved, e.g., cost reduction, effectiveness of service delivery, quality of working life, making the determination of the appropriate measure(s) particularly difficult. Ideally, the measure(s) would be specified during the design of the information system, and the evaluation of the implementation would involve only the making of the measurements, as specified. However, in practice, it is necessary to reassess the adequacy of any measure, in terms of the ideal of maximizing organizational utility.

304

Although the users of an information system, i.e., those who are to be informed by it, are not necessarily the only client, the solicitation of their evaluation of the system is in practice critical. User surveys, by means of questionnaires and interviews, permit the assessment of user appreciation of the system, which has been shown to be closely associated with involvement in system design and use [6]. Periodic assessment of user appreciation thus serves as a diagnostic method with which to monitor the impact of the system over the lifetime of its implementation.

Also helpful is the determination of the interpersonal use of the information system, i.e., the use of the system by one individual for the informing of another [7]. This permits the identification of indirect users of the system who might not otherwise be recognized, and provides a picture of the penetration of the system within the organization. Again, questionnaire and interview methods are useful for this particular aspect of utility analysis.

Techniques such as those just discussed should be of particular value for information systems designed to support managerial and planning processes, where the utilization is by nature sophisticated, and not easily observable.

The determination of the preferred information system implementation requires that alternatives to the present implementation be evaluated as well. Further, it is necessary to evaluate any transition implications. Indirectly, this provides for the assessment of the opportunity costs associated with the present implementation (the term "costs" is used here in the broadest sense).

Thus, the evaluation of an information system implementation cannot be separated from the evaluation of alternatives to it. Any such evaluation must inevitably reflect some judgment as to possibilities, as well as to present activities. For example, user appreciation of an information system must reflect perceived design opportunities not taken, e.g., in report specification and formatting, as well as knowledge of those design features actually implemented. This suggests that utility analysis might be conducted so as to provide specific feedback to possibility analysis. Research directed toward the development of tools toward this end would appear to be especially worthwhile.

REFERENCES

1. Henderson, J.M., and R.E. Quandt. *Microeconomic Theory: A Mathematical Approach*. McGraw-Hill, 1958.

2. Kriebel, C.H. "Modeling and Monitoring the Productivity of Computing and Information Services." *Proceedings, Ninth Annual Conference of the Society for Management Information Systems*. Los Angeles, California, September 1977.

3. Lientz, B.P., E.B. Swanson, and G.E. Tompkins. "Characteristics of Application Software Maintenance." *Communications of the ACM* 21 (6) (June 1978): 466-71.

4. Mason, R.O. "Measuring Information Output." *Information & Management* 1 (1978): 219-234.

5. Quirk, J. and R. Saposnik. *Introduction to General Equilibrium Theory and Welfare Economics*. McGraw-Hill, 1968.

6. Swanson, E.B., "Management Information Systems: Appreciation and Involvement." *Management Science* 21 (2) (1974): 178-188.

7. Swanson, E.B. "A Note on Interpersonal Information System Use." *Information and Management* 1 (1978): 287-294.

III. INSTRUMENTS AND TOOLS FOR ORGANIZATIONAL IMPLEMENTATION

Chairman: H.C. Lucas, Jr.

The title of this session indicated that the focus was on practical, instrumental support for systems design and implementation. It was understood that such means had to go beyond some eclectically compiled methods and techniques. So the final scope was rather broad; the session could be characterized "approach and philosophy-oriented" as well as dealing with practical instruments.

Ginzberg: "Early Diagnosis"

Mike Ginzberg sketched "the theoretical and empirical bases for ... a technique for assessing a system's probability of success before the system has been built".

1. The *Concept of Early Warning* assumes that in the initial stage of system development ("Definition"), requiring approximately 25 percent of the required resources, most key decisions affecting the system as the user will see it, and determining the ultimate system success or failure, are made. In this early stage, diagnosing the probability of ultimate success could (in the extreme case of cancelling a project) save up to 75 percent.

2. Empirical data exist pointing to the *availability of indicators* for ultimate success or failure:

> ... in cases where users were dissatisfied with the projects' outcome, their reports of the conduct of the implementation process differed markedly from the reports of the system designers involved in these projects ... regardless whether the system designer was satisfied or dissatisfied ... and no such difference occurred in cases where users were satisfied.

This is interpreted as a consequence of unrealistic user expectations—largely regarding "issues which should have been resolved at the definition stage"—maintained because of inadequate communication.

3. The findings are explained in terms of *Discrepancy theory*: dissatisfaction is the result of unrealistic expectations not met in the end. Satisfaction depends on the fit between expected and delivered features of the system. Thus, early warning indicators should be based on user expectations and satisfaction.

4. A *Program of Research* is described, dealing with the questions of
—Which expectations are most central?
—What constitutes a "realistic" expectation?
—How early in a project can these key expectations be reliably measured?

The program consists of
—an Exploratory Study (see below)
—a Longitudinal Field Study: when do expectations become stable?
—Action Research: can diagnosis data be used to manage projects into success?

The ultimate aim is on "easy to use tools".
5. The *Preliminary Study,* presently conducted within the framework of a major on-line information system development in the Trust Department of a major U.S. bank, deals with
—the verification of the existence of early warning indicators,
—identification of the best predictors,
—tools for the identification of realistic expectations in practice.

A Pre-Implementation Questionnaire focuses on supposedly promising perceptions and expectations:
a. reasons for developing the system
b. problem importance
c. adequacy of resources
d. expected usage pattern
e. expected impacts
f. expected difficulties of accomodating changes
g. evaluation criteria.

Results will be compared with post-implementation data. The first round of post-implementation data collection was underway by July 1978.

Questions and Discussion
centered around the following main points:
—Test of instruments before research
  The questionnaire was tested in cooperation with portfolio managers.
—Changes of users' expectations
  The phenomenon of users being dissatisfied with a system, but acting with it once it is implemented will be analysed in another questionnaire.
—Reasons for dissatisfaction
  Dissatisfaction might also be caused by inadequate participation, resulting in "premature" decisions before facts are sufficiently known.
—Degree of involvement
  There is no equal distribution of involvement: 10 of the portfolio managers are involved more deeply than the others.
—Distribution of expectations
  This subject was not investigated in the current study.

Kolf/Oppelland: "Concepts and Experiences with the PORGI Implementation Handbook"

The authors presented an approach and tools for system development, worked out in the research project PORGI at the BIFOA. They reported on the practical tests of some of these instruments—parts of the PORGI Implementation Handbook—in two system development projects within two German companies.

1. The *focus of the project* is on "organizational implementation", understood as a process of mutually adjusting the system components Man, Task, Information Technology, and Structure (*System Fit*). To arrive at this objective, "Process Fit" has to be established and maintained, e.g., the "consideration of the interests of those concerned with system design and application in building an adequate organization for the development process".

2. *Tools and Instruments* of the handbook "aim primarily at the analysis and diagnosis of the individual fit of a project at specific times during project life time" and at taking "corrective actions early enough to prevent possible ... or to solve existing problem situations".

The handbook consists of
—Descriptive Framework (common terminological basis)
—Procedural Scheme (sequence of design activities, associated with implementational aspects and hints at relevant tools)
—Pool of Methods
—Pool of Implementation Problems
—Pool of Design Concepts.

3. The Demonstration of *Practical Application* was tied to two cases.

Case 1 showed the use of PORGI instruments in the development of a new cost accounting and evaluation system in a large-scale German electrical industry enterprise. Emphasis was on "Process Fit"—especially critical due to the large number of people concerned with their different demands and interests.

Case 2 dealt with the development of a corporate financial planning model in a medium-sized pharmaceutical company. This case emphasized the "System Fit" side of the approach.

4. *Implications and Limitations* of the approach may be summarized as follows:
—System development in this sense is a particative socio-technical change process to be supported actively by management.
—Its application results in decrease of system development risks, but it requires additional expenses.
—It increases transparency of the development process; this implies a possible disclosure of hidden conflicts and problems. Therefore, it has to be applied cautiously and competently.
—It supposes the "technical side of development" to be sufficiently resolved.

—Instruments applicable only for initial phases?

The PORGI-Instruments focus on all activities throughout the whole process.

—Instruments to be used without training?

Training is regarded necessary because the instruments are embedded in a philosophy to be learned and accepted before application of tools.

—Who shall use the instruments?

It is suggested to make use of an external consulting arrangement to avoid pursuit of career aims and departmental interests.

—Had there been researcher influence on the situation in the reported cases?

Yes; but they tried to avoid the impression of manipulation.

CONCLUSIONS

1.   The session confirmed the impression of a need for practical instruments to facilitate implementation.

2.   Such tools will be needed to help diffuse techniques for design to designers/ analysts in the field.

3.   The methods still widely depend on individual skills; ways of transfer have to be investigated.

4.   The question of finding an adequate organizational arrangement for such instrumental support (e.g., external consultancy) is still unresolved.

21. Early Diagnosis of Implementation Failure: A Plan for Research*

by Michael J. Ginzberg

1 OVERVIEW

The development and operation of computer-based administrative systems consumes a significant, and growing, proportion of the resources of industrialized countries. In 1973, organizations in the United States alone spent roughly $26 billion for information processing [33]. A large percentage of this amount was spent to develop and maintain software systems. By one estimate, software costs amount to as much as 70 percent of total computer system costs [15].

Unfortunately, not all expenditures for system development prove to be fruitful. In both the research literature and the popular press, one can read about system development efforts which either failed completely or resulted in systems that did not fully meet the needs of the user organization. There is a growing consensus that these system development failures are not the result of technical faults in the systems themselves, but rather of deficiencies in the organizational and behavioral processes by which these systems are designed and implemented (e.g., [23; 34]).

Much of the research on system development and implementation has focused on identifying those organizational characteristics which appear to be particularly conducive to either success or failure of a system development effort. This is a *measurement* approach. While it certainly can give us insight into the nature of the implementation problem, it lacks the power of an alternative approach, one that focuses on the *management* of the implementation process. This latter approach recognizes the inherently dynamic nature of system development, and seeks to find ways in which the user and designer of an information system can most effectively influence and manage the process by which that system is developed.

There are at least two ways in which research guided by this management approach can contribute to improving the effectiveness of the system development process. One is by identifying those variables which are particularly important to successful system development and which are *controllable by* the system *designer or the user*. The other is by developing tools and procedures which designers and users can employ to manage the development process; that is, the tools which enable them to track and manipulate the controllable variables. The focus of this paper is the development of one such tool.

* This research was supported in part by a grant from the Faculty Research Fund of the Graduate School of Business, Columbia University.

2 THE CONCEPT OF EARLY WARNING

The development of an information system is a long and time-consuming process. This process can be divided into a number of sequential stages. Davis suggests three major stages and eight sub-stages [6]. Others have suggested different num- bers of stages. The specific number of stages is not important. What is important is to recognize that each stage entails a different type of activity; and, for most sta- ges, the activity of the preceding stage must be, completed before the new stage can be started.

Davis outlines the stages and sub-stages as follows:

Definition stage:	Feasibility Assessment
	Information Analysis
Physical Design Stage:	System Design
	Program Development
	Procedure Development
Implementation Stage:	Conversion
	Operation and Maintenance
	Post Audit

The *Definition* stage focuses on what the new system will do and how it will look to the user. The Information Analysis substage is what others have termed "Busi- ness System Design". The *Physical Design* stage takes the business system spe- cification developed during the Definition phase, and produces the design of a computer-based system to meet these specifications. During the *Implementation* stage, the physical system is installed, operated, and monitored.

There are important differences among the types of activities which occur at these three stages and among their outputs. At *Definition*, the central activity is *de- cision-making*; deciding what the system will do, what data will be collected, and how these data will be presented to the system users. The principal activity of the *Physical Design* stage is *decision implementation*. The key decisions made during Defi- nition are given a physical manifestation; that is, they are translated into the de- sign of a computer-based system to meet the business needs. The *Implementation* phase, of course, focuses on *physical implementation* of the completed system.

These differences in activities across the stages provide us with an opportunity to exercise significant leverage. By the end of the Definition stage, almost all key decisions about the system being developed have been made. It is at this stage that decisions about project goals, scope, and overall approach are made. This is also the stage at which the system as the user will see it—i.e., the business system—is designed. The available evidence shows that the apparent cause of many system failures is user dissatisfaction with the system scope (e.g., [14]), system goals—the problem addressed—(e.g., [9]), and the general approach to the business problem taken by the system (e.g., [7]). Since decisions about all of these questions are made during Definition, the importance of this stage to the ultimate success of the system should be apparent.

Clearly, decisions which affect a system development project's outcome are made at all stages of the project. Most of these decisions, however, are of little import to the user, as the user is (or at least should be) unaware of them. The major decisions about project scope, the general nature of the user interface, etc., should be, and usually can be, made early in the project; and, these are the decisions which are clearly visible to the user. The multitude of other decisions are either technical in nature and hence subordinate to the major design decisions (i.e., they should not change the basic "shape" of the system), or they relate to the process of system introduction. While these latter decisions can have a major impact on project success, they fall along a different dimension from the design decisions and are largely independent of them.

The concept of early diagnosis is, therefore, quite simple. If the key decisions which determine the ultimate success or failure of a system are made quite early in the project (i.e., at Definition), we should be able to assess the project's chances of success or failure at this early stage. If such assessments can be made with relative accuracy, this information can be used to guide further decisions about that project. That is, if the diagnosis indicates that failure (or substantial difficulty) is likely, management should decide whether to cancel the project or to attempt to redirect it, to manage it into success. Hopefully, the diagnostic data collected will help management decide which course of action is more appropriate.*

The value of early diagnosis does not depend on whether the project can be saved—i.e., managed into success—or not. Clearly one would prefer being able to rescue the project, but early diagnosis will still be of substantial value even in those cases where the project must be abandoned. The reason for this is the timing difference between decision flows and resource flows, as shown in Figure 1. Almost all key decisions which affect the overall "shape" of the information system are made during the Definition stage. This stage, however, typically accounts for no more than 25 percent of the resources required for system development and installation [6, p. 415]. Thus, it should be possible to make an accurate assessment of the likelihood of success or failure for the system when only a small part of the total cost of system development has been spent. Even if it should prove necessary to cancel the project, the savings would be substantial—approximately 75 percent of what would be spent were the system to be completed. And, of course, generally a project would not be abandoned unless it appeared that success was very unlikely, no matter what steps were taken.

In summary, the concept and potential value of the early diagnosis of implementation failure are clear. The issue that remains is how to operationalize this concept:

—what are the best indicators of the likelihood of success or failure of an MIS development project?
—how can these indicators be measured?
—when should they be measured?

---

* Making this choice is not the topic of this paper. For some guidance on how this choice might be made, see [2].

313

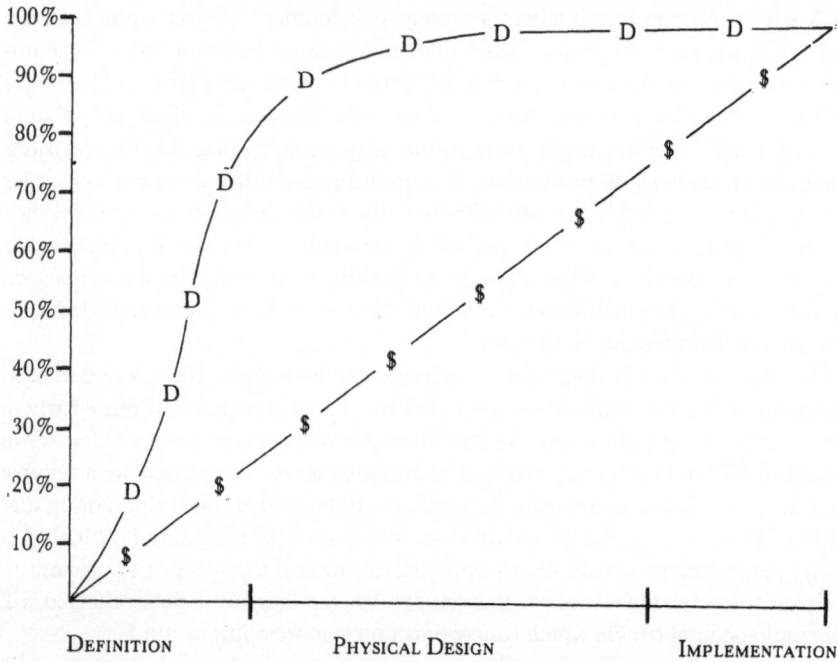

$—Development costs
D—Development decisions

Figure 1. Timing of Development Costs and Development Decisions.

In the remainder of this paper, we will explore these questions. First, we will consider the background evidence, empirical and theoretical, which suggests that early diagnosis should be possible. Then we will examine a program of research which addresses the questions posed above. Finally, we will examine in greater detail the first step in this program of research.

3   IS EARLY DIAGNOSIS POSSIBLE: THEORETICAL AND EMPIRICAL CLUES

A previous study of system implementation by Ginzberg [10] showed that in cases where users were dissatisfied with the projects' outcomes, their reports of the conduct of the implementation process differed markedly from the reports of the system designers involved in these projects. This difference occurred regardless of whether the system designer was satisfied or dissatisfied with the project; and no such difference occurred in cases where users were satisfied with the project (again, the designer's satisfaction or lack thereof did not matter).

This result could be interpreted to mean that in projects where users were dissatisfied, designers and users had failed to communicate adequately during system development. Designers assumed that agreement with users had been reached on a number of key issues (e.g., project goals and scope, responsibilities of users and designers) when, in fact, it had not. As a result, users held unrealistic expectations about the system, these expectations were not met, and the users were ultimately dissatisfied.

When the data were analyzed to determine at what stage of the project these disagreements most likely appeared, it was evident that in large measure they related to issues which should have been resolved at the Definition stage. Thus, the data, if interpreted as outlined above, would suggest that the basic disagreements which led to user dissatisfaction could have been identified early in the projects' lives. That is, they suggest that users and designers failed to reach agreement on key issues prior to or during the Information Analysis/Business System Design phase, and that these issues remained unresolved throughout the project.

The nature of the data collection for this study, however, renders this interpretation as just one of a number of possible interpretations. All data were collected after the projects had been completed, i.e., after the Implementation stage. Respondents were asked to describe what had happened in their projects by indicating the degree to which a number of descriptive statements were characteristic of the projects. Thus, it is possible that the particular responses of dissatisfied users were colored by their overall evaluation of the project, and that the apparent early warning indicators are merely artifacts. The questionnaire used in this study had been designed to try to guard against the biasing of responses, and the data do not give any reason to suspect that this problem exists. Nonetheless, in an "after only" design, one cannot be sure of time dependent phenomena which appear to be evident.

Although Ginzberg's study suggests most directly the possibility of early diagnosis in MIS development projects, the results of other empirical studies tend to support this possibility. Schultz and Slevin show that the user's expressed likelihood of using a system is positively correlated with his (or her) perception of the project's importance and belief that the technique being employed could successfully address the problem [31]. Zand and Sorensen show that in projects rated as exceptionally unsuccessful by designers, management could not state the problem clearly at the start of the project and felt that the problem being address-

ed was too large [39]. Other examples could also be cited, and these too would indicate that certain attitudes and perceptions held by users at the early stages of a
project are related to some measure of the project's success. Again, in each of
these studies data were collected at only one point during the project. Thus, the
problem of determining what is cause and what effect remains.

In summary, empirical studies of MIS implementation suggest the possibility
of early warning indicators. These studies have not demonstrated the existence of
indicators, nor have they addressed the question of *why* such indicators might
work. We can turn to another literature, that on job satisfaction, to find an answer to the latter question.

A number of theories have been proposed to explain why an individual is satisfied or dissatisfied with his job. One of these, Discrepancy theory [22], can provide insight into the reason it should be possible to find early warning indicators
of MIS project failure. Discrepancy theory looks at overall job satisfaction as being determined by satisfaction with individual aspects of the job. Satisfaction with
these individual aspects is defined as some function of what the person does receive compared to some reference quantity. Lawler suggests that this reference
quantity might be what the individual (1) felt he should receive, (2) wanted to receive, or (3) expected to receive [21]. If a discrepancy exists between what the individual does receive (or *perceives* he receives) and the reference quantity, he will
be dissatisfied with that job aspect. A number of studies have shown that individuals who hold unrealistic expectations about an organization prior to joining it,
exhibit considerable dissatisfaction once they have joined the organization and
find that their expectations will not be met (e.g., [35; 37]).

Lawler, in his review of this literature, discusses some of the observed consequences of job dissatisfaction [21]. While there is little relationship between job
satisfaction and job performance, there are strong negative relationships between
satisfaction and (1) absenteeism, and (2) turnover. Apparently, dissatisfaction
leads the individual to attempt to avoid the situation which gives rise to this dissatisfaction.

We can use these findings about job satisfaction to make certain inferences
about MIS development. First, they suggest that an individual whose expectations about an information system are unrealistic will likely be dissatisfied with
that system once it becomes available to him. Ineed, Keen has observed that in
the OR/MS/MIS area:

> ... to some extent implementation *is* the management of expectations—many fail-
> ures occur not because a "good" model was not delivered, but because the "right"
> one was not or because the user had excessively high expectations which led him to
> enthusiastically support the effort but which could never be met in practice [18, p.
> 19]

Thus, we would expect unrealistic expectations to lead to dissatisfaction with a
system; and satisfaction has been suggested as one measure of a system's success
(e.g., [10]). However, there are other dimensions of a project's outcome, and
many researchers have suggested that success or failure is appropriately measured

316

along one of these dimensions—most notably the amount of system *usage* [24; 36]. On the basis of the job satisfaction literature we can infer that a dissatisfied user will be less likely to use a system than will a satisfied user. Just as people dissatisfied with their jobs avoid them through absenteeism and turnover, the dissatisfied MIS user can avoid the system by limiting his use of it.

In summary, there are both empirical and theoretical bases for the contention that expectations formed early in an MIS development project should be related to the eventual success or failure of that project. Further, this should be the case whether we define success in terms of an attitudinal measure—satisfaction—or a behavioral measure—use. The remainder of this paper describes a program of research which aims to:

1. confirm the existence of early warning indicators for MIS development;
2. identify those indicators which best predict future success or failure; and
3. develop diagnostic tools and techniques which can be used in practice.

4   A PROGRAM OF RESEARCH

The ultimate aim of research into early warning indicators for system development is to produce a set of easy-to-use tools which will successfully diagnose incipient failure. There are, however, a number of questions which must be answered before this end can be attained. Among these are:

1. which expectations are most central to the user's response to the system?
2. what constitutes a "realistic" expectation?, and
3. how early in a project can these key expectations be reliably measured?

We have argued that unrealistic expectations about a system are likely to be harbingers of implementation failure. But, are all expectations equally important in this regard, or are some types of expectations more important than others? If the latter is the case, which types of expectations—that is, expectations about which aspects of a system—are most critical?

Unrealistic expectations can easily be defined after the fact as those expectations which were not met. Our problem, however, is to determine at the beginning of a development effort whether a user's expectations are realistic or not. To do this, we must define a set of realistic expectations at the Definition stage, and the question of how this set can be defined must be addressed.

Expectations are transient and malleable. As a project progresses, an individual's expectations can change or be changed. This raises the question of when key expectations become stable enough to be reliable indicators of the future.

Getting complete answers to all of these questions will, undoubtedly, be a long-term effort. To answer them, three separate, but logically interrelated, studies will be conducted. The first study addresses the questions of (1) the centrality of expectations, and (2) the definition of realistic expectations. This study will be described in greater detail in the following section.

Answering the third question posed above—when can key expectations be reliably measured—will be the primary objective of the second study. This will be a longitudinal study, tracking a number of MIS development projects from inception through completion. The conduct of this study will be pure *field research*. Expectation types identified as important in the first study will be monitored throughout the development process, and data on project success will be collected after implementation has been completed. These data will then be analyzed to determine at what point expectations become stable and reliable indicators of future outcomes.

Assuming the first two studies are successful, a third study will be conducted to assess the usefulness and practicability of the early diagnosis approach. This study will also be a longitudinal study of a number of MIS development projects. Unlike the second study, the approach in this third phase will be *action research*. Key expectations will again be monitored; but, this time when incipient problems are indicated, interventions will be made in an attempt to resolve these problems, to *manage* the project *into success*. While it will be impossible to tell for certain whether projects where interventions are made would have failed had they been left alone, the results of the second study should enable us to assess this, at least probabilistically. This third study, then, will enable us to assess the costs—monetary and nonmonetary—and benefits of early diagnosis.

5 PHASE 1

5.1 Searching for Key Expectations

Longitudinal field studies appear to be the best way to move early diagnosis from concept to practice. However, this type of research is quite time-consuming, and we have yet to show that early warning indicators in fact exist. Thus, a preliminary study is being conducted which will attempt:

1. to demonstrate that early warning indicators of implementation failure do exist;
2. to identify the types of expectations which can best serve as early warning indicators; and
3. to determine how to identify realistic expectations for a system under development.

This study is focusing on the implementation of a major on-line information system in the Trust Department of a large U.S. bank. The system (OLPM) was designed to support Portfolio Managers in their job of managing asset portfolios, consisting primarily of common stocks, debt instruments, and cash. The system was developed jointly by a team of bank employees—including Portfolio Managers, other portfolio-oriented personnel, and systems personnel—and employees of an external consulting firm. The system was installed in the bank in late 1977 and became operational and available for Portfolio Managers' use in early 1978.

The research project began in the latter half of 1977. At that point, the Definition stage had been completed, and the external consulting firm had finished the Physical Design and was ready to install the system. Portfolio Managers (the intended system users) had experienced little or no contact with the system (OLPM) from the time the Definition stage was completed until the start of the research project, a period of about 1½ years. Thus, we believed their expectations concerning OLPM would be similar to those held at the end of the Definition stage. In any case, if expectations are not sufficiently stable at this point in the project (just prior to installation), it is doubtful that early diagnosis can be of any use.

The plan of the research was to:

1. develop an instrument which would enable the capturing of key expectations about OLPM from Portfolio Managers, system developers, Trust Department management, and other potentially important Trust Department personnel;
2. administer that instrument to the relevant personnel in late 1977, just as OLPM was being installed; and
3. track project outcomes through periodic interviews with users, questionnaires, and the analysis of OLPM usage data.

5.2 Development of the Preimplementation Questionnaire

The first phase of this study required the identification of the expectation areas which were likely to be most important in predicting a user's response to an information system. This was accomplished by reviewing the literature on MIS and MS implementation to determine those variables which have been found to relate consistently to project outcomes. Keen has grouped this literature into seven categories [9]. Table 1 identifies the major findings in each category as well as selected references to the literature.

The findings listed in Table 1 are those which appear to receive some measure of consistent support in the literature. Many results which have received limited or conflicting support have not been included. This choice was made because it was felt that those aspects of implementation which have received greater empirical support as determinants of success are likely to be the most reliable early warning indicators. Recall that our focus in this study is on *expectations* about the system. Some of the research approaches directly address this question—e.g., the social change, user centered, and mutual understanding approaches. Variables found to be important in studies which followed these approaches could be incorporated directly into our research instrument. The remaining research approaches attempt to focus on "facts" about the implementation situation. For variables of this type, the preimplementation questionnaire can only measure the respondents' *perceptions* of these aspects.

After reviewing the literature, the implementation aspects which appeared to be the most promising sources of early warning indicators were perceptions of or expectations about:

1. the reasons for developing the system (goals and objectives);

Table 1. Key Findings of Implementation Research

Research Category	Key areas found to affect project outcome	Selected references
1. Failure study	—match between problem and solution —human versus technical orientation to system development	Ackoff (1967), Hall (1973), Argyris (1971), Mumford (1969)
2. Mutual understanding	—ability of each party to understand the methods and roles of the other —match between mode of presenting results and manager's style of cognitive functioning	Churchman and Schainblatt (1965), Mason and Mitroff (1973), McKenney and Keen (1974), Doktor and Hamilton (1973)
3. User centered (attitude-action models)	—favorable attitudes towards MS in general lead to favorable attitudes towards a specific project —favorable attitudes towards a project lead to high *intended* use	Manley (1975), Schultz and Slevin (1975), Keim and Kilmann (1975)
4. Factor study	—management support of project and of scientific approach —user involvement in system development —problem urgency and importance	Powers and Dickson (1973), Smith et al. (1973), Evan and Black (1967)
5. Organizational factors	—impact of OR/MS activity life cycle stage on type of project, degree of success	Rubenstein et al. (1967), Bean et al. (1975)
6. Contingency literature	—complex interaction of numerous factors, specifically dependent on the context	Hammond (1976), Huysmans (1975), Keen (1975)
7. Social change	—resolution of process issues—e.g., roles, goals, expected system impacts	Ginzberg (1975), Zand and Sorensen (1975).

2. the importance of the problem being addressed;
3. the adequacy of resources devoted to the system, including support, participation and understanding;
4. the way the system would be used;
5. the expected impacts of the system and their desirability;
6. the expected difficulty of accommodating the changes that would be caused by the system; and
7. the criteria which should be used to evaluate the system.

Perceptions of or expectations about some of these aspects can be assessed without much system specific information. For example, the types of resources needed to develop a system are basically the same for all computer-based systems. However, assessing perceptions of other aspects—e.g., goals, expected patterns of usage, expected impacts—requires some knowledge of the details of the particular system. In order to develop a questionnaire which could be used to assess these latter aspects as well as the former, a small sample of the members of all groups relevant to OLPM development was interviewed. These interviews focused on the specific reasons for developing OLPM, expected patterns of OLPM usage, expected impacts of OLPM, and criteria which should be used to evaluate the system. From the data gathered in these interviews, a preimplementation questionnaire to tap all of the key expectations about OLMP was developed.

5.3 Data Collection and Plans for Analysis

During December 1977 and January 1978, the preimplementation questionnaire was administered to all Portfolio Managers, Trust Department management, key

Table 2. Response Rates to Preimplementation Questionnaire

Group	Questionnaires distributed	Questionnaires returned	Response Rate
Portfolio Managers	44	38	86%
Department Management	3	3	100%
Development— External	4	4	100%
Development and Operations— Internal	6	5	83%
Other Trust Personnel	8	7	88%
Total	65	57	88%

development and operations personnel (both internal and external), and to a sample of other Trust Department employees who were likely to be familiar with OLPM. Response rates to the questionnaire were very high, as is shown in Table 2.

Preimplementation data were collected from systems users to enable testing of the following hypothesis:

H Users who hold realistic expectations about a system before it is implemented are more likely to judge that system as successful than are users who hold unrealistic expectations.

We have not yet specified how realistic expectations should be defined a priori. Indeed, answering this question is one of the objectives of this study. We can, however, logically deduce some possible sources of realistic expectations. A number of groups other than system users have a substantial impact on a system development effort. Central among these are the system developers and user management.

The system developers are key members of the design team as well as being the people who build the physical system. Their knowledge about the system is extensive, and their expectations about certain aspects of the system—especially mode of use and likely impacts—are likely to be realistic.

User management's impact on the system is not so direct as the designers', but can nonetheless be substantial. In the case of OLPM, management was clearly the client for the project, and there was active participation by Trust Department management in system development. Thus, management, too, may be a source of realistic expectations, particularly about project goals, objectives, and evaluation criteria.

For this study, the data gathered from three groups—management, internal development, and external development—will be used as the sources of a priori expectations, the benchmarks against which users' expectations can be measured. It is not yet known which of these groups can best serve as the source for realistic expectations, but this can be tested with data gathered after implementation. Two tests can be employed, reflecting two criteria. First, the expectations of these reference groups can be compared with what did in fact occur. This will tell us which groups' expectations were most *realistic* about each aspect of the system. However, our purpose in this research is to develop tools and techniques. Hence, a second test must be performed. This test will assess which groups' expectations were most *useful* in predicting user response to the system. Ideally, both tests will have the same result; but, this remains to be seen.

User training for OLPM took place during the late winter and spring 1978. The first round of postimplementation data collection occurred in July 1978. The sources of these data were (1) the OLPM usage logs, and (2) a questionnaire administered to Portfolio Managers and Trust Department management. This questionnaire (approximately half the length of the preimplementation questionnaire) focuses on impacts of, use of, reaction to, and satisfaction with OLPM.

322

These data will be used to address the questions and hypotheses set forth in this paper.

6 PRELIMINARY RESULTS, DISCUSSION, AND CONCLUSION

A preliminary analysis of the Phase 1 data has been quite encouraging and suggests that user expectations about a system can serve as predictors of user response to the system.* When additional data have been collected and analyzed, we should have a much better understanding of:

1. the value of expectations as predictors of success,
2. the relative importance of different types of expectations, and
3. the usefulness of designers' and management's expectations as standards of realism.

This improved understanding of the role of expectations should enable the development of diagnostic tools which could be used to monitor the progress of on-going system development projects. This type of monitoring would be an important tool for system developers. Before concluding, we should consider what this tool will contribute, how it will relate to other existing and emerging tools.

System developers already have many tools which they can use to aid them in MIS design and implementation. The majority of these tools focus on system design (e.g., flowcharting, decision tables, structured programming) or on the technical aspects of system implementation (e.g., PERT, formalized development methodologies). Only recently have tools which focus on the *behavioral* side of system implementation begun to emerge. Ginzberg describes one such tool—a prescriptive model of the phases of system development, focusing on the behavioral issues that must be addressed at each phase [11]. Essentially, this model can serve as checklist, posing questions which system developers and users must answer as the project progresses.

The PORGI project represents a much more ambitious attempt to develop this type of tool (see [34]). Kolf and Oppelland describe the progress to date of this project [20]. Briefly, they have succeeded in developing a comprehensive planning tool which enables system developers to diagnose the initial status of the organizational system and to develop an MIS implementation plan which takes account of the human element.

The early warning technique discussed in this paper will complement the PORGI (or similar) tools. While the latter focus primarily on implementation *planning*, early warning focuses on implementation *control*. Thus, the early diagnosis tool should be used in conjunction with the planning tools. The planning tools, through extensive analysis of the organization, can set the project on the track towards successful implementation. This does not, however, guarantee that success

---

* Analysis of this data has just begun and will not be included in this paper. A complete analysis of the data will be presented in a forthcoming paper.

323

will be achieved. The early diagnosis technique can be used to monitor project progress, to assure that the project is still on the road to success; and, it will do this with very little data. Thus, the combination of planning and monitoring tools should provide the greatest assurance of project success.

In conclusion, we should note that the tools discussed here—early diagnosis, PORGI, etc.—all focus on the behavioral side of system implementation. These tools are not meant to replace existing tools which support the technical aspects of design and implementation, but rather to complement them. For too long, the behavioral side has been ignored, and the result has been frequent difficulty, or even failure, in implementation. The emerging tools and techniques can correct this imbalance and improve our record of success in system implementation efforts.

REFERENCES

1. Ackoff, R.L. "Management Misinformation Systems." *Management Science* 14(4) (1967): B147-B156.

2. Alter, S.L. and M.J. Ginzberg. "Managing Uncertainty in MIS Implementation." *Sloan Management Review* 20(1) (1978): 23-31.

3. Argyris, C. "Management Information Systems: The Challenge to Rationality and Emotionality." *Management Science* 17(6) (1971): B275-B292.

4. Bean, A.S., R.D. Neal, M. Radnor and D.A. Tansik. "Structural and Behavioral Correlates of Implementation in U.S. Business Organizations." in R.L. Schultz and D.P. Slevin (eds.) *Implementing Operations Research/Management Science*. New York: American Elsevier, 1975.

5. Churchman, C.W. and A.H. Schainblatt. "The Researcher and the Manager: A Dialectic of Implementation." *Management Science* 11(4) (1965): B69-B87.

6. Davis, G.B. *Management Information Systems: Conceptual Foundations, Structure and Development*. New York: McGraw-Hill, 1974.

7. Dearden, J. and J. Lastavica. "New Directions in Operations Research." *Financial Executive* 38(10) (1970):24-33.

8. Doktor, R.H. and W.F. Hamilton. "Cognitive Style and the Acceptance of Management Science Recommendations." *Management Science* 19(8) (1973): 884-94.

9. Evan, W. and G. Black. "Innovation in Business Organizations: Some Factors Associated with Success or Failure of Staff Proposals." *Journal of Business* 40(1967):519-30.

10. Ginzberg, M.J. "A Process Approach to Management Science Information." Unpublished Ph.D. dissertation, M.I.T., 1975.

11. Ginzberg, M.J. "A Prescriptive Model for System Implementation." Research Paper No. 150A, Graduate School of Business, Columbia University, 1978.

12. Hall, W.K. "Strategic Planning Models: Are Top Managers Really Finding Them Useful?" *Journal of Business Policy* 3(2) (1973): 33-42.

13. Hammond, J.S., III. "A Contingent Framework for Management Science Implementation." Working Paper No. 76-5, Graduate School of Business Administration, Harvard University, 1976.

14. Harvey, A. "Factors Making for Implementation Success and Failure." *Management Science* 16(6) (1970): B312-B321.

15. Harvey, F.L. "The Developing Software Industry." *Infosystems* 23(7) (1976): 34-35.

16. Huysmans, J.H.B.M. "Operations Research Implementation and the Practice of Management." in R.L. Schultz and D.P. Slevin (eds.) *Implementing Operations Research/Management Science*. New York: American Elsevier, 1975.

17. Keim, R.T. and R.H. Kilmann. "A Longitudinal Investigation of Alternative Implementation Processes: Traditional versus Behavioral Model Building with the MAPS Design Technology." in P.G.W. Keen (ed.) *The Implementation of Computer-Based Decision Aids*. Center for Information Systems Research, M.I.T., 1975.

18. Keen, P.G.W. "A Clinical Approach to the Implementation of OR/MS/MIS Projects." Working Paper No. 780-75, Alfred P. Sloan School of Management, M.I.T., 1975.

19. Keen, P.G.W. "Implementation Research in OR/MS and MIS: Description versus Prescription." Research Paper No. 390, Graduate School of Business, Stanford University, 1977.

20. Kolf, F., and H.J. Oppelland. "Concepts and Experiences with the PORGI Implementation Handbook." presented at the BIFOA Symposium on the Design and Implementation of Computer-Based Information Systems. Bensberg/Cologne, 1978.

21. Lawler, E.E., III. *Motivation in Work Organizations*. Monterey, California: Brooks/Cole Publishing, 1973.

22. Locke, E.A. "What Is Job Satisfaction?" *Organization Behavior and Human Performance*. 4 (1969): 309-36.

23. Lucas, H.C., Jr. *Why Information Systems Fail*. New York: Columbia University Press, 1975.

24. Lucas, H.C., Jr. "The Use of Interactive Information Storage and Retrieval System in Medical Research." *Communications of the ACM* 21(3) (1978): 197-205.

25. Manley, J.H. "Implementation Attitudes: A Model and a Measurement Methodology." in R.L. Schultz and D.P. Slevin (eds.) *Implementing Operations Research/Management Science*. New York: American Elsevier, 1975.

26. Mason, R.O. and I.I. Mitroff. "A Program for Research on Management Information Systems." *Management Science* 19(5) (1973): 475-87.

27. McKenney, J.L. and P.G.W. Keen. "How Managers' Minds Work." *Harvard Business Review* 52(3) (1974): 79-90.

28. Mumford, E. "Implementing EDP Systems—A Sociological Perspective." *The Computer Bulletin* 13(1) (1969): 10-13.

29. Powers, R.F. and G.W. Dickson. "MIS Project Management: Myths, Opinions, and Reality." *California Management Review* 15(3) (1973): 147-56.

30. Rubenstein, A.H., M. Radnor, N.R. Baker, D.R. Heiman, and J.B. McColly. "Some Organizational Factors Related to the Effectiveness of Management Science Groups in Industry." *Management Science* 13(8) (1967): B508-B518.

31. Schultz, R.L., and D.P. Slevin. "Implementation and Organizational Validity: An Empirical Investigation." in R.L. Schultz and D.P. Slevin (eds.) *Implementing Operations Research/Management Science*. New York: American Elsevier, 1975.

32. Smith, R.D., J.R. Brown, R.H. Culhan and R.D. Amspoker. "Operations Research Effectiveness: An Empirical Study of Fourteen Project Groups." Presented at the Conference on the Implementation of OR/MS Models, University of Pittsburgh, 1973.

33. Strassmann, P.A. "Managing the Costs of Information." *Harvard Business Review* 54(5) (1976): 133-42.

34. Szyperski, N., F. Kolf, J. Claus and H.J. Oppelland. "The Organizational Implementation of Information Systems: A Design-Oriented Approach." PORGI Projektbericht No. 4, BIFOA, University of Cologne, 1976.

35. Wanous, J.P. "Organizational Entry: From Naive Expectations to Realistic Beliefs." *Journal of Applied Psychology* 61 (1976): 22-29.

36. Wynne, B. "Measuring the Immeasurable or Credibility in the Public Sector." *Interfaces* 8(1) (1977): 106-09.

37. Youngberg, C.F. "An Experimental Study of Job Satisfaction and Turnover in Relation to Job Expectations and Self Expectations." Unpublished doctoral dissertation, New York University, 1963.

38. Zand, D.E., and R.E. Sorensen. "Organizational Change and the Implementation of OR/MS Projects." in P.G.W. Keen (ed.) *The Implementation of Computer-Based Decision Aids.* Center for Information Systems Research, M.I.T., 1975.

39. Zand, D.E., and R.E. Sorensen. "Theory of Change and the Effective Use of Management Science." *Administrative Science Quarterly* 20(4) (1975): 532-45.

22. Concepts and Experience with the PORGI-Implementation Handbook

by Frank Kolf, Hans Jürgen Oppelland

1 PORGI-IMPLEMENTATION HANDBOOK: THE CONCEPT

The last decade has confronted system designers with the problem that they have to consider the requirements and restrictions of the human and organizational context in system development processes. There are lots of tools for supporting technical design activities but until now project management has lacked effective and efficient tools for handling the human and organizational problems from the beginning of system design.

The PORGI-approach of "organizational implementation" [16; 14] aims at a new understanding of the process of designing computer-based information systems (CBIS):

—Object of system development activities are not only technical but, simultaneously and equally important, the organizational and personal components of an information system (as a sociotechnical system).

—Organizational implementation is a *process of mutually adjusting* these different system components. (See a comparable "process view" of organizational implementation in [6; 7]) System development can only be successful (in technical as well as social terms) if activities to produce this fit between system components start with the beginning of the system development process.

The PORGI-approach differentiates two kinds of fit which have to be considered:

—*Process fit*, which means consideration of the interests of those concerned with system design and application in building an adequate organization for the development process;

—*System fit*, which means the degree of mutual adjustment between the system components "man, organizational structure, information technology and the task" to be supported.

The technical and social success of system development processes depends on the extent to which these fits have been made. Therefore, the tools and instruments of the PORGI-Implementation Handbook (IHB) aim primarily at the analysis and diagnosis of the individual fit of a project at specific times during project lifetime and at taking corrective actions early enough to prevent possible problem situations or to solve existing problem situations.

The basis elements of the PORGI-IHB are therefore [17; 14]:

—The *Descriptional Framework* (DF) which serves as a common terminological basis for all tools and guidelines of the IHB. The DF contains all those principal elements which constitute specific implementational situations.

—The *Procedural Scheme* (PROC) consists of a sequence of well-known design activities. Associated with the different design activities are implementational aspects and specific tools to support the analysis of these aspects.

—The *Pool of Methods* (METH) consists of instruments, tools and methods for analyzing and diagnosing implementational situations. The abovementioned PROC points to such aspects which have to be considered in the view of organizational implementation. Problem-oriented questionnaires, checklists, lists of criteria, etc., support the analysis and diagnosis of constellations of variables which are relevant to organizational implementation activities in this specific situation.

—The *Pool of Implementation Problems* (PROB) for contextual analysis and diagnosis consists of specific implementation problems which can be identified by a situational profile. These profiles describe those empirical situations in which that specific implementation problem has occurred repeatedly. Descriptions of implementation problems use the categories of the descriptional framework and are based, e.g., on those problems which have been identified in our expert interviews to be typical for specific situations [30]. Objective of the diagnosis is the comparison of the characteristics of the individual situation and the situative profile of the implementation problems of PROB in order to identify possible problem areas in the actual situation.

—The *Pool of Design Concepts* (CON) supports the solution of these problems identified by the use of METH and PROB in offering appropriate implementational actions. The description of these design concepts is also oriented at the categories of DF. The design concepts contain as possible implementational actions proposals to correct (or confirm) social and organizational behaviour and its rules regarding the different aspects of:
   —organization and procedures of design and implementation process
   —design of mutually adjusted system components.

2 PRACTICAL APPLICATION OF PORGI-TOOLS

We will discuss some of our instruments and tools and preliminary empirical experiences with their application in two CBIS-projects which were performed in two German companies.

The discussion will primarily focus on the instruments for planning the Process Fit (Case 1) and those for planning the System Fit (Case 2).

The structure of the cases is as follows:

—Results of the initial situational analysis

—Explication of the status of the project at the time of involvement of the PORGI-team (e.g., defining the project phase and relevant OI-aspects according to PROC)

—Explanation of the PORGI-tools used in that specific phase (METH)

—Results of the application of PORGI-tools

—Design-recommendations for the solution of specific problems diagnosed according to CON.

2.1 Initial Situational Analysis

Some difficulties may arise from our orientation of looking at system development as a whole—beginning from the early moment of problem statement and analysis to the end at system use and evaluation—by the fact that often methodical implementation support is supposed to be an actual problem in the later phases of system design processes. In our view every system design project has its individual history before it actually becomes a "project". Let us see how we try to meet these difficulties.

To assure successful application of PORGI-implementation support instruments we designed a special checklist SIT which enables us in an initial diagnosis to review the history of a system development project from the early beginning up to the actual situation. Usually the informations and answers for SIT were given from project group members of the analyzed system development project.

This SIT checklist contains fifty items regarding:

—*task*

the actual state of task performance in the division or department considered, its existing dp-support, and intended changes (16 items).

—*organizational structure*

aspects especially focussing on relationships between planning managers and subordinates and system-(dp-) specialists (15 items).

—*personal area*

special dp-knowledge and system design experience of those planning managers and subordinates concerned with system development (4 items):

—*design process*

aspects of project history, existing rules to form project organization structures, and the kind and degree of involvement and participation of different organization members in system design process until now (15 items).

The portion of this PORGI-SIT checklist (see SIT-17.0 in Table 1) may give an idea of those questions it contains. Some main topics of this checklist—regarding those concerned with system development, their function in system usage, the degree of their concern, and the kind of participation they have experienced until now—can be represented in the PORGI-table BTR-BET. This table may be used in all diagnoses performed during the design process—starting with rough information about initiating phase (as in our case), continuing with proposals or demands for adequate participation, and demonstrating all together the changes in design process organization and perhaps increase of process fit.

Table 1. Portion of Checklist PORGI-SIT

IV. DESIGN PROCESS

The questions of this section focus on aspects of project initiation, organization of the project, those concerned and their kind and degree of involvement or participation.

36.   Is this project included in a long-
range dp-development plan?

        a) yes   ☐
        b) no   ☐

37.   Who did initiate this project?

        a) top management   ☐
        b) planning department (manager of)   ☐
        c) organizational department   ☐
        d) dp-department/system
           system development department   ☐
        e) hardware/software supplier   ☐
        f) external consultant   ☐

38.   What were the reasons for the initiation of
the project?

        a) improving coordination of planning activities   ☐
        b) saving man-power   ☐
        c) speeding up information supply   ☐
        d) more detailed information supply   ☐
        e) more extended information supply   ☐

2.2 Case 1: Application of PORGI-Instruments for Planning the PROCESS FIT

We started practical tests of PORGI-instruments in a well-known large-scale enterprise of the German electronic industry. Its department for data processing has been willing to cooperate with us in application of methodical instruments in system development processes. This department has started the development of a new cost-accounting and evaluation system (CAES) for its own hardware and software development projects, which should replace the different existing subsystems. We joined this project (CAES) in a phase called "planning phase I", which has to be ended with a rough version of the system design concept.

Because of the possible difficulties mentioned in section 2.1, we used the checklist PORGI-SIT for an initial analysis of this CBIS-project CAES and its actual implementation situation, the results of which are shown in Table 2 (BTR-BET).

Table 2. PORGI Table BTR-BET I: Results of Case I

No. (1)	Div: Division / Dp: Department / Bd: Board (2)	Name of organizational member/unit (3)	Function in system use (4)	Number of organizational members (5)	Kind of concern: 0/1/2 (+/−) — Task assignment (6)	Work flow (7)	Decision autonomy (8)	Responsibility (9)	Information (10)	Work quality (11)	Work load (12)	Control (13)	Kind of participation: G/D/M/I — Problem analysis (14)	Goal definition (15)	Feasibility study (16)	Coarse design (17)	Detailed design (18)	Realization (19)	Introduction (20)	Evaluation (21)	Project management (22)	Project control (23)
1	Dp.		2	40		(1)	0		(1)				I	I								
2	Dp.		1 3	300		0	0		1				I	I								
3	Dp.		1 3	400		0	0		1				G	G	G	G						
4	Dp.		1 3			1	0		1				I	I								
5	Dp.		1 3	500		1	0		1				G	G	G	G						
6	Dp.		1 3			0	0		1				I	I								
7	Dp.		(1)			0	0		1				G	G								
8	Dp.		1 3	400		1	0		1				G	G	(D)	(D)						
9	Dp.		1 3	60		1	0		1				G,D	G,D	G,D	G,D						
10	Dp.												G	G	G,D	G,D						
11	Bd.												G	G	G	G						
12													-	-	D	D					x	x

—The system development implies little technological innovation, but much standardization of procedures.

—Directly concerned with system application are about 200 project leaders (the users)—with perhaps 2,000 subordinates all about (this is the amount summed up from column (5) in Table 2), which could be seen as indirectly concerned—and a project-group of six members concerned with system design (the designers).

—The user project-groups belong to different subdepartments for hardware and software research and development, organizational development, maintenance tasks, and others.

—They are a hetereogeneous group with different demands and interests. The designers are members of the subdepartment for organization and data processing and were partly supported by members of the subdepartments for accounting and software development.

The organization and the PORGI-group members agreed to proceed along the PORGI—PROCEDURAL—SCHEME. As we identified the planning phase I of the project CAES as similar to our section (6) of design activities—*design concept—rough version* (see Table 3, PROC-3.0, where we marked the mentioned topics)—the O.I. aspects for which PORGI provides methodical implementation support are:

—identification of those concerned and

—determination of those to be involved

—planning of fit between the system components

(personal(man), task, organizational structure, information technology)

—analysis and evaluation of system and process fit.

Diagnosis with SIT in this case led us to the conclusion to concentrate the application of PORGI-instruments mainly on aspects of design process organization and additionally on some aspects of tuning system components and consideration of organizational consequences. We therefore decided to apply a special combined questionnaire composed of different sets of questions from the existing (general) PORGI-checklists/questionnaires BTR, BET, and FIT. We chose such questions for each aspect, which should supply that information we need to organize the design process so that interests and needs of those concerned could be met adequately and mutual adjustment of system elements could be achieved (= process fit). The questionnaire focuses on the following aspects:

—function and competency of those concerned with system usage, e.g.,

—supply of input

—preparing alternatives

—operating the system

—ratification of the results

—receiving output

Table 3. PROC-3.0

Design Activities	OI-Aspects	Analytical Tools

5. Organizing the Project
—Institutionalization of the
  —Control level
  —Project management
  —Level
  —Task forces
—Planning of
  —needed resources
  —design activities
  —milestones
	—Identification/Determination of
	  people to be involved
	—Determination of coordination and
	  decision rules
	—Determination of principles for the
	  documentation of the system and the
	  project
	—Task assignment according to
	  —qualification
	  —motivation
	  —availability
		PORGI-Questionnaire 70-110
		PORGI-Analytical-Scheme
		PORGI-Questionnaire BTR
		PORGI-Checklist BET
		PORGI-Pool of potential
		implementation problems (PROB)
		Cooperation models from
		PORGI-CON

6. Design Concept—Rough Version
—Analysis of relations between the
  components of the existing system
—Generation of alternative solutions
  for system components
—Evaluation of alternatives and
  selection of a specific alternative
—Design of concepts for the system
  components
	—Identification/Determination of
	  people to be involved
	—Planning of FIT between
	  —Man
	  —Task
	  —Structure
	  —Information Technology
	—Analysis and evaluation of FIT
		PORGI-Checklist BTR
		PORGI-Checklist/Questionnaire BET
		PORGI-Checklist/Questionnaire FIT

333

—expected or known changes for *task-oriented* aspects of work resulting from system development and their importance for those concerned, e.g.,
  —task assignment
  —work flow
  —decision autonomy
  —responsibility
  —information
  —quality of own work
  —work loads/stress
  —control by others

Additional questions on aspects of work normally belonging to this context had been removed because of the restriction of questioning only representatives of those concerned, and not those concerned themselves; these questions refer to (e.g.):
—expected or known changes for *person-oriented* aspects of work resulting from system development and their importance for those concerned, e.g.,
  —personal image
  —influence
  —chances for promotion
  —salary
  —work satisfaction
  —work load/stress
  —self-esteem

These first aspects are aimed at identifying those concerned and the degree of their concern; the following aspects concentrate on the kind of experienced participation and its evaluation for past phases of system design, the desired participation in future phases, the experienced and desired rules for the election of re·presentatives of a user group, whose members cannot participate at all, and the experienced and desired kind of information exchange and opinion foundation in those represented groups.

Some of these items are shown in the selected part of our questionnaire (CAES-Q) shown in Table 4.

In order to support the tuning of system components and the interpretation of questionnaire results we added some questions which refer to the evaluation of system concept, personal and organizational consequences of system implementation, proposals for preparing and managing the system introduction, and personal data (age, sex, education, professional experience) from the PORGI-checklist/questionnaire FIT.

The CAES-Q questionnaire was answered by the representatives of the involved subdepartments during a session for presentation and tuning the rough version of the CAES concept at the end of the planning phase I.

Table 4. CAES-Q.

PARTICIPATION	Ratification	Responsible performing	Cooperation Consultancy	Receiving information	Not involved
1. What kind of participation have you experienced in the past phase of system development?					
2. What kind of participation would have been appropriate for you?					
3. What kind of participation do you desire for the future phases of system development?					

Please note reasons, when kinds of participation experienced differ from the appropriate resp. desired ones:

. . . .

ELECTION OF REPRESENTATIVES	Hierarchy	Qualification	Available time	Co-worker proposal	Other
1. On what kind of criteria are elections of representatives for system design participation based?					
5. On what kind of criteria do you think that elections should be based?					

Please note the arguments for your desire, if it differs from your experience:

. . . .

335

We would like to call special attention to some remarkable aspects of the interpretation of answers to the CAES-Q questionnaire:

—In *no case* is the experienced kind of *participation* evaluated to be *too intensive*.
—Only 25 percent of those concerned call the kind of participation they experienced unconditionally *satisfactory*, 75 percent desired a more intensive kind of participation.
—*Active cooperation* in system design by giving suggestions, consultancy, etc., and *participation in decision responsibility* is evaluated to be rather more *positive or ideal* than any other more passive kind of participation, such as only receiving information about system design activities or results.
—The *more importance* expected or known changes have for those concerned, the more they desire an *intensive and active participation* in system design.
—The intensive kind of participation of those concerned clearly corresponds with their ability
　—to realize the extent and importance of personal and organizational consequences of system implementation,
　—to consider possible problem solutions and to create constructive proposals for organizational changes,
and corresponds with their level of aspiration to get qualified support for system introduction.
—The attitude towards system development of those concerned is rather positive, their evaluation is more critical but also differentiated if they have experienced a more intensive participation. Much too little participation tends to result in an emotionally influenced distance to system development or neglect of its impact.

These statements confirm the importance of consideration in system design process organization. They led to the following proposals:
—to increase the openness and transparency of the system design process by providing more intensive information about it, beginning, for instance, with the feedback of questionnaire results;
—to document the individual's participation in system design activities in writing invitations, protocols, circulars, etc., in order to consider people's self-assessment and self-confidence, but also to achieve clear responsibility;
—to consider competence of user department's representatives and the experienced criteria of representatives' election,
—to ask those concerned (their respective representatives) the kind of participation they desire in the next phase of system design.

The CAES-project group accepted these proposals and realized the underlying ideas. Feedback of questionnaire results was given together with a protocol explaining the critical aspects and a short additional questionnaire regarding the participation demands. All these questionnaires were filled out completely and returned to the CAES-group. Organization of participation in the planning phase II of CAES has been altered due to the results of this questionnaire.

2.3 Case 2: Planning the System Fit

The application of tools and instruments for planning the System Fit was tested in another CBIS-project in a medium-sized pharmaceutical company. Our initial situational analysis by use of SIT resulted in the following statements:

—The company is organized in functional divisions (finance, marketing, production, etc.) and operates a rather small DP-department (in terms of available hardware and especially manpower), which reports to the vice-president of finance.

—It is a company policy to buy software rather than to make it, if possible.

—A preliminary statement of the company regarding the objectives of that CBIS-project focused on the design and implementation of a corporate financial planning model (further referred to as the CFP-project) by use of that software package.

—The initially stated requirements were:
  —to simulate different alternatives (regarding, e.g., sales volume, prices, costs, etc.);
  —to state the consequences of these alternatives for the profit and loss-statements and balances of the next five years;
  —to set up a five-year-financial plan;
  —to deduce a procurement plan for raw materials;
  —to perform sensitivity analyses for specific groups of costs;
  —to deduce a capacity and investment plan.

—The company's major expectations regarding the involvement of the PORGI-team were:
  —in general, support in dealing with organizational and human aspects of that CBIS-project;
  —specifically, to support in:
    —reaching a problem analysis and definition which is based upon the common consensus of all persons and departments concerned with the CBIS-project and the use of the system;
    —reaching a project specification (including user requirements and organizational requirements) which is systematically based and takes into consideration the interests of the different persons and departments involved as well as necessary organizational changes in the technical design of the system;
    —identifying needs for organizational changes early in the project and developing organizational solutions.

The company and the PORGI-Team agreed to proceed along the Procedural Scheme PROC, shown in Table 5.

According to PROC, in Problem Definition and Analysis specific Design Activities have to be performed under special consideration of different implementational aspects shown in table BTR-1.

We will focus our intention primarily on the application of those analytical tools especially marked in the third column of PROC:

Table 5. PROC-1.0

Design Activities	OI-Aspects	Analytical Tools
1. Problem Definition		
Identification and Description of the problem —Information about the problem —Evaluation of the problem —Decision about the realization of Problem analysis	Identification of the "interested" people —Who has the problem? —Who articulates the problem? —Who participates in the evaluation (priorities, etc.) of the problem? —Who decides upon the realization of the Problem Analysis?	**PORGI-Checklist BTR** PORGI-Descriptional Framework **PORGI-Checklist PROB** Group-evaluation-methods (e.g., BASYC) PORGI-Questionnaire BEW
2. Problem Analysis		
—Analysis of the different elements of the problem and its context —Analysis of possible causes —Specification of the requirements for the system components	—Analysis of problematic areas in/between the system components —Man —Task —Structure —Information Technology —Identification of the interests of the people concerned —Group consensus about the required characteristics of the different system components	**PORGI-Checklist PROB** PORGI-Questionnaire 1-69 **PORGI-Questionnaire INFBED** PORGI-Checklist INN Group-evaluation-methods **PORGI-Checklist ZIE** PORGI-Criteria-List EIG-1; AUS-1

—PORGI-Checklist BTR
—PORGI-Checklist PROB
—PORGI-Questionnaire INFBED
—PORGI-Checklist ZIE.

By use of the BTR Checklist (see the abstract) we identified those individuals and organizational units affected by the new system. The results are shown in Table 6, BTR-BET I Case 2. The organizational units are neutralized (col. 3), the functions in system usage (col. 4) differ from "Supply of inputs" (= 1), "Preparing alternatives" (= 2), "Operating the system" (= 3), "Ratification of the plan" (= 4) to "Receiving output" (= 5), the numbers of concerned people in the different Divisions (Div), Departments (Dp), Board of Directors (BD) or Vice-Presidents (VP) are shown in column 5 and different aspects of being concerned (cols. 6 to 13) are shown.

From that diagnosis we were able to identify those members of the organization who are strongly affected by the new system and should therefore be participants in the phases Problem analysis/definition and project specification. The Problem analysis/definition was performed by the use of the PORGI-Checklist PROB (Table 7).

We assume that a CBIS-project is initiated to solve a specific problem by designing a new sociotechnical solution. With the term "problem" is associated "the difference between some existing situation and some desired situation" [32]. The objective of Problem analysis/definition is therefore to describe that unsatisfactory situation in a way which gives a picture that is accepted by all members affected by that situation. The PORGI-checklist PROB is based upon those major categories of our Descriptional Framework which may describe problem situations which shall be solved by designing a new system.

By checking the items and associated problem causes, PROB serves as a guide for discussion and interviews with all those people who have been identified in Table 1, BTR-BET I. As an example some items regarding the planning task to be supported by the new system are shown in Table 8, PROB-3.0. Additionally the system components man, organizational context and information technology are covered in the same way. The PORGI-team applied this checklist in eight interviews with those people in the CBIS-project who are most concerned by the new system. Some of the results of this problem analysis are:
—Length of planning process: More and more members of Boards of Directors ask for plan-alternatives and What-if-questions, which can no longer be handled with the existing resources and within the allocated time.
—Problem level of planning: financial planning was up to now a "residual activity", not an area of strategic activity. The business trends led the Board of Directors to the expectation that there is an urgent need for active strategic financial planning, but, for that task, available tools are insufficient.
—In that context the financial consequences of investments get a much higher priority, but the existing information about production capacities supplied by the technical division is insufficient from the financial director's point of view.

Table 6. PORGI Table BTR-BET I: Results of Case 2

No. (1)	Div.: Division / Dp: Department / Bd: Board (2)	Name of organizational member/unit (3)	Function in system use (4)	Number of organizational members (5)	Task assignment (6)	Work flow (7)	Decision autonomy (8)	Responsibility (9)	Information (10)	Work quality (11)	Work load (12)	Control (13)	Problem analysis (14)	Goal definition (15)	Feasibility study (16)	Coarse design (17)	Detailed design (18)	Realization (19)	Introduction (20)	Evaluation (21)	Project management (22)	Project control (23)
	Div.	1	1 5	2-3	1	1	1+	1	1+	0	1+	0										
	VP	2	1 5	1	2	2	2+	2	2+	2+	2+	0										
	Div.	3	1 5	2-3	0	1	0	0	1+	0	1+	0										
	Div.	4	1 5	3-5	1	1	2+	2	1+	0	1+	1+										
	Dp.	5	1 2 3 5	1	2	2	2+	2	2+	2+	2+	0										
	Dp.	6	1 2 5	1	2	2	2+	2	2+	2+	2+	0										
	Div.	7	2 4 5	2	2	2	2+	2	2+	2+	2+	0										
	BD	8	4 5	5	1	2	2+	1	2+	1+	2+	0										
	Dp.	9	3	1-2	2	2	0	1	0	1+	0	0										
		10	5	60	0	0	0	0	1+	0	0	0										
		Externe Sw																				
		Suppl Externe																				
		PORGI-team																				

Table 7. PORGI-Checklist PROB

1. Who (person, organizational unit) will be affected by the application of the system currently being developed? The following five functions have to the differentiated and the respective symbols (1 to 5) have to be marked in col. 4 of table BTR-BET I:

    column 2:   person or organizational unit

            Div = Division
            VP = Vice President
            Dp = Department
            BD = Board of Directors
            etc.

    column 3:   name/acronym of unit

    column 4:   functions in system usage

            1 = supply of inputs
            2 = preparing alternative solutions
            3 = operating the system
            4 = ratification of the plan
            5 = receiving outputs

2. How many people in these units (dep., div., etc.) will be affected regarding the different functions? Specify in column 5.

3. Will there be expected/planned changes by the use of the new system regarding the following aspects:

    column 6: task assignments
    column 7: work flow
    column 8: decision autonomy
    column 9: responsibility
    column 10: information
    column 11: quality of own work
    column 12: work load
    column 13: control by others

The technical director insists that it is very difficult to define capacities, the financial director assumes that a possible fear of losing freedom of activity may be the cause.

—The workload for the planners is quantitatively too high, but qualitatively they feel a need for more challenge of their intellectual abilities and an overload of administrative work (''calculating'').

—Some members of the organization did not realize (at least from the Board of Directors' point of view) that the company had grown very rapidly in recent

Table 8. PROB-3.0

Characteristics of the problem situation	Possible causes

System component: planning TASK

1. Time structure of task
   —Planning horizon   too short; lack of long-range perspectives
   —Length of planning process   too long; insufficient possibility to answer changes in market conditions
   —Initiative for planning process   unsystematic ad hoc planning

2. Level of task
   —Problem-level   only operative planning, no integration with strategic planning
   —Considered units   isolated unit plan, integration with other units is insufficiently handled

3. Complexity of task
   —Number of different activities   too high; not to be handled with available methods and/or resources
   —Intellectual requirements   too low; permanent coordination problems with other units performing
   —Degree of detail   similar activities

4. Work load   too big; permanent performing in over-time
   too low; people feel no "challenge"

---

years and therefore their patterns of cooperation and communication had not been changed appropriately. Therefore, there was a tendency to isolate, e.g., the manager of the financial accounting department from all design activities, although he would have to play an important role in system use.

—The CBIS-project was primarily initiated by the vice-president of finance and his division dominated all design activities up to now. But the new system would be an integrated system covering all company functions and the interests of the other functions had been up to now insufficiently considered.

—The results of the organizational analysis showed that the organization structure did not have any organizational unit (staff, committee, etc.) to handle an *integrated* planning process.

This picture was complemented by the results of the questionnaire INFBED which had to be answered by the participants. The objective of that question-

Table 9. INFBED-4.0

3.2 **Fit**: to which degree does the current situation fit your requirements for accuracy?

| almost completely | sufficiently | partly | unsatisfactorily | not at all |

3.3 **Need for change**: should this situation be changed by the new system?

| indispensable | necessary | not necessary | not, if possible | definitively not |

Please specify
what should be   _____
changed: _____

4. **Alternatives**: that is, to have alternative solutions for a specific problem.

4.1 **Importance** of this aspect for your activities.

| very important | important | partly important | not important | not at all important |

4.2 **Fit**: to which degree does the current situation fit your requirements for alternative solutions?

| almost completely | sufficiently | partly | unsatisfactorily | not at all |

naire (see, as an example, page 4.0 of INFBED) is to get an individual assessment of the *current* supply of information regarding the aspects actuality, availability, accuracy, supply of alternatives, possibility of what-if-questions, covered planning horizons. Each of these aspects had to be assessed on a five-point scale by the participants regarding the questions of:

—*Importance* of an aspect (1 = not at all important, 5 = important);

—*Fit* of current supply of information and information need (1 = not at all, 5 = almost complete);

—*Need for change* (1 = definitely not, 5 = change is indispensable).

For some aspects the participants have the opportunity to specify the required changes.

Some of the results are shown in Table 10.

Table 10. Mean Scores for INFBED.

Problem aspects Information Aspects	Importance	Fit	Need for change
Actuality	(4.6)	3.6	3.4
Availability	3.8	3.4	(4.0)
Accuracy	2.6	3.8	3.4
Alternatives	(4.8)	(2.6)	(4.2)
Simulation	(4.8)	(2.8)	(4.4)
Planning horizon	4.2	3.8	3.4

Most interesting are those information aspects which have a mean score in "Need for change" near 1 (should definitively not be changed) or 4 and more (change is necessary or indispensable). In this CBIS-project the aspects availability, alternatives and simulation show scores which indicate that the participants are not satisfied with the current situation (low scores in Fit) and require the appropriate changes. An additional possibility of analyzing these results is description by profiles which show the differences between the responding participants and therefore enable us to initiate actions which take into account individual needs and assessments.

All this information forms the basis for design recommendations and a project specification with the PORGI-checklist ZIE, shown in Table 11. The objective of ZIE is to consider the major problem aspects and required changes and to translate these into operational design requirements. In this way we get a project specification which is accepted by all participants and forms the basis for evaluation activities during the project and at the end: during the project at specific milestones for the analysis of the fit of the different system components (by use of specific PORGI-tools not shown here) and comparison with the planned status. If variances exist, corrective actions can be initiated early in the project, and at the end of the project, when the system becomes operational and users as well as designers evaluate whether the objectives of the project have been met or not.

Some of the major recommendations for the next phases and major elements of the project specification by use of ZIE were:

Table 11. ZIE-1

1. System Objectives

   1.1 Which status shall the different elements of the problem situation have at the end of the project?

      ⟶ results of PROB, INFBED, INN

   1.2 What shall be reached/hindered by that status?

      1.2.1 Functional effects regarding the system components
      1.2.2 Economic effects (see IHB-List of Criteria AUS-3)
      1.2.3 Social effects (see IHB—List of Criteria GA-FIT)

   1.3 In which area (person, unit) shall these effects be realized?

   1.4 At what time shall these effects be realized?

      1.4.1 Date of handing-over the system
      1.4.2 Length of transition-period
      1.4.3 Date of routine-operation

   1.5 Evaluation

      1.5.1 Which status/event indicates the realization of planned objectives?
      1.5.2 Which measure indicates the realization of planned objectives?

—Major objective is the qualitative improvement of the five-year planning system, which shall be consistent with the one-year plan.

—Special emphasis shall be on the objective of making possible an *active* role in financial planning.

—Transparency of capacities and capacity planning has to be improved.

—The Board of Directors wants alternative plans for the next five years and expects about five to ten alternatives as sufficient.

—The requested possibility of asking "What-if-questions" shall focus on costs of material, personnel, advertising, R & D, overhead (more than DM 50,000 a year), licences, prices, sales.

—The actuality of information about major issues of other divisions shall be improved (at a maximum of two or three days).

—The analyzed requests of the users show a strong interest in an on-line interactive version of the system, which should be realized when the technical conditions (new release of operating system) are realized.

—Output formats should be flexibly adaptable according to the different interests of the users.

—The application of the new system shall enable those members of the organization who prepare alternative plans to do a more challenging job and less routine work.

—The organizational context has to be changed so that there is an organizational unit available for the preparation of alternative plans. This unit should represent the interests of all divisions.

—Transparency between the divisions shall be improved. This may have been reached already by means of the proposed "inter-divisional" planning group.

—The participation of those members of the organization affected by the new system shall be oriented to their individual degree of being affected.

Our recommendations for the next activities of the project focused primarily on two aspects:

—Project presentation for all "affected" members (topics and participants) to solve the diagnosed problem of the insufficient participation aspects.

—Elaboration of organizational solutions for the "planning group" parallel to technical design activities.

3 IMPLICATIONS AND LIMITATIONS OF THE PORGI-APPROACH

The PORGI-concept of organizational implementation of CBIS—mutually adjusting the technical, organizational and social system components and adequate involvement of those organization members concerned—implies an understanding of system development as a *participative sociotechnical* (and therefore organizational) *change process*. It is true that such change processes need active support by responsible management levels.

Application of methodological instruments for a satisfactory organization of the design and change processes (process fit) and adequate tuning of system components (system fit) results in increase of system success respective to decrease of system development risks but demands additional expenses (time, manpower, etc.). Because of the difficulties in evaluating the benefits of these tools in "hard-dollar-terms", *management has to take account of these additional expenses* for realizing a successful application of these instruments.

The applications of PORGI-instruments rigorously increases transparency of system development processes: it makes it possible to disclose technological, organizational but even more personal problems and conflicts in system design. What we have experienced is that problem disclosure and analysis demands a good deal of neutrality and independence (professional expertise and experience are of course presumed), which possibly only an external consultant may have. What we yet do not know is whether and how to avoid disclosure of such problems or conflicts that cannot be solved or handled adequately because of either lack of appropriate problem and conflict solving procedures in the practised management style or organization members' insufficient willingness or capability to solve such conflicts. In the above-described cases of PORGI-instruments application, we tried to anticipate problems potentially disclosed in the analysis, discuss available problem solutions and possible consequences of either the conscious solution of the problem or the conscious "not-solution" of the disclosed problem or neglect of possible existing latent conflicts. In every case the client organization in respect to

346

its management has to take the responsibility for the application of PORGI-instruments. Thus we are rather certain to disclose only problems or conflicts which can be solved, but are not certain of disclosing all existing problems which should be solved for economic and social satisfactory results of system development.

The traditional "classical" activities of system design concentrate on the question: which technological alternative is the best (most efficient) one to solve a given, predefined task? Concentration of PORGI-tools on planning and control of the fit between technological and organizational/human system components supposes that this question has been or will be answered during system development. The PORGI-approach does not support answers to this difficult and in many cases very unclear question. But this limitation has been chosen deliberately. The authors feel that the solution of those problems discussed in this paper are as crucial to system success as the organization of technological solutions. In that way our intention is not to substitute but to complement existing technological research and instruments with respect to certain variables extremely relevant to system success.

REFERENCES

1. Bariff, M.L., and E.J. Lusk. "Cognitive and Personality Tests for the Design of Information Systems." *Management Science* 23(8) (1977): 820-29.

2. Barkin, S. *An Investigation Into Some Factors Affecting Information System Utilization.* Unpublished Ph.D. thesis, University of Minnesota.

3. Benbasat, I., and R.G. Schroeder. "An Experimental Investigation of Some MIS Design Variables." *Management Information Systems Quarterly* 1 (March 1977).

4. Churchman, C.W., and A.N. Schainblatt. "The Researcher and the Manager: A Dialectic of Implementation." *Management Science* 11(4) (1965): B69-B87.

5. Dyckman, T.R. "Management Implementation of Scientific Research: An Attitudinal Study." *Management Science* 13(10) (June 1967): B612-B621.

6. Ginzberg, M.J. *A Process Approach to Management Science Implementation.* Unpublished Ph.D. thesis, M.I.T., 1975.

7. Ginzberg, M.J. "A Study of the Implementation Process." Research Paper No. 120. Graduate School of Business, Columbia University, New York, 1975.

8. Hansel, J., F. Kolf. "Projektplanungs- und -steuerungsmethodiken im Rahmen der Gestaltung computergestützter Planungs- und Entscheidungssysteme." PORGI-Projektbericht No. 7, Cologne (BIFOA) 1977.

9. Hawgood, J., E. Mumford, F.F. Land and C.M. Reddington. "The Evaluation and Management of Computer-based Systems: An Interdisciplinary Approach." *Information Processing 71.* Amsterdam, 1972.

10. Hawgood, J., F.F. Land, and E. Mumford. "Comparison of alternative strategies and systems." *Datenverarbeitung im Europäischen Raum.* Vienna, 1972, pp. 283-87.

11. Hawgood, J., F.F. Land, and E. Mumford. "Quinquevalent Quantification of Computer Benefits." in A.B. Frielink (ed.) *Economics of Informatics.* Amsterdam, 1975, pp. 171-80.

12. Hawgood, J. "A Formal Framework for Participative Benefit Assessment." Paper prepared for IFIP-Congress 77, Toronto, Canada, 1977.

347

13. Hedberg, B., and E. Mumford. "The Design of Computer Systems." in (Mumford and Sackman, 1975), pp. 31-59.

14. Kolf, F., and H.J. Oppelland. "A Design-Oriented Approach in Implementation Research: The Project PORGI." Paper prepared for the International Symposium on Design and Implementation of Computer-Based Information Systems, BIFOA, Bensberg/Cologne, Sept. 18-20, 1978.

15. Kolf, F., U. Dortans, and M. Schübeler. "Methodische Hilfsmittel zur Erleichterung der Teilnahme des Managers an der Gestaltung von entscheidungsorientierten Informationssystemen." BIFOA-Forschungsbericht No. 72/13, Cologne, 1973.

16. Kolf, F., J. Claus and H.J. Oppelland. "Grundlagen und Konzeption eines Modells zur Beschreibung organisatorischer Implementierungssituationen." PORGI-Projektbericht No. 1, Cologne (BIFOA) 1977.

17. Kolf, F., H.J. Oppelland, D. Seibt and N. Szyperski. "Instrumentarium zur organisatorischen Implementierung von rechner-gestützten Informationssystemen." *Angewandte Informatik* 20 (1978): 299-310.

18. Kolf, F., H.J. Oppelland, D. Seibt, N. Szyperski. "Tools for Handling Human and Organizational Problems of Computer-Based Information Systems." Paper prepared for Second Conference of the European Co-operation in Informatics (ECI) on Information Systems Methodology, Venice, Italy, October 10-12, 1978.

19. Land, F.F. "Evaluation of Systems Goal in Determining a Design Strategy for a Computer Based Information System." *The Computer Journal* 19(4) (1976): 290-94.

20. Little, J.D.C., and L.M. Lodisch. "A Media Planning Calculus." *Operations Research* 17(1) (1969): 2-35.

21. Little, J.D.C. "Models and Managers: The Concept of a Decision Calculus." *Management Science* 16 (1970): B466-B485.

22. Lodisch, L.M. "CALLPLAN: An Interactive salesman's Call Planning System." *Management Science* 18(4) (1971): B25-B40.

23. Lucas, H.C., Jr. *Why Information Systems Fail.* New York, London, 1975.

24. Mitroff, I., and T. Featheringham. "On Systemic Problem Solving and the Error of the Third Kind." *Behavioral Science* 19(6) (1974): 383-93.

25. Mitroff, I. "Towards a Theory and Measure of Total Problem Solving Performance." in P.G.W. Keen (ed.) *The Implementation of Computer-Based Decision Aids.* Proceedings of a Conference sponsored by the Center for Information Systems Research, April 3-5, 1975, Cambridge, Mass.

26. Mumford, E. "A Comprehensive Method for Handling the Human Problems of Computer Information." *Proceedings of the IFIP-Congress 1971*, Loubljana, Ta-5, pp. 105-09.

27. Mumford, E. *Systems Design for People. Economic evaluation of computer based systems.* Book 3. Manchester, 1971.

28. Mumford, E. Job satisfaction. A study of computer specialists. London, 1972.

29. Mumford, E., and H. Sackman (eds.) *Human Choice and Computer.* Amsterdam: North-Holland, 1975.

30. Oppelland, H.J., F. Kolf, and J. Claus. "Dokumentation der Ergebnisse einer Expertenbefragung zur Entwicklung und Einführung rechnergestützter Informationssysteme." PORGI-Projektbericht No. 5, Cologne (BIFOA) 1977.

31. Parson, T., and E. Shils. *Towards a General Theory of Action.* Boston, 1951.

32. Pounds, W.F. "The Process of Problem Finding." *Industrial Management Review* 11(4) (1969): 1-19.

33. Sorensen, R.E., and D.E. Zand. "Improving the Implementation of OR/MS Models by Applying the Lewin-Schein Theory of Change." in (Schultz and Slevin, 1975), pp. 217-36.

34. Szyperski, N. "Gegenwärtiger Stand und Tendenzen zur Entwicklung betrieblicher Informationssysteme." in H.R. Hansen, M.P. Wahl (eds.) *Probleme beim Aufbau betrieblicher Informationssysteme*. Munich, 1973.

35. Weir, M. "The Effectiveness of Computer Systems in Creating Satisfying Jobs for Users; a Method of Assessment." in A.B. Frielink (ed.) *Economics of Informatics*. Amsterdam, 1975, pp. 421-26.

36. Zand, D., and R. Sorensen. "Theory of Change and the Effective Use of Management Science." *Administrative Science Quarterly* 20(4) (1975): 532-45.

37. Zand, D., R. Sorensen. "Organizational Change and the Implementation of OR/MS Projects." in (Mumford, 1971 [26]).

D
Review

CHALLENGES AND CONSEQUENCES FOR FUTURE RESEARCH ON IMPLEMENTATION

by Norbert Szyperski and Thilo Tilemann

1 INTRODUCTION

Future research on design and implementation of information systems is confronted with many different expectations. A major prerequisite for success seems to be a conscious regard of the problems that have been experienced in research and implementation practice in the past. A closer look at these problems will reveal various aspects for further reflections. Analyzing pitfalls in practice and limitations of research results must lead not only to "inventories of misery", but can as well help to find challenges for future work in a positive sense.

According to recent discussions [e.g., 7] we want to differentiate at least three different groups of problems in the implementation process:
—problem analysis and implementation of conceptual ideas (e.g., problem fitting of model concepts)
—technical implementation, including programming, testing and documentation
—organizational implementation relating primarily to the conditions of men and organizational structure.

These problem areas traditionally are discussed relating only to the specific information system actually being planned. On the background of manifold evolutions in information and communication technologies [e.g., 4; 24] however, the contextual nature of developing a single information system puts an increasing importance on comprehensive approaches to plan the informational infrastructure of a company. This aspect is reinforced by the growing necessity to integrate information systems planning into the overall planning activities of the firm's development.

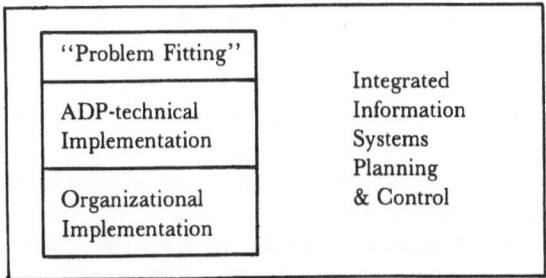

Figure 1. Problem sets of the Implementation Processes

On the basis of the problems perceived both in the proper areas of single systems projects and in integrated systems planning (Figure 1) this paper tries to identify major challenges in implementation and suggests some consequences for future research activities.

2 ACTUAL CHALLENGES IN INFORMATION SYSTEMS IMPLEMENTATION

In planning and implementing new technologies the main problem is actually not so much the availability of technologies and resources but the lack of knowledge on how to combine and to make use of these technologies and resources. The implementation of new technologies must take into account processes, structures and personal factors of the individual organization. Especially less advanced companies and agencies need basic help to cope with these problems.

The difficulties encountered in practice in using results from implementation research can be illustrated by the following example: Implementation experts are still discussing whether implementation is to be regarded as a phase or as an overall aspect in the development process. The perception that implementation can relate to different objects makes clear that implementation problems may occur in different phases. Following the understanding of a growing group of people, design can include implementation of methods into a logical systems concept, programming can mean implementation of logical concepts into the computer, and "conventional" implementation comprises the introduction of a physical system into an organization.

2.1 Technical Implementation Problems

Within the technical group of implementation problems we usually have to cope with activities such as problem analysis, systems design and ADP-technical implementation. Earlier approaches dividing these activities into separate steps have proven to be dangerous. Especially the development of large and integrated systems with multiple influences between single steps cannot be mastered by the traditional phase schemes. Until now organizational alternatives to the separate steps concepts, however, are not really satisfying. Relating to the group of technical problems, therefore, we would like to emphasize the difference between
—implementation of general ideas or methods (e.g., from Management Science or Operations Research) into individual solution concepts, and
—the implementation of model concepts into programs.

The implementation of general methods or abstract model types into an individual application situation is perceived as an urgent problem by a growing number of scientists and professionals. This may be partially due to the overestimation of the multiple applicability of standard software [10] and to the evolving perception of the individuality of application needs. Implementation research however has until now neglected the methodologies for problem analysis and design.

Specific methods are lacking and the existing general ones are poorly used. Several efforts actually being made in requirements analysis and specification [16; 31] prove the difficulties in closing the methodological gap. Further research may be more successful if it puts more emphasis on problem contents instead on formal techniques. A better problem orientation in this sense could lead to more efficient problem analysis techniques and better recommendations for the choice between economic methods or solution alternatives.

For the ADP-technical implementation such a vast amount of principles, methods and techniques is offered that compatibility and choice problems arise in practice. Available software techniques differ or contradict each other considerably in the premises and areas of applications. Though common in mechanical engineering, the achievement of equal production results cannot be guaranteed with division of labor between different programmers.

Software-technological methods usually are isolated approaches. By supporting only specific parts or layers of the whole process they often cannot be integrated into comprehensive instruments for the whole life cycle of a program. For some steps, as for example documentation or quality control of software, we find only poor methodological aids. In addition, besides the own problems of software techniques, their influence on the organization of systems development has not been investigated in depth.

Software design procedures should be better reflected on the conceptual level before they are cast into programs themselves. Not all design procedures seem to be programmable. Software-technological design approaches need not only to be completed and further developed but must as well be integrated into comprehensive "Application System Technologies" simultaneously regarding all factors that influence systems implementation. Developing tools for technical implementation also means giving advice on how to structure the manual tasks corresponding to those controlled by programs.

2.2 Organizational Implementation Problems

The ways of dealing with problems of organizational implementation differ considerably between theory and practice. While research is piling up factor, impact, relational and recently also somewhat comprehensive studies, practice usually is muddling through or at best using methods as we can find in project management handbooks.

A considerable part of the research studies use definitions which are not operational enough for practitioners. Especially the impact studies tend to neglect situative conditions and try to explain impacts by monocausal approaches. Other studies using relatively small samples investigate different factors, which cannot be compared. Due to the lack of a common frame of reference, research results often cannot be integrated, and monocausality in certain areas produces contradicting results. Common to all of these studies is the retrospective view which naturally provides a poor aid for systems planning.

Among the developments derived from the efforts of consultants, project management methods are the most important. They provide good support for the administration of projects. Constructive aids for system development and situational recommendations to use certain methods or instruments, however, are lacking.

In long-term projects, factors like value systems, qualifications of people and organizational structures become variables. Concerning the relationships between these variables and the technological alternatives Harold Sackman's experiences with U.S. government agencies seem to be worthy of some reflection: new technologies do not necessarily bring up changes in work organization. So an implementation of tele-conferencing did not change human communication patterns severely, but accentuated them and stimulated people to meeting personally.

Compared to the tools available for the software-technical implementation of planning systems [11] the supply of tools to change man's conditions is rather poor. This inconvenience assumes a growing importance by the continuing shift to user participation in systems development.

Normally the success of implementation heavily depends on the fit between the new system and the organization. System planners therefore are confronted with the question of with which state of the organization does the system have to cope. Especially projects with several years of development become dependent on reliable forecasts and/or plans of organizational change. On the other hand, the discussions on organizational amendments should take into account the dynamics of informational infrastructure, too.

Organizational dynamics are not only reflecting user behaviour or other internal processes, but are also considerably affected by dynamics from outside the organization. Environmental changes—in market structures and economic conditions, as well as in technology and other fields—can, however, induce problems the solutions for which are superior tasks of strategic management [9].

2.3 Requirements of Strategic Information Systems Planning

The management of information resources and the planning of the informational infrastructure of a company go far beyond the problem of implementing and using a single computer-aided system. Problems of information systems planning are quite often problems of information resource management as well. Both areas of activities are still trying to delimit their boundaries. For the following let us assume that both include the determination of the fields of activity of information systems, of their goals and of the resources necessary for their contribution to the realization of the company's success potential. This implies two essential challenges:

—to take a strategic approach to information systems planning and
—to integrate information systems planning into overall corporate planning activities.

Strategic reflections on the long-term development of information and communication systems have been, until now, established only in a few advanced companies. There exists, however, a bulk of reasons for the other companies to start thinking in this dimensen [28]:

—Innovations of information technology bring up new opportunities for the company's operations and impose problems calling for, at least, a response.
—The growing volume of funds invested in the informational infrastructure of a company makes investment planning necessary.
—The need of qualified personnel to develop and operate this infrastructure calls for long-term personnel planning.
—The time necessary to develop complex information systems makes forecasts of future application situations indispensable. Resulting organizational problems may ask for planned organizational change.
—Decisions on technical equipment (e.g., networks and hardware) cannot easily be reversed.
—Changing products and markets of a company lead to new informational requirements.

Strategic problems usually go beyond the authority of an individual project manager. As it is often hard to identify the man in charge of implementation problems of a single project, it seems to be still harder to find a responsible person for the broad scope of questions involved in information systems planning. Complexity and strategic importance of these questions are a challenge for general management.

Quite a number of tools and approaches are offered for the solution of common strategic problems in business [2]. The research on specific tools for information resource management however can be regarded to be in an embryonic state. This has been argued on one hand to refer to a lack of empirical surveys. On the other hand maybe university research has missed to advise practice how to contribute to this research and to find appropriate experimental research designs. However recent efforts in empirical research are providing considerable contributions [15; 18; 22; 25].

The arguments for strategic planning mentioned above make it obvious that this effort should be integrated with the strategic reflections on the development of the whole company.

Another reason for integration may be derived from West Churchman's statement that the quality of a management information system (MIS) can at best be equal to the quality of the corresponding management system [3]. Since MIS development projects may stimulate amendments in the management system [30], the quality of a new MIS sometimes can even be better than the quality of the management system has been at the moment when the MIS development started. However, it may be dangerous to rely on unplanned effects. In many corporations long-term planning approaches are necessary to provide the cultural conditions that make a corporate setting ready to accept new information technologies. The success of the introduction of information systems depends on the plans for instructing, motivating, training and coaching the members of the organization.

357

This interdependence assumes a growing importance with new information and communication systems calling for deeper changes in organization than traditional data processing systems did.

Another argument for integration is based on the fact that technological innovations become mature for practical use at different points in time. After management operation systems, MIS came up in the 1960s, office automation systems started in the late 1970s and new communication systems will have to be integrated with the other systems in the near future. In spite of their step-by-step occurrence these innovations are influencing each other and, thus, call for joint planning.

Regarding technological trends in office automation, telecommunications, value added networks, etc., the use of new technologies may well become a strategic factor for companies. Integrated planning has to compare, for example, whether the competitive position may better be supported by investing limited resources in an office technology or in the production workshops.

In quite a lot of corporations an integration on the strategic level is impossible. Often there are no formalized strategic planning activities of the common business. In other cases long range planning of information systems is impossible be-. cause of the instable behaviour of an organization. The failure of the Planning Programming Budgeting System for a five-year horizon in U.S. Agencies with a one-year budget environment provides an impressive example.

In a recent analysis we found not only encouraging developments of empirical research in the planning area [29]:

—Although growing in number since 1970, studies on corporate planning and planning situations often describe "inventories of misery" only.

—Corresponding to relatively large samples (more than a quarter of the studies compare over 100 companies) the trend is to numerical analysis. However, a combination of the results is nearly impossible because of the lack of replication of the same questions.

—A more encouraging development is marked by the trend to better documentation, e.g., of the conceptualization of variables, statistical methods and samples used.

The analysis confirms the necessity of technological research. Especially the restricted potential for innovations in empirical research constitutes a principal barrier for the deduction of technologies related to the design or use of new systems.

3 CONSEQUENCES FOR FUTURE RESEARCH

Reflections on future research should not only regard the actual problems in practice [e.g., 13], but also take into account current trends in research activities. Corresponding to the urgent needs for help in information systems planning and implementation the emphasis of research is already shifting to the generation of technological knowledge [1; 14].

The design of programs for future research in this area will have to be based on

Key Subjects	Methodological Consequences
Think about a common frame of reference for implementation	Develop new concepts of interdisciplinary research
Catch up with work in related disciplines	
Discover stereotypes in problem and solution patterns	Amend collection and documentation of empirical data
Find indicators for human behaviour in innovation processes	
Analyze system life cycles	Make control and evaluation of large information bases possible
Develop techniques for system problem fitting	
Amend and integrate software-technologies	Develop alternatives to separate step phase schemes of application system engineering
Develop instruments for the diagnosis of organizational settings	
Develop tools for strategic planning and control of the informational infrastructure of a firm	Develop new designs of action research in the form of "research by development"
Transfer research results into practice	

Figure 2. Synopsis of Consequences for Future Research.

at least two categories of consequences: firstly, a set of challenging subjects of research, and secondly, a couple of measures which should lead to a more efficient research methodology. Figure 2 tries to give a synopsis of some consequences resulting from the previous analysis. A strictly horizontal co-ordination of research subjects and methodological consequences is not intended, although certain relations cannot be ignored.

3.1 Concentration on Key Subjects

1. The immense expenses for research efforts, especially for empirical research work on the one hand, and the still remaining problems in combining the results of different studies are symptomatic of the lack of a common frame of reference. Physics and Chemistry, for example, have at their disposal well standardized systems of technical terms, problem areas and corresponding solutions. In the area discussed here it would be too early to standardize similar systems, but it seems to be urgent to discuss and think about a common frame of reference for the scientists involved. This might also provide the means for a better integration of implementation approaches from different disciplines corresponding to the growing demands of system implementers for comprehensive turn-key instruments.

2. System developers usually do not use the full scope of knowledge offered by psychology. Behavioral scientists seem to work with psychological research results that are several years old, and economists seem to work with behavioral science research results that are even older. They should be more aware of the advances that are being made in related disciplines and integrate them into their own work. An example has been set by Mitroff who picked up Guilford's work on intelligence [8] and investigated questions of information handling, resistance and cognitive style [17]. Today valuable insights could be derived from information, decision and communication psychologies.

3. The rather isolated work of different research groups presumably hides parallels in problems and solutions. More analysis is needed to discover potential stereotypes in changes of technologies, methods and organizations. In order to be useful as a basis for the development of implementation methodologies, these analyses should follow at least two objectives: identify comprehensible application areas to permit manageable methodologies, and avoid a vast amount of "single-purpose machines" by concentrating on stable solution patterns that occur with sufficient frequency.

4. Further analysis should reveal possibilities of how to achieve innovation without manipulating the people concerned. Analysis results should be able to aleviate the fear of a growing number of people that they are being forced to do something they do not want to do. A major problem in this issue consists in getting the right indicators. In order to find them, a lot of variables have to be tested for, i.a., their stabilizing influence or their dominance over other indicators. This could also provide a valuable basis for a-priori reflections on why systems succeed.

5. Life cycles of computer-aided systems have not been analyzed thoroughly

enough until now. This might, however, provide valuable insights not only into the system of models and computers, but also into their organizational environment. The conditions under which models live reflect changes in organizational attitudes and structures, and in personal knowledge and capacity. A closer look might reveal to what extent the functional features of models or modeling systems, and how much the users' minds made-up about these are determining model life cycles.

6. Quite a number of information systems have failed because they have not reached a sufficient problem fit [13; 20]. Methods and models often have proven to be incompatible with planning problems and processes. Practice is suffering from a lack of techniques to adjust system concepts to the tasks they shall support [32]. Although efforts in this area are meant to solve intellectual problems, more help could be provided. A promising starting point seems to be a better differentiation of system types (e.g., by degrees of integration and autonomy) and of types of system changes (e.g., dependent on existing systems and development technologies used).

7. Relating to the software level, implementation aids will have to differ between at least two alternatives. The choice of standardized application software on the one hand, and the development of individual programs, perhaps with programming methodologies, on the other hand, call for different approaches in problem fit checking and user participation. Representation and documentation of programs being fairly well supported by now, more emphasis should be given to the design aids and to integrating the separate approaches into a comprehensive software technology.

8. On the other hand, practice needs more information on the behavior of organizations and their members in implementation processes. Transparency of the present situation and of future developments of an organizational setting can be provided by the use of structured instruments of diagnosis [12]. The results of diagnosis may lead to specific measures of instructing, motivating, training and coaching members of the organization. Causal relations and processes forming the context for these measures should be further investigated.

9. Concerning the strategic problems related to information system planning and resource management, the supply of tools is very poor. Especially new technologies make these problems highly important and critical for organizations. So, tools should be developed for strategic analysis as well as for the related control mechanisms. A special task of these control mechanisms must be to overcome potential crisis within an organization.

10. A common objective behind all these tasks must be to close the gap between implementation research and practice. Researchers should aim at providing more understandable publications and more methods of sufficient practicability in terms of operationality, efficiency and expense. They should support practitioners in becoming aware of the implementation game. A basic knowledge about players, playground, rules and possible strategies is a prerequisite for getting into implementation processes. The long-term goal of research, however, is to offer a practicable multi-staged and multi-dimensional implementation methodology.

3.2 Methodological Consequences

1. At present there are quite different groups working on implementation problems. Caused by the broad spectrum of disciplines involved in research on the development of computer-based information systems there are at least three groups in action:

—specialists for computer and telecommunication technologies trying to get these systems to run in organizations

—management scientists and operation researchers discussing how to get methods and models used within problem solving processes

—political and social oriented researchers interested in how to analyze organizational situations and to achieve acceptance of new systems and programs.

Regarding their rather isolated work the mere idea of interdisciplinary research seems not to be sufficient. For an efficient realization of this idea deeper reflections on organization and communication in research projects seem to be necessary.

2. The quality of the collection of research data—especially within living organizations—should be amended. This includes the documentation of the behavior of the organizations. Several experiences in implementation processes [23] support the assumption that fascinating causalities can be found between certain conditions and the related processes and patterns of behavior. The engineering example should guide the direction. Instead of sending special researchers with a special project into a special organization it should become more common to get a great part of the empirical data out of the normal control of the daily use of advanced technologies within organizations.

3. Current research is characterized by very special analyses and subsequently very small pieces of research results. The combination of these results is often very difficult and does not often yield operational knowledge. Refering to data out of the non-technical area, which by their nature can not be seized by automated monitors, additional problems arise. Procedures should be developed which by partial description and/or on a stochastical basis make these data controllable. For the long-term goal of comprehensive analyses a lot of design problems and, last but not least, the huge amount of effort to make them longitudinal will have to be mastered.

4. The experiences with numerous attempts to divide developing processes into distinct stages led to the understanding that an isolation of single stages would not be very helpful. Problem solving in practical development as well as in research processes often moves simultaneously in several of these stages. Therefore, the actual trend to decomposing these processes no further than necessary (for a rough relation of some types of activities and instruments to some stages) should be promoted.

5. New concepts of action research seem to be worth developing and testing. Compared to traditional research approaches they will have to master more conditions and their results may be valid only for a shorter time and a narrower field. Taking into account feedbacks from practical experience and real life evolutions

of research subjects in the course of time they might, however, provide more and better knowledge on planning, implementing and controlling information systems. That asks for "Research by Development" strategies [e.g., 26; 27; 21; 23].

REFERENCES

1. Ansoff, I.H., and R.C. Brandenburg, "A Program of Research in Business Planning," *Management Science* 13 (1967): B219-B239.

2. Ansoff, H.I., R.P. Declerck and R.L. Hayes (eds.). *From Strategic Planning to Strategic Management*. London et al., 1976.

3. Churchman, C.W. *The Design of Inquiring Systems*. New York, 1971.

4. Diebold (ed.). *Diebold Management Report*. Frankfurt, 1978.

5. Dittmann, E.L. "Ansätze zur Abbildung der Miniwelt in Datenstrukturen," *Angewandte Informatik* (2) (1978): 50 et seq.

6. Ginzberg, M.J. "A Detailed Look at Implementation Research." MIT-Working Paper 753-4, Nov. 1974.

7. Ginzburg, M. "Steps toward more effective Implementation of MS and MIS," *Interfaces* 8(3) (1978): 57-63.

8. Guilford, J.P. *Personality*. New York, 1959.

9. Heinen, E. *Grundlagen betriebswirtschaftlicher Entscheidungen: Das Zielsystem der Unternehmung*. 2nd ed., Wiesbaden, 1971.

10. ISIS-Software-Report 1/78, Munich, 1978.

11. Hurst, E.G. and T. Tilemann. "Characteristics of Planning Systems," in A. Ralston and C.L. Meek (eds.). *Encyclopedia of Computer Science*. New York: Petrocelli/Charter, 1976, Col. 1077-1081.

12. Kolf, F., H.J. Oppelland, D. Seibt and N. Szyperski. "Tools for Handling human and organizational Problems of Computer-based Information Systems," in G. Bracci and P.C. Lockemann (eds.). *Information Systems Methodology*. Berlin et al.: Springer, 1978, pp. 82-119.

13. Lucas, H.C. Jr. *Why Information Systems Fail*. New York: Columbia University Press, 1975.

14. Mason, R.O. and I.I. Mitroff. "A Program for Research on Management Information Systems," *Management Science* 19(5) (1973): 475-487.

15. McLean, E. and J.V. Soden. *Strategic Planning for MIS*. New York et al., 1976.

16. McGowan, C. and R. McHenry. *Software Management*. New York: Petrocelli/Charter, 1976.

17. Mitroff, I.I. "Solipsism: An Essay in Psychological Philosophy," *Philosophy of Science* 38 (3) (1971): 376-395.

18. Neumann, S. and E. Segev. "User Evaluation of Information Characteristics." Working Paper 558/78, Tel Aviv University, 1978.

19. Nunamaker, J.F. Jr., R.B. Konsynsky, H.O. Thomas and C. Singer. "Computer-Aided Analysis and Design of Information Systems," *Communic. of the ACM* 19 (12) (1976): 674 et seq.

20. Rosenkranz, F. "Status and Future Use of Corporate Planning and Simulation Models: Case Studies and Conclusions." in H.D. Plötzeneder (ed.). *Computer Assisted Corporate Planning*. Stuttgart/Chicago: Science Research Ass., 1977, pp. 143-179.

21. Schreiner, G., "Analyse der Einsatzmöglichkeiten von Action Research im planungswissenschaftlichen Kontext." Dissertation, Cologne, 1976.

22. Schultz, R.L. and D.P. Slevin (eds.). *Implementing Operations Research/Management Science.* New York/Amsterdam, 1975.

23. Seibt, D. "Analyse der Anwendung der Strategie 'Forschung durch Entwicklung' in den BIFOA-Projekten ISAS, CORPIS und SIMMIS." BIFOA-Projektbericht. Cologne, 1978.

24. SHARE Inc. (ed.). *Data Processing in 1980-1985, a Study of Potential Limitations.* New York et al.: John Wiley, 1976.

25. Swanson, E.B. "Management Information Systems: Appreciation and Involvement," *Management Science* 21(2) (1974): 178-88.

26. Szyperski, N. "Zur wissenschaftsprogrammatischen und forschungsstrategischen Orientierung der Betriebswirtschaftslehre," *Zeitschrift für betriebswirtschaftliche Forschung* 23 (1971): 261-282.

27. Szyperski, N. "Forschungsstrategien in der Angewandten Informatik—Konzepte Erfahrungen," *Angewandte Informatik* 16 (1974): 148-53.

28. Szyperski, N. and F. Kolf. "Integration der strategischen Informationssystem-Planung in die Unternehmungs-Entwicklungsplanung," in H.R. Hansen (ed.), *Entwicklungstendenzen der Systemanalyse.* Munich/Vienna, 1978.

29. Szyperski, N. and D. Müller-Böling. "Empirische Forschung und Forschung durch Entwicklung: Ein Plädoyer zur Nutzung von Ergebnissen und Techniken der empirischen Forschung bei der Verfolgung des technologischen Wissenschaftsziels." Arbeitsbericht Nr. 20, Seminar für betriebswirtschaftliche planung, University of Cologne, 1979.

30. Szyperski, N., D. Seibt, A. Harrmann and K.H. Hauer. "Entwicklung eines computergestützten Informationssystems zur administrativen Steuerung einer Unternehmung (ISAS)." Bundesministerium für Forschung und Technologie, Forschungsbericht Dv 76-05. Leopoldshafen, 1976.

31. Teichroew, D. and E. Hershey: "PSL/PSA—A Computer Aided Technique for Structured Documentation and Analysis of Information Processing Systems." Second International Conference on Software Engineering, Oct. 1976.

32. Tilemann, T. "Anleitungen zum Entwurf von Rechenmodellen für betriebliche Planungsaufgaben." APIS-Projektbericht Nr. 11. Cologne: BIFOA, 1978.

List of Participants

Baan, Wilhelm, Dr.
Rheinisch-Westfälische Elektrizitätswerke AG, Essen/FRG
Bleuel, Bernhard, Dipl.-Volksw.
Mannesmann AG Hüttenwerke, Essen/FRG
Burwick, Horst, Dr.
Gesellschaft für Mathematik und Informatik, Aachen/FRG
Clausen, Hasse
Center for Datamatik, Copenhagen/Denmark
Domsch, Michel, Prof. Dr.
Hochschule der Bundeswehr, Hamburg/FRG
Dröschel, Wolfgang, Dipl.-Math.
Gesellschaft für Mathematik und Datenverarbeitung mbH, Bonn/FRG
Fürtjes, Heinz-Theo, Dipl.-Kfm., Dipl.-Volksw.
Betriebswirtschaftliches Institut für Organisation und Automation an der Universität zu Köln, (BIFOA), Köln/FRG
Garmers, Hartwig, Dipl.-Kfm.
Betriebswirtschaftliches Institut für Organisation und Automation an der Universität zu Köln (BIFOA), Köln/FRG
Ginzberg, Michael, Prof., Ph.D.
Graduate School of Business, Columbia University in the City of New York, New York/USA
Griese, Joachim, Prof. Dr.
Lehrstuhl für Betriebsinformatik, Universität Dortmund, Dortmund/FRG
Grochla, Erwin, Prof. Dr. Dr.h.c.
Seminar für Allgemeine Betriebswirtschaftslehre und Organisationslehre der Universität zu Köln and Betriebswirtschaftliches Institut für Organisation und Automation an der Universität zu Köln (BIFOA), Köln/FRG
Höring, Klaus, Dipl.-Ing., Dipl.-Wirtsch.-Ing.
Betriebswirtschaftliches Institut für Organisation und Automation an der Universität zu Köln (BIFOA), Köln/FRG
Kallio, Kari
OY Nokia AB, Helsinki/Finland
Kampffmeyer, Hermann, Dipl.-Kfm.
Siemens AG, München/FRG
Klaus, Hans-Günther, Dr.
Betriebswirtschaftliches Institut für Organisation und Automation an der Universität zu Köln (BIFOA), Köln/FRG

Kolf, Frank, Dipl.-Kfm.
Betriebswirtschaftliches Institut für Organisation und Automation an der Universität zu Köln (BIFOA), Köln/FRG
Kotthaus, Rolf, Ing. grad.
Standard Elektrik Lorenz AG, Stuttgart/FRG
Kriebel, Charles H., Prof., Ph.D.
Graduate School of Industrial Administration, Carnegie Mellon University, Pittsburgh, Pa./USA
Land, Frank, Dr.
London School of Economics and Political Science, London/Great Britain
Langen, Bernhard, Dipl.-Kfm.
Betriebswirtschaftliches Institut für Organisation und Automation an der Universität zu Köln (BIFOA), Köln/FRG
Lekow, Hubertus von, Dipl.-Ing.
SANOL Schwarz-Monheim GmbH, Monheim/FRG
Lucas, Jr., Henry C., Prof., Ph.D.
Graduate School of Business Administration, New York University, New York/USA
Luther, Frank, Dipl.-Kfm.
Betriebswirtschaftliches Institut für Organisation und Automation an der Universität zu Köln (BIFOA), Köln/FRG
Marock, Jürgen, Dr.
Gesellschaft für Mathematik und Datenverarbeitung mbH, Bonn/FRG
Müller-Merbach, Heiner, Prof. Dr.
Institut für Betriebswirtschaftslehre, Technische Hochschule Darmstadt/FRG
Mumford, Enid, Prof.
Manchester Business School, University of Manchester/Great Britain
Oppelland, Hans-Jürgen, Dipl.-Ing. (Wirtsch.-Ing.)
Betriebswirtschaftliches Institut für Organisation und Automation an der Universität zu Köln (BIFOA), Köln/FRG
Podger, David N., Dr.
Manchester Business School, University of Manchester/Great Britain
Rosenkranz, Friedrich, Priv.-Doz., Dr.
Ciba Geigy AG, Basel, and Universität Basel/Switzerland
Sackman, Harold, Prof. Ph.D.
Manchester Business School, University of Manchester/Great Britain
Schönfeld, Werner, Lic. rer. pol.
Sandoz AG, Basel/Switzerland
Schuler, Wolfgang, Dr.
Gesellschaft für Information und Dokumentation, Heidelberg/FRG
Seibt, Dietrich, Prof. Dr.
Universität Essen - GHS, and Betriebswirtschaftliches Institut für Organisation und Automation an der Universität zu Köln (BIFOA), Köln/FRG

Szyperski, Norbert, Prof. Dr.

Seminar für Allgemeine Betriebswirtschaftslehre und Betriebswirtschaftliche Planung der Universität zu Köln and Betriebswirtschaftliches Institut für Organisation und Automation an der Universität zu Köln (BIFOA), Köln/FRG

Swanson, E. Burton, Prof., Ph.D.

Graduate School of Management, University of California, Los Angeles/USA

Tilemann, Tilo, Dr.

Betriebswirtschaftliches Institut für Organisation und Automation an der Universität zu Köln (BIFOA), Köln/FRG

Welke, Richard J., Prof., Ph.D.

Faculty of Business, McMaster University, Hamilton, Ontario/Canada

Windler, Albrecht, Dipl.-Kfm.

Betriebswirtschaftliches Institut für Organisation und Automation an der Universität zu Köln (BIFOA), Köln/FRG

COLOPHON

setter: Expertext, Alphen aan den Rijn
printer: Samsom Sijthoff Grafische Bedrijven, Alphen aan den Rijn
binder: Callenbach, Nijkerk
cover-design: Wim Bottenheft